The Epistle of James

McMaster Divinity College Press
**Linguistic Exegesis of
the New Testament, Volume 1**

The Epistle of James

Linguistic Exegesis of an Early Christian Letter

EDITED BY
JAMES D. DVORAK
AND
ZACHARY K. DAWSON

PICKWICK *Publications* · Eugene, Oregon

THE EPISTLE OF JAMES
Linguistic Exegesis of an Early Christian Letter

Linguistic Exegesis of the New Testament, Volume 1
McMaster Divinity College Press

Pickwick Publications
An Imprint of Wipf and Stock Publishers
199 W. 8th Ave., Suite 3
Eugene, OR 97401

McMaster Divinity College Press
1280 Main Street West
Hamilton, Ontario, Canada
L8S 4K1

www.wipfandstock.com

PAPERBACK ISBN: 978-1-4982-2458-1
HARDCOVER ISBN: 978-1-4982-2460-4
EBOOK ISBN: 978-1-4982-2459-8

Cataloguing-in-Publication data:

Names: Dvorak, James D., editor. | Dawson, Zachary K., editor.

Title: The epistle of James : linguistic exegesis of an early Christian letter / edited by James D. Dvorak and Zachary K. Dawson.

Description: Eugene, OR: Pickwick Publications, 2019 | Linguistic Exegesis of the New Testament 1. | Includes bibliographical references and indexes.

Identifiers: ISBN 978-1-4982-2458-1 (paperback). | ISBN 978-1-4982-2460-4 (hardcover). | ISBN 978-1-4982-2459-8 (ebook).

Subjects: LCSH: Bible.—James—Criticism, interpretation, etc. | Bible. New Testament—Language, style.

Classification: BS2785.52 L37 2019 (print). | BS2785.52 (ebook).

Manufactured in the U.S.A.

07/11/19

Contents

Series Preface

Linguistic Exegesis of the New Testament (LENT), a series of structured edited volumes, contributes to the growing body of literature on linguistic and exegetical analysis in New Testament studies by focusing on linguistic method in exegetical practice. To accomplish this goal, we have designed the volumes to be instructive in and usable for multiple contexts and purposes. Each volume in this series provides a collection of linguistically informed exegetical analyses of a sub-corpus of the New Testament. The purpose and benefit of this simple idea is to provide a consistent and unified linguistic perspective across each volume, and, thereby, each sub-corpus of the New Testament. Multi-contributor volumes often lack methodological consistency and rigor. Such volumes may exemplify varying methods, or no method at all. Another limiting feature of such volumes is that they cover a wide range of test cases from different textual sources. Such volumes, when they are used, are often mined for the one or two essays that pertain to a scholar's or student's topic of research, while the rest of the volume is deemed irrelevant. This series has in mind a more useful way of applying its linguistic methodology in that it brings together methodologically similar studies that all focus on the same specific set of New Testament texts. As a result, we believe the nature of these volumes lends itself to the needs of independent researchers, professors, and scholarly pastors, while at the same time facilitating the pedagogical aims of the typical seminary exegetical course as supplementary texts.

Although the volumes in the LENT series cover the breadth of the New Testament, the volumes do not aim to offer comment on every single verse in the New Testament. All too often, traditional commentaries that aim for comprehensiveness end up merely parroting existing resources without making a contribution to the body of scholarship already available. The more recent development of exegetical handbooks has not, unfortunately, avoided this pitfall of repetition that does not advance our understanding of the texts. They tend to reflect the diminished exegetical capacity of most students of Greek. Instead, exegetical handbooks, when in the hands of students (and others), tend to become crutches for learning Greek; they are essentially used as parsing guides. By contrast, as potential supplementary texts for seminary or graduate-level seminars, and even valuable sources for scholars, the volumes in this series provide a favorable alternative to the often-used exegetical commentary or handbook because they have explicit methodological aims and exemplifications. Further, they have clear advantages over commentaries because the essays in this series are not bound to a linear treatment of the text that often becomes cumbersome to wade through with their numerous comments on basic textual features, interaction with other commentators, and the many other features that make commentaries the pedantic genre of biblical scholarship that they are. Instead, each essay within the series is autonomous, addresses its own topic, and argues its own thesis. This demonstrates for students how linguistically-informed exegetical analysis can be creatively and productively used when applied according to a defined linguistic methodology. Further, to answer the question "What benefit will learning Greek have for my ministry or scholarship?" a synthesizing concluding chapter in each volume provides an additional instructive essay on the various kinds of exegetical payoff that arise from the essays in the volume. It is our hope that this feature will be viewed as a valuable addition by those who use these books.

Traditional series often reflect a spectrum of methodologies from various critical perspectives, traditional historical-grammatical analysis, or, more recently, theologically-driven exegesis. The result of this methodological eclecticism means that from volume to volume the linguistic perspectives represented in a series may shift to suit the goals of each individual author. The LENT series, by contrast, aims to introduce methodological consistency across the canon, and thus all of the studies in each volume approach the task of exegesis from a structural-functional linguistic perspective. *Functional* linguistics involves a top-down perspective when analyzing the way linguistic elements work in a text. On this view, a text is seen as having a broad social and/or literary function (i.e., its genre) reflected in the type of language used in a given context (i.e., its register), and the sub-units within the text, including the units of discourse, the paragraphs, sentences or clauses, and word groups are all seen as having a functional meaning within this broader framework. The label *structural* narrows the scope of functional linguistics by introducing a complementary bottom-up priority, whereby the functional potential of texts is inextricably tied to the formal features of those texts. In short, structural-functional linguistics excludes a focus on some things traditionally understood to be part of some functional analyses (such as, for example, prototypes and conceptual schemata), while instead focusing on the close relationship between semantics (understood as meaning potential), syntax, lexis, and morphology.

The LENT series has been planned, so far, to make up a nine-volume series of books, divided according to various sub-corpora in the New Testament. Each subdivision of the New Testament has been selected on the basis of the similar content contained in those texts, balanced by the aim of having each volume cover a suitable amount of content from within the New Testament. Each essay is written from a structural-functional linguistic perspective as defined above, but the ways in which linguistics informs and shapes the individual essays vary from author to author. The analyses and arguments as well as the methods used to make them are all filtered through the same linguistic perspective. This allows for creative ways of marshaling the wide range of resources of the linguistic models that are situated within the structural-functionalist perspective. This means that the essays are linguistically challenging, but they are more valuable for that fact, because they encourage thinking in terms of models and methods for engaging the biblical texts, rather than focusing on the static and bland re-labelling of morphological features and posturing on theological issues that are only tangentially related to the text itself. We believe that the volumes in LENT will encourage new and creative interaction with the biblical texts by exemplifying innovative exegesis relevant to the sets of New Testament books that researchers, pastors, and students are already engaged in studying.

The first volume of this series only covers one book, while most of the other volumes will group together related New Testament books or potentially sub-corpora of various types. We see the first volume, a compilation of linguistic analyses on the Epistle of James, as a great way to kick off this series because James is a short letter not immediately related to the other letters of the New Testament. The following volumes, which will not necessarily be published in this order, are designated to cover the following New Testament books:

- The Synoptic Gospels
- The Johannine Writings (the Gospel of John, the Johannine Epistles, and Revelation)
- Acts
- Romans and Galatians
- The Corinthian and Thessalonian Correspondences
- Ephesians, Philippians, Colossians
- Paul's Personal Correspondences (1–2 Timothy, Titus, Philemon)
- Early Jewish-Christian Writings (1–2 Peter, Jude, and Hebrews)

Stanley E. Porter,
Zachary K. Dawson,
and Ryder A. Wishart
Series editors

Contributors

Zachary K. Dawson is a PhD candidate in New Testament at McMaster Divinity College, Hamilton, ON, Canada.

James D. Dvorak is Professor of Greek and New Testament at Oklahoma Christian University, Oklahoma City, OK.

Benjamin B. Hunt holds an MA in New Testament from McMaster Divinity College, Hamilton, ON, Canada.

Ji Hoe Kim is a PhD student in New Testament at McMaster Divinity College, Hamilton, ON, Canada.

Christopher D. Land is Assistant Professor of New Testament and Linguistics at McMaster Divinity College, Hamilton, ON, Canada.

Stanley E. Porter is President, Dean, and Professor of New Testament, as well as holder of the Roy A. Hope Chair in Christian Worldview, at McMaster Divinity College, Hamilton, ON, Canada.

Jonathan M. Watt is Professor of Biblical Studies at Geneva College in Beaver Falls, PA.

Cynthia Long Westfall is Associate Professor of New Testament at McMaster Divinity College, Hamilton, ON, Canada.

Xiaxia E. Xue is Assistant Professor of Biblical Studies at China Graduate School of Theology in Hong Kong.

Abbreviations

AA	*American Anthropologist*
AB	Anchor Bible
AC	*Acta Classica*
AE	*American Ethnologist*
ARA	*Annual Review of Anthropology*
ATR	*Anglican Theological Review*
BAGL	*Biblical and Ancient Greek Linguistics*
BBB	Bonner biblische Beiträge
BDAG	Baur, Walter, et al. *Greek-English Lexicon of the New Testament and Other Early Christian Literature.* 3rd ed. Chicago: University of Chicago Press, 2000.
BDF	Blass, Friedrich, and Albert Debrunner. *A Greek Grammar of the New Testament and Other Early Christian Literature.* Translated and revised by Robert W. Funk. Chicago: University of Chicago Press, 1961.
BECNT	Baker Exegetical Commentary on the New Testament
BHL	Blackwell Handbooks in Linguistics
BibInt	*Biblical Interpretation*
BibInt	Biblical Interpretation Series
BLG	Biblical Languages: Greek
BNTC	Black's New Testament Commentaries
BTB	*Biblical Theology Bulletin*
BSac	*Bibliotheca Sacra*
BZ	*Biblische Zeitschrift*

BZAW	Beihefte zur Zeitschrift für die alttestamentliche Wissenschaft
CBQ	*The Catholic Biblical Quarterly*
ConJ	*Concordia Journal*
CQ	*The Classical Quarterly*
CSCO	Corpus scriptorum christianorum orientalium
CTL	Cambridge Textbooks in Linguistics
CTR	*Criswell Theological Review*
CurBS	*Currents in Research: Biblical Studies*
DEL	Describing English Language
ECHC	Early Christianity in Its Hellenistic Context
ELS	English Language Series
ES	*Economy and Society*
GAP	Guides to Apocrypha and Pseudepigrapha
GBS	Guides to Biblical Scholarship
GCWCRB	*Gifu City Women's College Research Bulletin*
HTR	*Harvard Theological Review*
HvTSt	*Hervormde teologiese studies*
IBC	Interpretation: A Bible Commentary for Teaching and Preaching
IBS	*Irish Biblical Studies*
ICC	International Critical Commentary
IJES	*International Journal of English Studies*
JAOS	*Journal of the American Oriental Society*
JBL	*Journal of Biblical Literature*
JCPS	Jewish and Christian Perspectives Series
JEAP	*Journal of English for Academic Purposes*
JETS	*Journal of the Evangelical Theological Society*
JGRChJ	*Journal of Greco-Roman Christianity and Judaism*
JSJSup	Supplements to the Journal for the Study of Judaism
JSNT	*Journal for the Study of the New Testament*
JSNTSup	Journal for the Study of the New Testament Supplement Series

KEK	Kritisch-exegetischer Kommentar über das Neue Testament (Meyer-Kommentar)
KNT	Kommentar till Nya Testamentet
LASBF	*Liber Annuus Studii Biblici Franciscani*
LB	*Linguistica Biblica*
LBR	Lexham Bible Reference Series
LBS	Linguistic Biblical Studies
LEC	Library of Early Christianity
LENT	Linguistic Exegesis of the New Testament
LNTS	Library of New Testament Studies
LS	*Language in Society*
LW	Martin Luther. *Luther's Works.* Edited by Jaroslav Pelikan and Helmut Lehman, 55 vols. Philadelphia and St. Louis: Fortress and Concordia, 1955–1986.
MBSS	McMaster Biblical Studies Series
MJT	*Midwestern Journal of Theology*
MSJ	*The Master's Seminary Journal*
NCBC	New Cambridge Bible Commentary
Neot	*Neotestamentica*
NICNT	New International Commentary on the New Testament
NICOT	New International Commentary on the Old Testament
NIGTC	New International Greek Testament Commentary
NIVAC	NIV Application Commentary
NLC	*Nottingham Linguistic Circular*
NovT	*Novum Testamentum*
NovTSup	Supplements to Novum Testamentum
NSBT	New Studies in Biblical Theology
NTM	New Testament Monographs
NTOA	Novum Testamentum et Orbis Antiquus
NTS	*New Testament Studies*
NTTS	New Testament Tools and Studies
OLS	Open Linguistics Series
ÖTK	Ökumenischer Taschenbuch-Kommentar
PNTC	Pillar New Testament Commentary

RB	*Revue biblique*
RBS	Resources for Biblical Study
RevExp	*Review and Expositor*
ResQ	*Restoration Quarterly*
SBG	Studies in Biblical Greek
SBJT	*The Southern Baptist Journal of Theology*
SBLDS	Society of Biblical Literature Dissertation Series
SBLSBS	Society of Biblical Literature Sources for Biblical Study
SE	*Studia Evangelica*
SemeiaSt	Semeia Studies
SNTG	Studies in New Testament Greek
SNTSMS	Society for New Testament Studies Monograph Series
ST	*Studia Theologica*
STDJ	Studies on the Texts of the Desert of Judah
SUNT	Studien zur Umwelt des Neuen Testaments
SWBA	Social World of Biblical Antiquity
SymS	Symposium Series
THKNT	Theologischer Handkommentar zum Neuen Testament
TJ	*Trinity Journal*
TLL	Topics in Language and Linguistics
TSAJ	Texte und Studien zum antiken Judentum
TSL	Typological Studies in Language
TynBul	*Tyndale Bulletin*
WATSA	What Are They Saying About. . .
WBC	Word Biblical Commentary
WTJ	*Westminster Theological Journal*
WUNT	Wissenschaftliche Untersuchungen zum Neuen Testament
ZECNT	Zondervan Exegetical Commentary on the New Testament
ZNW	*Zeitschrift für die neutestamentliche Wissenschaft und die Kunde der älteren Kirche*

1

Introduction

JAMES D. DVORAK AND ZACHARY K. DAWSON

THE EPISTLE OF JAMES has endured centuries of critique and criticism; nearly every commentary on the epistle discusses this to a greater or lesser extent. This discussion tends to be diachronic and often draws attention to what have been negative or pessimistic views of the epistle. Timothy George reminds us that James was not quoted by any Church Father of the second century, that the letter does not appear in the Muratorian canon, and that it received very little attention during the time between Augustine and Luther.[1] Although both Calvin and Zwingli held relatively positive views of James,[2] it has been Luther's now (in)famous pessimistic characterization of James as "an epistle of straw" (or "a right strawy epistle") that has endured from the period of the Reformation.[3] Luther made this comment as he compared the letter of James with the letters of Paul—and for Luther there was really no comparison at all, since, to his way of thinking, James "has nothing of the nature of the Gospel about it."[4] He also questioned the letter's canonicity, and even though he included it in the first edition of his German New Testament, he relegated it to the back of the book (with Jude, Hebrews, and Revelation) and omitted its page numbers from the table of contents.[5] Four centuries later, another Martin—the critical scholar Martin

---

1. George, "Right Strawy Epistle," 21.

2. See ibid., 24–28.

3. Luther, "Prefaces to the New Testament," 362.

4. Ibid.

5. Ropes, *Epistle of St. James*, 106.

Dibelius—carried on the pessimistic view of James. Dibelius questioned whether James was even a letter at all, claiming that because the document as a whole "lacks continuity in thought," it was impossible to locate within it an "epistolary situation" making it "impossible to consider Ja[me]s an actual letter."[6] Further, Dibelius characterized James as "paraenesis," which he defined as "a text that which strings together admonitions of general ethical content."[7] As such, the document "provides no opportunity for the development and elaboration of religious ideas"[8] and, thus, as Dibelius forthrightly states, James "has no theology."[9]

However, during the decade of the 1980s, critical biblical interpretation underwent a significant paradigm shift (in the Kuhnian sense).[10] More and more interpreters were approaching the biblical text with questions that traditional (historical-)critical methods were not equipped to answer. As a result, scholars began drawing upon methodologies, especially from the humanities and the social sciences, that had thentofore been utilized outside the discipline of biblical studies. Some scholars attempted to integrate these methods with traditional criticism, while others developed entirely new models and methodologies.[11] During this time, scholarly interest in the letter of James began to reemerge for various reasons—and in a much more positive light.[12] In a recent survey of this scholarship on the letter of James, Alicia Batten highlighted four distinct areas of research into the letter that have developed significantly over the past several decades: the letter's structure and genre; authorship and audience; thematic issues; and relation to the sayings of Jesus.[13] These topics continue to engage the scholarship of the previous generations in various ways, but often with different presuppositions and, thus, contrasting results. Scholars continue to propose new arguments and nuances to issues associated with the text through a proliferation of models and methods. Some of these have yielded more fruit than others. For example, John

6. Dibelius, *James*, 2.

7. Ibid., 3

8. Ibid., 21.

9. Ibid.

10. See Kuhn, *Structure of Scientific Revolutions*.

11. See now volumes 1 and 2 of Porter and Adams, eds., *Pillars in the History of Biblical Interpretation*.

12. See McKnight, *Letter of James*, 9–10.

13. Batten, *What Are They Saying*.

Elliott's rhetorical analysis, bringing to bear on the letter the insights of social-scientific criticism (particularly the notion of purity and pollution in antiquity) concluded that the unifying theme of the letter was "wholeness-holiness."[14] This study made use of social-scientific criticism, a critical methodology that, we think, aided in identifying convincingly the central theme of the letter, namely wholeness and holiness. This has provided a foothold for further exegesis; in fact, other scholars have even used the holiness motif to structure entire commentaries on James.[15] For a document once disparaged as anemic Christian discourse, the Epistle of James has come to be seen as communicating a profound message about whole (holy) living.

The chapters in this volume represent an attempt to continue pushing the study of James forward, and all of them endeavor to do so through applying modern linguistic models that, to a greater or lesser extent, make use of Systemic Functional Linguistics (SFL). SFL as a paradigm for biblical interpretation has been used in New Testament studies now for nearly three decades, but its potential and value have often been underestimated if not overlooked. One reason for this may be that the idea of utilizing specialized methods runs the risk of being inaccessible to those who are not familiar with their specialized terminology. The contributors to this book make a conscious effort to mitigate this potential hindrance for our readers. A related reason as to why SFL has been underappreciated is that scholarly engagement with such works requires a thorough grasp of modern linguistic theory, and even a specific school therein, which was wholly developed outside of biblical studies proper. On one end of the spectrum, there appears to be a lack of willingness of some biblical scholars to become interdisciplinary in their scholarship (this is certainly not always the case) out of a desire to maintain a tight grip on the familiar categories of traditional Greek grammar that modern linguistic theory often challenges. On the other end of the spectrum, instead of approaching biblical texts fully from within a linguistic theory, which requires a comprehensive understanding of the theory, methodological eclecticism is often promoted as virtuous because it "takes the best" from any given theory or model and applies it to biblical interpretation. The problem with this is that what constitutes the best parts of other methods is arbitrary

14. Elliott, "Epistle of James," 71–81. Elliott was highly influenced by Wuellner, "Der Jakobusbrief," 5–66.

15. E.g., Moo, *Letter of James.*

and is often used expressly to serve as an apologetic for predetermined conclusions, enlisting exegesis in the service of dogma as it were, and not as descriptive components of a critical method to investigate biblical texts afresh. While SFL displays a lot of diversity in itself, as well as in how it is applied, it seemed advantageous to us, and wholly within the interdisciplinary currents of biblical scholarship, to compile a volume that has a common thread running through various linguistic studies on the book of James. We hope that our readership will see the value in using a functional linguistic approach for biblical interpretation as a result of the chapters this volume offers on the Epistle of James.

In the first chapter Cynthia Long Westfall addresses one of the biggest questions concerning the book of James: its structure and purpose. Westfall claims that there is "a direct relationship between the structure of a discourse and its message, which is directly related to its purpose." As a means, then, of uncovering the structure and purpose of the letter, Westfall employs an SFL-informed discourse analysis procedure on the first chapter of James that she systematically carries out in a four-step methodology. As a result, she sees the structure and purpose of Jas 1 as "a series of comparisons that serve to summarize the readers' problems and ethical failings, which encompass most of the major themes in the rest of the discourse, and serve to urge the readers to make life-giving choices in each case." The fruit of Westfall's study is offered in the form of a complete outline of Jas 1 at the end of her essay.

Again, one of the perennial issues concerning the Epistle of James has been the question of the letter's structure and genre—i.e., is James truly a letter? If so, how does it hang together? In chapter 2 Stanley E. Porter responds to Martin Dibelius's classic declaration that James has no continuity of thought. Porter begins his paper by addressing the question: What is cohesion? Clarifying the difference between cohesion and coherence, Porter uncovers a category mistake made by many contemporary commentators. By explaining that coherence is a category that belongs to the ideational metafunction of language, and that cohesion belongs to the textual metafunction, Porter disentangles the discussion that so often conflates the two categories. Since a text can be cohesive, and still lack coherence, but not vice versa, the logical order to approach the issue of structure in James is to determine if the text has cohesion, and then address the question of coherence. To do this, Porter makes use of cohesive harmony theory, which was developed in SFL by Ruqaiya Hasan.

By isolating the imperative independent clauses of the letter, Porter uses forty-eight clauses to evaluate the cohesion and cohesive harmony of the Epistle of James by identifying the major content words and their respective cohesive chains and their chain interactions. The linguistic data collected by this analysis effectively establish the cohesive harmony of all five chapters of the letter. As a result, Porter finds that, by way of cohesive harmony analysis, the number of different types of sections in the Letter of James proposed by Dibelius is undermined, and because cohesive harmony analysis supports a definable textual relationship between the textual metafunction (cohesion) and the ideational metafunction (coherence), a way forward for addressing the actual coherence of the letter is paved because the letter displays a high cohesive harmony.

Following Porter's chapter on cohesion in James, the third chapter then takes up one of the most, if not the most, difficult issues in the Epistle of James with regard to its coherence. In his recent commentary, Dale Allison concludes that Jas 2:18 is either corrupt or "James expressed himself so poorly that we cannot offer any clear exposition of his words."[16] In this chapter Christopher Land proposes that 2:18 may actually make good sense within Allison's proposed context of situation, despite Allison's failure to recognize this. James addresses a general Diaspora audience, yet he calls for a Jesus-like eschatological faith to issue forth in a Jesus-like understanding of true Torah observance. The person in 2:14–17 espouses such a faith yet lacks the concomitant mercy; by contrast, the interlocutor of 2:18–26 disclaims such a faith altogether. Attentiveness to this distinction clarifies the subsequent references to the *Shema* and to Abraham and Rahab. With this proposed interpretation, Land offers a new, contextually insightful, and coherent view of one of the most problematic passages in the New Testament.

The next two chapters apply methods of intertextual analysis to James. One lexeme that has attracted much attention from scholars in the Epistle of James is δίψυχος because no use of this term is known prior to its occurrence in James (1:8; 4:8). Studies have inquired into the morphology and background of δίψυχος, even making strong cases that James himself coined the term. Picking up the conversation in chapter 4, Ji Hoe Kim attempts to sharpen understanding of this term by analyzing the theme of "doubleness" or "double-mindedness" in the Epistle of James of which δίψυχος is a key contributor, but also how this theme

16. Allison, *Epistle of James*, 472.

5

is intertextually related to James's literary environment. Kim notes that it has often been observed that double-mindedness harkens back to the *Shema* (Deut 6:4–5), which commands that Israel be whole—the conceptual opposite of being divided—with regard to one's allegiance to God. However, Kim argues that it is not sufficient to link the *Shema directly* to James's use of δίψυχος because of the conceptual gap between the undivided commitment to Yahweh in the *Shema* and the double-minded attitude toward God in the Epistle of James. The intertextual relationship, argues Kim, needs to be understood through the tradition of the *Shema* as it develops in other texts. As a result, using a set of linguistic tools informed by SFL, Kim argues the thesis that James uses δίψυχος so as to engage a pre-existing Old Testament theme that originated with the *Shema* by echoing the double-mindedness language in Hos 10:2. Thus, the key to understanding how δίψυχος contributes to the theme of doubleness in James is not simply to analyze it morphologically, but rather to analyze it thematically and intertextually, which sets the Epistle of James against a more informed contextual backdrop.

In chapter 5 Xiaxia Xue observes that the role of Rahab, who is mentioned in Jas 2:25, has been overshadowed by the emphasis placed on Paul and Abraham in previous intertextual analyses of Jas 2:14–26. Xue explains that one cannot grasp the intertextual meaning created in the Epistle of James simply by analyzing how the letter relates to Abrahamic texts or how the letter reacts to understandings of Paulinism as other scholars have done. This is because James deliberately juxtaposes the historical figure of Abraham with Rahab for a specific purpose. Xue works from the premise that *textual* juxtaposition of these characters in Jewish history logically leads to an *intertextual* juxtaposition, and so one will not understand the intertextual significance of one of these without seeing how the other compares and contrasts in the larger backdrop of texts that the community shares. Xue implements an intertextual analysis for James 2:14–26 to focus on how the roles of Abraham and Rahab are juxtaposed in the letter. Xue's methodology depends on Jay Lemke's SFL-informed model for intertextual analysis. Unlike previous intertextual studies of James, Xue connects the Second Temple Jewish backdrop of both of these characters to the context of situation the letter addresses, which brings into clearer focus why the writer would wish to invoke a harlot alongside the father of Israel. That both of these characters of Israel's history who occupied radically different social classes and occupations were used by

God reinforces the notion that God does not show partiality, and so those who are God's people should follow likewise, even attending to those who are socially marginalized and poor. Xue makes the additional argument that when emphasis on the intertextual juxtaposition is accurately grasped the James-Paul tension between faith and works slackens.

Chapters 6 through 9 are grouped together because they all address the interpersonal metafunction in the letter of James. In the sixth chapter Zachary K. Dawson analyzes the rhetorical and interpersonal functions of the diatribe in Jas 2:14–26. The rhetorical structure of James is a topic that has been addressed many times in recent scholarship under various methods, but with virtually no agreement on the rhetorical structure of the letter. Further, whereas James is often viewed as exhibiting ancient forms of argumentation (e.g., diatribe) and regarded for its sophisticated Hellenistic Greek style, Dawson sees the purposes and effects of James's language on the letter's recipients as inadequately answered by contemporary commentators. At once in the same essay, Dawson proposes a fresh model by which new light is shed on how the diatribal style functions in James with regard to the tenor (interpersonal) relations at play, which in turn reveals how and why James rhetorically organizes the letter in the way he does. After surveying the scholarly landscape on rhetoric in James, Dawson illustrates a social theory of discourse adapted from Critical Discourse Analysis (CDA) by which to interpret types of discourse based on the social structures and events that constrain them. While the study of how ancient modes of argumentation functioned in antiquity is helpful for understanding how they function in New Testament documents, Dawson claims that because early Christian documents belonged to a different social domain than those of the wider society, the practice of using types of discourse such as diatribe becomes reinvested and reoriented around the social structures within the early Christian social domain. The system of Engagement, a linguistic model developed by systemic-functional linguists J. R. Martin and P. R. R. White is then adapted for New Testament Greek to analyze the interpersonal semantics of Jas 2:14–26, and thereby identifies the ideological strategies at work in the letter that attempt to negotiate values and beliefs around points of sociological struggle. Dawson concludes that the linguistic patterns evidenced in this part of the letter reveal James's personal disposition toward his audience, and shows how he seeks to (re)establish relations of power and solidarity with his addressees as he attempts to persuade them to adopt beliefs and behaviors characteristic of his ideology (theology).

In chapter 7 James D. Dvorak focuses on James's use of questions. He argues that James does not ask questions merely to demand information from the readers; rather, he uses questions as a means of positioning or repositioning his readers in such a way that they would be more likely to adopt or to adopt again a particular ideological (i.e., theological) point of view and its attendant values. In support of this thesis, Dvorak makes several moves. First, he argues that the ideological purpose of the letter of James is the resocialization of the readers, since, from James's perspective, they had forsaken the core values and ideology of the group of Jesus-followers and replaced them with worldly values and ideology. In the second move, Dvorak lays out a two-part sociolinguistic model for analyzing questions. The first part of the model describes the basic grammar and syntax of questions, with special attention given to identifying questions as open or closed. The second part of the model is based on a functional linguistic model known as Appraisal Theory, especially the portion of the theory that deals with Engagement, which Dvorak uses to demonstrate how James's questions realized the kinds of interpersonal meanings that would, at least potentially, position his readers to (re-) align themselves with the values that James promoted. Finally, Dvorak completes the chapter with an analysis of a number of specific questions that James asked his readers in the letter, offering an interpretation of each from the perspective of the theory and model that he proffered.

It may strike the casual reader of the Epistle of James as surprising that James in one breath would call his addressees brothers and sisters, but in the next breath call them adulteresses, sinners, and double-minded ones. Noting that forms of address in the Epistle of James are pervasive, Benjamin Hunt in chapter 8 explores how these forms of address were utilized by James to create and maintain interpersonal relations with the community he writes to. Hunt brings insight from social-scientific criticism into contact with the SFL model, which facilitates a means of describing interpersonal meaning within a first-century Mediterranean context. The first part of the essay develops a linguistic model that maps the interpersonal semantic choices available to a person speaking Greek in the first century when addressing others. This model is then employed to examine forms of address in James as indicators of the relationship James is attempting to prescribe between himself and the community he writes to. Arguing that James's use of forms of address are deliberate and calculated, Hunt's essay provides an explanation of why James chose to address his addressees as he did, as well as the intended and potential rhetorical effect this had on his addressees.

In chapter 9 Jonathan Watt takes on the question of whether James uses anti-language, the theory of language developed by Michael Halliday to describe how features of language in anti-societies function to defend an alternate social reality and challenge the standards of the majority society. Watt begins by describing the main features of Halliday's seminal essay on anti-languages, making note of some of the limitations the study presents for wider applications. After considering other test cases of anti-language studies, one even involving the application of the theory to Qumran Hebrew, Watt engages the discussion of the applicability of the theory within New Testament studies. Finding that using Halliday's original case studies to describe notions of "relexicalization" and "metaphorization" in New Testament documents, particularly in the Gospel of John, has presented certain logical issues, Watt moves carefully into describing the linguistic phenomena characteristic of James's letter, making comparisons to Halliday's anti-language study along the way. Though James exhibits many features of anti-language, Watt aptly judges that without sufficient contextual matching, it is unnecessary and unwise to consider James's language "anti" even if it functions persuasively via similar linguistic avenues. Watt finishes his essay by providing some considerations for ongoing study.

In the conclusion, we suggest that the linguistic methods put to work throughout this volume offer a greater heuristic return than the tired models and methods of contemporary exegetical commentary writing. To do this, we selected a recently-published commentary that appears in a well-known and typically well-respected commentary series—a commentary that, we believe, represents well what is considered to be high quality exegetical commentary writing—and we offer our critique. Our critique reveals a number of significant shortcomings, not merely of the interpretations it seeks to advance, but in regards to the paradigm in which it operates and the models and methods it deploys. Along the way, we interject where, in our opinion, the functional sociolinguistic readings offered in this volume (and others like them) give greater insight into the meanings made in the Epistle of James.

The papers described above pave new ground for linguistic study of the New Testament, and particularly for James. Several of the current academic discussions are engaged by these studies, and new light has been shed on them through methods of linguistic criticism, and all within the SFL model. There is no doubt that the topics discussed in these studies will continue to generate press, and so it is our hope that others will engage our linguistic analyses on the Epistle of James as they seek new insights into this early Christian letter.

BIBLIOGRAPHY

Allison, Dale C., Jr. *A Critical and Exegetical Commentary on the Epistle of James*. ICC. New York: Bloomsbury T. & T. Clark, 2013.

Dibelius, Martin. *James: A Commentary on the Epistle of James*. Revised by Henrich Greeven. Translated by Michael A. Williams. Hermeneia. Minneapolis: Fortress, 1975.

Elliott, John H. "The Epistle of James in Rhetorical Social Scientific Perspective: Holiness-Wholeness and Patterns of Replication." *BTB* 23 (1993) 71–81.

George, Timothy. "'A Right Strawy Epistle': Reformation Perspectives on James." *SBJT* 4 (2000) 20–31.

Kuhn, Thomas S. *The Structure of Scientific Revolutions*. 3rd ed. Chicago: University of Chicago Press, 1996.

Luther, Martin. "Prefaces to the New Testament" (1522), *LW* 35, edited by E. Theodore Bachmann, 355–411. Translated by Charles M. Jacobs. Revised by E. Theodore Bachmann. Philadelphia: Muhlenberg, 1960.

Moo, Douglas J. *The Letter of James*. PNTC. Grand Rapids: Eerdmans, 2000.

Porter, Stanley E., and Sean A. Adams (eds.). *Pillars in the History of Biblical Interpretation, Volume 1: Prevailing Methods before 1980*. MBSS 2. Eugene, OR: Pickwick, 2016.

———. *Pillars in the History of Biblical Interpretation, Volume 2: Prevailing Methods after 1980*. MBSS 2. Eugene, OR: Pickwick, 2016.

Ropes, James Hardy. *A Critical and Exegetical Commentary on the Epistle of St. James*. ICC. Edinburgh: T. & T. Clark, 1916.

Wuellner, Wilhelm H. "Der Jakobusbrief im Licht der Rhetorik und Textpragmatik." *LB* 43 (1978) 5–66.

2

Mapping the Text

How Discourse Analysis Helps Reveal the Way through James

CYNTHIA LONG WESTFALL

INTRODUCTION

A S I WAS WRITING this paper, one of my students at McMaster Divinity College asked me whether or not discourse analysis would make a difference in the way he would preach a sermon about a passage.[1] Like my student, before making the effort to attempt to even read a discourse analysis of a given book, many biblical scholars ask: "What is the exegetical payoff of discourse analysis?" Discourse analysis is a relative newcomer to biblical studies.[2] Since it is a linguistics-based discipline, it requires effort to learn linguistic theory and terminology.

1. Several years ago, an earlier version of this chapter was presented at the invitation session of the New Testament Greek Language and Exegesis section of the ETS Annual Meeting in San Francisco on November 17, 2011. The session topic was "Discourse Analysis as a Tool for New Testament Exegesis" and the title of this paper was "James 1:1–27: A Systemic Functional Linguistics Approach." I wish to thank the section chair and moderator Martin Culy for overseeing the project and giving helpful feedback. It was agreed that each participant would take a section from James and do a discourse analysis of that section, each utilizing their distinctive methodologies and approaches to exegesis. I also wish to thank my co-presenters and co-panelists Steven E. Runge and Erwin Starwalt. A special thanks is due to Stephen Levinsohn who provided helpful feedback and encouragement.

2. For an overview of Discourse Analysis in New Testament studies, see Westfall, *Hebrews*, 23–27. However, there are a growing number of studies and publications within the last ten years.

The book of James is an excellent place to demonstrate exegetical pay-off. After having suffered from the neglect of scholarship, it has slowly emerged into the light of interest. However, one of the biggest questions about the book concerns its structure and purpose.[3] While discourse analysis is used to analyze many different patterns at the discourse level, it is a natural approach to the examination of structure. According to my approach to discourse analysis, there is a direct relationship between the structure of a discourse and its message, which is directly related to its purpose. While this study will not be able to offer a full analysis of the book, it will offer significant insight on the structure and purpose of Jas 1, which is probably one of the most difficult sections in the book. The discourse analysis will show that the first chapter is mapped on a series of comparisons that serve to summarize the readers' problems and ethical failings, which encompass most of the major themes in the rest of the discourse and serve to urge the readers to make life-giving choices in each case.

METHODOLOGY FOR DETERMINING DISCOURSE STRUCTURE

Linguistic Theory

Discourse analysis is a discipline of linguistics rather than a methodology.[4] It looks at language as discourse above the sentence level. Discourse analysis draws on and informs work from such diverse fields as psychology, speech-language pathology, informatics, computer science, philosophy, biology, human anatomy, neuroscience, sociology, anthropology, and acoustics. That is to say, in practice it is synthetic and may utilize insight from any discipline that is relevant. Any of these disciplines may provide a lens through which patterns are analyzed in a text. There are

---

3. As noted below, many assume that the discourse has no unifying theme, and describe it in such a way that the flow of thought resembles a pastiche. For example, Nida et al., described it as a collection of exhortations related by "stream of consciousness" (*Style and Discourse*, 118).

4. For an overview of sources for discourse analysis, see Westfall, *Discourse Analysis*, 22 n. 1. Brown and Yule's *Discourse Analysis* is still a good introduction to Discourse Analysis, though the field has expanded significantly since 1984. Another source that is helpful is Shiffrin et al., *Handbook of Discourse Analysis*. There have been a growing number of recent works that represent a variety of linguistic approaches including Gee, *Introduction to Discourse Analysis*; Gee, *How To Do Discourse Analysis*; and Strauss and Feiz, *Discourse Analysis*.

an infinite number of possibilities of what you can do with it. I have been primarily interested in using discourse analysis to identify text structures and build a mental representation of the text that is grounded in the formal features of the discourse.[5]

I have adopted Halliday's Systemic Functional Linguistics (SFL) as my primary theory.[6] SFL studies how language is used to communicate in social interaction (the functional element), and treats language as a network of systems, or interrelated sets of options for making meaning. The battle cry of SFL is "Trust the text!" which means that the focus of the study of language should be on real, ordinary language in use.[7] Along that line, in this study the biblical text is treated as having the properties of real language. I assume that the biblical text has coherence, relevance, cohesion, and prominence, which are basic properties that define a text. The simplest way to describe my methodology is that it is based on formal and semantic patterns of continuity and variation, which produce cohesion and prominence.

Analytical Procedure

I employ a four-step methodology[8] to analyze the structure of the

5. For a description of arriving at a mental representation of the text, see Dooley and Levinsohn, *Analyzing Discourse*, 51–53.

6. For an introduction to SFL, see Halliday and Matthiessen, *Introduction to Functional Grammar*. For a brief summary of discourse analysis of the New Testament based on SFL, see Reed, *Discourse Analysis of Philippians*, 16–122. For a fuller description of my model as illustrated by various New Testament texts and applied to Hebrews, see Westfall, *Discourse Analysis*, 28–87.

7. The argument behind this statement is that the analysis of language should be textually based, and that form and meaning are inseparable. Trusting the text involves the assumption that the author has a purpose in the way he or she structures the text and that the formal features reflect meaning and should affect interpretation. See Sinclair and Carter, *Trust the Text*. John Sinclair first summarized SFL's textually based approach in an earlier article: "Trust The Text." As Brown and Yule assert, "We assume that every sentence forms part of a developing, cumulative instruction which tells us how to construct a coherent representation" (Brown and Yule, *Discourse Analysis*, 134).

8. My approach is structured around SFL's three dimensions of context and three metafunctions of language as charted in Halliday and Hasan, *Text and Context*, 40, and discussed throughout their work with some variations. I follow their chart in associating cohesion with mode (the textual metafunction). I associate topic with the properties of field (the ideational metafunction) because it involves the distillation of ideational meanings. I associate prominence, with tenor (the interpersonal metafunction) because it is a strategy that orchestrates the recipients' involvement with the text.

discourse at and above the sentence level in the text, working through the text in a linear manner.[9]

1. Grouping with patterns of cohesion and variation

2. Identifying topics within the groupings

3. Locating patterns of prominence and main clauses

4. Determining the relationship to the co-text

While I cannot explain in detail all the formal and semantic data in the text that are used to analyze each of these discourse functions, I can refer you to my *Discourse Analysis of the Letter to the Hebrews* where there is an attempt to describe in detail the various devices that authors used to create cohesion, topics, and prominence in a unit and at the level of discourse. However, I can briefly explain the steps.

GROUPING BY COHESION AND VARIATION

The first step is to locate the way that the author groups the text above the sentence level into sub-units, units, and sections. This is done through analyzing the cohesion patterns.[10] Cohesion refers to how an entire discourse hangs together, but we may also detect cohesion patterns that glue text together and group the text at lower levels in the discourse. In our textual analysis and translation work, the cohesion patterns in Greek should be the foundation and basis of our paragraph and section structures, rather than an attempt to locate "breaks" based on intuitive notions about topic.[11] In Greek the author creates cohesion with patterns of continuity. The sentence structure is the starting point for determining cohesion.[12] Above the sentence level, an author glues sentences together

---

See also Westfall, *Discourse Analysis*, 78–87.

9. This requires preliminary observation and hypotheses of what constitutes a section in the discourse, but the process should be self-correcting by the end of the process and test the preliminary determination of each unit of study for analysis.

10. For the theory and a description of cohesion, see Halliday and Hasan, *Cohesion in English*. See also Westfall, *Discourse Analysis*, 30–31, 37–55.

11. This methodology and approach is in direct contrast with the text-linguistic approach of Mark Taylor, whose "cohesion analysis" has a starting point of "cohesion shift analysis," where the first step discerns where the shifts occur based on shifts in predetermined "cohesion fields." However, there is no rigorous methodological attention given to the actual patterns of cohesion and continuity in the fields. See Taylor, *Text-Linguistic Investigation*, 42–43, 45–58.

12. Sometimes notions about the topic override the basic sentence structure, and

into units with a number of strategies that utilize repetition of formal and semantic features.[13] The repetition creates units with spans and cohesive ties, but an author also uses sequencing, staging, and logical relationships. In a complementary way, the author also uses variation of formal and semantic features to group the discourse. Grouping with variation is done with a shift in patterns, and also with features that are marked or emphatic (such as the nominative of direct address). However, the author also uses variation in the discourse to create prominence. Therefore, patterns of continuity in the discourse must be given priority over variation or discontinuity at the beginning of the process.[14] The assumption of the coherence of a discourse means that the text is relevant and it makes sense. Discrete units will form cohesive ties with each other to reinforce and clarify a relationship between them that makes sense.

Identifying Topic within the Grouping

"Topic" refers to what a speaker or writer is talking about within a given unit of analysis. This is arguably the most important step because our sense of the topic is the interpretive frame that we place on the discourse.[15] When we place subheadings in our translations or commentaries, they often become more powerful than the text itself. However, there has been

---

a commentary, translation, or even the editors of the critical Greek text will begin a paragraph or even a section in the middle of a sentence. The integrity of clause complexes should be respected as a rule of thumb.

13. See Westfall, *Discourse Analysis*, 39–55, who demonstrates relationships between grammar and lexis and grouping.

14. This is in contrast with George Guthrie's methodology, because his first step is to locate "cohesion shifts," in a variety of formal and semantic "cohesion fields," which calculates the variation or breaks in the discourse. Furthermore, shifts in topic and "genre" are considered to be part of the variation, so preconceived notions about topic and discontinuity in the "genre" (exposition and exhortation) are included at the first step, which creates a somewhat circular process. Also, the method tends to confuse prominence with a "break" in the discourse. See Guthrie, *Structure of Hebrews*. But also see Taylor, *Text-Linguistic Investigation*, who applies Guthrie's methodology to the discourse of James. The different methodology results in different outcomes.

15. See Brown and Yule, *Discourse Analysis*, 140, who state, "There are, of course, many ... easily recognisable thematisation devices used in the organisation of discourse structure. Placing headings and sub-headings within a text is a common thematisation device in technical or public-information documents.... What these thematisation devices have in common is not only the way they provide 'starting points' for paragraphs in a text, but also their contributions to dividing the whole text into smaller chunks. This 'chunking' effect is one of the most basic of those achieved by thematisation in discourse."

little control on what counts for evidence in the identification of topics or the decisions on subheadings—the process appears to be primarily an intuitive process in most translations and commentaries and even in some discourse analyses.

After we identify how the author groups the discourse, we are in a better position to identify topics in each unit, or answer the questions: What is a discourse unit about? What accounts for all of the data or information in the unit? Often this involves (1) the identification of semantic and identity chains of the participants and how they interact and/or (2) the linear information flow.[16] However, there are times that other factors may play a large role in identifying the topic when the reader cannot identify clear semantic chains. The units and sections can be organized around an episode, a character, a topic, or other features such as a repeated phrase or a group of commands. There are formulaic discourse structures such as a problem-solving procedure, an instruction manual, recipe formats, or stereotypical scenes, stories, or characters. A description of the information flow takes into account the linearization of the unit, including the starting point and the ending point. The starting point is the "theme" in that it connects back with the previous discourse and serves as a point of departure for further development. The end point or destination concludes the unit and points the way forward to the rest of the discourse. The function of the starting point and ending point can be consistent with the occurrence of prominence in the discourse.

Locating Patterns of Prominence and Main Clauses in a Unit

Authors utilize emphatic elements both to chunk or group the text and to create prominence. High and low-level shifts in the discourse will often be marked by emphatic features and by changes in the grammar and lexical patterns. Clusters of emphatic features highlight clauses or clause complexes as being "main" or "central" or to place the emphasis on one sentence over another.[17] Prominence is signaled by formal and

16. For a description and illustration of semantic chains and identity chains, see Westfall, *Discourse Analysis*, 49–53. For a description of different types of repetition, see Hoey, *Patterns of Lexis*, chapter 3.

17. For definitions of prominence, see Reed, *Discourse Analysis of Philippians*, 105–6; Callow, *Discourse Considerations*, 49–68; Wallace, "Figure and Ground," 208. For "main" or "central" clauses, see Reed, *Discourse Analysis of Philippians*, 107; Callow, "Patterns of Thematic Development," 195. For an overview of prominence and features that contribute to prominence, see Westfall, *Discourse Analysis*, 31–36, 55–78.

semantic features that elevate or set apart the content. Prominent clauses are highlighted both by emphatic formal features and from a semantic relationship with the rest of the passage so that they will reflect the purpose of the unit. The formal features include: marked choices and variation in grammar, the use of discourse markers, conjunctions, word order, deixis, the use of emphatic words or phrases, and repetition. Semantic prominence involves devices such as the use of extra words, vividness, crowding the stage, the use of certain figures or concepts that the author assumes are of particular interest to the readers, and the use of logical relationships that distinguish between mainline material and support material. Authors highlight the clauses that are central with clusters of these features that create "zones of turbulence."[18] One clause will therefore be more prominent in a paragraph or section than another on the basis of the confluence of these emphatic indicators.

Determining the Relationship to the Co-text

As Brown and Yule have stated, "Text creates its own context."[19] The co-text is the textual content that surrounds the passage, and the interpretation of any text is constrained by its co-text. The recognition of cohesive ties on the formal and semantic levels between a section of a text and its co-text is a study of both the text's coherence and cohesion. It contributes directly to understanding the place of a section of text in the general structure of a text and locating the text's global themes. This final analysis works toward building a mental representation of the entire text.

ANALYSIS OF JAMES 1

James has been one of the classic structural enigmas in the New Testament and some are still convinced by Dibelius's claim that there is no unified train of thought.[20] There have already been several linguistic-based discourse studies of the structure of this intriguing epistle.[21] It poses an

---

18. "Zones of turbulence" is a term introduced by Longacre (*The Grammar of Discourse*, 38). The discontinuity in a zone of turbulence must be more than the observation of the odd or peculiar, but rather a detection of a constellation of features including marked grammar and lexis, discourse markers associated with variation, emphasis and/or salience, and extra words that are often embedded by syntax which add detail or information.

19. Brown and Yule, *Discourse Analysis*, 50.

20. Dibelius, *James*, 2.

21. Varner, *Book of James*; Taylor, *Text-Linguistic Investigation*; Cheung, *Genre*.

interesting challenge for discourse analysis to see if an analysis above the level of the sentence can detect some coherence in the discourse.

The first chapter is a valid unit in the discourse for preliminary analysis. On the one hand, it begins with the salutation and the letter opening in 1:2, and there is an identifiable shift in 2:1 with a nominative plural of direct address, which is fronted in the thematic position for the first time, along with a second person plural imperative introducing a second person plural span with an arguably large unit in 2:1–13, which demonstrates a significant shift.

The salutation is typical of the Hellenistic Greek letter.[22] It identifies the sender James, his relationship as a servant of Jesus Christ, and the recipients: the twelve tribes of Israel.[23] This formulaic greeting contains no thematic material, though the identity and relationship of the sender and recipients are relevant to the meaning of the discourse. However, it will be excluded from the rest of the analysis.

Tracing Cohesion Patterns/Grouping in James 1:2–27

OVERVIEW OF THE COHESION IN JAMES 1

There are patterns in Jas 1 that group the text at a number of levels. The grammatical features include the grammatical and semantic organization of the discourse into sentence units of primary and dependent clauses.[24] Lexical repetition and paraphrase also group the discourse. However, ch. 1 is primarily mapped on the semantic pattern of contrast that characterizes the entire first chapter. The contrasts set Jas 1 apart from what follows.

Perhaps it goes without saying that the point of departure of the discourse in vv. 2–3 is not a contrast with the epistolary opening in v. 1. It is the letter's initial command/exhortation to count it all joy when you fall into various problems because it produces patience (ὑπομονήν); it forms multiple cohesive ties with the following co-text. The repetition of

---

22. See White, *Greek Letter*.

23. This does not give us a great deal of internal information about the interpersonal register, though one can detect that the author assumes a certain status and authority with the recipients through the use of the imperative and passing judgment on behavior and doctrine.

24. The imperative in 1:7 is an exception to the other imperatives that advance the discourse in James, but it is marked as support material with a γάρ, which is not the case with the other imperatives.

patience (ὑπομονή) in v. 4 as the subject of the third person imperative creates a sub-unit composed of two sentences in 1:2–4.

Most analyses group 1:2–4 with 1:5–8 based on the repetition of "lack": "one who is perfect and complete lacks nothing," and "if anyone lacks wisdom they should ask God."[25] While this repetition forms a cohesive tie, it is a cohesive tie between two discrete sub-units.[26] There is a contrast in 1:5–8 between a person who asks for wisdom in faith (1:5) and one who asks for wisdom but doubts (1:6–8).[27] The contrast forms its own discrete unit around the repetition of asking God (αἰτείτω/2x) with doubting/one who doubts (διακρινόμενος/2x), and anaphora in vv. 7–8 (ὁ ἄνθρωπος [human] and the proverbial ἀνήρ refer to ὁ . . . διακρινόμενος in v. 6).

The contrast in 1:5–8 initiates the pattern that is characteristic of ch. 1: there is a series of contrasts in which a person, character type, or behavior is introduced and receives a positive evaluation and is contrasted with the opposite type of person, opposite character type, or opposite behavior, which receives a negative evaluation.[28] The contrasts are char-

25. McCartney, for example, finds one unit in 1:2–8 and labels it "Faith and Wisdom," which does not adequately convey the information in 1:2–4 (*James*, 83–84). The end of the stages of endurance in v. 4 is not lacking anything (ἐν μηδενὶ λειπόμενοι), and v. 5 forms a cohesive tie with λειπόμενοι to introduce their first contrast: if anyone needs/lacks wisdom (εἰ δέ τις ὑμῶν λείπεται σοφίας). This forms a clear cohesive tie between the first sub-unit and the first comparison, but does not compete with or negate the stronger cohesive ties between 1:2–4 and 1:12. Dibelius dismisses the tie as "superficial" (*James*, 76), and Varner suggests that these linkages have been "overplayed" (*Book of James*, 46).

26. Therefore, the assumption that "link words" create discontinuity is rejected as an oxymoron. Repetition creates cohesion. So-called "link words" can signal cohesion between two discrete units and contribute to the texture of the discourse.

27. The imperative addressed to the one who asks but doubts is expanded with support material including a second command.

28. In an expanded discourse analysis, we could further analyze and compare the composition of the contrasts at the clause level. While James somewhat varies the strategies to create contrasts, the dominant pattern is a positive imperative followed by a negated imperative "Do X; do not do Y," which could be demonstrated in half of the primary contrasts (1:5–8, 19–21, 22). However, in the fourth contrast, James gives a positive evaluation of the first element (μακάριος) without a command before prohibiting the opposite behavior with a negated imperative (1:12–15). This, perhaps, could be contested as a formal contrast, but the one who endures in trials is set up as the antithesis of the person who blames God for being tempted. Within the context of contrast, this would be taken as another example, though it could be read as summative. In regard to the other contrasts, James simply relies on antonymy in order

acterized by the imperative[29] and the conjunction δέ, which marks a new development.[30] Though the syntax may vary in some of the contrasts, they are characterized by a positive element paired with a negated element (Do X; do not do Y). However, the order is reversed in the last two contrasts concerning the mirror illustration and the different types of religion, and negations are not used in the contrasts between the poor and rich and the mirror illustration.[31]

1. The one who asks in faith vs. the one who doubts (vv. 5–8)

2. The poor vs. the rich (vv. 9–11)

3. The one who endures when tested vs. the one who blames God when tested (vv. 12–15)[32]

---

to contrast the rich and poor, which is all that is needed for the reader to follow and understand the contrast in play (1:9–11). This leaves the supportive illustration that contrasts behavior of looking in a mirror (1:23–25), and the concluding contrast of deceptive religion with pure religion (1:26–27). The element of contrast cannot be in doubt in these two variations of the pattern. If anything, the variation of the pattern in the last contrast draws attention to it.

29. Taylor finds the use of third person imperative verbs in 1:4–19 as "the unique function of chapter 1" (Taylor, *Text-Linguistic Investigation*, 1). See also Cheung, *Genre*, 65. However, note that while the third person singular imperative is used in 1:5–13, the second person plural imperative is used in 1:19–27, which varies the rhetorical impact, among other pragmatic effects.

30. As Runge argues, δέ is a coordinating conjunction that has "the added constraint of signaling a new development," something like steps in an argument (*Discourse Grammar*, 31). This is consistent with what is meant by my indication that δέ signals a moderate discontinuity in emphasis in the discourse but is more explanatory concerning the semantics of how it functions (Westfall, *Discourse Analysis*, 66).

31. The question is: Why did James omit negation in these cases? The simple answer is that he did not need it in either case because the contrast was already clear, and/or negation would be awkward in serving the point. In the case of the poor and rich, they are antonyms, which form a semantic contrast, and he is not making a "Be poor, not rich" statement, so negation did not serve James's purpose at this point. In the case of the illustration, it supports or expands the preceding contrast of being doers of God's word, not only hearers in v. 22, which uses the "X not Y" pattern.

32. The pattern of contrasts and the repetition of trials/temptations (πειρασμόν/ πειραζόμενος) as the point of contrast between the two kinds of people should disambiguate the cohesion patterns and remove doubt that 1:12 forms a sub-unit with 1:13–15. This has generally been the understanding of most commentators. However, it must be acknowledged that some recent commentators place 1:12 with 1:9–11: e.g., Johnson, *Letter of James*, 174–76; Penner, *Epistle of James*, 144–47; Moo, *Letter of James*, 71–72; McCartney, *James*, 100; Taylor, *Text-Linguistic Investigation*, 49. This group of analysts finds that the meaning of "testing" has shifted to "temptation" at

4. Being quick to hear vs. being an angry person with ethical impurity (vv. 19–21)

5. Being doers of the word vs. being only hearers of the word (v. 22)

6. The contrast between the two people who look in the mirror (vv. 23–25)

7. Useless religion vs. pure religion (vv. 26–27)

The semantic repetition of relatively short units composed of contrasts makes the strongest contribution to the cohesion of the first chapter, and this particular pattern of contrast is discontinued at 2:1.[33] However, two parts of ch. 1 are outside of the pattern of contrasts: 1:2–4 and 1:16–18.

The two parts of the chapter that do not belong to the series of contrasts occur with asyndeton, the second person plural imperative, and the nominative plural of direct address (ἀδελφοί μου) in 1:2, 16, and 19. The variation in the use of conjunctions,[34] the marked features, and the interruption of the discourse pattern (the series of contrasts), are consistent with zones of turbulence that mark shifts in the discourse.[35] Ἀδελφοί μου is an emphatic discourse marker that James typically uses at shifts in the discourse.[36] The shifts in vv. 16 and 19 are made more emphatic than they would have been with the occurrence of the address ἀδελφοί μου because

1:13, so that there is a shift in topic. I suggest that this kind of analysis comes from grouping with intuitive notions of topic as a first step, and confuses the Greek lexis with the "meaning" of the glosses we use in our English translations. There is a shift from the temptation or challenge being a noun to it being a verb in which temptation is experienced by the subject. That does not change the nature of the trial or temptation, or obviate the cohesive tie, but it does change the relationship of the subject to temptation.

33. However, the choice between two ways characterizes the discourse, which Varner describes as "the bi-polar choices that James sets before his readers" (*Book of James*, 68).

34. I do not argue that asyndeton marks "breaks" as a function (continuity should be assumed when there is no conjunction), but a variation in the discourse pattern of the author's use of conjunctions contributes to a shift when it occurs with other marked features (Westfall, *Discourse Analysis*, 46).

35. See Varner's chart on the relationship between the nominative of address and the grouping into sections (*Book of James*, 35).

36. The occurrence of the address ἀδελφοί μου at shifts is a characteristic of the discourse; see 1:2, 16, 19; 2:1, 5, 14; 3:1, 10, 12; 5:12, 19. But see also ἀδελφοί without the possessive in 4:11; 5:7, 9, 10.

it involves the readers more personally with the text.[37] The two verses create a pivotal shift in the chapter, which divides the series of contrasts into two units.[38] The deictic use of "Know [this] brothers and sisters!" in 1:19 points to the following material in the second unit.[39] However, the command/prohibition "Do not be deceived!" and the following description of God in 1:16–18 form the strongest cohesive ties with the preceding unit, which will be discussed below.

COHESION IN 1:2–18

The first unit shows distinct patterns of continuity and variation. A set of three distinct contrasts is framed by 1:2–4 and the shift in 1:16–18. The two sub-units with the second person plural imperatives vary from the pattern of the characteristic third person imperatives in the contrasts. The first unit is marked by a point of departure and a destination that share common features.

In addition, within the first unit, there are strong cohesive ties that glue the unit together. The strongest cohesive ties are between 1:2–4 and 1:12, formed by the repetition of the challenges of trials or temptation, endurance, and testing that were introduced in 1:2 (ὑπομένει, πειρασμόν, δόκιμος).[40] Furthermore, cognates of πειρασμός (trial/temptation)

37. The occurrences of the emphatic nominative plural of direct address in such close proximity is unusual, because James uses the nominative plural of direct address to shift to a new unit or section throughout the discourse. However, the same features that are used to create shifts are also used to indicate prominence in central sentences and conclusions.

38. As Runge argues, this variation from the pattern of contrasts "exploits patterns and expectations. Humans are wired to recognize patterns. When patterns are broken or expectations are unmet, the standard response is to associate some new meaning with the change" (*Discourse Grammar*, 16). This statement comes in his discussion on prominence, and illustrates well how and why prominence may be used by authors to chunk the discourse.

39. The verb ἴστε in 1:19 could be an indicative, which may be taken as connecting with the previous conclusion in 1:16–18. However, the occurrence with the nominative plural of direct address makes an imperative more likely, given the collocation of the imperative with the nominative plural of direct address in James. There are sixteen occurrences of ἀδελφοί μου in James. Of the fifteen other occurrences, eleven occur with an imperative, three occur with a rhetorical question, and only one other case occurs with the indicative in 3:10, though it occurs with a verb that indicates necessity and so should be categorized as exhortation: οὐ χρή, ἀδελφοί μου, ταῦτα οὕτως γίνεσθαι ("my brothers and sisters, these things should not happen!").

40. The difference produced by the procedure of finding cohesion patterns as the first step is in marked contrast with Taylor, who first locates "cohesion shifts" on the

are repeated five more times in vv. 13–15 (πειραζόμενος, πειράζομαι, ἀπείραστός, πειράζει, πειράζεται), which not only glue the contrast together, but also strengthen the ties of the contrast with 1:2–4.[41] In addition, the expected end product of perfection (τέλειοι) in 1:2–4 forms a lexical and semantic cohesive tie with the description of the Father giving every perfect gift (πᾶν δώρημα τέλειον) in 1:17. The cohesion is extended and strengthened by multiple ties between 1:5–8 and 1:17 with the references to God who gives good gifts and the description of God who gives generously to all who ask. The description of God being without variation or shifting shadow in 1:17 forms a tie with the antonymy of the description of the double-minded person who is unstable in all their ways in 1:8.[42] In 1:18 the choice of God to give birth to us forms strong cohesive ties not only with the adjacent sexual innuendo in the process of temptation from lust to conception to birth to death (1:14–15), but also forms an inferred tie with the process toward maturity in 1:2–4. The reference to first fruits indicates a clear hope in a future in God's plan. Therefore, these formal, lexical, and semantic ties confirm that 1:2–4 is the point of departure for a unit that has its destination in 1:18.[43] How-

---

basis of a problematic methodology and asserts that a "high-level cohesion shift" occurs before and after 1:12 (Taylor, *Text-Linguistic Investigation*, 48). However, Taylor also finds an *inclusio* between 1:2–4 and 1:12 as well as ties with 1:5–8 and 9–11, so he takes it as a summary (Taylor, *Text-Linguistic Investigation*, 60–61).

41. This is in agreement with Laws, *Epistle of James*, 13; and Davids, "James 1:13," 386–92. Contra Taylor, who locates a semantic shift with the form and meaning of the repeated cognates. Taylor asserts that even though there is a repetition of cognates, there is a shift from noun to verb and, "If the semantic shift from 'testing' to 'temptation' is granted, then a corresponding shift occurs in the subject and actor fields from the 'one who perseveres' to 'the one who is tempted'" (*Text-Linguistic Investigation*, 49). With Taylor's criteria, contrasts would have a tendency not to form a unit, though they are clearly two parts of a whole unit. As Davids argues, "Is it not true that here πειραζόμενος has a completely different meaning from πειρασμόν in 1:12?" (*Epistle of James*, 80). He argues against the idea that "link words" indicate a lack of continuity, a position that is consistent with the linguistic theory of the function of repetition in creating cohesion.

42. This is in agreement with Cheung, *Genre*, 62.

43. James is also concerned with deception in the first and third contrasts in the second unit (1:22, 26), but the command not to be deceived in 1:16 (μὴ πλανᾶσθε) is concerned with the readers' theology about God, which is a concern in the first unit, while the concerns in 1:22 (παραλογιζόμενοι ἑαυτούς) and 1:26 (ἀπατῶν) are with self-deception about one's own righteousness and piety. Therefore, James's concern about deception characterizes the entire chapter, but the ties between the two units are not strong, as the semantics, lexis (non-cognates), and grammar are different.

ever, note that the strong cohesive ties have not included the contrast between the poor and the rich in 1:9–11. Yet, since the author has given powerful indications through formal and semantic features that this unit is a group, and with strong cohesion in the repeated pattern of contrasts, the relationship between 1:9–11 and its surrounding co-text must be explained by the identification of the unit's topic in order to determine or infer the plausible relevance of 1:9–11 to the rest of the unit.[44]

COHESION IN 1:19–27

The second unit is framed by emphatic formulaic discourse markers in 1:19 and its destination in the third contrast in 1:26–27. However, the destination is determined mostly by the formulaic point of grouping and marked point of departure in 2:1–13. The shift is strengthened because the distinctive pattern of contrast that characterized ch. 1 is discontinued at 2:1.[45]

In 1:19, a shift is created by the command to "know" (ἴστε), together with the nominative plural of direct address with the possessive (ἀδελφοί μου), strengthened by the appositional "beloved" (ἀγαπητοί).[46] The rest of the contrasts follow one another consecutively without significant variation.

The first contrast begins with the third person imperative that everyone/every human (πᾶς ἄνθρωπος) should be (ἔστω) quick to hear, slow to speak, and slow to anger. The behavior that receives a positive evaluation is hearing, with a negative evaluation of speech and anger within the command. The command is supported by the negative evaluation of the opposite behavior, which is signaled by γάρ: the anger of a

---

44. Grice's maxims assert that there is a general agreement between participants in conversation: cooperation, quality, quantity, relevance, and manner. Authors strive to be relevant for their readers, and readers interpret texts with the assumption that the texts are relevant; see Grice, *Studies in the Way of Words*, 22–40. While these maxims form the basic assumptions of Relevance Theory, they are also consistent with the linguistic concept of coherence and with the assumptions about the text in SFL.

45. The assertion that the pattern of contrast is discontinued in 2:1 is not to say that James does not use contrast in 2:1–13, but that the elements in the contrast function differently than the contrasts in ch. 1, and the contrast is an extended one rather than the use of aphorism (the use of terse sayings written in a laconic and memorable form), which characterized the first chapter.

46. There is a textual variant with some manuscripts reading ὥστε, but ἴστε has stronger support from Alexandrian and Western witnesses. In James, the nominative plural of direct address tends to occur with the imperative or rhetorical questions.

person (proverbial use of ἀνδρός) does not achieve the righteousness of God. The contrast is followed by a command: Therefore (διό), getting rid of filth and evil, receive the word implanted that can save you. The conjunction διό is inferential, indicating that the reason for the command is the preceding contrast.[47] The semantic link between them is that 1:21 rephrases the command in 1:19b with a direct second person plural command that is more explanatory. James equates the positive behavior of being quick to hear (ταχὺς εἰς τὸ ἀκοῦσαι) with receiving God's word, which is confirmed by the following qualification in v. 22 not to be hearers of God's word only (μὴ μόνον ἀκροαταί). Therefore, 1:19–21 forms a highly cohesive sub-unit.

The second contrast qualifies the first contrast: Be doers of the word and not merely hearers who deceive themselves (1:22). This is followed by an illustration of doing and hearing only with a contrast of two types of people who look in a mirror, so that the two contrasts in 1:22–25 form a sub-unit together rather than two separate contrasts. A cohesive tie is formed with the first unit with the warnings against deception (1:22//1:16). Also, the concluding phrase that the one who does the word will be blessed (μακάριος) in what he/she does forms a cohesive tie with the formulaic blessing in the first unit (1:25//1:12).[48] While these links with the first unit contribute to the coherence and texture of the section, they do not override the dominant patterns of continuity and variation.[49]

---

47. Taylor finds a shift between 1:20 and 1:21 because he finds shifts in the cohesion field, though he allows that the "conjunction διό effects a smooth transition as the author draws out the implications of the statement regarding the wrath of God (1.20)" (*Text-Linguistic Investigation*, 51). The problem is that it overrides the author's discourse signal, which indicates a semantic relationship that must be explored as a cohesive device.

48. However, the tie is relatively weak. The syntax is not the same and the only word in common is μακάριος. The additional parallels that Taylor finds to support an *inclusio* are not convincing (ibid., 62). The other *inclusios* he finds in 1:16 and 1:19 (based on ἀδελφοί μου ἀγαπητοί) and 1:13 and 1:21 (κακῶν and κακίας) are similarly unconvincing because of the way that ἀδελφοί μου functions at shifts in the discourse (see n. 36 above) and because the ties between κακῶν and κακίας are not strengthened by semantics or grammar, so they do not override the more dominant patterns of cohesion (ibid., 63). This illustrates the tendencies to process repetition as *inclusio* which indicates breaks in the discourse apart from a robust understanding of cohesion.

49. The detection of *inclusios* as a second step in Taylor's analysis (following Guthrie's model) prioritizes the lexical repetition (or paraphrase) of sometimes one word over other formal indications of structure, so that conjunctions, discourse markers, and semantic patterns of repetition may be overlooked by the procedure. See ibid.,

The final contrast between worthless religion and pure and undefiled religion (1:26–27) is not stated with imperatives, and the person with the negative evaluation is placed first, but it still fits the pattern of contrast and the contrast accounts for all of vv. 26–27. The description of religion with purity language (pure and undefiled [καθαρὰ καὶ ἀμίαντος]—keep oneself from being polluted by the world [ἄσπιλον]) and the negative evaluation of the one who does not control their tongue—forms multiple strong cohesive ties to controlling the tongue and anger (1:19, 20) and getting rid of moral filth and evil (1:21) in the first contrast. There is also a general unexpressed semantic tie between piety and the practice of religion and the spiritual disciplines of hearing and doing the word of God (1:22–25). A weaker cohesive tie is formed by the warnings against self-deception in vv. 16 and 22. The three contrasts form a very close cohesive unit without significant variation in 1:19–27, along with significant ties with the first unit, including the use of the pattern of contrast, and lexical ties, which unify the first chapter.

Concluding Remarks about Cohesion Patterns

On the basis of the formal features, lexical cohesion and patterns of contrast, we can form an overview of the grouping in Jas 1. If we weigh all of these factors, the discourse in ch. 1 contains two units in 1:2–15 and 1:16–18 that form a section. Each part has three contrasts if it is recognized that the two people who look in the mirror are illustrations of the difference between hearers and doers of the word.

A. Unit 1

   1. Point of departure: Consider it all joy when you encounter various trials and temptations (vv. 2–4)

   2. First set of contrasts

      a. The one who asks for wisdom in faith vs. the one who doubts (vv. 5–8)

      b. The poor vs. the rich (vv. 9–11)

      c. The one who endures vs. the one who is tempted by their own desires (vv. 12–15)

60–64 for his location of *inclusio* in ch. 1.

      3. Destination: Don't be deceived, every good gift is from the Father (vv. 16–18)

  B. Unit 2

      1. Point of departure: Know, my beloved brothers and sisters! (1:19a)

      2. Second set of contrasts

         a. Being slow to speak vs. human anger (vv. 19b–21)

         b. Being doers of the word vs. hearers; e.g.: The two people who look in the mirror (vv. 22–25)

         c. Worthless religion vs. true and pure religion (vv. 26–27)

      3. Destination: pure and undefiled religion (third contrast)

Identifying Topics

The recognition of units assists in locating the common thread or topic running through the units that have been located in the section. Following the formulaic salutation in 1:1, it is established that while there are patterns that characterize the entirety of Jas 1 that create a unit, there are two sub-units in the chapter: 1:2–18 and 1:19–27. The lexical and semantic repetition in vv. 2–18 in each contrast involves the collocation of trials or problems with positive outcomes or evaluations. The common semantic thread in each contrast in vv. 19–27 is the collocation of associations of piety (Scripture and religion) with positive action.

Consider Yourselves Blessed in the Midst of Your Problems if You Endure Them (1:2–18)

In the first unit, there are two identity chains, consisting of people whose actions receive a positive evaluation in contrast with people who receive a negative evaluation. The readers form a third identity chain that has the potential to identify with either side or choose between options. There is also a semantic chain of trials/temptations that sometimes conflates with the identity chains.

    The author utilizes rote repetition and paraphrase in vv. 2 and 12 to form cohesion and highlight the topic in vv. 2–18 through the interaction of these ties:

1:2 Πᾶσαν χαρὰν ἡγήσασθε, ἀδελφοί μου, ὅταν πειρασμοῖς περιπέσητε ποικίλοις
γινώσκοντές ὅτι τὸ δοκίμιον ὑμῶν τῆς πίστεως κατεργάζεται ὑπομονήν

1:12 Μακάριος ἀνὴρ ὃς ὑπομένει πειρασμόν

This repetition suggests that the unit in vv. 2–18 is about problems or trials that the recipients are encountering. The repetition sandwiches and constrains the contrast between the poor and the rich, framing and identifying poverty (and probably the behavior of the rich; cf. 2:1, 6–7; 4:13–16; 5:1–6) as a specific and perhaps the quintessential challenge for the readers, which is confirmed by the repeated references to the poor and rich in the discourse.[50] Poverty is usually understood as a problem universally, and a reader who is experiencing problems with poverty would easily infer a relationship between various kinds of trials (πειρασμοῖς . . . ποικίλοις) and one's own personal destitution.

The general principle is given in v. 2: The readers are told to consider it all joy (πᾶσαν χαρὰν ἡγήσασθε) when they encounter various trials, because trials are an opportunity to go through a productive process that results in maturity (1:2a–3). Therefore, the readers can rejoice (inferred) because problems are an opportunity to gain wisdom—God will give generously if they ask for it in faith (vv. 5–8).[51] People who have the problem of poverty can rejoice (paraphrased from καυχάσθω) in their high position. People who are tempted can rejoice because they are blessed (μακάριος) if they endure—specifically, they will receive the crown of life (1:12).

However, there is also the potential of a negative outcome in response to external problems. The contrasts give corresponding examples of behavior or circumstances that will not be blessed in the same way that serve both as clarifying illustrations and warnings. In contrast with those who receive wisdom, those who ask for wisdom while doubting will not receive anything from God because they are double-minded and unstable in all their ways. In contrast with the poor, the rich must "take pride" in the humiliation (ἐν τῇ ταπεινώσει) of having a transitory position in life (1:10–11).[52] Therefore, in the second contrast James suggests

50. See 2:1–13; 4:13–17; and 5:1–6. Concern about the rich and poor is one of the more dominant themes in the discourse.

51. As Varner suggests, the repetition of λείπω (vv. 4, 5) may indicate that wisdom is what is lacking to be perfect and complete (*Book of James*, 54). If so, James wants the readers to consider its ready availability as good news.

52. The rich definitely receive a negative evaluation, though it is not one of

that it is the rich rather than the poor that have the true problem.[53] In the third contrast, those who endure trials and receive a crown of life stand in contrast with a person who blames God for experience of being tempted. The second person, who blames God, is deceived about God's nature and their own responsibility. The second person does not "endure" by definition, because their lack of understanding involves an ethical problem (a failure to admit one's own evil desire), and this may result in a process parallel to 1:3 that ends in death (1:14–15).[54] The concluding command in 1:16–18 urges the readers not to be deceived in their theology about God. This points out the theological basis of any productive response to problems. In order to have the right attitude in the midst of external challenges, and to receive the benefits, it is imperative that the readers believe in the basic goodness and consistency of God, have the conviction that he has constructive intentions toward them personally by having given birth to them by the word of truth (and so is committed to their growth to maturity) (1:18//1:5), and that he gives good gifts.

These problems or challenges are, for the most part, external challenges rather than ethical shortcomings (the lack of wisdom is not so much a fault or foolishness as a need for discernment and insight in a particular problem or situation). The topic may be summarized as: Consider yourself blessed in the midst of your challenges if you endure them.[55] The series of contrasts may then be viewed through the lens of having the right attitude in the midst of specific challenges and problems because of the potential of positive outcomes. After the introduction to the benefits of enduring trials, the specific trials are illustrated by a contrast that pro-

---

condemnation as much as a perspective—the rich do not have trials like the poor have, and their source of blessing in riches is transitory. We will see that the rich may have a spiritual problem and may be a problem to the Christian community. McCartney finds the concept of taking pride in humiliation difficult semantically (*James*, 96), but it is extremely close to the same kind of oxymoron in which the Greco-Roman culture held that a woman's honor was her shame.

53. As McCartney says, "the rich man is viewed as a man in danger" (ibid., 95). This is not to say that the negative evaluation at this point in the text is a harsh criticism or even a polemic as 5:1–6 is.

54. As it says in Heb 11:6, in order to have a faith that pleases God, one must believe that God rewards those who seek him.

55. Similarly, Blomberg and Kamell's main idea for 1:1–11 is: "Christians should respond to trials by rejoicing at the maturity they can foster, by asking God for wisdom, and by viewing them as leveling experiences that often invert the roles of rich and poor" (Blomberg and Kamell, *James*, 44).

vides semantic antonymy: the wrong attitude toward trials and incorrect theology about God results in a negative outcome. In the first unit, the negative outcomes receive the most expansion and therefore the most emphasis.

Pursue Righteousness through Action and Self-control (1:19–27)

As in the preceding unit, in the second unit there are two identity chains, consisting of groups whose actions receive a positive evaluation in contrast with groups, or characteristics, that are representative of a type of people or an option that receive a negative evaluation. The readers form a third identity chain that has the potential to identify with either side or choose between options. Similarly there are two semantic chains that are formed by the contrast between kinds of actions that characterize the groups. Finally there is the semantic chain of a desired goal or outcome that could be shared information between the author and hearers; it involves righteousness, being blessed, and religion, and this is central to the topic as the primary motivation for the readers' choice between types of options or actions, and it is in contrast with the goal of endurance in the first unit.

It was most tempting to find the semantic chain of God's word as the topic in the second unit (vv. 21, 22, 23, 25 [λόγος and νόμος]), but while that accounts very well for 1:19–25, it leaves 1:26–27 hanging primarily with a formal relationship with what precedes. Is there a way that 1:26–27 relates to the preceding material so that it may be perceived as less of a *non sequitur*? The suggestion that the religious/religion in vv. 26–27 (θρησκός/ θρησκεία) is a paraphrase of "doing the word" may seem plausible, but it is slightly strained—religion is a broader term that would encompass a relationship to God's word, not the other way around. Also, the illustration of pure and undefiled religion does not neatly parallel the actions described in doing the word or fit a comprehensive summary of what the word of God teaches. Therefore, an effort to establish the word of God as the dominant semantic chain may overlook other features that better account for the passage. On the other hand, in v. 20, the goal of "producing the righteousness of God" (δικαιοσύνην θεοῦ . . . κατεργάζεται) is an inferred goal of being quick to hear, and an expected outcome of receiving the engrafted word.[56] The outcome of applying the word or the law

---

56. The assertion that anger does not produce the righteousness of God implies

is being blessed in whatever one does, which is comparable to achieving righteousness. Producing or achieving the righteousness of God may also be a category that encompasses the legitimate goal of pure and undefiled religion. Therefore, "achieving God's righteousness" may be an adequate description of a semantic chain that interacts with the actions that receive a positive evaluation.[57] In ch. 2, James will use the word "faith" to interact with what is being described here, in that the outcome or evidence of faith is righteousness (see particularly 2:21–26).

What every comparison has in common is a concern with ethical purity, a contrast between types of action, and a form of self-control involved in making choices between the options—one type of action receives a positive evaluation and the other type of action receives a negative evaluation. The first contrast in 1:19–21 compares being quick to hear (which is paraphrased as receiving the engrafted word of God) with hasty speech, anger, filth, and wickedness. Unlike anger, being quick to hear consists of the kind of action that will produce the righteousness of God. The second contrast in 1:22–25 compares simply hearing God's word without making any adjustments with doing it with continual attention and taking action. Constantly examining and applying God's word results in producing the righteousness of God—those who do it are blessed in what they do. The third contrast in 1:26–27 compares a person who professes to be religious without controlling their speech with the practice of pure and undefiled religion that involves pragmatic care for the poor (widows and orphans) and ethical purity. The care of the poor and ethical purity describes actions that are consistent with producing

----

that hearing (τὸ ἀκοῦσαι), which is placed in direct contrast with anger (ὀργή), does produce the righteousness of God, and that is a primary goal. The command to receive the engrafted word while laying aside all filth and wickedness further defines or describes what is in view with being quick to hear—the readers are to be quick to hear God's word, which is associated with producing the righteousness of God, and which is in contrast with hasty speech, anger, filth, and wickedness.

57. Cheung argues that the concerns of the working of God's righteousness, acting in accordance with God's word, and being religious refer to the singular concern of perfection (*Genre*, 66). Being perfect and complete is the work and the goal of the process of the endurance of external challenges in 1:2–4, and the goals in 1:19–27 are consistent with that goal. However, at this level in our procedure, this anticipates too much—we need to limit our focus to the unit. In addition, labeling the goal "perfection" may carry implications and interpretive baggage that "being mature and complete" does not.

the righteousness of God. Therefore, we have an interaction of the semantic chains of righteousness and action.

The chain that involves some form of self-control or willpower includes not only being *slow* to speak, *slow* to anger (v. 19), and *bridling* the tongue (v. 26), but also *laying aside* filth and wickedness (v. 21) and *enduring* or *remaining* and *to look* at God's word (the perfect law) (v. 25). The actions of speech and anger are associated with a negative evaluation, but they involve pitfalls or problem areas that cannot be avoided, so self-control is necessary in dealing with them. Therefore, the readers are to work against all the actions that receive a negative evaluation by practicing various forms of self-control as well as exercising the will to get rid of bad behavior and give constant attention to God's word.

Therefore, the topic of the unit in 1:19–27 has pursuing the righteousness of God (including the discipline of hearing and practicing God's word, and the practice of true religion) as a goal as reflected in ethical choices between options and the use of self-control in regard to areas that are pitfalls and in regard to actual filth and wickedness.

Prominence

The most prominent points in Jas 1 correspond with the same features that create the shifts in the discourse, particularly the use of the nominative of direct address and the second person plural imperatives, but additional features create zones of turbulence that indicate central sentences and focuses the readers' attention on the relevant information.

PROMINENCE IN 1:2–18

The first sentence in the opening of the letter in 1:2–3 is a zone of turbulence that is consistent with the point of departure of a discourse. It utilizes the nominative plural of direct address, the second person plural with the imperative and in pronominal form, concatenation of terms[58] and begins and ends with salient features that are of interest to the reader: all happiness and the positive outcome of the process of endurance. The introduction of problems, challenges, or trials that they have fallen into (πειρασμοῖς περιπέσητε ποικίλοις) is arguably a topic of central relevance—these readers are facing serious challenges, and James takes those

---

58. Concatenation is a rhetorical device where a word from one series is repeated in the next series, also called *gradatio*. See Brosend, *James and Jude*, 34–35; Dibelius, *James*, 72.

challenges on immediately. Therefore, the opening of the letter strongly engages the readers with multiple techniques that grab the attention and interest. In 1:4, the third person command "Let endurance have its perfect result" (ἡ δὲ ὑπομονὴ ἔργον τέλειον ἐχέτω) is the primary clause of the conclusion of the opening, stressing a desired outcome of being perfect and complete, lacking in nothing, which is relatively less prominent than the second person plural engagement in 1:2–3, but still quite prominent through the use of the imperative and salience.

Each command and its support in ch. 1 has a measure of prominence, but third person singular commands are not as emphatic as the second person plural commands—primarily because they engage the reader less. The three contrasts in the first unit are associated with third person imperatives and in the first two contrasts the imperatives occur with δέ:

1:5   Εἰ δέ τις ὑμῶν λείπεται σοφίας, αἰτείτω παρὰ τοῦ διδόντος θεοῦ

1:6   αἰτείτω δὲ ἐν πίστει μηδὲν διακρινόμενος

    1:7   μὴ γὰρ οἰέσθω ὁ ἄνθρωπος ἐκεῖνος (support material)

1:9   Καυχάσθω δὲ ὁ ἀδελφὸς ὁ ταπεινὸς ἐν τῷ ὕψει αὐτοῦ

1:10   [Καυχάσθω] ὁ δὲ πλούσιος ἐν τῇ ταπεινώσει αὐτοῦ

*1:12   Μακάριος ἀνὴρ ὃς ὑπομένει πειρασμόν

1:13   μηδεὶς πειραζόμενος λεγέτω ὅτι ἀπὸ θεοῦ πειράζομαι

While not perfectly symmetrical, the third person imperatives play a major role in forming the contrasts between the different types of individuals. In each contrast, the description of the person who receives the negative evaluation receives the greater prominence within the contrast. Generally, the second element in the contrast receives the emphasis, all things being equal.[59] In this case, the negation of the second element also

---

59. All things being equal, the second element in a contrast above the sentence level is prominent: "Prominence above the sentence level in contrasts and comparisons is the same in principle as contrastive focus at the level of clause or phrase, where the speaker/writer raises a claim and then contradicts it or replaces it with a newer, more relevant claim" (Westfall, *Discourse Analysis*, 69). Replacement is clearest in the "not X but Y" contrasts, which is slightly different from the negation patterns throughout Jas 1. In the first series of contrasts, the "X not Y" pattern is used, but the negated element receives the most expansion, so that the first element is more relevant, but the description of the negated element serves as a warning to the reader. In the second series, the first contrast is semantic rather than formal and the first element is

qualifies that emphasis, but nevertheless, the descriptions are expanded more, which is consistent with the prominence of a second element in the contrast.[60] The prominence of the negated element in the contrast serves as a warning.

In the first contrast, the positive example of asking for wisdom is described in 1:5, while the one who asks doubting is described with expansion in 1:6–8, and receives a second command as well. In the second contrast, there is a command to the poor to take pride, and then there is an ellipsis of the command to the rich in 1:10, so that the command for the rich must be understood from the command for the poor in v. 9, which serves to form the contrast even more closely. However, then the expansion in the support material in vv. 10b–11 places the prominence on the challenges of the rich: they are humiliated because they, and all from which they derive worldly honor, will fade away. The use of imagery is salient and effective in depicting the rich as being the ones that have a problem, but its prominence is part of the contouring of the discourse without competing with the dominant structure of the contrasts.[61]

The third contrast in vv. 13–15 is not introduced with a command, but rather utilizes a formulaic blessing that paraphrases the opening of the letter in 1:2–4. It has relative prominence over the first elements in the other two contrasts because of that variation.[62] However, the command concerning a person who blames God for temptation receives a similarly disproportionate expansion in vv. 13–15 like the second element in the other two contrasts. The extended sexual innuendo and metaphor ending

emphatic because it is supported by the second element. In the second contrast, the syntax throws prominence on the first element, as well as the expansion.

60. While we could say that the focus is on the second element of the contrast (as usual), since the contrasts involve primary clauses with the exception of 1:10, "prominence" is a better term since it involves emphasis above the sentence level.

61. One of the issues in discussing emphasis or prominence is that every sentence, every paragraph, and every section has various kinds of emphasis, so that prominence is relative and a discourse is contoured by nature with levels of prominence. Therefore, there is a tendency to locate one emphatic feature and give it significance at too high a level in the discourse. There is another tendency to intuitively identify the passage that seems most prominent in a discourse, and then explain why it is prominent by identifying its emphatic features (which they will surely find), but prominence must be determined by a passage's relationship to the co-text—perhaps the next passage has even more of the same emphatic features, or has other features that highlight it even more.

62. The formulaic blessing μακάριος ἀνήρ repeats a common pattern from the LXX wisdom literature (cf. Ps 1:1).

in death in the description of temptation is even more salient than the graphic description of the rich,[63] but again, as much as it captures the attention, it does not compete with the more prominent points of the passage.

The conclusion in 1:16 is the most prominent point since 1:2–4, because it repeats the second person plural present imperative (though it is a prohibition: μὴ πλανᾶσθε) and the nominative of direct address with the more emphatic ἀδελφοί μου ἀγαπητοί. It has little information in that it only warns against deception. However, that warning highlights the nature of God as the framework in which the challenges that the readers face must be understood.

PROMINENCE IN 1:19–27

The second unit is emphatically introduced with an emphatic imperative and the nominative plural of direct address: "Know [this] my beloved brothers and sisters!" (Ἴστε, ἀδελφοί μου ἀγαπητοί). Its function is deictic—it gives prominence to what follows. It creates a decisive shift in the discourse and draws attention to the following contrast in vv. 19b–21.

The patterned occurrence of imperatives changes in 1:19–27. The first and second contrasts are introduced each with δέ and with one third person imperative, but the third contrast has no imperative and both elements are joined with asyndeton.[64] Furthermore, the emphasis is on the person who receives a positive evaluation as his or her actions receive the most focus, emphatic markers, and/or description.[65]

The first "contrast" is introduced with a third person imperative and δέ, which is less emphatic in form than the formulaic introduction to the unit: every person should be quick to hear, slow to speak, and slow to anger (ἔστω δὲ πᾶς ἄνθρωπος ταχὺς εἰς τὸ ἀκοῦσαι, βραδὺς εἰς τὸ λαλῆσαι,

---

63. Scholars have noted the rhetorical impact of the description of the process of temptation, conception, birth, and death. Davids observes, "For the first time in the work [James] drops into a so-called diatribe style with imaginative dialogue and closing exhortation" (*Epistle of James*, 80).

64. The function of asyndeton in discourse is a matter of debate. It is my position that the absence of a signal is just that. The reader is left to infer the logical relationship of the clause to the discourse, but continuity is always assumed as a primary property of discourse. Others suggest that asyndeton "creates breaks" or is emphatic because it is a deviation from the expected norm.

65. Technically, the person who hears the word and does not do what it says receives a little more description than the one who puts it into practice. But other features emphasize the positive behavior, including the formulaic blessing.

βραδὺς εἰς ὀργήν). The negative alternative is briefly stated in the indicative and marked with a γάρ as support material rather than being stated with a δέ and an imperative: a person's anger [ὀργὴ . . . ἀνδρὸς] does not achieve the righteousness of God.[66] Therefore, this is not a formal contrast, but rather a command that is elaborated with the negated element. However, the "do X; do not do Y" pattern is still clear, though the "do not do Y" element is joined with a conjunction that signals support material. The rhetorical effect is to make the positive element, which occurs first, more prominent than the negated element. Then the "contrast" is concluded with a more prominent command in the second person plural to receive the engrafted word, which is able to save them (δέξασθε τὸν ἔμφυτον λόγον τὸν δυνάμενον σῶσαι τὰς ψυχὰς ὑμῶν). This command has a cohesive tie with "quick to hear" in that receiving the engrafted word is a function of hearing. The prominence in the passage is placed on the exhortation for the readers to be people who, in effect, are quick to hear or receive God's word. The prominent shift and emphasis in v. 19 ultimately points to the second person plural imperative with the salient outcome of salvation in v. 21 and creates the greatest prominence in the second unit.[67]

The next highest point of prominence in the second unit is in the second contrast in v. 22, but it is adjacent to the second person imperative in v. 21. James commands the readers to be doers of the word, not only hearers who deceive themselves (γίνεσθε δὲ ποιηταὶ λόγου καὶ μὴ μόνον ἀκροαταὶ παραλογιζόμενοι ἑαυτούς). We may suggest that the structure is similar to the contrast between the poor and rich, and that there is an ellipsis of γίνεσθε in the second element of the contrast, but the focus is on the one who practices the word, and the second element of the contrast is negated. The contrast is supported by the illustration of the two individuals who look in the mirror. The description of the one who hears the word without doing it receives slightly more expansion than the description of the person who practices God's word. This is counter-balanced by the formal focus in the command, the emphasis on the description

66. This is another good example of the inclusive or proverbial use of ἀνήρ (cf. 1:12). It is consistent with use of the masculine for the default gender, meaning that any person's wrath does not achieve the righteousness of God. It is similar to the patterned use of ἀνήρ in Proverbs (LXX).

67. The prominence within the first contrast in the second unit is counter-expectation. It is not formally in one of the contrasted elements, and it is not in a conclusion as was 1:16.

of the word (v. 25b), and the formulaic blessing pronounced on the one who practices the word (v. 25c). The formulaic blessing concludes the contrast. While prominent, it is not as prominent as the second person plural imperative in the contrast's point of departure in 1:22.

The final contrast is devoid of most markers that indicate formal prominence in comparison with the relative prominence within the unit or the two units within the chapter.[68] There are no second person plural references to engage the readers or salient examples. However, there are some features that merit attention, if only to illustrate how relative prominence may be created. The focus in 1:26 is indicated by deixis: τούτου μάταιος ἡ θρησκεία. The preceding description of the religion of a person who did not control their tongue is summarily dismissed: This religion is useless! Similarly, there is deixis in 1:27 that throws the focus on the description of pure and undefiled religion: Pure and undefiled religion before the God and Father *is this* (αὕτη ἐστίν). The description of valid religion is emphatic because of expansion. While this places a certain focus on the goal of the choices, the unit ends with relatively low prominence in comparison with the prominent points in the rest of the unit: there is more prominence in 1:19, 21, 22, and 25. This may be counter-expectation to what one expects of the destination of a unit.

The prominence in the second unit falls on 1:21 and 1:22, which belong to different contrasts, but are adjacent and closely tied together by formal and semantic repetition. They reinforce each other and contribute to their mutual prominence. The primary clauses that are emphasized are: receive or hear the word of God, but be doers of the word and not only hearers, which stresses a theme that is global in the discourse. However, while we may say that these two sentences are central in the unit by virtue of their prominence, they do not account for the information in the third contrast.

---

68. McCartney suggests that the last two verses "both summarize the preceding material and effectively encapsulate the concerns for 'word-worthy' and 'faith-ful' behavior that occupy the remainder of James's letter" (*James*, 127). However, 1:26–27 lacks the markers of prominence that would indicate that these verses play this kind of major function in the discourse. The importance of the ideas cannot be denied, but the low prominence indicates that James is not highlighting these verses as central sentences.

PROMINENCE IN THE SECTION 1:2–27

As the two units form a section by virtue of the repetition of contrasts among other features, we may attempt to locate prominence in the discourse at the level of the section. The most prominent point in the section is the highest point in the first discourse, which is the point of departure for the section in 1:2–4. Both the prominence and the content of 1:2–4 suggest that it is a central sentence in the section. The process of endurance has the goal of being perfect or complete and lacking nothing in 1:4. This encompasses the goals of the second unit, and therefore, the point of departure may account for the entire section.

Relationship with the Co-text

There are multiple links between ch. 1 and the rest of James. In fact, elements in the first chapter may be connected to virtually each part of James. In addition, discourse patterns are established that continue to be used throughout the text: the use of the nominative plural of direct address and the use of the imperative as the point of departure of a unit.[69] The significance of the first chapter can be illustrated by showing that every major issue in 1:2–27 is repeated later in the discourse.[70]

The issue of trials or temptation (1:2–4; 12–15) forms cohesive ties with various points in the discourse. It particularly forms ties with the description of the rich who are exploiting them, dragging them into court, and insulting their name (2:6–7). It also has ties with the exhortation to have patience in suffering like Job and the prophets in 5:7–12.

- The issue of endurance (1:2, 3, 4, 12) similarly forms cohesive ties with the exhortation to have patience in suffering in 5:7–12.

- The issue of wisdom (1:5) forms cohesive ties particularly with the description of the wisdom from above (3:13–18).

- The issue of faith (1:3, 6) forms multiple cohesive ties with 2:1–3 (faith is inconsistent with favoritism), the discussion of faith and action in 2:14–26 and the prayer offered in faith (5:15). Prayer and faith collocate in 1:6 and 5:15.

69. Varner makes the observation about how 1:2 initiates the pattern (*Book of James*, 45–56).

70. Blomberg and Kamell suggest that the three key themes of the letter are trials/temptations, wisdom, and issues of riches and poverty (*James*, 43). However, the multiple ties in ch. 1 appear to extend beyond these themes.

- The issue of the prayer (1:6) forms strong cohesive ties with the concluding section of the discourse in 5:13–18 on prayer.

- The description of the double-minded person who doubts (1:8) forms a cohesive tie with James's description of their problems that are causing fights and quarrels in 4:8: purify your hearts you double-minded!

- The issue of the rich and the poor forms a cohesive tie between 1:9–11 and the discussion of favoritism illustrated by the treatment of the poor and rich in 2:1–13, the warning against boasting about plans to engage in trade and make a profit in 4:13–17, and the polemic against the rich in 5:1–6.

- The issue of temptation and the connection with lust, sin, and death (1:13–15) forms cohesive ties with the description of the quarrels and fights that James claims they are having in 5:1–9. It forms a more remote tie to judging one another in 4:11–12.

- The issue of the tongue and uncontrolled speech (1:19, 26) forms cohesive ties with the need to control the tongue and the polemic against it (3:1–11), and the tie is strengthened with the collocation of the tongue and the use of a bridle (1:26; 3:3).[71]

- Perhaps being quick to speak and quick to anger rather than quick to hear, slow to speak, and slow to anger (1:14) is also related to judging one another (4:11–12), but James certainly links the passage with the reference to being a doer of the law rather than a judge of the law (1:22–25).

- The relationship between righteousness and action along with being a doer of the word form strong cohesive ties between 1:19–27 and the discussions about favoritism and faith without works in 2:14–26.

- Concerns about contamination from the world and purity in 1:21, 27 form cohesive ties with 4:4–8, which includes "wash your hands, you sinners, and purify your hearts you double-minded" (4:8). Other concerns with contamination are included in the polemic on the tongue (3:6, 9–12), the purity of wisdom (3:17), and the corruption of wealth (5:2–3).

71. In 1:26, a verb/participle is used to express bridling (μὴ χαλιναγωγῶν γλῶσσαν) and in 3:3 the noun is used (χαλινοὺς εἰς τὰ στόματα βάλλομεν).

In other words, most of the primary themes in Jas 2–5 appear in ch. 1, and virtually every theme in ch. 1 occurs somewhere in the following four chapters, though the point that is being made about the themes is not usually the same. Therefore, it is not saying too much to suggest that since the primary entities or tokens that are introduced in ch. 1 are repeated elsewhere in the discourse, ch. 1 accounts for the rest of the discourse in some way. Some have suggested that ch. 1 forms an overview, a table of contents, or that 1:19–27 is an introduction while 1:2–18 is a prologue.[72] However, that requires some manipulation of the text, and ignores the distinctive topical structure of the two units. Therefore, I suggest that James begins the discourse by referring to the things that are his and the readers' central and most relevant concerns: their problems and their ethical failings, and he places them all in a theological framework in the beginning that lays the foundation for the rest of the letter, but does not constitute a formal introduction.[73] His good news is that they can experience joy and blessing in the midst of all their challenges and problems. However, their joy and blessing is contingent on their endurance, their theology about God, and praxis combined with self-control. If the readers are truly going through an unusual period of challenges and trouble (as both the text and the plausible historical context may suggest), then James is addressing felt needs and his concerns in a dramatic and productive manner that earns a hearing for the rest of his letter.[74]

CONCLUSION

The structure of Jas 1 must be analyzed above the sentence level to detect the patterns that are formed in the discourse, and the formal features of the discourse must be recognized rather than beginning with intuitive notions of topic structure. If the contrasts throughout the chapter

---

72. McCartney suggests that 1:2–27 is an "overview of the life of faith" (*James*, 81), but the argument is more specifically related to problems than a broad theme of life in general. Some find a double opening statement: an introduction (1:2–11) with a recapitulation (1:12–25) (Francis, "Form and Function," 110–26; Davids, *Epistle of James*, 22–28; Blomberg and Kamell, *James*, 43–44).

73. As McCartney suggests, the vividness of the text in verses such as 2:2, 15 and 4:13 "suggest[s] something more than general hypothetical situations. James appears to have heard some disturbing news and he is addressing real problems" (*James*, 37).

74. The venue of Palestine for the place of origin, and perhaps the location even for some of the recipients provides a context that contained these kinds of problems. For a discussion on this, see McCartney, *James*, 36–37.

are recognized as discrete sub-units, then the formal structure of the discourse falls into place. The formal structure has to be the starting point for determining the topic. Determining the topic and the logical connections within the units has involved some interpretive inference. However, it is the nature of language to supply these kinds of connections in a discourse rather than to assume discontinuity and incoherence. The following outline provides a plausible functional representation of the section that is a result of the preceding discourse analysis:

James 1:2–27

How You Should Respond to the Issues that You Are Facing

I. Consider yourself blessed in the midst of your problems if you endure (1:2–18)

Point of departure: Rejoice because problems are an opportunity to become mature through perseverance (1:2–4)

A. A problem is an opportunity to gain wisdom (1:5–8)

1. Ask God for wisdom in faith and you will get it (1:5)

2. But do not ask for wisdom with doubt or you will get nothing (1:6–8)

B. The problem of poverty is really an opportunity to be lifted up (1:9–11)

1. A person with the challenge of being poor can take pride in their high position in God (1:9)

2. The rich must embrace humiliation—they are the ones with the problem (1:10–11)

C. Problems are an opportunity for blessing (1:12–15)

1. A person who faces their problems with perseverance is blessed (1:12)

2. No one facing problems should make the mistake of blaming God for their temptation to sin (1:13–15)

Conclusion: Do not be deceived about the nature and role of God because he is the source of all of these benefits (1:16–18)

II. Pursue righteousness through action and self-control (1:19–27)

   A. Righteousness is achieved by receiving God's word (1:19–21)

      1. Every person needs to be quick to listen to God's word, but slow to speak and slow to become angry (1:19)

      2. An angry person does not achieve God's righteousness (1:20)

         (v. 21 is the point)

      3. Conclusion: Receive God's word and throw away impurity and evil

   B. Put God's word into action and you will be blessed (1:22–25)

      1. There are two ways to respond to God's word (1:22)

         a. Be a doer of God's word (1:22a)

         b. Do not only be a hearer of God's word and deceive yourselves (1:22b)

      2. An illustration of the two ways to respond to God's word (1:23–25)

         a. One who looks in the mirror and walks away forgetting (1:23–24)

         b. One who looks in the mirror attentively and constantly then takes action (1:25)

   C. Valid religion involves self-control and action (1:26–27)

      1. A person's religion is worthless if they cannot control their speech (1:26)

      2. A person who practices pure and undefiled religion takes practical action: they take care of orphans and widows (1:27)

As James believes that all of these contrasts represent issues that are relevant to the readers, they will all be addressed again in the rest of the discourse. However, James places a summary of all the issues that encompasses their problems and ethical failings at the beginning of the discourse, and gives the readers a series of choices. In order to make the right choices, they need to have an essential understanding about the goodness of God and they need to constantly put God's word into practice. Then they may choose between being a person who is blessed, mature, significant, and productive or being a person who fails in every goal that matters and misses every opportunity.

BIBLIOGRAPHY

Blomberg, Craig L., and Mariam J. Kamell. *James*. ZECNT. Grand Rapids: Baker, 2008.

Brosend, William F. *James and Jude*. Cambridge: Cambridge University Press, 2004.

Brown, Gillian, and George Yule. *Discourse Analysis*. CTL. Cambridge: Cambridge University Press, 1983.

Callow, Kathleen. *Discourse Considerations in Translating the Word of God*. Grand Rapids: Zondervan, 1974.

———. "Patterns of Thematic Development in 1 Corinthians." In *Linguistics and New Testament Interpretation: Essays on Discourse Analysis*, edited by David Alan Black, 194–206. Nashville: Broadman, 1992.

Cheung, Luke L. *The Genre, Composition and Hermeneutics of James*. Carlisle, UK: Paternoster, 2003.

Davids, Peter H. *The Epistle of James*. NIGTC. Grand Rapids: Eerdmans, 1982.

———. "The Meaning of Ἀπείραστός in James 1:13." *NTS* 24 (1978) 386–92.

Dibelius, Martin. *James: A Commentary on the Epistle of James*. Revised by Henrich Greeven. Translated by Michael A. Williams. Hermeneia. Minneapolis: Fortress, 1975.

Dooley, Robert A., and Stephen H. Levinsohn. *Analyzing Discourse: A Manual of Basic Concepts*. Dallas: SIL International, 2001.

Francis, Fred O. "Form and Function of the Opening and Closing Paragraphs of James and 1 John." *ZNW* 61 (1970) 110–26.

Gee, James Paul. *An Introduction to Discourse Analysis: Theory and Method*. 4th ed. London: Routledge, 2014.

———. *How To Do Discourse Analysis: A Toolkit*. 2nd ed. London: Routledge, 2014.

Grice, H. P. *Studies in the Way of Words*. Cambridge, MA: Harvard University Press, 1989.

Guthrie, George H. *The Structure of Hebrews: A Text-Linguistic Analysis*. NovTSup 73. Leiden: Brill, 1997.

Halliday, M. A. K., and R. Hasan. *Cohesion in English*. ELS. London: Longman, 1976.

———. *Language, Context and Text: Aspects of Language in a Social-Semiotic Perspective*. Geelong, Australia: Deakon University, 1985.

Halliday, M. A. K., and Christian M. I. M. Matthiessen. *An Introduction to Functional Grammar*. 3rd ed. London: Hodder Arnold, 2004.

Hoey, Michael. *Patterns of Lexis in Text*. DEL. Oxford: Oxford University Press, 1991.

Johnson, Luke Timothy. *The Letter of James*. AB 37A. New York: Doubleday, 1995.

Laws, Sophie. *A Commentary on the Epistle of James*. BNTC. London: A. & C. Black, 1980.

Longacre, Robert. E. *The Grammar of Discourse*. TLL. 2nd ed. New York: Plenum, 1996.

McCartney, Dan G. *James*. BECNT. Grand Rapids: Baker Academic, 2009.

Moo, Douglas J. *The Letter of James*. PNTC. Grand Rapids: Eerdmans, 2000.

Nida, Eugene A., et al. *Style and Discourse: With Special Reference to the Text of the Greek New Testament*. Cape Town, South Africa: Bible Society, 1983.

Penner, Todd C. *The Epistle of James and Eschatology: Re-reading an Ancient Christian Letter*. JSNTSup 121. Sheffield: Sheffield Academic, 1996.

Reed, Jeffrey T. *A Discourse Analysis of Philippians: Method and Rhetoric in the Debate over Literary Integrity*. JSNTSup 136. Sheffield: Sheffield Academic, 1997.

Runge, Steven E. *Discourse Grammar of the Greek New Testament: A Practical Introduction for Teaching and Exegesis*. LBR. Peabody, MA: Hendrickson, 2010.

Shiffrin, Deborah, et al., eds. *The Handbook of Discourse Analysis*. BHL. Malden, MA: Blackwell, 2001.

Sinclair, John M. "Trust the Text." In *Advances in Systemic Linguistics: Recent Theory and Practice*, edited by Martin Davies and Louise Ravelli, 5–19. OLS. London: Pinter, 1992.

Sinclair, John, and Ronald Carter. *Trust the Text: Language, Corpus and Discourse*. London: Routledge, 2004.

Strauss, Susan, and Parastou Feiz. *Discourse Analysis: Putting Our Worlds into Words*. London: Routledge, 2013.

Taylor, Mark Edward. *A Text-Linguistic Investigation into the Structure of James*. LNTS 311. London: T. & T. Clark International, 2006.

Varner, William. *The Book of James: A New Perspective: A Linguistic Commentary Applying Linguistic Analysis*. The Woodlands, TX: Kress Biblical Resources, 2010.

Verseput, Donald J. "Wisdom, 4Q185, and James." *JBL* 49 (1998) 253–67.

Wallace, Stephen. "Figure and Ground: The Interrelationships of Linguistic Categories." In *Tense-Aspect: Between Semantics and Pragmatics*, edited by Paul J. Hopper, 201–23. TSL 1. Amsterdam: Benjamins, 1982.

Westfall, Cynthia Long. *A Discourse Analysis of the Letter to the Hebrews: The Relationship between Form and Meaning*. LNTS 297. London: T. & T. Clark International, 2005.

White, John Lee. *The Form and Function of the Body of the Greek Letter: A Study of the Letter-Body in the Non-literary Papyri and in Paul the Apostle*. SBLDS 2. Missoula, MT: Scholars, 1972.

3

Cohesion in James
A Response to Martin Dibelius

STANLEY E. PORTER

INTRODUCTION

IN HIS RECENT COMMENTARY on the letter of James, Dale Allison indicates that questions regarding the structure of the book have been posed from the earliest days of critical discussion. These questions have persisted from the time of Luther to the present.[1] However, one figure looms most significantly in this debate: Martin Dibelius. In his now classic commentary, first published in 1921 in the Meyer commentary series[2] and then translated in the Hermeneia series, Dibelius from the outset engaged in a brief analysis of the content of the letter; the beginning of his commentary reads, "The results of this analysis are indeed complex, but they do lead to the recognition of one consistent feature of Ja[me]s: *the entire document lacks continuity in thought.* There is not only a lack of continuity in thought between individual sayings and other smaller units, but also between larger treatises."[3] Dibelius is quick to note that this is "not to say that the letter has no coherence of any sort," although

---

1. Allison, *James*, 76–81. A similar perspective is found in Moo, *James*, 44–45. In one of the most recent treatments, Jackson-McCabe seems to see more agreement on the basic outline than I see in the secondary literature ("Enduring Temptation," 162, 165).

2. See Dibelius, *Brief des Jakobus*.

3. Dibelius, *James*, 1–2; cf. 34–38.

it certainly, so he thinks, lacks the coherence of a Pauline letter.[4] Allison acknowledges the influence of Dibelius, while also noting that, "[a]lthough rejection of Dibelius is the current consensus, there remains no agreement as to what to put in its place."[5] Allison's survey of some of the recent proposals shows that not only is there lack of agreement, but there are widely divergent means by which such proposals are formulated and a corresponding range of proposed alternatives. They range from rather problematic macro-chiastic patterns to minimalist outlines that provide only the hint of a cohesive book.

In this paper, I wish to return to the notion of Dibelius regarding the lack of continuity in the book of James. Dibelius poses this as a problem of James lacking continuity of thought, and in that sense he is correct to associate that with the issue of coherence. However, I wish to pose an even more fundamental question regarding the cohesion of James. If coherence is concerned with continuity of thought, cohesion is concerned with continuity of textual structure. In other words, examination of cohesion is an attempt to identify the patterns that define the text of James as a text that "holds together." There have been several previous studies of James along potentially promising linguistic lines,[6] but in this paper, I specifically pursue the matter of the cohesion of James from a Systemic Functional Linguistics (SFL) perspective, in particular by means of a modified form of what is called cohesive harmony analysis.[7]

WHAT IS COHESION?

Before we can explore whether or what type of cohesion is to be found in the book of James, we need to discuss what cohesion is. Cohesion is

4. Ibid., 2.

5. Allison, *James*, 77; cf. Jackson-McCabe, "Enduring Temptation," 162–64.

6. See Taylor, *Text-Linguistic Investigation*; and Taylor and Guthrie, "Structure of James," 681–705. However, I must admit that I do not find Taylor's (and Taylor and Guthrie's) macro-chiastic pattern for the body of the letter at all convincing. Varner (*James*) uses a linguistic approach that has many similarities to mine, but he does not concentrate upon cohesion, although he is concerned with the textual metafunction. Cf. also Varner, "Main Theme," 115–29.

7. See Halliday and Hasan, *Cohesion in English*; and more particularly, Hasan in Halliday and Hasan, *Language, Context, and Text*, 89–94; cf. Hasan, "Coherence and Cohesive Harmony," 181–219; Parsons, *Cohesion and Coherence*, esp. 5–30, for an overview of issues and opinions; Cloran et al., "Models of Discourse," esp. 651–54; and Scott, "Peace and Cohesive Harmony," 89–96. Cf. Thompson, *Introducing Functional Grammar*, 179–80, on cohesion and coherence.

a sub-category of the textual metafunction of language (from a SFL perspective). By that, I mean that when we examine the means by which a text is constituted as a text (its mode), cohesion is a sub-set of all of the various means that are available to create that text. All of these various means constitute the textual metafunction. Cohesion is one part of this. Cohesion itself can be said to be any linguistic means found at the word group level or higher (and especially at the clause level) by which an author unites or ties together the various elements of language to constitute a text. These elements may include several types of devices. One of the major ways by which cohesion is created is through repetition of identical lexical items, different lexical items with similar or related meanings, different lexical items that refer to the same entities, and the like. Another way by which cohesion is created is through the use of similar lexico-grammatical elements, such as repetition of tense-forms, mood-forms, personal reference (whether by means of pronouns or verbal affixes), and the like. A final way by which cohesion is created (although I am not attempting to be inclusive here) is by means of a variety of other elements. These other elements may include (but are not restricted to) conjunctive structures (conjunctions and the like), syntactical patterning, and even sound patterning.

There are two major questions that arise when discussing cohesion. The first is how one calculates the number and type of ties used within a discourse to constitute an adequate number of elements to constitute sufficient cohesion. This has been discussed in some ways in some recent works that attempt to formulate patterns of cohesive usage, especially cohesive harmony analysis. Cohesive harmony analysis, a significant step forward for discussion of cohesion, brings cohesion as textual into interaction with the ideational. In other words, it brings the constitutive and organizational elements of the text into relationship with elements of the ideational metafunction. As helpful as cohesive harmony analysis is, it is difficult to see whether it can provide convincing analyses of how much cohesion is enough and how much is too little,[8] and whether it can deal with the problems of James. Such studies are better at formulating comparative results between examples, but not determining the threshold for cohesion, as Hasan admits regarding levels of cohesion.

---

8. These and related issues have been noted from the outset, by both Hasan (in Halliday and Hasan, *Language, Context, and Text*, 90, 93–94) and some of her appreciative critics, such as Parsons (*Cohesion and Coherence*, 23–25).

The second question is the relationship between cohesion and coherence. Above I mentioned that in studies of James there is often discussion of coherence, with debate continuing over what constitutes the overriding ideas and their organization within the letter. I believe that, in some ways, discussion of James has suffered from a category mistake. Many of the disputes over the understanding of the letter purport to be over coherence, when they are in fact over cohesion. In other words, virtually all commentators find the ideas within the book of James understandable. This is not the problem. The problem is that these same commentators are not convinced that they understand how the ideas relate to each other. They then have in the past concluded that the book lacks coherence. Coherence is concerned with the field of a discourse, and in that way realized by the ideational metafunction. Cohesion, however, is concerned with the mode of a discourse, and realized by the textual metafunction. The relationship between the two is complex, and they cannot be equated, as they appear to be in many studies of James. This confusion is seen in the fact that many, if not most, analysts of James attempt to use their discussion of coherence to posit structure (cohesion) and then determine genre, without fully realizing that they are mixing categories and even strata of analysis. Even more contemporary commentators admittedly struggle to find unifying ideas within the book. Failure to find such ideas is often seen as an indication that the book is, to use Luther's words, "chaotic."[9] I contend that this reveals not a problem primarily focused upon coherence but upon cohesion, and one that can be, at least in theory, addressed by cohesive harmony analysis, because it brings together both textual and ideational metafunctions.

As a general rule (there may be exceptions, but I am wary of them), a cohesive text may not have coherence, but a coherent text will have cohesion, even if minimal. Hasan states that "Texture is thus essential to textual unity, and cohesion is the foundation on which the edifice of coherence is built." This means that "variation in coherence is the function of variation in the cohesive harmony of a text."[10] I believe that we can see that, in fact, the book of James does have cohesion, even if we are not all able to agree on its coherence. To show this, I will use a modified form of cohesive harmony analysis.

---

9. Luther's words are often cited. See, for example, Allison, *James*, 76.

10. Hasan in Halliday and Hasan, *Language, Context, and Text*, 94.

EVIDENCE OF COHESION AND COHESIVE
HARMONY IN JAMES

Cohesion is the basis of cohesive harmony analysis in the SFL framework. There are two major dimensions to a cohesive harmony analysis. The first is a description of the cohesive chains. The second is the chain interactions that occur. Rather than undertaking a complete cohesive harmony analysis of the book of James, I instead will focus upon a more limited type of cohesive harmony analysis as evidence of cohesion and the basis for some comments on organization, especially in those sections that have posed problems in establishing its "coherence," to see if there is a legitimate claim to be made for a foundation of cohesion for coherence. I focus upon two dimensions of cohesive harmony—cohesive chains formed on the basis of semantic domains, and clauses that will form the basis of cohesive harmony chain interaction, that is, the major identifiable clauses in which the chains play a part at the clause level and within the clause at the group level.

In Dibelius's treatment of the issue of the genre of the letter, he discusses the problems with its organization, what he calls its "literary technique and its 'style.'"[11] He finds at least three different organizational principles stylistically at play within the letter. James 1:2–27 and 5:7–20, clearly to him, reflect "the form of the brief or expanded saying . . . and these sayings are usually strung together quite loosely, requiring their designation as *series of sayings* as opposed to groups of sayings."[12] James 2:1—3:12, what he calls "the core of the writing," he says "is composed of three expositions, each having characteristics of a treatise."[13] These three treatises, according to the table of contents, are on partiality (2:1–13), faith and works (2:14–26), and the tongue (3:1–12). James 3:13—5:6 consists of a number of "smaller, self-contained units" (3:13–17; 4:1–6; 4:13–16) and "less unified texts and even isolated sayings like 3:18 and 4:17. Here one may speak of groups of sayings."[14]

Many commentaries observe that there are a number of literary or stylistic features within James that could be seen as cohesive devices (though they do not, so far as I have seen, use this language very often,

---

11. Dibelius, *James*, 1.
12. Ibid., 1 (italics his).
13. Ibid.
14. Ibid.

an exception being Luke Cheung).[15] Allison, for example, offers lists of catchword connections, wordplays, assonance, consonance and alliteration, parallelism, aphoristic style, and even antithetical formulations that might be examined in this light.[16] Most of these features, however, are confined to single verses and hence function at the clause or clause complex level, rather than providing more extended cohesive indicators. Although Cheung also seems to confuse (or at least fails to differentiate) cohesion and coherence,[17] he offers an insightful analysis of the book of James, what he recognizes many people might call a "discourse analysis."[18] One of the major features that he identifies is the use of commanding language in the book.[19] He recognizes that such language plays an important role, even if he does not see its role in creating cohesion for the book as a whole. I believe that we can do better than that and that, on the basis of a modified cohesive harmony analysis (that is, a version suitable for analysis of an ancient Greek book), we can determine structure once we have seen cohesion that leads to coherence.

I begin by providing a list of the major clauses (or clause complexes) within James that have imperatives within them. I do not include embedded clauses with imperatives and I do not include clauses based upon fixed form imperatives (such as ἰδού). I have used the OpenText.org displays as a means of defining the clausal boundaries. I generally do not include content clauses that constitute their own embedded clauses. I realize that my conclusions are subjective and may well be questioned by others. I have started with this position to initiate such study, realizing that others may take a different approach. My examination of James results in 48 clauses for analysis. For each major content word (I exclude pronouns and function words), I provide the Louw-Nida semantic domain number

15. See Cheung, *Genre*, 53.

16. Allison, *James*, 82–85. I am surprised that Allison does not cite James Hope Moulton's work on the style of James (nor does he appear to know Moulton's *Prolegomena*).

17. Cheung, *Genre*, 53.

18. Ibid., 57.

19. See ibid., 37; cf. 23; cf. Allison, *James*, 80. Cheung uses the commanding language as a major factor in determining that James is an instance of Jewish wisdom parenetic literature. However, on p. 37, I am unclear on his interpretation of the statistics regarding imperatives and claiming that James has more, proportionately, than 1 Thessalonians and 1 Peter, when this is not true if he includes "imperatival participles," which he seems to want to do. See also pp. 65, 71, 72, 75, 77–79, 81 (note that he incorrectly refers to the negative prohibition, when a prohibition is negative by definition).

or numbers, with those with three or more domain occurrences within the sample being placed in bold to indicate a cohesive chain. I believe that three occurrences is the minimal number to form a cohesive chain. I realize that in a number of the instances there are multiple domains listed for a given word. I do not simply list all of the domains provided by the Louw-Nida lexicon, but include those that, at least in my opinion, may be viable domain options. I believe that this is in keeping with the nature of the semantic domains, in which semantically related words generally have closer domain numbers. Such instances may indicate that such lexemes have broader and overlapping semantic domains.

The so-called imperative clauses (numbered) and their domains for each content word are as follows (those with three or more domain occurrences in bold; see below):[20]

1. Jas 1:2: Πᾶσαν χαρὰν (**25**) ἡγήσασθε (**31**), ἀδελφοί (**10, 11**) μου . . . γινώσκοντες (**28**)

2. Jas 1:4: ἡ δὲ ὑπομονὴ (**25**) ἔργον (42) τέλειον (88, 73, **79**, 68) ἐχέτω (57, 18, **90**)

3. Jas 1:5: αἰτείτω (**33**) παρὰ τοῦ διδόντος (57, **13**, **90**) θεοῦ (**12**) πᾶσιν ἁπλῶς (**57**) καὶ μὴ ὀνειδίζοντος (**33**)

4. Jas 1:6: αἰτείτω (**33**) δὲ ἐν πίστει (**31**), μηδὲν διακρινόμενος (30, **31**, **33**)

5. Jas 1:7–8: μὴ γὰρ οἰέσθω (**31**) ὁ ἄνθρωπος (9) . . . ἀκατάστατος (37) ἐν πάσαις ταῖς ὁδοῖς (41) αὐτοῦ

6. Jas 1:9–10: Καυχάσθω (**33**) δὲ ὁ ἀδελφὸς (**10, 11**) ὁ ταπεινὸς (88, **87**) ἐν τῷ ὕψει (**87**) αὐτοῦ, ὁ δὲ πλούσιος (57, 59) ἐν τῇ ταπεινώσει (88, **87**) αὐτοῦ

7. Jas 1:13: μηδεὶς πειραζόμενος (27, **88**) λεγέτω (**33**) ὅτι Ἀπὸ θεοῦ (**12**) πειράζομαι (27, **88**)

8. Jas 1:16: Μὴ πλανᾶσθε (**31**), ἀδελφοί (**10, 11**) μου ἀγαπητοί (**25**)

9. Jas 1:19: Ἴστε (**28**, 32, 29), ἀδελφοί (**10, 11**) μου ἀγαπητοί (**25**) [probably is imperative]

---

20. There may well be other clauses that are disputed besides those that I have mentioned above. Some may also question the amount of material that I have included or excluded in the given clauses or clause complexes.

10. Jas 1:20: ἔστω (13) δὲ πᾶς ἄνθρωπος (9) ταχὺς (67) εἰς τὸ ἀκοῦσαι (24, 33, 31, 36, 32), βραδὺς (67) εἰς τὸ λαλῆσαι (33), βραδὺς (67) εἰς ὀργήν (88)

11. Jas 1:21: διὸ ἀποθέμενοι (85, 68) πᾶσαν ῥυπαρίαν (88) καὶ περισσείαν (59, 78) κακίας (88) ἐν πραΰτητι (88) δέξασθε (57, 34, 18) τὸν ἔμφυτον (85) λόγον (33, 90) τὸν δυνάμενον (74) σῶσαι (21, 23) τὰς ψυχὰς (26, 23, 9) ὑμῶν

12. Jas 1:22: Γίνεσθε (13) δὲ ποιηταὶ (42) λόγου (33) καὶ μὴ ἀκροαταὶ (24) μόνον (58) παραλογιζόμενοι (88) ἑαυτούς

13. Jas 2:1: Ἀδελφοί (10, 11) μου, μὴ ἐν προσωπολημψίαις (88) ἔχετε (57, 18, 31) τὴν πίστιν (31) τοῦ κυρίου (12) ἡμῶν Ἰησοῦ (93) Χριστοῦ (53, 93) τῆς δόξης (79, 76, 33, 87)

14. Jas 2:5: Ἀκούσατε (24, 33, 31, 36, 32), ἀδελφοί (10, 11) μου ἀγαπητοί (25)

15. Jas 2:18: δεῖξόν (28, 33) μοι τὴν πίστιν (31) σου χωρὶς τῶν ἔργων (42), κἀγώ σοι δείξω (28, 33) ἐκ τῶν ἔργων (42) μου τὴν πίστιν (31)

16. Jas 2:24: ὁρᾶτε (24, 30, 32) ὅτι ἐξ ἔργων (42) δικαιοῦται (34, 88, 56) ἄνθρωπος (9) καὶ οὐκ ἐκ πίστεως (31) μόνον (58)

17. Jas 3:1: Μὴ πολλοὶ (59) διδάσκαλοι (33) γίνεσθε (13), ἀδελφοί (10, 11) μου, εἰδότες (28, 32) ὅτι μεῖζον (78) κρίμα (56, 30) λημψόμεθα (57, 90)

18. Jas 3:13: δειξάτω (28, 33) ἐκ τῆς καλῆς (88) ἀναστροφῆς (41) τὰ ἔργα (42) αὐτοῦ ἐν πραΰτητι (88) σοφίας (32)

19. Jas 3:14: μὴ κατακαυχᾶσθε (33)

20. Jas 3:14: μὴ καὶ ψεύδεσθε (33) κατὰ τῆς ἀληθείας (72)

21. Jas 4:7: ὑποτάγητε (36) οὖν τῷ θεῷ (12)

22. Jas 4:7: ἀντίστητε (39) δὲ τῷ διαβόλῳ (12), καὶ φεύξεται (15, 13) ἀφ' ὑμῶν

23. Jas 4:8: ἐγγίσατε (15) τῷ θεῷ (12), καὶ ἐγγιεῖ (15) ὑμῖν

24. Jas 4:8: καθαρίσατε (53) χεῖρας (8), ἁμαρτωλοί (88)

25. Jas 4:8: καὶ ἁγνίσατε (88) καρδίας (26), δίψυχοι (31)

26. Jas 4:9: ταλαιπωρήσατε (25)

27. Jas 4:9: καὶ πενθήσατε (25)

28. Jas 4:9: καὶ κλαύσατε (**25**)

29. Jas 4:9: ὁ γέλως (**25**) ὑμῶν εἰς πένθος (**25**) μετατραπήτω (**13**) καὶ ἡ χαρὰ (**25**) εἰς κατήφειαν (**25**)

30. Jas 4:10: ταπεινώθητε (**87**) ἐνώπιον κυρίου (**12**), καὶ ὑψώσει (81, **87**) ὑμᾶς

31. Jas 4:11: Μὴ καταλαλεῖτε (**33**) ἀλλήλων, ἀδελφοί (**10, 11**)

32. Jas 4:13: Ἄγε (**91**) νῦν οἱ λέγοντες (**33**) . . .

33. Jas 5:1: Ἄγε (**91**) νῦν οἱ πλούσιοι (**57**)

34. Jas 5:1: κλαύσατε (**25**) ὀλολύζοντες (**25**) ἐπὶ ταῖς ταλαιπωρίαις (**22**) ὑμῶν ταῖς ἐπερχομέναις (**15, 39, 13**)

35. Jas 5:7: Μακροθυμήσατε (**25**) οὖν, ἀδελφοί (**10, 11**), ἕως τῆς παρουσίας (**15**) τοῦ κυρίου (**12**)

36. Jas 5:8: μακροθυμήσατε (**25**) καὶ ὑμεῖς

37. Jas 5:8: στηρίξατε (**74**) τὰς καρδίας (**26**) ὑμῶν

38. Jas 5:9: μὴ στενάζετε (**25, 33**), ἀδελφοί (**10, 11**), κατ᾽ ἀλλήλων

39. Jas 5:10: ὑπόδειγμα (**58**) λάβετε (**18, 57**), ἀδελφοί (**10, 11**), τῆς κακοπαθείας (**24**) καὶ τῆς μακροθυμίας (**25**) τοὺς προφήτας (**53**), οἳ ἐλάλησαν (**33**) ἐν τῷ ὀνόματι (**33**) κυρίου (**12**)

40. Jas 5:12: Πρὸ πάντων δέ, ἀδελφοί (**10, 11**) μου, μὴ ὀμνύετε (**33**), μήτε τὸν οὐρανὸν (**1**) μήτε τὴν γῆν (1, **2**) μήτε ἄλλον τινὰ ὅρκον (**33**)

41. Jas 5:12: ἤτω (**13**) δὲ ὑμῶν τὸ Ναὶ ναὶ (**69**) καὶ τὸ Οὒ οὔ (**69**)

42. Jas 5:13: προσευχέσθω (**33**)

43. Jas 5:13: ψαλλέτω (**33**)

44. Jas 5:14: προσκαλεσάσθω (**33**) τοὺς πρεσβυτέρους (**9**) τῆς ἐκκλησίας (**11**)

45. Jas 5:14: καὶ προσευξάσθωσαν (**33**) ἐπ᾽ αὐτὸν ἀλείψαντες (**47**) ἐλαίῳ (**6**) ἐν τῷ ὀνόματι (**33**) [τοῦ] κυρίου (**12**)

46. Jas 5:16: ἐξομολογεῖσθε (**33**) οὖν ἀλλήλοις τὰς ἁμαρτίας (**88**)

47. Jas 5:16: καὶ εὔχεσθε (**33**) ὑπὲρ ἀλλήλων

48. Jas 5:20: γινωσκέτω (**28, 32**) ὅτι ὁ ἐπιστρέψας (14, **31, 41**) ἁμαρτωλὸν (**88**) ἐκ πλάνης (**31**) ὁδοῦ (**41**) αὐτοῦ σώσει (**21**) ψυχὴν

(23, 9) [αὐτοῦ] ἐκ θανάτου (23) καὶ καλύψει (79) πλῆθος (59) ἁμαρτιῶν (88)

The domain notation of these 48 clauses result in the following number of total occurrences within the sample, with those with three or more occurrences specified according to domain name:

- Domain 1: 2x

- Domain 2: 1x

- Domain 6: 1x

- Domain 8: 1x

- Domain 9: 6x—People

- Domain 10: 12x—Kinship Terms

- Domain 11: 13x—Groups and Classes of Persons and Members of Such Groups and Classes

- Domain 12: 10x—Supernatural Beings and Powers

- Domain 13: 8x—Be, Become, Exist, Happen

- Domain 14: 1x

- Domain 15: 5x—Linear Movement

- Domain 18: 4x—Attachment

- Domain 21: 2x

- Domain 22: 1x

- Domain 23: 4x—Physiological Processes and States

- Domain 24: 5x—Sensory Events and States

- Domain 25: 18x—Attitudes and Emotions

- Domain 26: 3x—Psychological Faculties

- Domain 27: 2x

- Domain 28: 7x—Know

- Domain 29: 1x

- Domain 30: 3x—Think

- Domain 31: 15x—Hold a View, Believe, Trust

- Domain 32: 7x—Understand

- Domain 33: 32x—Communication
- Domain 34: 2x
- Domain 36: 3x—Guide, Discipline, Follow
- Domain 37: 1x
- Domain 39: 2x
- Domain 41: 4x—Behavior and Related States
- Domain 42: 6x—Perform, Do
- Domain 47: 1x
- Domain 53: 3x—Religious Activities
- Domain 56: 2x
- Domain 57: 9x—Possess, Transfer, Exchange
- Domain 58: 3x—Nature, Class, Example
- Domain 59: 4x—Quantity
- Domain 67: 3x—Time
- Domain 68: 2x
- Domain 69: 2x
- Domain 72: 1x
- Domain 73: 1x
- Domain 74: 2x
- Domain 76: 1x
- Domain 78: 2x
- Domain 79: 3x—Features of Objects
- Domain 81: 1x
- Domain 85: 2x
- Domain 87: 6x—Status
- Domain 88: 19x—Moral and Ethical Qualities and Related Behavior
- Domain 90: 4x—Case
- Domain 91: 2x
- Domain 93: 2x

These semantic domains constitute the basis for what I am calling cohesive chains in my implementation of a cohesive harmony analysis. These cohesive chains are chains formed by semantically related lexis, here according to semantic domains rather than on the basis of similar lexical choice (or differentiation of identity or similarity chains, the categories used by Hasan).[21] These results can be displayed in relation to both the cohesive chains and the imperative clauses. This display lists the numbered clauses of the text vertically (sometimes referred to as representing the logogenetic unfolding of the text, a concept to which I will return below)[22] and the semantic domains constituting the chains horizontally listed. Such a configuration is designed to display the semantic domains that are used as the text linearly develops. Whereas most cohesive harmony analyses include every clause of the text (most of much shorter texts than that of James), I am only displaying the clauses with imperatives, as the commanding element (parenetic in nature) is what is generally considered to be the agreed upon structural backbone of the book of James. The individual lexical items of a text, in this case the book of James, may be differentiated in relation to the role they play in cohesive chains. These lexical items may be referred to as either relevant or peripheral tokens of their types. Relevant tokens are those that appear within cohesive chains and peripheral tokens are those that do not. I am concerned here with relevant tokens, the focus of cohesive harmony analysis. Within the selected imperative clauses of James, there are a total of 257 tokens identified (note, however, that some lexemes are designated as belonging to several domains), and 219 of these tokens are members of cohesive chains and hence relevant tokens (defined as containing three instances or more; the number of tokens would increase if chains were constituted on the basis of two instances). Those that are not in such cohesive chains are peripheral tokens (38 tokens of 257, roughly 15 per cent). This represents roughly a percentage of 85 per cent of tokens as relevant. I note again, however, that I am only including lexical items within the imperative clauses. The result is 28 cohesive chains based upon their respective semantic domains. This seems like a large number for consideration, as some of

21. I note that Hasan's similarity chains use a very loose notion of semantic domains, although when they are represented, they often consist of a very limited number of lexical items. See Hasan in Halliday and Hasan, *Language, Context, Text*, 90.

22. See Scott, "Peace and Cohesive Harmony," 90, 91, 93, 95, 96.

them have relatively few members within a book as large as James. To narrow the discussion, I am more concerned here, however, with the cohesive chains with semantic domains of greater textual significance, as indicated by their frequency and distribution throughout the book of James. The results of the cohesive chain analysis are displayed in Table 1 below on pp. 58–60, with the chains of greater significance indicated in bold font. Also, lines are not drawn to separate domains 9, 10, 11, and 12 to highlight their semantic similarity and the significance these groups of words play in the cohesive harmony of the letter.

The analysis has narrowed down the number of important cohesive chains to eleven, with four of them grouped together because of their semantic similarities. These are focal chains within the text. Several observations can be made about these eleven (or perhaps better, eight) focal chains. The first is that semantic domain 33, Communication, forms the largest (by instances) and most extensive (by scope over the entire book) cohesive chain. This should not be surprising, as many, if not most books within the New Testament have a preponderance of this semantic domain (that is, it has the highest density of any semantic domain within the New Testament).[23] However, before we dismiss this evidence too quickly as not significant for cohesion in James, I wish to note that, despite the failure of domain 33, Communication, to distinguish the content of the letter of James from other writings within the New Testament, the cohesive chain does form a set of cohesive ties that extend from the opening to the closing of the book (Jas 1:5 to 5:16, insofar as the imperative clauses are concerned). In this sense, James is no different from other books of the New Testament, in that cohesion is formed around the notion of communication (a type of cohesive chain interaction between the chain and the imperative). Such cohesion does not guarantee coherence, but it does at least place the letter of James within the same textural realm as most of the other books of the New Testament, rather than it being easily dismissed as incohesive.

23. See Porter and O'Donnell, "Semantics and Patterns," 182.

Table 1.

	1.	2.	3.	4.	5.	6.	7.	8.	9.	10.	11.	12.	13.	14.	15.	16.	17.	18.
90			x								x					x		
88		x			2	2				x	3	x	x			x		2
87					3								x					
79		x											x					
67										3								
59					x					x						x		
58												x				x		
57		x	2		x					x		x				x		
53																		
42		x								x			2	x			x	
41				x														x
36									x			x						
33			2	2		2	x			x	x	x	x	x	2		x	x
32								x	x				x			x	x	x
31	x			2	x			x		x			2	x	2	x		
30				x												x	x	
28	x								x					2		x	x	
26										x								
25	x	x						x	x				x					
24										x		x		x		x		
23											2							
18		x								x		x						
15																		
13			x							x		x				x		
12			x				x					x						
11	x				x		x	x		x	x					x		
10	x				x		x	x		x	x					x		
9				x					x	x					x			

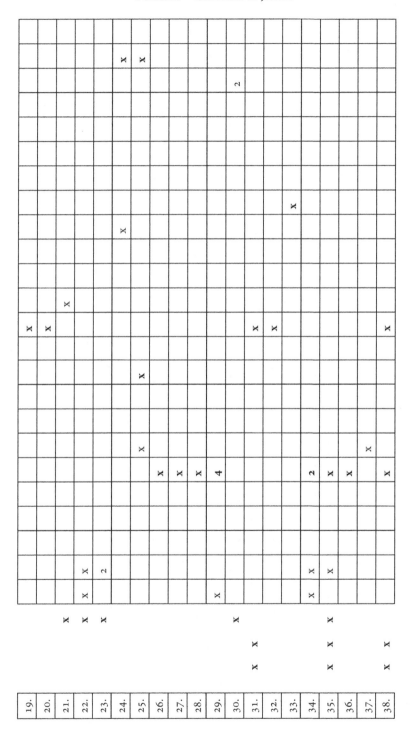

	90	88	87	79	67	59	58	57	53	42	41	36	33	32	31	30	28	26	25	24	23	18	15	13	12	11	10	9
39.							x		x				x						x	x		x			x	x	x	
40.													2													x	x	
41.																								x				
42.													x															
43.													x															
44.													x													x		x
45.		x											2												x			
46.													x															
47.													x															
48.		2		x		x					2			x	2		x				2							x

The next important set of semantic domains comprise domains 9 (People), 10 (Kinship Terms), 11 (Groups and Classes of Persons), and 12 (Supernatural Beings), all of which are concerned with various "beings." As a whole, this group of domains includes a greater number of instances than domain 33 (although a number of tokens are classified in two domains, 10 and 11), with 41 tokens as opposed to 32. The cohesive chain that is formed around Beings concerns various types of beings that are addressed within the letter of James and extend from the opening to the closing of the book (Jas 1:2 to 5:20). This cohesive chain makes clear that the book of James is texturally configured to involve various types of being as the addressees or participants. I will examine the possible cohesive chain interaction of these first two chains further below.

There are, however, a number of other domains that, while they are not as populated as the previous two sets, also form important cohesive chains. The first of these is semantic domain 25 (Attitudes and Emotions). There are eighteen tokens in this domain, which extends roughly the length of the book, from Jas 1:2 to 5:10 (James ends at 5:20). The tokens are not as evenly distributed throughout the book as are those above, with no instance occurring in Jas 3. Nevertheless, there are a number of instances in James 1:2—2:10 and 4:9—5:10. The indication is that attitudes and emotions play a significant role in the discourse at least at a number of places. The distribution of this cohesive chain has implications for organizational analysis of the book. This will be discussed more below.

A second domain of significance is domain 88 (Moral and Ethical Qualities and Behavior). This domain, like domain 25, has a relatively large number of tokens (19), but its distribution is somewhat more restricted than that of domain 25. Domain 88 extends from Jas 1:4—4:8, but then does not have another instance until Jas 5:16. This distributional pattern may well tacitly underlie some of the comments that have been made regarding the book of James and its lack of coherence, as lexis for moral and ethical qualities (at least in the imperative clauses) is not distributed evenly throughout the book and tends to be found in the first three chapters.

The next set of semantic domains to note are domains 31 (Hold a View, Believe, Trust) and 57 (Possess, Transfer, Exchange). They are not related semantically (note the separation in numbers within the Louw-Nida semantic domain lexicon), but they have similar distributional patterns. Semantic domain 31, with 15 tokens, is found predominantly in the first half of James (Jas 1:2—2:24), with one instance in Jas 4:8 and two more in 5:20. Semantic domain 57, with 9 tokens, is also found predominantly in the first half of James (Jas 1:4—3:1), with one further instance in Jas 5:10. Both of these cohesive chains will be examined in regard to the organization of James below.

The final semantic domains to mention here, domains 28 (Know) and 42 (Perform, Do) have fewer tokens than those already mentioned above. Domain 28, with 7 tokens, is found exclusively in the first half of the letter (Jas 1:2—3:18), apart from a single instance in Jas 5:20. Domain 42, with 6 tokens, is also found exclusively in the first half of the letter (Jas 1:4—3:13). These two cohesive chains will also be examined below regarding organization of the letter.

This summary presents the basic evidence of the cohesive chains and their numerical and distributional significance within at least the imperative clauses of the book of James. There is enough evidence on the basis of this set of data to see that there is little grounds for claiming that there is no cohesion to the book of James. There are two major cohesive chains (around domain 33 and domains 9, 10, 11, and 12) that provide strong cohesive ties for the entire book—even if their content does not provide a firm basis for establishing the field of the discourse.[24] These two major sets of chains do identify communication with beings as important cohesive ties that establish the texture of the letter. This is a significant finding. However, the other cohesive chains do not support this textual cohesion, as they are fairly restricted to the first half of the discourse, roughly up to the middle verses of Jas 3 or perhaps a little later in some instances.

Cohesive chain interaction is designed to be able to overcome some of the limitations noted above in the data from cohesive chains. These chains are important for seeing broad patterns of lexis within the text, in this instance grouped by semantic domains in an attempt to reinforce or help to configure the field of the discourse. As Hasan states, "Although the chains go a long way towards building the foundation for coherence, they are not sufficient; we need to include some relations that are characteristic of those between the components of a message."[25] That is, these individual tokens may be components of the message, but we need to find

---

24. See Hasan in Halliday and Hasan, *Language, Context, and Text*, 90.

25. Ibid., 91.

a way to examine the message (clause) itself. These chains by themselves do not go far enough in showing how the lexical choice—used for cohesive purposes—interacts at the group level (attribution) or clausal level with the transitivity system to establish the field of the discourse and hence its coherence. That is provided, at least in part, by cohesive chain interaction. Cohesive chain interaction is concerned with how two or more cohesive chains interact with one another at the lexicogrammatical level as part of clausal structure. Hasan has proposed that such chain interaction should include a minimum of two members of one chain interacting in the same way with two members of another chain.[26] She argues that two is the minimal number to establish distinct interaction (every member of a chain has at least one instance of interaction, by definition) and to identify similarities typical of a discourse. In the analysis below, I will extend the analysis in several different ways, because of the size and configuration of my corpus, so that the imperative forms in the clauses constitute one cohesive chain. This will form the basis for analysis of interaction with other chains. I also extend the notion of chain interaction to include the presence of a token within a cohesive chain within the imperative clause, whether it performs the same lexicogrammatical role or not. This is designed to capture the interaction within the clause, even if the lexicogrammatical function is not identical.

We can identify two types of chain interaction in the data that I have gathered from the book of James. The first is broad types of interaction and the second is specific types of interaction. The interaction involves relevant tokens of two types: central tokens, in which interaction occurs, and non-central tokens, in which interaction does not occur. I am concentrating upon a sub-group of central tokens, those that are found within the above identified cohesive chains. Further, the notion of chain interaction is necessarily different for Greek than it is for English as presented in a variety of English treatments of the topic, not least because some of the primary interactants, such as the explicit subject, are not required in Greek, and hence not required as an interactive element. This is especially true of the imperative clauses that I have identified as central to the cohesive harmony of James. This severely reduces the cohesive interactive patterns available, if one insists on the same configurations for each interaction (e.g., actor action, action acted-upon),[27] so that Hasan's

26. Ibid.

27. Hasan has identified only lexical cohesion, not lexicogrammatical cohesion,

notion of two members interacting might also be reformulated in relation to grammatical cohesion (with the imperative). Nevertheless, there are a number of useful interactive patterns worth observing.

The broad type of interaction concerns some general patterns of interaction. I observe first that all but two of the clauses (as defined above) have the imperative form itself interacting with at least one of the focal cohesive chains listed above as having identifiable significance (the only two that do not are Jas 5:8 and 12), a percentage of roughly 95 per cent. This includes every one of the imperative clauses found from Jas 3:14—4:9, many of which consist only of the imperative itself as the domain-identified component (e.g. Jas 3:14; 4:9 thrice), as well as such instances as Jas 4:13 and 5:1 (it is debatable whether the initial imperative should be included; it is identified as a Discourse Marker, domain 91, by Louw-Nida), and 5:8, 13 (twice), 16. Further, in 37 of 40 possible instances, the imperative (without consideration of its semantic domain) interacts with one or more of the focal chains, roughly 93 per cent of the instances. Perhaps even more significantly, two or more identified focal cohesive chains (9, 10, 11, and 12, 25, 28, 31, 33, 42, 88) are found in 30 of 40 possible clause complexes, or 75 per cent of the possible instances (as noted above, not all clauses have two or more identified domains because they consist of a single verbal element). More specifically, one finds the presence of cohesive chains 9, 10, 11, and 12, 25, 33, and 88 in 42 of 48 clauses (roughly 88 per cent). One further notes the presence of members of cohesive chains 25, 33, or 88 in 41 of 48 of the imperative clauses (roughly 85 per cent). Tokens of chains 25 and 88 together are found in only one clause (Jas 1:4), but cohesive chain 25 or 88 is found in 25 of the 48 clauses (roughly 53 per cent). Cohesive chain 33 and at least one token of one of the other focal chains is found in 18 of 25 clauses (72 per cent). This high percentage indicates (or rather, reinforces) the significance of the imperative clauses, as well as the focal chains of the letter, those cohesive chains that interact with the largest number of other chains.[28] This by itself shows a high percentage of central token interaction (and their significance in focal chains), sufficient to establish widespread cohesion

---

which I am introducing here as a possible interactive cohesive chain. See ibid., 93. For some other comments on the shortcomings of her model, besides those of Parsons (noted above), see Martin, "Cohesion and Texture," 42–43.

28. Hasan in Halliday and Hasan, *Language, Context, and Text*, 94.

and a high degree of cohesive harmony (although admittedly such a statement requires comparative data for its full significance).

The specific interaction concerns lexicogrammatical patterns in which members of different chains interact in specific ways. There are a number of patterns that can be identified, which further establish central tokens and focal chains. The major pattern concerns the cohesive chain interaction of the imperative itself. The imperatives are found with the following domains from among the central domains: 33 (18x), 25 (7x), 31, 28, and 13 (a cohesive chain though not a focal chain as I have identified it above) (5x), and 57 (4x). In six instances when the imperative belongs to domain 33 it interacts with cohesive chains 9, 10, 11, or 12, while in all five instances when the imperative belongs to domain 31 it interacts with these chains, as either nominatives of address or the objects of address. There are no instances within the imperative clauses identified with an explicit subject where the second person imperative is used, although one third of them interact with the nominative of address (11 of 33). Imperatives in the third person, where they have explicit subjects, express those subjects using members of either chains 9, 10, 11, or 12 (3x) or chain 25 (2x).

I draw this analysis to a close with some observations on the impact of these findings for organization of the book of James. The cohesive harmony analysis shows above all that there are a number of cohesive chain interactions that extend throughout the letter that establish a high level of cohesive harmony. The book of James satisfies all three criteria that Hasan establishes as pertaining to a coherent text. These include a high percentage of relevant as opposed to peripheral tokens. Second, James has a high degree of central or non-central tokens, and within the group of central tokens the largest number are parts of focal chains. Third, there is a clear pattern of interaction, especially in relation to cohesive chains 9, 10, 11, and 12 and 33, among the focal chains. Cohesive harmony analysis, however, can also offer insights into the organization of the text. As noted above, Dibelius outlined the letter as consisting of a number of different types of sections. These are not readily defensible in light of the cohesive harmony analysis offered above, which evidences strong cohesive chain interaction throughout the letter and involving a number of focal cohesive chains. An analysis of the major moves within the discourse on the basis of cohesive harmony indicates that the letter is divided into two parts. The first part extends from Jas 1:2—4:8. Focal chains 33, 28,

41, 57, and 88 all interact within this first part of the letter, although there is a reduction of interaction from Jas 3:14—4:8, in which only chains 12 and 88 interact with the imperative verbs (note also, however, that cohesive chains 13 and 15 are active in this closing section). This first part of the letter can be classified as focusing upon communicating with others the importance of moral and ethical qualities and behavior (encompassing especially both cohesive chains 41 and 88). The second part extends from Jas 4:9—5:20.[29] The intensity of the chain interaction is not as high as it was in the first part, although focal chains 33 and 25 are active with chains 9, 10, 11, and 12. Even though the chain interaction is not as high as in part one, the second part continues the cohesive textual pattern found in the first part, as if Jas 4:9 and following are an extension of the section from 3:14—4:8. This second part can be classified as focusing upon communicating with others regarding attitudes and emotions. In that sense, part two might well be seen as an extension, development, or specification of part one of the letter of James—at least so far as cohesive harmony analysis may play a part in such analysis. I realize that this organizational pattern does not represent that found in commentaries and other treatments of the book. Nevertheless, the analysis that I have provided seems to indicate this pattern of development.

CONCLUSION

This has been an exploratory study in cohesive harmony analysis. As Hasan states regarding cohesive harmony analysis, "variation in coherence is the function of variation in the cohesive harmony of a text."[30] The cohesive harmony of a text is predicated upon its cohesion as established by its cohesive chains. Cohesive harmony analysis suggests that there is a definable textual relationship that exists between the textual metafunction (as seen in cohesion) and the ideational metafunction, so that one can establish how the textual features of an instance of language use can activate the field of a discourse. In this study of the book of James, we have seen that there are a number of focal cohesive chains that interact

29. See Varner, *James*, 154–55, for some helpful insights. Cf. Jackson-McCabe, "Enduring Temptation," esp. 174–77, who sees a significant break in this general area. His discussion of coherence, however, is formulated along the usual lines as noted above. See the contrasting argument in Dibelius, *James*, 228–29 and 230–31. See also Davids, *James*, 165–70; McCartney, *James*, 217–18, 220–21. Contra Taylor, *Text-Linguistic Investigation*, 66–67.

30. Hasan in Halliday and Hasan, *Language, Context, Text*, 94.

with each other and with the imperative verbs of a number of clauses in order to establish both cohesion and cohesive harmony. Whereas there are those who have argued against the coherence of the book of James, on the basis of the cohesive harmony analysis presented above, we must conclude that the book of James constitutes a text with high cohesion, high cohesive interaction, and hence high cohesive harmony.

BIBLIOGRAPHY

Allison, Dale C., Jr. *A Critical and Exegetical Commentary on the Epistle of James*. ICC. New York: Bloomsbury T. & T. Clark, 2013.

Cheung, Luke L. *The Genre, Composition and Hermeneutics of James*. Paternoster Biblical and Theological Monographs. Carlisle: Paternoster, 2003.

Cloran, Carmel, et al. "Models of Discourse." In *Continuing Discourse on Language: A Functional Perspective Volume 2*, edited by Ruqaiya Hasan et al., 647–70. London: Equinox, 2007.

Davids, Peter H. *The Epistle of James*. NIGTC. Grand Rapids: Eerdmans, 1982.

Dibelius, Martin. *Der Brief des Jakobus*. Revised by Heinrich Greeven. 10th ed. KEK. Göttingen: Vandenhoeck & Ruprecht, 1959.

———. *James: A Commentary on the Epistle of James*. Revised by Henrich Greeven. Translated by Michael A. Williams. Hermeneia. Minneapolis: Fortress, 1976.

Halliday, M. A. K., and Ruqaiya Hasan. *Cohesion in English*. London: Longman, 1976.

———. *Language, Context, and Text: Aspects of Language in a Social-Semiotic Perspective*. Geelong, Victoria, Australia: Deakin University Press, 1985.

Hasan, Ruqaiya. "Coherence and Cohesive Harmony." In *Understanding Reading Comprehension: Cognition, Language, and the Structure of Prose*, edited by James Flood, 181–219. Newark, DE: International Reading Association, 1984.

Jackson-McCabe, Matt. "Enduring Temptation: The Structure and Coherence of the Letter of James." *JSNT* 37 (2014) 161–84.

Louw, Johannes P., and Eugene A. Nida. *Greek-English Lexicon of the New Testament Based on Semantic Domains*. 2 vols. New York: United Bible Societies, 1988.

McCartney, Dan G. *James*. BECNT. Grand Rapids: Baker, 2009.

Martin, J. R. "Cohesion and Texture." In *The Handbook of Discourse Analysis*, edited by Deborah Schiffrin et al., 35–53. Oxford: Blackwell, 2003.

Moo, Douglas J. *The Letter of James*. PNTC. Grand Rapids: Eerdmans, 2000.

Parsons, Gerald. *Cohesion and Coherence: Scientific Texts: A Comparative Study*. Nottingham: Department of English Studies, University of Nottingham, 1991.

Porter, Stanley E., and Matthew Brook O'Donnell. "Semantics and Patterns of Argumentation in the Book of Romans: Definitions, Proposals, Data and Experiments." In *Diglossia and Other Topics in New Testament Linguistics*, edited by Stanley E. Porter, 154–204. JSNTSup 193. Sheffield: Sheffield Academic, 2000.

Scott, Claire. "Peace and Cohesive Harmony: A Diachronic Investigation of Structure and Texture in 'End of War' News Reports in the Sydney Morning Herald." In *ISFC 36: Challenges to Systemic Functional Linguistics: Theory and Practice*, edited by Y. Fang and C. Wu, 89–96. Beijing and Sydney: The 36th ISFC Organizing Committee, 2010.

Taylor, Mark Edward. *A Text-Linguistic Investigation into the Discourse Structure of James*. LNTS 311. London: T. & T. Clark International 2006.

Taylor, Mark Edward, and George H. Guthrie. "The Structure of James." *CBQ* 68 (2006) 681–705.

Thompson, Geoff. *Introducing Functional Grammar*. 2nd ed. London: Hodder Education, 2004.

Varner, William. *The Book of James: A New Perspective: A Linguistic Commentary Applying Discourse Analysis*. The Woodlands, TX: Kress Biblical Resources, 2010.

———. "The Main Theme and Structure of James." *MSJ* 22 (2011) 115–29.

4

Torah Observance without Faith

The Interlocutor of James 2:18 as a Critic of Jesus-Faith

Christopher D. Land

INTRODUCTION

IT IS AXIOMATIC AMONG practitioners of New Testament scholarship that our task as interpreters operates both with respect to the texts of the New Testament and with respect to its various contexts. So although the field is replete with different interpretive methods, some of which focus more on the texts (e.g., textual criticism, linguistics, literary criticism, etc.) and others more on their contexts (e.g., historical criticism, social-scientific criticism, etc.), one must eventually draw together the texts and contexts so as to produce interpretive readings. A recent example along these lines is Dale Allison's ICC commentary on the Epistle of James.[1] As regards historical context, Allison proposes a second-century *Sitz im Leben* for the epistle, suggesting that it emerged from a form of Christian Judaism closely related to (or perhaps belonging to) Ebionitism.[2] As regards literary context, however, Allison affirms some under-appreciated arguments made by earlier scholars and suggests that the letter construes a first-century Christian Jew addressing first-century diaspora Judaism.[3] The commentary as a whole, then, aims to understand the Epistle of James in relation to these two disparate contexts, both of which must

1. Allison, *Epistle of James.* See also Allison, "Fiction of James," 529–70; Allison, "Polemic against Paul," 123–49; Allison, "Jewish Setting," 154–62.

2. Allison, *Epistle of James,* 48–50.

3. Allison, *Epistle of James,* 37–38.

be considered, according to Allison, if the interpreter wishes to fully appreciate the text.

It is not my intention in this essay to discuss the merits or demerits of Allison's proposed *Sitz im Leben*, since I am entirely unconcerned here with the historical circumstances under which the text of James was actually produced.[4] Rather, my interest is the interpretive context that Allison describes as a "literary fiction," whereby "James presents itself as a letter from a Jerusalem authority to Jews in the diaspora."[5] As Allison rightly observes, irrespective of one's conclusions regarding the historical circumstances surrounding the production and reception of the text we now possess, a first-century letter is what the text purports to be, and so the first task of the reader is to interpret the wording of the text in connection with a first-century context.[6] To put this in the terminology of epistolary theory, it is within the *epistolary situation* of the Epistle of James that our readings must initially operate.[7] Or, to put it instead within the framework of Systemic Functional Linguistics, we cannot adequately explain what the wording of a text means, or why it means this, until we have developed an explicit description of the text's *context of situation* and have explained how that context both emerges from the wording of the text and informs our attempts to make sense of its wordings.[8] My thesis in this essay is that Allison has rightly discerned the context of

4. Let it suffice to say that, while I affirm an important distinction between the context of situation construed by a text and the actual historical situation in which it was produced, I am not fully convinced by Allison's arguments that the two are a half-century apart in the case of our Epistle of James.

5. Allison, *Epistle of James*, 38.

6. As Allison observes, the context construed by the wording of the text must be taken seriously, and "one can hardly promote some other interpretation by remarking upon this fiction's historical implausibility" (Allison, *Epistle of James*, 38). I note here in passing that some of the historical implausibility that Allison perceives would seem to be the result of outdated assumptions about the place of the Christian movement within Judaism in the earliest decades of its existence (see, e.g., Allison's affirmation of Ropes's remark about "the promptness of the separation of Christians and Jews in the diaspora" and his offhand rejection of the possibility that a first-century Christian Jew might feel a sense of responsibility for the instruction of all diaspora Jews [*Epistle of James*, 38]).

7. A good example of an epistolary approach is Dippenaar, "Reading Paul's Letters," 141–57.

8. I discuss Systemic Functional Linguistics (SFL) and its notion of context of situation in Land, *Integrity*, chapter 2. A standard introduction to SFL is Halliday, *Introduction to Functional Grammar*.

situation construed by the Epistle of James, but failed to see the bearing it has on the interpretation of Jas 2:18 in particular and of Jas 2:18–26 in general. I will begin with a summary of Allison's work, before turning to a consideration of the text itself.

ALLISON'S READING OF JAMES 2:18

Context of Situation

Regarding the context of situation that is construed by the Epistle of James, there is nothing remarkable in Allison's claim that the Epistle presents itself as a letter written to Jews in the diaspora by James the brother of Jesus; the dispute, like the proverbial devil, is in the details. Most important for my purposes here is Allison's opinion that the Jews who are ostensibly addressed by the letter are not necessarily *Christ-following* Jews. A diverse and geographically dispersed Jewish audience consisting only *in part* of Christ-followers would, Allison argues, explain why James is so infamously lacking in distinctively Christian ideas and expressions and why the letter sometimes seems to be saying things that would be quite unexpected on the assumption that only Christians are being addressed.[9] In adopting this position, Allison is not an innovator; in fact, he is able to cite a lineage of interpreters that stretches back at least to the Venerable Bede.[10] Nor is Allison a lone voice in contemporary scholarship, since there are others who share the general contours of his view.[11] It is safe to say, however, that only a small minority of modern scholars have been intentional about reading James as a letter addressed to diaspora Judaism broadly conceived, and so the interpretive implications that go along with adopting such a context of situation have not been fully appreciated.

---

9. Allison, *Epistle of James*, 33–35. A number of passages seem to problematize this reading, but Allison rightly shows that few of them are truly problematic (e.g., 1:18, 25; 5:7–8, 14; see *Epistle of James*, 36–37). James 2:1 is the most difficult text, and it is at this point that Allison's proposal has been seen to fall short (e.g., Marcus, "Twelve Tribes," 436). Below, I will demonstrate that even 2:1—without textual emendation—can be read within Allison's proposed context of situation.

10. Allison mentions especially Bede, Grotius, Moulton, and McNeile (see *Epistle of James*, 38–43), but also provides a lengthy list of relevant authors (*Epistle of James*, 116 n. 23).

11. See the recent authors included in Allison's aforementioned list, to which I would add Kaden, "Stoicism," 97–119.

Later in this essay, I will examine Jas 1:1—2:17 in order to demonstrate that Allison's description of the letter's context of situation does indeed make good sense of the letter's beginning. First, however, I wish to consider Allison's treatment of Jas 2:18.

The Interlocutor

In order to understand Allison's discussion of Jas 2:18, one must begin with his remarks concerning 2:14–26 as a unit, since it is his identification of these verses as a unit and his understanding of their function that most directly set him up for the difficulties he experiences with the interlocutor in 2:18. Unfortunately, there is little that can be said about Allison's delimitation of 2:14–26 as a unit, because he does not explicitly defend his decision to segment the letter at 2:14, being content simply to describe the internal structure and coherence of 2:14–26.[12] Accordingly, I will defer discussion of the status of 2:14–26 as a textual unit and will proceed immediately to the alleged function of these verses.

Recognizing that 2:14–26 is not the beginning of a discourse, Allison discusses the literary setting of these verses and correctly observes their continuity relative to James's earlier remarks concerning mere speech instead of action (1:22–25; 2:12), true religion as service to others (1:26–27; 2:1–7), and the importance of loving one's neighbor (2:8). For James, "religion is walking, not talking; it is halakah, a way of life, not dogma."[13] Despite these opening remarks, however, Allison more or less ignores 2:1–13 in his discussion of 2:14–26, aside from occasional remarks that note an ongoing concern with eschatological salvation.[14] Certainly, nothing about 2:1–13 is deemed programmatic for the interpretation of 2:14–26. Instead, Allison turns to a different interpretive context in order to understand what he reads: "This commentator . . . must also conjecture a particular historical setting beyond the literary context. As interpreters have always recognized, the language of Jas 2.14–26 at many points echoes Paul . . . and it is hard to avoid surmising

12. Regarding 2:14–26, Allison merely remarks, "The argument is complete in itself" (*Epistle of James*, 443).

13. Allison, *Epistle of James*, 444.

14. A notable exception occurs on p. 458, where Allison notes that "the anarthrous noun [πίστις] signals a new subject beyond 2.1–13." As will become clear, I find the repetition of πίστις (see 2:1) more significant than its simply being anarthrous, since the lack of an article can be explained in other ways.

that Jas 2.14–26 contains some sort of reaction to Paul or Paulinists."[15] So strong is the pull towards this conjectured context that Allison cannot even imagine resisting it ("Indeed, one wonders whether any informed readers of the New Testament have ever read Jas 2.14–26 wholly on its own terms, without thinking about Paul").[16] He even goes so far as to accuse Johnson of begging the question, simply because Johnson thinks that the meaning of these verses "must be determined not with reference to another author, but from their place in the composition's argument."[17] For Allison, then, the exegesis of Jas 2:14–26 *must* be predicated on the intertextuality that exists between Jas 2 and Paul's letters and by the function of that intertextuality in some historical context wherein James is a response to Paul.

In keeping with this deeply entrenched presumption, Allison insists that "the burden of the section [2:14–26] is not to establish that genuine faith will produce works . . . [or] that salvation requires both faith and works." To the contrary, "James is rejecting a view which allegedly claims that faith does not need works, a view associated with a scriptural argument that he seeks to overturn."[18] The earlier appeals for action have given way to a dogmatic concern, and now "James is not trying to change bad behavior but to refute a defective opinion."[19] In short, the function of 2:14–26 is to refute a Pauline argument to the effect that faith does not need works, and the role of the interlocutor in 2:18 must somehow relate to these conflicts surrounding Paul.

One of the most striking things about Allison's discussion of 2:14–26 is the way that it repeatedly assumes and topicalizes *faith*. The passage is said to be about whether faith (which is assumed) produces works (which are at issue); or it is said to be about whether salvation requires both faith (which is assumed) and works (which are at issue). Later, I myself will observe that Jas 2:2–17 presumes the importance of faith and demands the outworking of faith in appropriate action, and so I have no quibble with the summary expression *faith needs works*. The problem is

---

15. Allison, *Epistle of James*, 444. See also Kloppenborg, "Judaeans or Judaean Christians," 134: "Jas 2.14–26 presuppose[s] a debate that arose within the Jesus movement" (and similarly on p. 124).

16. Allison, "Polemic against Paul," 126.

17. Johnson, *Letter of James*, 247.

18. Allison, *Epistle of James*, 443.

19. Ibid., 448.

that Allison *continues* to assume and to topicalize faith when presenting the view that Jas 2:14–26 allegedly opposes and when discussing the interlocutor in 2:18.

For Allison, 2:14–26 serves to reject an opposing point of view according to which *faith* (which is assumed) *does not need works* (which are the issue), with a key indicator of this conflict being the dissenting interlocutor introduced in 2:18.[20] Yet the interlocutor in question does precisely the opposite of what this reading would predict! Instead of assuming faith (along with James) but distancing himself from works (against James), the interlocutor distances himself from faith (which James has hitherto assumed) but agrees on the importance of having works (thus granting the very thing for which James is allegedly arguing). "*You* have faith," the interlocutor insists (and here note the fronted and contrastive redundant pronoun). Then, much to the chagrin of commentators, "And as for me, *I have* works"—which is to say, *Stop telling me to do something that I think I am already doing*, not, *Stop telling me that I must do something that I think I need not do.*

How does Allison cope with this annoyance? If the overall function of Jas 2:14–26 is to insist, within a historical context shaped by the Apostle Paul, that Christians must not neglect works, who is this interlocutor and why does he say absolutely nothing to challenge the idea that people must have works? One might imagine that a good strategy, given Allison's *Sitz im Leben*, would be to identify the interlocutor as a non-Christ-following Jew of the sort who needs to have his concerns about the Christian movement assuaged as regards the importance of works (i.e., Torah observance). Hence, "You (a Christian) have faith, whereas I (a Torah-observant Jew) have works."[21] This objection would be relevant to second-century concerns about emerging Christianity, and the reading potentially explains why the interlocutor is introduced as a dissenter

20. Allison writes: "Is it not . . . natural to see Pauline ideas or slogans as somehow informing James . . . ? This is all the more so as Jas 2.14–26 is more denial than affirmation, less commandment than clarification. *Not only does James here directly address someone with an opposing point of view*, but the section, although preceded by an imperative . . . and followed by an imperative . . . is itself bereft of moral exhortations" (*Epistle of James*, 448 [emphasis mine]).

21. Something like this was proposed by Zahn, although he has gained few supporters. See Zahn, *Introduction to the New Testament*, 97–98, and the response in Ropes, *Epistle of St. James*, 214.

even though he, like James, affirms the importance of works.[22] In the end, however, Allison rejects this possibility, citing the wording of v. 19. He does not like Zahn's suggestion that v. 19 continues to report the speech of a non-Christian Jewish interlocutor, and he sees no point in attempting to make sense of v. 19 as James's response to such an interlocutor. After all, Allison reminds us, dissent between James and a Torah-observant Jew would make very little sense given "the likelihood that the passage is in part a response to Paul."[23] In the end, after surveying a wide range of other explanations—none of which I will outline here, since interested readers can consult the literature for themselves—Allison concludes that "not one of these explanations satisfies" and that he himself "is unable to offer anything better in their place."[24]

When it comes to the interpretation of 2:18, therefore, Allison is flummoxed. Having decided in advance that 2:14–26 is a reaction to Paul, he assumes an opposing voice proclaiming that *faith does not need works*, and consequently he is unable to make sense of the interlocutor's words.[25] He can conclude only that "James expressed himself so poorly that we cannot offer any clear exposition."[26] Indeed, we should rather entertain the possibility that an explicit reference to Paul has been removed, leaving the text as its stands corrupt.[27] It would seem that Allison is so convinced by his mirror reading that, having gazed intently into the mirror, he is prepared to walk away and forget what the text looks like!

Summary and Prospectus

What we are dealing with, I suggest, not only in Allison's commentary but in virtually all of the literature on Jas 2, is the imposition of foreign concerns onto the interpretation of Jas 2—concerns that assume not just a Pauline mission but the neglect of actual Torah observance among early

22. Allison insists (rightly, in my opinion) that the interlocutor is represented as a dissenter in relation to the views James espouses just prior to 2:18 (Allison, *Epistle of James*, 468–71).

23. Ibid., 471.

24. Ibid., 471.

25. In actual fact, Allison blatantly dismisses the idea that v. 18 might actually mean what it says. He writes, "As we have seen, the issue being discussed stems from Pauline theology, which raises the problem of *faith without deeds, not deeds without faith*" (*Epistle of James*, 470 [emphasis mine]).

26. Ibid., 471.

27. Ibid., 471 n. 253.

"Christians."[28] Yet these concerns are being imposed onto a text that projects, as its ostensibly epistolary situation, a devout, Torah-observant Christian Jew addressing diaspora synagogue communities whose members—we must surely assume, in the absence of any clear evidence to the contrary from within the text itself—will have taken the importance of Torah observance for granted. In actual fact, I suggest, it is *only* the perceived intertextuality with Paul that activates Allison's interpretive framework; nothing in the wording of the text implies anyone's disagreement with the principle that *faith needs works*. Moreover, Allison's interpretive framework does not enrich the interpretation of the text's wording, but produces interpretive difficulties.

Now, because Allison sees the letter as a literary fiction, he can perhaps ignore the inherent implausibility of diaspora synagogue communities needing to be convinced that righteous works are in principle necessary. After all, not all literary fictions are equally plausible. To my mind, however, Allison has missed an opportunity to explore how the social dynamics of his own proposed context of situation (namely, first-century Judaism, *inclusive* of the early Christian movement) can actually resolve some longstanding questions surrounding the wording of 2:18 and the function of Jas 2. Specifically, I think that 2:18 makes very good sense when read in connection with first-century Jewish debates concerning what it means to obey Torah, with the main issue between James and his interlocutor being the relative importance of eschatology and the extent to which eschatological expectations should motivate seemingly inappropriate behavior (e.g., refusal to honor the rich). In 2:18, an unnamed diaspora Jew distances himself from the radical faith James has been espousing with regard to the future fate of the rich and poor (which I will here call Jesus-faith), asserting that he already does Torah and has no interest in James's Jesus-faith; James retorts that Jesus-faith is at the heart of Judaism and insists (once again) that asserting one's own obedience to Torah is not the same thing as actually doing Torah. In other words, the interlocutor in 2:18 does not inject into the discourse a dispute over the importance of works in relation to an assumed faith, but a dispute over the place of Jesus-faith within Judaism.[29]

---

28. The questionable status of this longstanding assumption can be seen very clearly in a number of fields of study, including historical Jesus studies, Pauline studies, and Matthean studies.

29. In all fairness, I must point out that Allison cannot be faulted *in principle* here. He himself observes, "The audience ostensibly addressed—Jews of the diaspora—contains

In what follows, I will develop this hypothesis by drawing attention to details in the wording of Jas 1–2 that construe first-century diaspora Judaism as the primary context of situation within which the wordings ought to be understood. I will then observe that within this primary context of situation, nobody has minimized the importance of doing Torah, as though Jas 2:14–26 is concerned to distance the Jesus-movement from such ideas by openly refuting them. Instead, some of James's implied readers are perhaps thinking that they can do Torah without adopting the radical views of Jesus, and the goal of Jas 2 is to show that Jesus-faith, which entails the adoption of Jesus's radical eschatological ethic, is the natural—nay, *necessary*—outworking of a desire to obey Torah.

THE PRECEDING CO-TEXT

Because my argument in this essay concerns the relative coherence of Jas 2:18 within the context of situation observed by Allison himself, I will not attempt to build an entirely independent case in support of this proposed context. Instead, I will string together a series of Allison's own observations with the aim of showing that Jas 1:1—2:17 makes sense remarkably well within an overarching context of situation in which everyone affirms the importance of Torah observance, including not only the ostensible author of the letter but everyone in the diaspora communities that are ostensibly being addressed.[30] Near the end of the section, I will begin to develop my thesis by showing that, for the sake of argument, James *temporarily* assumes his readers' universal acceptance of the appeal for Jesus-faith in 2:1, with the implausibility of this rhetorical assumption serving to explain the appearance of an imaginary interlocutor in 2:18.

The Addressees

Ἰάκωβος θεοῦ καὶ κυρίου Ἰησοῦ Χριστοῦ δοῦλος ταῖς δώδεκα φυλαῖς ταῖς ἐν τῇ διασπορᾷ χαίρειν (Jas 1:1).

Christian Jews and non-Christian Jews . . . It follows that we should consider 2.14–26 from two points of view and ask not only what a Christian Jew might have made of the section but also what a non-Christian Jew might have made of it" (*Epistle of James*, 455). My point is only that he too easily imagines a mid-first-century diaspora synagogue needing to be told about the importance of doing Torah. In general, Christian interpreters have been far too quick to imagine first-century Jews jettisoning their cultural and religious heritage.

30. Here again, I am dialoging with Allison for the sake of convenience, without meaning to minimize the contributions of other scholars who have treated the issues.

"Since the onus is on those who have argued against a prosaic [as opposed to metaphorical] reading of 1:1, and since . . . their arguments are far from demonstrative, we are encouraged to reconsider the view that Jas 1:1 is designed in the first place to make one think of the literal twelve tribes of Israel and so of Jews in general, not Christians in particular."[31] Here, I suggest, Allison is exactly right. Taken in isolation, the language of Jas 1:1 very naturally suggests diaspora Jews, and so those who see the author addressing specifically *Christian* Jews (or even Christians in general) must find things in the letter that do not fit with a very general diaspora audience but require a more specifically Christian one. As both Allison and Kloppenborg have recently argued, however, the passages that have been brought forward are (almost?) all intelligible within a letter written to both Christian *and* non-Christian Jews.[32]

Perfection and Perfect Work

Ἡ δὲ ὑπομονὴ ἔργον τέλειον ἐχέτω, ἵνα ἦτε τέλειοι καὶ ὁλόκληροι ἐν μηδενὶ λειπόμενοι (Jas 1:4).

Regarding Jas 1:4, Allison endorses the work of Klein and observes that "ἔργον and ἔργον τέλειον refer to a person's lifework as judged by God."[33] Which is to say, James is thinking eschatologically here, and his concern is that his readers will be judged in accordance with the quality of their work (i.e., their deeds). Allison also suggests that, for diaspora Jewish readers familiar with the Torah, such ideas will have evoked the command of Deut 18:13, which demands of Israel, "You must be perfect [LXX: τέλειος] before the Lord your God."[34] Deuteronomy 18 urges Israel to heed the Law of Moses (Deut 18:9–14)—and (interestingly enough) to heed the voice of the Prophet whenever he comes (Deut 18:15–22)—in a way that displays single-minded devotion to the Lord amidst the alternative beliefs and practices characteristic of surrounding nations.[35] For my

31. Allison, "Fiction of James," 545.

32. In addition to Allison, *Epistle of James*, 36–37, see also Kloppenborg, "Judaeans or Judaean Christians," 120–27. The obvious exception to this claim is the very troublesome reference to Jesus-faith in Jas 2:1, which both Allison and Kloppenborg—following a number of earlier authors—excise from the text (see my alternative solution below).

33. Allison, *Epistle of James*, 154.

34. Ibid., 155.

35. Note James's appeal for wholeness and condemnation of double-mindedness

purposes here, what matters is that diaspora Jews will have been able to make sense of James's opening remarks about eschatological judgment and perfect work by relating his remarks to the doing of Torah.

Receiving Torah and Doing the Work of Torah

Πᾶσα δόσις ἀγαθὴ καὶ πᾶν δώρημα τέλειον ἄνωθέν ἐστιν . . . ἀπεκύησεν ἡμᾶς λόγῳ ἀληθείας εἰς τὸ εἶναι ἡμᾶς ἀπαρχήν τινα τῶν αὐτοῦ κτισμάτων . . . ἀποθέμενοι πᾶσαν ῥυπαρίαν καὶ περισσείαν κακίας ἐν πραΰτητι, δέξασθε τὸν ἔμφυτον λόγον (Jas 1:17–21).

Γίνεσθε δὲ ποιηταὶ λόγου καὶ μὴ μόνον ἀκροαταὶ . . . ὁ δὲ παρακύψας εἰς νόμον τέλειον τὸν τῆς ἐλευθερίας καὶ παραμείνας, οὐκ ἀκροατὴς ἐπιλησμονῆς γενόμενος ἀλλὰ ποιητὴς ἔργου, οὗτος μακάριος ἐν τῇ ποιήσει αὐτοῦ ἔσται (Jas 1:22–25).

The above wordings have often been understood in relation to distinctly Christian ideas (e.g., the Christian gospel, Christian conversion, Christian baptism, Christian obedience, etc.). Allison, however, makes good sense of these exhortations within a context in which James is addressing diaspora Jews. In support, Allison notes that: (1) "if we take the epistolary fiction seriously, it is altogether natural to identify ἡμᾶς with the Jewish people"; (2) "God gives birth to Israel in Deut 32.18"; (3) various Jewish texts speak about Israel as first fruits; (4) Jewish literature manifests strong associations between the Torah and "truth," and some texts use the phrase "word of truth" with reference to Torah; and perhaps most significantly of all, (5) "the λόγος of 1.22 is the same as 'the law of freedom' in 1.25, and the latter . . . is the Torah."[36]

On this reading of Jas 1, God is said to have given perfect gifts to James and his diaspora readers (i.e., to Israel), including a word of truth and word of freedom that has been implanted within them (i.e., Torah).[37] When we ask what it means for James and his readers to *obediently receive* this word of truth and freedom, however, the answer we find in the text

---

in Jas 1:2–8, as well as his appeal for purity in relation to the defiling influence of the world in Jas 1:27.

36. See Allison, *Epistle of James*, 282–83.

37. Much could be said about the manner in which this implanting was understood by first-century Jews, including the likely influence of Stoicism, but this would take me far afield of my present concerns. Let it suffice to say that identifying a Jewish background here does not in any way preclude wider influences.

is that it means to look intently into their "perfect law, the law of liberty" (Jas 1:25) and to *do what it says.*[38] As in Deut 30, therefore, the word is near, in the heart—so that it might be observed (30:14; cf. 30:2, 6, 8, 10). Whatever else he or she is, the doer of Jas 1 is a doer of Torah.[39]

Doing Torah and Showing Mercy

θρησκεία καθαρὰ καὶ ἀμίαντος παρὰ τῷ θεῷ καὶ πατρὶ αὕτη ἐστίν, ἐπισκέπτεσθαι ὀρφανοὺς καὶ χήρας ἐν τῇ θλίψει αὐτῶν (Jas 1:27).

Εἰ μέντοι νόμον τελεῖτε βασιλικὸν κατὰ τὴν γραφήν· ἀγαπήσεις τὸν πλησίον σου ὡς σεαυτόν, καλῶς ποιεῖτε· εἰ δὲ προσωπολημπτεῖτε, ἁμαρτίαν ἐργάζεσθε ἐλεγχόμενοι ὑπὸ τοῦ νόμου ὡς παραβάται. ὅστις γὰρ ὅλον τὸν νόμον τηρήσῃ πταίσῃ δὲ ἐν ἑνί, γέγονεν πάντων ἔνοχος (Jas 2:8–10).

Granting that James is exhorting diaspora Jews to become perfect by living out Torah, it remains to ask what this means and why James feels a need to say it. Does the text perhaps assume that some kind of mass apostasy is affecting diaspora Jewish communities, as though Jews around the Mediterranean are deciding *en masse* that they should no longer bother to obey Torah? Here we must carefully avoid mirror reading and remember that a Jew can appeal for Torah observance even when addressing Jews who are themselves deeply passionate about obeying Torah. (Were it otherwise, how would we explain the teachings of Jesus himself?) Since nothing in the wording of the epistle suggests that its addressees are rejecting Torah observance *in principle*, we should proceed on the assumption that James is exhorting Torah-conscious Jews to obey Torah *in a certain way*—namely, in a way that shows mercy to the poor.[40]

Recognizing the force of these general observations, Allison suggests that Jas 2:1–13 is a discourse "ostensibly aimed at synagogue members who tend to disparage co-religionists less fortunate than themselves

38. As Allison writes with respect to Jas 2:14, "For a Jew such as James, 'works of the law' and 'good works' would scarcely be distinguished. This is all the more apparent since . . . 1.25 clearly associates the law with ποιητὴς ἔργου" (*Epistle of James*, 461).

39. Allison writes: "Given the νόμον in v. 25, it is natural to suppose that ποιητὴς ἔργου denotes one who does the work that Torah demands" (ibid., 343).

40. Kloppenborg correctly observes that "James's argument in 2.8–13 and 2.14–26 presumes that the addressees are, or claim to be, Torah observant" ("Judaeans or Judaean Christians," 119).

while honoring the wealthy, even when the latter take them to court (v. 6) and bring disrepute to their religion (v. 7)."[41] Accordingly, the point being made in the opening part of Jas 2 is *not* the abstract point that Torah should *in principle* be obeyed; it is the *practical* point that obeying Torah means refusing rich oppressors the honor to which they feel entitled. There may well have been "some Christians . . . among the poor," and James may be "seeking here, as elsewhere, to maintain or make room for them in the community," but the argument—although it sounds remarkably like Jesus—is firmly grounded in the authority of the Law of Moses.[42] James is asking his readers to "complete the royal law" by loving their neighbors (2:8) so as to not be "convicted by the law" (2:9), or again, to "keep the whole law" (2:10) so as not to become "transgressor[s] of the law" (2:11). As *diaspora Jews* they should "speak and act as people who are going to be judged by a liberating law" (2:12), remembering that "judgment without mercy will be shown to anyone who has not been merciful" (2:13).

Given all of this, one might expect Allison to treat the remarks in 2:14–17 concerning the relationship between faith and works in a similar manner, as a discussion concerned with the difference between *espousing* Torah (i.e., faith) and *obeying* Torah fully (i.e., works, with a focus on acts of mercy). This, however, Allison does not do. Instead, as we have already seen, he leaps from the remark in 2:14 ("Can faith save you, if you say you have faith but you do not have works?") to the inference that "James is rejecting a view which allegedly claims that faith does not need works."[43] Notably, this goes beyond what is explicit in the wording of our text, since the diaspora Jew envisioned in 2:14–17 speaks *only* about faith (πίστιν λέγῃ τις ἔχειν), saying nothing whatsoever about works. Moreover, it moves outside of the general context of situation construed by the letter, given that Jews at this time took it for granted that their Jewish faith needed to work itself out in righteous actions.[44]

So then, is Allison correct that Jas 2:14–17 rejects the view that faith does not need works? Yes, in the sense that every positive assertion

---

41. Allison, *Epistle of James*, 376.

42. Ibid., 376.

43. Ibid., 443.

44. See ibid., 448. Which is to say, a diaspora audience, all things being equal, will have shared James's opinion that mere faith cannot save someone who has no works. To posit a much more specific context in which someone is arguing to the contrary would seem to require justification from the explicit wording of the text.

implies the denial of a corresponding negative. But it does *not* follow that there is someone else in the context of situation of James's letter who actually espouses the corresponding negative. To the contrary, all of Jas 1:1—2:17 suggests otherwise. Repeatedly, James has pointed out the potential that exists for division within the individual, for inconsistencies between what people understand or espouse and how people actually behave, and nothing in 2:14–17 suggests any departure from this. So if one of James's diaspora readers claims to have faith but does not do works of mercy, the problem in view is not a defective understanding of the importance of works in general but a failure to actually *do* the specific works with which James is here concerned. Really, the problem of *faith without works* is, within the context established by Jas 1:1—2:13, *Judaism without mercy.*[45] There is no sign of any significant transition at 2:14, but only a continuing development of that which was made explicit in 2:1: James wants his Jewish readers to have a faith that does not tolerate favoritism.

Eschatology and Jesus-Faith

Ἀδελφοί μου, μὴ ἐν προσωπολημψίαις ἔχετε τὴν πίστιν τοῦ κυρίου ἡμῶν Ἰησοῦ Χριστοῦ τῆς δόξης (Jas 2:1).

At this point we come finally to the critical issue of Jas 2:1, which is the only place that James speaks explicitly about Jesus-faith. Does the reference to Jesus-faith in 2:1 have any bearing on the interpretation of the *faith without works* problem addressed later in 2:14–17? And does it have anything to do with the interlocutor who emerges in 2:18?

Allison, commenting on πίστις in 2:14, observes that "one must judge its connotations from the immediate context."[46] He rightly, in my opinion, suggests that its uses in Jas 1:3, 6 and 2:5 implicate "whole-hearted allegiance and commitment to and unconditional trust in God," but he wrongly places a question mark over the usage in 2:1 and he wrongly describes the uses in 2:14, 17, 18, 20, 22, and 24 as having a distinct meaning that implicates "something close to intellectual consent . . . like

45. Although Allison repeatedly speaks in his commentary about Jas 2:14–26, the discussion in 2:14–17 is not self-evidently discontinuous with what precedes it. It calls for action rather than mere possession or confession, picking up a point made first in 1:22 and then developed right up to 2:13. What is more, 2:14–17 cites mercy towards the poor and vulnerable as its only example of what it means for faith to have works, thereby picking up a concern articulated not only in 1:27 but also developed throughout 2:1–13.

46. Allison, *Epistle of James*, 458.

a purely professed or confessed faith."[47] These errors, I suggest, stem from Allison's failure to perceive how 2:1 functions in the wider discourse, and even more specifically, from his failure to perceive how its reference to Jesus functions. Accordingly, I will argue in what follows that 2:1 very intentionally introduces Jesus-faith into a discourse that has previously assumed only Jewish faith, with the various uses of πίστις differing not as regards the meaning of πίστις but only as regards what is being trusted or believed. I will then show how James's intentional reference to Jesus-faith in 2:1 sets up the arrival of an interlocutor in 2:18.

As is well-known, Allison excises the words ἡμῶν Ἰησοῦ Χριστοῦ from Jas 2:1, preferring to treat them as a scribal interpolation.[48] He does so in part because of perceived grammatical difficulties, but also because an overt confession of Jesus-faith by the letter's ostensible addressees does not make any sense to him given the consistency with which the letter construes a general diaspora audience.[49] Here I will propose a reading of 2:1 that makes sense of the text as it has been passed down to us, that makes sense in relation to a general diaspora audience, and that makes sense of the interlocutor who arrives in 2:18. My reading thus eliminates one of the major difficulties that prompts Allison to emend the text, as well as the various difficulties that prompt him to declare 2:18 inexplicable.

I will develop my argument in two steps. First, I will show that the Jesus-faith of 2:1 should be understood in relation to the eschatological and ethical views espoused throughout the surrounding co-text, such that—in this context, at least—the most salient thing about Jesus-faith is that it entails being mindful of future judgment, mindful of what God's coming kingdom means for the poor, and consequently merciful in the way that one treats the poor. Second, I will show that Jas 2:1 does not in fact presume that its readers are Christ-followers; rather, it presumes that they wish to obey Torah and so exhorts them to have Jesus-faith, with the unspoken premises being that the eschatological and ethical teachings

---

47. Ibid., 458.

48. As part of his excursus on this issue, Allison provides a list of scholars who endorse the emendation (ibid., 382–84).

49. The present essay will not address the alleged grammatical difficulties. I note, however, that the inclusion of the Greek term δόξα can hardly be deemed unexpected in a discourse that is fundamentally concerned with social status and with the appropriate and inappropriate bestowal of honor.

of Jesus sum up the teaching of Torah and that trusting Jesus is itself the natural outworking of a desire to obey Torah.

Here, then, is the wording that opens Jas 2: μὴ ἐν προσωπολημψίαις ἔχετε τὴν πίστιν τοῦ κυρίου ἡμῶν Ἰησοῦ Χριστοῦ τῆς δόξης. Notably, this wording comes on the heels of a remark about widows and orphans and about the dangers of worldly influences. Moreover, it is followed by an elaborating discussion (note the γάρ in 2:2) that very clearly contrasts mercy towards the poor with deference towards the wealthy and influential. It would seem logical, therefore, to suppose that James sees the faith invoked in this verse as being somehow relevant to the treatment of Jews who are economically vulnerable. Its relevance, I suggest, derives from the fact that James understands Jesus-faith (τὴν πίστιν τοῦ κυρίου ἡμῶν Ἰησοῦ Χριστοῦ) to entail the very things at issue in the discourse. For James, Jesus-faith is Jewish, and it endures testing so as to produce the perfect work God requires, namely, a life of full obedience to the teachings of Torah. More specifically, James understands Jesus-faith to be a form of Jewish faith that stresses the points he develops in 2:1–17, including eschatological expectations ("Has not God chosen those who are poor in the eyes of the world to be rich in faith and to inherit the kingdom he promised to those who love him?") and the present implications of those expectations ("Judgment without mercy will be shown to anyone who has not been merciful"). In essence, Jesus-faith is relevant to what James is doing in his letter, because for James, Jesus-faith encapsulates the kind of eschatologically-oriented and ethical Judaism he seeks to inculcate among his diaspora readers.

As regards the development of James's discourse, the above understanding of 2:1 entails that James is not introducing a new idea or teaching into his discourse when he invokes the notion of Jesus-faith in 2:1. All along he has had in view Jesus's teachings about the coming judgment and about how Jews ought to live in the meantime, and all along James has been exhorting his Jewish readers to think and act in accordance with the teachings of Jesus of Nazareth. What is new is simply his decision to explicitly name these things "Jesus-faith."

What then, of the fact that 2:1 describes Jesus as "*our* Lord Jesus Christ"? And what about the inherent implausibility of a scenario in which diaspora Judaism, broadly conceived, is construed as *having* Jesus-faith?[50]

---

50. For a discussion of some authors who have, in fact, understood the verse in this way, see Allison, "Fiction of James," 544–45.

Here, I suggest, we must very carefully differentiate between that which the wording of 2:1 assumes, that for which the wording of 2:1 appeals, and that which is actually the case within the letter's context of situation. By calling Jesus "our Lord," James construes the lordship of Jesus over both himself and his diaspora readers as an indisputable fact. But this does not imply that his addressees actually recognize the lordship of Jesus over themselves, nor does it entail that James actually expects them to.[51] To the contrary, the casual phrase "our Lord Jesus Christ" indicates only that James himself, as a servant of the Lord Jesus Christ (1:1), views his lord as lord of all Israel, and that he wishes to treat this lordship as something non-negotiable. The lordship of Jesus is thus assumed, but nothing is assumed as regards the reader's stance towards Jesus.

As further evidence for this last point, I note that where James does speak in 2:1 about a posture of trust and belief towards Jesus on the part of his addressees, he does not use a similar wording such as "*your* faith in our Lord Jesus Christ" but instead urges his diaspora Jewish addressees to have Jesus-faith. Unfortunately, this appeal for Jesus-faith is obscured by most English translations, which inadvertently encode the assumption that James's readers already purport to have Jesus-faith. The NRSV translates, "Do you with your acts of favoritism really believe in our glorious Lord Jesus Christ?" which implies that James is calling into question something that would otherwise be assumed: namely, that his readers believe in Jesus Christ as Lord.[52] For its part, the NIV avoids encoding this assumption, producing the more neutral instruction, "Believers in our glorious Lord Jesus Christ must not show favoritism," but this fails to convey the fact that James is not making a general statement about believers but instead is directly appealing to his readers.[53] More wooden is the KJV, which reads, "Have not the faith of our Lord Jesus Christ, the Lord of glory, with respect of persons," but by moving the words *with respect of persons* to the end, the King James translators have altered the focus and scope of the negative particle, leaving the impression that James is telling

---

51. Here I differentiate between wanting something (which is almost always the case when one asks for something) and expecting something (which is only sometimes the case, since, as all children know, you can't always get what you want).

52. I will not extensively discuss the interrogative reading of 2:1, because I find the imperative reading more likely in the present context. It should be noted, however, that treating 2:1 as an interrogative would not invalidate my larger hypothesis.

53. Probably, I assume, the translators of the NIV felt safe in obscuring this because they expected readers of the NIV to view the letter as one addressed to Christians.

his readers how *not* to live out their Jesus-faith—with their Jesus-faith once again assumed.

A truly helpful rendering of the Greek, I suggest, needs to convey that the focus of the negative particle in 2:1 is the opening prepositional phrase ἐν προσωπολημψίαις ('in favoritism') and that the scope of the negative particle may or may not extend so as to encompass the verb and its arguments ('have Jesus-faith'). The focus of the negative is significant because it indicates that James is not prohibiting Jesus-faith *per se* but a favoritism that he finds incompatible with Jesus-faith (something recognized by all of the above translations); the uncertain scope of the negative is significant because it indicates that James could be prohibiting a discriminatory Jesus-faith or else *appealing for* a Jesus-faith that is by nature opposed to favoritism (a reading that none of the above translations permit). Given that nothing in the letter so far has suggested that James's diaspora readers unanimously espouse Jesus-faith, I suggest that this last reading is the most likely one, with 2:1 meaning something like: *Without showing favoritism, have the faith of our Lord Jesus Christ of glory.* Which is to say, *I'm concerned to discourage social injustice among you, and in line with this I urge you to embrace Jesus-faith.*

Notice that, on this reading of the syntax in 2:1, James is explicitly urging his readers to have Jesus-faith, a move that introduces into the letter the implicit possibility that some of his readers will reject the appeal. This implicit possibility is, I suggest, completely ignored throughout 2:1–17, with the discourse proceeding on the assumption that its readers are sympathetic to the appeal in 2:1 and consequently willing to treat Jesus-faith as encapsulating their Jewish faith in the God of Israel, their expectation of divine judgment, and their commitment to live in obedience to Torah. This is why the scenario in 2:2–7 elaborates 2:1 using second person plural references, why the exhortations in 2:8–13 concerning obedience to the law continue to use second person plurals, and why the person who espouses faith but lacks works is introduced simply as "someone" but immediately illustrated as "one of you" (2:14–15). In all of this, James is making the rhetorical assumption that his readers' Jewish faith is in fact Jesus-faith—since Judaism, for James, is truly manifested in Jesus—and so his focus is not so much on faith itself but on the works of mercy that must follow. But is James making a fair assumption? Will diaspora Jews in the first century have agreed that "the faith of our Lord Jesus Christ of glory" encapsulates their own understanding of Judaism?

It is this very obvious question, I suggest, that explains the arrival of an interlocutor in 2:18, who takes issue not with the importance of works but with James's Jesus-faith.

Summary

Why does an interlocutor suddenly emerge in Jas 2:18, and what is his problem? Given the context of situation construed by the preceding co-text of Jas 1:1—2:17, I suggest, *the dissent has more to do with the questionable status of Jesus-faith within diaspora Judaism than it does with the questionable status of works within early Christianity.* Or, to put things a bit differently, the central issue that prompts the arrival of a dissenter in 2:18 is not the entirely unexpected question *Must people do the works of Torah in order to be declared righteous?* but questions that are already at issue in the discourse: namely, *What does righteous obedience to Torah actually look like in an unjust world?* and *Are the diaspora communities actually doing Torah?*

In my opinion, nothing in Jas 1:1—2:17 presumes a "works free" form of faith (whether Jewish or Christian) and nothing suggests a reaction to an alternative stream within the emerging Christian movement (whether Pauline or otherwise). The critiques in the text are all leveled at un-merciful expressions of Judaism, such that James's appeals for Jesus-faith and for works of mercy constitute an *intra-Jewish apologetic.* Moreover, within the parameters of this context of situation, the most likely counter-argument is not one that denies the importance of works (since even un-merciful expressions of Judaism persist in espousing obedience to Torah, including acts of mercy) but one that denies the importance of Jesus-faith (since it is actually the radical social activism of Jesus that is the true focus of the discourse and the most likely source of controversy). The difference between the available readings and my own thus comes down to this: on most readings, all of the voices that are operative within the discourse, including both explicit and implicit voices, take for granted the importance of faith (and in some readings, even Jesus-faith specifically); by contrast, I think that 2:1–17 appeals for Jesus-faith as though Jews who want to obey Torah will *of course* see Jesus-faith as integral to a truly Torah-observant life, with the interlocutor of 2:18, who calls this assumption into question, voicing an essentially anti-Jesus sentiment.[54]

54. This is true even of Zahn, who most closely approximates my reading, in that he sees v. 18b as the continuation of the interlocutor's objection, such that the

A PROPOSED READING OF JAMES 2:18

Consider the following outline of James 2, which, for the sake of clarity, presents only the barest scaffolding of the text:

μὴ ἐν προσωπολημψίαις ἔχετε τὴν πίστιν τοῦ κυρίου ἡμῶν Ἰησοῦ Χριστοῦ (*Without showing favoritism, have the faith of our Lord Jesus Christ!*) (2:1). [Hereafter follows various remarks about social inequality, about God's choice of the poor as heirs of the kingdom, about future judgment, and about works of mercy as an essential part of doing Torah—which is to say, remarks about things proclaimed by Jesus.]

Ἀλλ᾽ ἐρεῖ τις· σὺ πίστιν ἔχεις, κἀγὼ ἔργα ἔχω (*But someone will say, "You have faith; as for me, I have works!"*) (2:18a). [Hereafter follows various remarks about the essential role that faith plays in Judaism and about the faith and works taught in Torah—which is to say, remarks that establish continuity between Jesus's proclamation and the teaching of Torah.]

The main thing to notice from this outline is the very clear two-part structure whereby 2:1–17 is balanced by 2:18–26. The first part opens with an appeal for faith; the second part opens with someone explicitly rejecting this appeal. The first part implies that the adoption of Jesus-faith correlates with true Torah observance; the second part opens with a dissenter who directly challenges this correlation by laying claim to works independently of faith.

Perceiving this overall structure allows us to see that, whereas 2:1–17 insists that Jesus-faith must work itself out in social justice, 2:18–26 insists that Jesus-faith is in fact the Jewish faith taught in Torah. And this in turn allows us to explain why James persists in saying that his interlocutor's faith must produce works, even after the interlocutor has implicitly rejected James's appeal for faith. In the end, the fundamental disagreement between James and his interlocutor is not whether the Jewish faith (in general) must produce works (in general), but what specific *kind* of faith is taught in Torah and what specific *kind* of works this faith must produce.

---

interlocutor pledges to show his own faith (*Introduction to the New Testament*, 98).

The Objection in 2:18a

Let us consider a hypothetical diaspora Jew who has heard James's condemnation of favors towards the rich and decided to object.[55] Is such a person likely to deny the importance of works? Hardly. Even if he wants to maintain the status quo of social inequality and avoid the works of mercy prescribed by James, our hypothetical Jew is unlikely to admit it! And he is even less likely to challenge in any general fashion the implicit necessity of Torah observance that underlies James's exhortations, because in asking for obedience to Torah, James makes a request that *no real Jew can in principle reject.* Instead, our hypothetical interlocutor must *grant* the importance of works and take issue with something else.

So then, what sort of objections might have been leveled against James's argument by his first-century Jewish contemporaries? If we can anticipate possible objections, we can perhaps better understand where the interlocutor in Jas 2:18 might be coming from. One obvious objection to Jesus—and hence to his brother as well—would be that full Torah observance is possible without the acceptance of Jesus's radical ethic. This, I suggest, is precisely what we are seeing when the interlocutor of Jas 2:18 insists, in the context of a debate about whether or not people actually do the works commanded in Torah, "I have works." Second, a plausible objection might be that Jesus—and hence also his brother—has inappropriately tied full Torah observance to belief in a particular apocalyptic eschatology, when in fact it is possible to be Torah-observant without adopting this eschatology and its radical socio-political implications. This, I suggest, is precisely what we are seeing when the interlocutor in Jas 2:18 distances himself from faith, saying, "It is you, James, who has faith."

In sum, the main thrust of Jas 2:1–17 is summed up in its opening exhortation ("Without tolerating favoritism, have the faith of our Lord Jesus Christ of glory") and the subsequent rhetorical question ("Has not God chosen the poor in the world to be rich in faith and to be heirs of the kingdom that he has promised to those who love him?"). Even the insistence in 2:14–17 that faith needs works is fundamentally concerned with eschatological and ethical concerns about social justice. And against this apocalyptic backdrop, the interlocutor in 2:18 does not arrive in order to inject Pauline theology, but in order to challenge the eschatology

---

55. I will not trouble myself with the historical plausibility of such a figure, since rhetorical straw men are often implausible.

and ethic that underlie the exhortation in 2:1–17. In more colloquial language, the interlocutor is saying, "Don't be ridiculous, James. I'm a righteous, Torah-observant Jew irrespective of whether or not I buy into your radical Jesus movement and its radical ideas about divine judgment and justice."

The Retort in 2:18b

The reading of 2:18a that I have just proposed is more-or-less the same as one proposed by Zahn many years ago, in that the interlocutor is a non-Christian Jew who seeks to distance himself from Jesus Christ and those who follow Jesus.[56] My reading differs from Zahn's, however, in that I see the second half of v. 18 as the beginning of James's response rather than as a continuation of the interlocutor's objection.[57]

Let us consider, then, how James reacts when a hypothetical diaspora Jew steps forward and says, "You have faith; I have works." His response is to say, "Show me your faith without works, and I will show you my faith by my works." This seems confusing, at first glance, because there are two major points of disconnect. First, whereas the interlocutor distances himself from faith, James's retort construes his interlocutor as a person of faith. Second, whereas the interlocutor lays claim to works, James's retort construes him as having none. These difficulties, however, are more imaginary than real, and they dissipate as soon as we remember the obvious fact that *people only disagree when they disagree*. So what is the nature of the disagreement here? Is it whether faith needs works? No. The disagreement is not at all about the relationship that exists in principle between faith and works. It is about Judaism and about what Torah demands as regards faith and works. The interlocutor aims to support his actions (or inactions, as the case may be) by disputing James's definition of Jewish faith and hence James's expectations as regards righteous works;

56. Zahn writes: "There is thus introduced into the discussion between James and the τίς of ii. 14 a speaker who is represented as really a third person, and that, too, of another faith. But this third person must be a Jew, not a pagan" (Zahn, *Introduction to the New Testament*, 97).

57. According to Zahn, even 2:19 is part of the interlocutor's objection. Hence, "It is not until ii. 20 that James begins to speak again, and resumes the thought of ii. 17" (ibid., 97). Concerning this, Allison writes, "One problem with this conjecture is that it implausibly has the outsider claim πίστιν" (*Epistle of James*, 471). It is not at all clear to me why a first-century Jew should be prevented from laying claim to faith. In fact, as I understand the text, it is *James* who points out his interlocutor's faith.

James, on the other hand, aims to define Judaism in such a way that his interlocutor is found deficient as regards both faith and works. In effect, the interlocutor in 2:18a proclaims, "You can keep your faith, James; I don't need it. You see, I'm already obeying Torah quite apart from your nonsense about a coming kingdom that will displace the rich and vindicate the poor!" James then reacts in 2:18b by saying, "Go on, then! Keep on indicating your Jewish faith to me without actually doing Torah. I too will indicate my Jewish faith, by actually doing Torah."[58]

An interesting question at this point is why James will not allow his interlocutor to self-identify as a non-believer. My answer is that James, in keeping with early Christianity in general, sees the obedience of faith as something at the heart of Judaism and even at the heart of Torah itself. Consequently, he cannot tolerate the insertion of a wedge between believing and doing, or between Judaism (as works) and "Christianity" (as faith), but must immediately point out that Judaism is *founded* on faith. For James, the real question is not whether a Jew believes, because there is no such thing as an unbelieving Jew; the question is whether a Jew believes and behaves in accordance with what is taught in the Torah. To see how James develops this point, however, we must look beyond 2:18 in order to consider the subsequent co-text.

THE SUBSEQUENT CO-TEXT

My hypothesis in this essay is that Jas 2:18a accepts the importance of works but objects to the assumed necessity of Jesus-faith, which raises a very obvious question: Why does 2:18b–26 continue to argue that faith cannot stand alone but must be combined with works? The answer I have given is twofold: (1) James regards faith as inherent to Judaism, and his imaginary interlocutor is someone who self-identifies as a Jew; and (2) James rejects his interlocutor's claim to have works, diagnosing a defective Jewish faith that produces mere lip-service rather than actual acts of mercy. In this section, I will examine the co-text that follows 2:18 with the goal of demonstrating that these verses confirm my hypothesis. Here I cannot cite Allison's observations as frequently, because our readings

---

58. Zahn objects that it is hard to imagine James asserting his own works in this manner (*Introduction to the New Testament*, 97). Yet this is not all that hard to imagine, given Jesus's aggressive discourse in Matt 23. There Jesus warns his hearers not to honor the teachers of the law and the Pharisees: "Be careful to do everything they tell you, but do not do what they do, for they do not practice what they preach" (Matt 23:3).

diverge quite sharply, but I will nevertheless continue to employ Allison as my primary dialogue partner.

The Shema

Δεῖξόν μοι τὴν πίστιν σου χωρὶς τῶν ἔργων, κἀγώ σοι δείξω ἐκ τῶν ἔργων μου τὴν πίστιν. σὺ πιστεύεις ὅτι εἷς ἐστιν ὁ θεός, καλῶς ποιεῖς· καὶ τὰ δαιμόνια πιστεύουσιν καὶ φρίσσουσιν (Jas 2:18b–19).

"The Christian character of πίστις goes unremarked and, in view of the recipients named in 1.1, cannot be assumed. Certainly the faith of v. 19 . . . is not distinctively Christian. It rather characterizes Judaism."[59] In making this observation, Allison grasps something very important about Jas 2:17–26: its ostensible author is seeking to move people beyond a faith that "characterizes [all of] Judaism" and towards a faith that is "distinctly Christian." The move, however, is presented as a move *within* Judaism, from a defective Jewish faith *without works* to an obedient Jewish faith *with works*. Accordingly, the argument is made with reference to the teaching of Torah, which functions for all parties as the definition of the works that God requires.

By beginning his retort with an invocation of the Shema, James establishes that faith is at the very heart of the Jewish religion, in Deuteronomy's call for Israel to believe and to confess that God is one. As regards true Jewish religion, however, the question is not whether Jews must have faith (they must), but what *kind* of faith they must have and whether their faith issues forth in appropriate works. "You yourself believe that God is one," James points out to his Jewish interlocutor. But will this faith by itself produce the perfect work God requires and hence a favorable divine judgment? The demons, at least, know to shudder in fear. By contrast, this foolish interlocutor does not realize that his professed works will afford him little protection when the books are opened and human beings are judged according to the divine standard.

Since Torah has been the assumed standard throughout the preceding discourse, we anticipate at this point that James will now expound Torah in order to demonstrate that Jewish faith encompasses much more than the Shema. And indeed, this is what he does, citing Abraham and Rahab in order to demonstrate how a person can embrace and live out Jewish faith in such a way that God will declare that person righteous.

59. Allison, *Epistle of James*, 459.

Abraham and Rahab

Ἀβραὰμ ὁ πατὴρ ἡμῶν οὐκ ἐξ ἔργων ἐδικαιώθη ἀνενέγκας
Ἰσαὰκ τὸν υἱὸν αὐτοῦ ἐπὶ τὸ θυσιαστήριον; (Jas 2:21)

ὁμοίως δὲ καὶ Ῥαὰβ ἡ πόρνη οὐκ ἐξ ἔργων ἐδικαιώθη
ὑποδεξαμένη τοὺς ἀγγέλους καὶ ἑτέρα ὁδῷ ἐκβαλοῦσα; (Jas
2:25)

Regarding the manner in which James discusses Abraham and
Rahab, a great deal has been said, although much of the literature is
concerned with the Christian doctrine of justification and the relevant
Pauline texts usually cited in formulations of it. Since my concern here is
to explore how the references to Abraham and Rahab function within the
discourse of Jas 1–2 and within its ostensible context of situation, I am
more interested in scholarly observations like the following: "The verses
[vv. 20–24] balance and stand in antithesis to the two examples in vv.
15–19—someone ignoring the needy, demons believing that God is one.
One should note, however, that Abraham and Rahab behave in unethical
ways: the patriarch seeks to kill his son, and the harlot tells lies."[60] In the
first sentence of this quotation, Allison rightly observes that, for James,
both Abraham and Rahab exemplify a proper Jewish faith-in-action,
complementing the negative examples in 2:1–17. It is actually Allison's
second sentence, however, that I have found the most helpful in my exploration of how the scriptural examples in Jas 2:20–26 continue James's
response to his imaginary interlocutor.

The basic thesis I wish to argue as regards Abraham and Rahab is as
follows: James invokes these two individuals chiefly to demonstrate that
Torah itself prescribes *more than Shema-faith* and *more than socially-ac-
ceptable works*, with the point being to move the interlocutor (and more
importantly, the readers who are overhearing the imaginary debate) to
accept James's radical Jesus-faith and Jesus-ethics as the epitome of obedience to Torah. I will begin by discussing the nature of Abraham and
Rahab's faith, before turning to the nature of their works.

Regarding Abraham's faith, I note Allison's observation that "trials—for which Abraham was famed—are a means of testing faith, and
besting them results in the 'patient endurance' that 'produces a perfected
work.'"[61] Here Allison observes a connection between the traditional

---

60. Ibid., 481.
61. Ibid., 488–89.

character of Abraham, a man tested by God, and the testing endured by James's readers (and especially the poor among them) as they await the eschaton (Jas 1:1–15; see above). So in effect, when James writes concerning Abraham that "faith was perfected by works," we are prompted to envision Abraham as a man who, in the midst of trials, lived out the very *kind* of faith to which James has been calling his readers. Abraham did not simply believe that God is one—he had the kind of faith that looks to the future realization of God's promises. He did not merely believe in the unseen God—he had faith in an as-yet-unseen future. One suspects that, like the author of Hebrews (Heb 11:17–19), James intends for us to see that it was Abraham's *future-oriented faith* in the promises of the One True God that enabled him to *do the work* asked of him in Gen 22:2 (cf. Gen 17:16, 19; 21:12).

Turning to the example of Rahab, I note that Allison quotes with approval the words of Jonathan Edwards: "Had Rahab the Harlot said to the spies, 'I believe that God is yours, and Canaan yours, but dare not show you any kindness', her faith had been dead and unactive, and would not have justified her."[62] Edwards correctly observes that Rahab's faith cannot be reduced to belief in the God of Israel, since it also entailed belief in God's promise to give Israel the land of Canaan. Here too, therefore, we see that James is concerned with a certain kind of faith, namely, the future-oriented kind that looks beyond the present social order. We can add the following, then, to the fifteen potential explanations that Allison considers for James's surprising reference to Rahab: James is trying to push his interlocutor (and his readers as well) beyond the Shema and towards the recognition that Torah itself demands an eschatological trust in the future work of God.[63] Rahab acts mercifully towards the spies precisely because she knows, through her faith in the promises of Israel's God, *who it is that will eventually inherit the land* (cf. Jas 2:5).

By citing the lives of Abraham and Rahab, James grounds in scripture the eschatologically-oriented Jewish faith that he espouses throughout his letter. But this is not all that he does. In keeping with the Allison quotation above, we must also consider the "unethical" nature of Abraham and Rahab's righteous deeds. Why should seemingly unethical examples

---

62. Edwards, *Blank Bible*, 1172, cited by Allison, *Epistle of James*, 499.

63. In the end, after discussing no fewer than fifteen different attempts to explain why James invokes Rahab, Allison concludes that we should probably allow for "several explanations at once" (*Epistle of James*, 504).

be cited, when so many others are available? Because the heart of the problem being confronted in Jas 2 is *the social acceptability* of injustice within the diaspora communities. And how do these particular examples challenge the interlocutor in 2:18? They pose a challenge, I suggest, because Abraham and Rahab's faith makes them willing to do things that most people would deem not simply inappropriate but heinous.

Between the two of them, Abraham and Rahab betray two of the most deeply ingrained conventions that order human society: (1) concern for one's family (Abraham); and (2) loyalty to one's people (Rahab).[64] James thus demonstrates from their examples, found within Torah itself, that his Jesus-inspired teachings are not as outlandish as the interlocutor of Jas 2:18 seems to think. Is Jesus-faith outlandish and unconventional? Are Jesus's teachings about family and society a threat to diaspora Judaism? Perhaps so. But if diaspora Jews wish to fully obey the teaching of Torah, they *must* move beyond their belief in the God of Israel and allow their beliefs about God's future acts to motivate socially inappropriate behavior. In this way, Allison himself sums up the main point of Jas 2: "Showing partiality to the rich is not an issue of etiquette but a matter of Torah."[65]

Summary

In his retort to the interlocutor of Jas 2:18, James upbraids the dissenter for being foolish. "Do you want to know," he writes, "that faith without works is useless?" The problem is not, however, that the interlocutor is an "unbeliever." Rather, as a Jew, he is (despite his rhetoric to the contrary) a person of faith. Nor is the problem an alleged denial of the importance of works. Rather, as we would expect of a righteous Jew, the interlocutor lays claim to righteous works. Really, the problem with the interlocutor (according to James, at least) is that his Jewish faith is deficient, with the result that his works are deficient as well.

Is Allison correct, then, that the problem with the faith discussed in 2:14–26 is that it is "something close to intellectual consent . . . like a purely professed or confessed faith"?[66] I think not. Rather, the problem

---

64. My explanation is very similar to the one proposed by Pemble, *Vindiciae Fidei*, 219 (cited by Allison in ibid., 504), except that I draw out the social aspects more than does Pemble.

65. Allison, *Epistle of James*, 401.

66. Ibid., 458.

is that the interlocutor's faith is too limited, and that Torah itself shows through the examples of Abraham and Rahab that something more is required. In order to be a righteous Jew, the interlocutor should be mindful of what God has revealed about the future and willing to do what God has asked even if it entails socially-disruptive behaviors. Once again, therefore, we find that the issue in Jas 2 is not whether faith needs works, but what Jewish faith really entails and what obedience to Torah really entails. The point is to tell diaspora Jews how to do what they already know they must do: they must love the Lord wholeheartedly and they must fully obey his law—and so, looking ahead to the coming of divine justice, they must refuse to honor wealthy and powerful people over and against those who are weak and oppressed.

CONCLUSION

Concerning the oft-cited discussion of Abraham in Jas 2:20–24, Allison writes: "James . . . appeals to Abraham to teach that justification is by works and not by faith alone."[67] While this is true as far as it goes, I would add that nobody within the ostensible epistolary setting of James's letter seems inclined to disagree. Rather, the letter manifests an intra-Jewish disagreement over the kind of faith taught in Torah and the kinds of works this faith should produce, with even the interlocutor of 2:18 operating under the assumption that works are an integral part of the faithful Jewish life. In truth, the focus of the discourse is on social justice and on the way that the perpetuation of injustice can become socially acceptable even among the people of God, with James appealing to Abraham in order to demonstrate to his fellow Jews that Torah itself encourages the radical, future-oriented, and socially-inappropriate obedience that characterizes Jesus-faith. In the end, the emphasis on works throughout Jas 2 does not serve to promote a Torah-observant form of Christian Judaism as an alternative to Paulinism, but rather to promote a Jesus-inspired form of Torah observance among diaspora Jews who may be showing insufficient mercy towards the poor and vulnerable in their midst.

Where does this leave us as regards the relation of Jas 2 to Paul's letters? Supposing that one is predisposed to accept a late date for the Epistle of James, one can still argue that Jas 2 is functional in a second-century setting as a means of advancing Ebionite Christianity as a legitimate form of Judaism, with Paul lurking in the background even though his ideas find

67. Ibid., 426.

no overt expression anywhere in the letter and even though nothing in the letter directly presupposes distinctly Pauline ideas. If we set aside the presumption that James is one of the later New Testament writings, however, my reading potentially challenges the widely held belief that the author of Jas 2 was to some degree familiar with the arguments made in Romans and Galatians.

For his part, Allison dismisses the idea that Jas 2 addresses a general religious problem whereby religious belief does not always issue forth in the behaviors expected of a religion's adherents.[68] The main reason that he finds such a reading unconvincing, however, is that there are a number of similarities between James and Paul's letters that are difficult to explain (according to Allison) unless James is reacting to Paul.[69] Moreover, "To the best of our knowledge, it was Paul, in response to issues arising from the Gentile mission, who first turned the relationship of faith to works into a topic for discussion."[70] Allison's arguments, however, can easily be made to go the other way.

On the one hand, nothing in James's discussion about the relationship of faith to works represents a significant innovation relative to Jesus's own teachings. James's point is simply that Jews ought to live out their Jewish faith in appropriate works, with Jesus-faith functioning for James as the ideal Jewish faith and Jesus's ethical teachings summing up the required works. The discourse is entirely continuous with the opening of the letter, in that it is still about how Jews should navigate the time of testing that precedes final judgment, and its message is still that they should navigate it by obeying the commands of God. Even by Allison's own reckoning, "James' use of Abraham in this connection is altogether natural, *perhaps indeed more natural than the Pauline reading* (which avoids referring to the Aqedah)."[71] Indeed, we might even say that James brings together the various elements in Jas 2 in a way that fits comfortably within first-century Judaism broadly conceived.

Paul, on the other hand, offers a far more subtle analysis of the Abraham narrative than does James. Whereas James's letter is solely concerned

---

68. Ibid., 449–50.

69. See esp. ibid., 444–57.

70. Ibid., 448.

71. Ibid., 483 (emphasis mine). Elsewhere, Allison writes: "Paul's application is idiosyncratic. James, by contrast, stands in the well-attested interpretive tradition that related Gen 15.6 to the Aqedah. . . . [And so James] can write in the confidence that informed and sincere readers will concur with him" (ibid., 493).

with Jewish readers, Paul wants to demonstrate that Abraham serves as an example not only to Jews but *also* to non-Jews, and so he teases out a number of details that are ignored in James's reading. Specifically, Abraham was declared righteous *as a non-Jew* on the basis of the faith that he had *before* he displayed his faith in the Akedah and even *before* he enacted the rite of circumcision and became a Jew. The future-oriented faith in question was in fact the belief that, through Isaac, God would make him the father of *many* nations. And the object of Abraham's justifying faith was *not* the promise that God would produce through Isaac a special (Jewish) nation, nor the promise of blessings for that nation contingent upon their doing the works commanded by Moses, but a broader promise that applies both to Jews and to non-Jews and that finds its fulfillment ultimately in Jesus. These details, unparalleled in other early Jewish literature, are well-suited to an argument that seeks to move beyond the more-or-less traditional reading of the Abraham narrative found in Jas 2 by exploring implications of the Abraham narrative for non-Jews. By contrast, it is difficult to explain why Jas 2 fails to invoke any of these innovations, if it constitutes a response to them.

Obviously, this is not the place to offer a fresh reading of Romans and Galatians on the assumption that Paul is self-consciously interacting with the Epistle of James. It seems to me, however, that such a project is warranted. The interlocutor in Jas 2:18 is most certainly not a Pauline interlocutor, and nothing in Jas 1–2 presupposes anything resembling Paul's most distinctive theological ideas. So if intertextuality suggests a deliberate interaction between the Epistle of James and the letters of Paul, scholars should stop invoking James's imaginary interlocutor as evidence of dissent and start looking more closely at Paul's opening conditional in Rom 4:2 (εἰ Ἀβραὰμ ἐξ ἔργων ἐδικαιώθη ["if Abraham was justified by works"]), a wording that, to my mind, deliberately invokes James's conclusion from the Abraham narrative that ἐξ ἔργων δικαιοῦται ἄνθρωπος ("a person is justified by works").[72] Here, I think, more than in the usual readings of Jas

---

72. Allison's entire argument hinges on a directed relationship between two intertextually-related texts: "The more that text A has reminded readers of text B, the more likely it is that text A was in fact designed to do just that" (Allison, "Polemic Against Paul," 126). Yet few, if any, of Allison's arguments are concerned to establish which is text "A" and which is text "B," because he has already committed himself to the view that James is pseudonymous and late. Thus in some cases, he begs the question that I am raising here (e.g., "Paul is the first Greek writer known to us to use δικαιόω in the passive + instrumental ἐκ. . . . It shows up in James three times" [*Epistle of James*, 445]).

2, there is a reasonable chance of success for scholars who wish to argue that the intertextuality between the Epistle of James and Paul's letters is indicative of a deliberate interaction between them in the form of point and counter-point.

BIBLIOGRAPHY

Allison, Dale C., Jr. *A Critical and Exegetical Commentary on the Epistle of James*. ICC. New York: Bloomsbury T. & T. Clark, 2013.

———. "The Fiction of James and Its *Sitz im Leben*." *RB* 108 (2001) 529–70.

———. "Jas 2:14–26: Polemic against Paul, Apology for James." In *Ancient Perspectives on Paul*, edited by Tobias Nicklas et al., 123–49. NTOA/SUNT 102. Göttingen: Vandenhoeck & Ruprecht, 2013.

———. "The Jewish Setting of the Epistle of James." *In die Skriflig* 49 (2015) 154–62.

Dippenaar, Michaelis Christoffel. "Reading Paul's Letters: Epistolarity and the Epistolary Situation." *Taiwan Journal of Theology* 15 (1993) 141–57.

Edwards, Jonathan. *The Blank Bible*, Part 2. Works of Jonathan Edwards 24.2. New Haven, CT: Yale University Press, 2006.

Halliday, M. A. K. *Halliday's Introduction to Function Grammar*. Revised by Christian M. I. M. Matthiessen. 4th ed. London: Routledge, 2014.

Johnson, Luke Timothy. *The Letter of James: A New Translation with Introduction and Commentary*. AB 37. New York: Doubleday, 1995.

Kaden, David. "Stoicism, Social Stratification, and the Q Tradition in James: A Suggestion About James' Audience." In *James, 1 & 2 Peter, and Early Jesus Traditions*, edited by Alicia J. Batten and John S. Kloppenborg, 97–119. LNTS 478. New York: Bloomsbury T. & T. Clark, 2014.

Kloppenborg, John S. "Judaeans or Judaean Christians in James?" In *Identity and Interaction in the Ancient Mediterranean: Jews, Christians and Others: Essays in Honour of Stephen G. Wilson*, edited by Zeba A. Crook and Philip A. Harland, 113–35. NTM 18. Sheffield: Sheffield Phoenix, 2007.

Land, Christopher D. *The Integrity of 2 Corinthians and Paul's Aggravating Absence*. NTM 36. Sheffield: Sheffield Phoenix, 2015.

Marcus, Joel. "'The Twelve Tribes in the Diaspora' (James 1.1)." *NTS* 60 (2014) 433–47.

Pemble, W. *Vindiciae Fidei*. Oxford: 1629.

Ropes, James Hardy. *A Critical and Exegetical Commentary on the Epistle of St. James*. ICC. Edinburgh: T. & T. Clark, 1916.

Zahn, Theodor. *Introduction to the New Testament*. Volume 1. Edinburgh: T. & T. Clark, 1909.

5

Minding the Gap

Linking the Thematic Relationship between Δίψυχος (Jas 1:8 and 4:8) and the Shema (Deut 6:4–5) through Hos 10:2

JI HOE KIM

INTRODUCTION

IN HIS 1990 ARTICLE, "Is *dipsuchos* (Jas 1:8; 4:8) a 'Christian' Word?" Stanley E. Porter described the stagnation of scholarly discussion pertaining to the semantic background of the term δίψυχος in the Epistle of James.[1] Throughout the history of discussion of this term, the search for the source of James's use of δίψυχος ("double-minded") has resulted in a range of hypotheses. Some attributed its origin to Greek words with the prefixed δι,[2] a morpheme that apparently carries the Hellenistic concept of dualism of mind.[3] Others suggest that it derives from the the Hebrew word *yetzer* as used in Rabbinic Judaism.[4] Another view is that δίψυχος

---

1. Porter, "Is *dipsuchos* a 'Christian' Word," 474. Porter argued convincingly that James coined the word *dipsuchos* in Jas 1:8 and 4:8 and that this expression subsequently appeared only in Christian writings (ibid., 473–74, 77). The literal rendering of δίψυχος would be "double-souled" or "double-spirited." See Ropes, *Epistle of St. James*, 143. The major dictionaries tend to advocate for "double-minded" (see BDAG, 253; LSJ, 440).

2. Martin, *James*, 20.

3. Allison, *Epistle of James*, 187 n. 171.

4. Seitz, "Antecedents," 211–18; cf. Davies, *Paul and Rabbinic Judaism*, 17–35; Adamson, *Epistle of James*, 60.

reflects Essene psychology as found in the Qumran writings.[5] Still others make the case that δίψυχος is simply a Roman idiom.[6] The common issue among most arguments about this term is that the methodologies used to find the background of James's language usually do not go beyond searching for semantically related terms and/or concepts from contemporary texts. Compiling instances where "double-minded" language is conveyed, however, does little more than confirm what is already known—that is, the concept of a divided mind was present in the first-century thought-world. In an attempt to move the discussion of this term forward, the present study goes beyond searching for semantic equivalent terminology by investigating the thematic origin which δίψυχος should be read against and connected to.

Numerous scholars claim that δίψυχος in Jas 1:8 and 4:8 harkens back to the theme of the *Shema*, the total allegiance to the one God, in Deut 6:4–5.[7] However, this view has suffered from being repeated over and over in commentaries to the point where scholars generally take this link for granted rather than firmly substantiating their position. My primary objective here, then, is to present a more linguistically astute methodology to firmly establish the thematic linkage between double-mindedness in James and the *Shema* in Deut 6:4–5.

The first problem one encounters when attempting to make an intertextual link between δίψυχος and the *Shema* is that the command of the *Shema* is the conceptual antithesis to the notion of double-mindedness. Richard Bauckham clearly delineates the issue as follows:

> Moreover, the commandment's requirement of devotion 'with all your heart and with all your soul' is the implicit opposite of the attitude James calls 'double-minded' (1:8; 4:8, representing the Hebrew expression 'with a heart and a heart,' i.e. 'with a double heart': Ps. 12:3; 1 Chr. 12:33; 1QH 12:14; 4QTQahat 1:9; 4Q525 4:6). The double-minded have divided loyalties, wanting to be friends with the world as well as with God (4:8). In relation to God they are at best half-hearted, whereas the *Shema*ʿ requires wholehearted love of God alone.[8]

5. Wolverton, "Double-Minded Man," 166–75; Seitz, "Afterthoughts," 327–34.

6. Seitz, "Two Spirits," 82–95; Laws, *Epistle of James*, 60–61; Marshall, "Δίψυχος," 349–51.

7. Allison, *Epistle of James*, 189; Bauckham, *Wisdom of James*, 145; Davids, *Epistle of James*, 74; McKnight, *Letter of James*, 91–92; Moo, *Letter of James*, 63.

8. Bauckham, *Wisdom of James*, 145.

In my opinion, this issue is well addressed but not well treated. What has not been convincingly explained is in what ways James's expression of divided mind is legitimately linked back to undivided loyalty to God.

In order to make an intertextual connection between δίψυχος and the *Shema* I will take two steps. First, I will trace the thematic thread that ties this lexeme into the *Shema* tradition in spite of the presence of conceptual contrast. This task entails developing a clearly-defined method for assessing intertextual thematic relations among texts.[9] I recognize that there is a critical problem here in that conceptual parallels and thematic parallels have never been distinguished in this conversation. For instance, Hellenistic Greek writers made use of the *concept* of dualism of

---

9. Julia Kristeva, a literary critic, is generally considered to have first coined the term "intertextualité" in her essay "Word, Dialogue and Novel," 34–61. Mary Orr argues that the concept of intertextuality belongs to Roland Barthes, Kristeva being indebted to Barthes. See Orr, *Intertextuality*, 20. For other works discussing the origin of the notion of intertextuality, see Yoon, "Ideological Inception," 61–65; Emadi, "Intertextuality," 10. Steve Moyise ("Intertextuality," 14–15) recognizes two biblical works as first introducing the concept of intertextuality into biblical scholarship, one of which is Richard Hays's *Echoes of Scripture in the Letters of Paul* (1989). In this book, Hays frequently uses the phrase "intertextual echo," which refers to an implicit connectedness between the Old Testament and the New Testament. According to Samuel Emadi, the publication of Hays's book boosted biblical scholars' interests in this field of research and the subsequent appropriation of the term intertextuality ("Intertextuality," 8–9). Emadi notes, however, that "intertextuality is an integral part of a radical deconstructionist hermeneutic and postmodern worldview" (ibid., 10). For this reason, some are opposed to adopting the term for biblical studies. However, its orginal meaning in literary criticism is significantly altered by those who employ it in biblical studies, which can lead to confusion surrounding the term in general. See Hatina, "Intertextuality," 41–42; Miller, "Intertextuality," 305; Porter, "Use of the Old Testament," 84; Yoon, "Ideological Inception," 68.

In this study I will use the term "intertextuality" in a linguistic sense. Halliday understands intertextuality as the "dialectical" relation between text and context: "the text creates the context as much as the context creates the text" (Halliday in Halliday and Hasan, *Language, Context, and Text*, 47). The meaning of a text is shaped through the interaction with the pre-text (i.e., what has been said, repeated, remembered, and shared among members of a community that comprises the verbal and non-verbal environment). In this vein, the intertextual network among texts is taken into account as an essential part of the interpretation of a text. Jay Lemke, a systemic-functional linguist, also makes a similar point when he notes that "Intertextuality is an important characteristic of the way we use language in social communities. The meanings we make through texts, and the ways we make them, always depend on the currency in our communities of other texts we recognize as having certain definite kinds of relationships with one another" ("Intertextuality," 3). See also Lemke, "Discourses in Conflict," 32.

mind, but none of them discusses the *theme* of one's mind being divided in relation to allegiance to a deity. Rather, the Hellenistic dualism is often associated with a theme of hesitation in decision-making between two alternatives or divided opinions as to a certain matter.[10] This point will be dealt with in more detail later. Toward that end, the term echo as defined by Porter will be employed to study the use of Old Testament themes or traditions in the New Testament.[11] In order to identify the theme associated with δίψυχος in James I will adopt linguistic tools—namely, semantic domain theory as developed in biblical Greek studies by Johannes P. Louw and Eugene A. Nida and lexical chain analysis as used from a Systemic Functional Linguistics perspective (hereafter SFL).

Second, I will propose Hos 10:1–2 is the possible bridge that fills the conceptual gap between the *Shema* and James's use of δίψυχος.[12] In addition, I will demonstrate that this intertextual relation is best explained from a developmental perspective in which Hos 10:1–2 constitutes the intermediate stage between an earlier stage of the *Shema* tradition and a later stage represented in James's invocation of it. Although Hos 10:1–2 has received relatively less attention in comparison to Ps 12:2, 1 Chr 12:33, and Sir 1:28 (in scholarship that engages James's use of δίψυχος), the language used to express the divided mind of Israel toward God in Hos 10:1–2 possesses the closest thematic relation with James's use of δίψυχος. This will establish that James uses δίψυχος so as to encapsulate a pre-existing Old Testament theme, the *Shema*, by echoing the double-mindedness language in Hos 10:2.

DEFINING INTERTEXTUAL TERMS: THEME, TRADITION, AND ECHO

The New Testament was not produced in a vacuum, and thus it should be read and interpreted in light of or in dialogue with a network of writings composed of the Old Testament as well as other contemporary writings

10. For Hellenistic texts connoting the concept of a divided mind see Homer, *Il.*, 1:188–89; 16:435; 20:32; Theognis 91; Herodotus, *Hist.* 6.109; Plato, *Resp.* 554D; Xenophon, *Cyr.* 6.1.41; and Epictetus, *Ench.* 29.7. See Porter, "Is *dipsuchos* a 'Christian' Word," 474–75.

11. Porter, *Sacred Tradition*, 43–46.

12. Many works fail to recognize Hos 10:2 as a significant text here. Martin (*James*, 20) and Allison (*Epistle of James*, 186–91) also do not mention Hos 10:2. Davids shows uncertainty as to the relation between Hos 10:2 and Jas 1:8 (*Epistle of James*, 74). Moo, however, does make reference to Hos 10:2 (*Letter of James*, 63).

in the first century, such as those from Second Temple Judaism.[13] In order to trace an Old Testament theme or tradition (see below) that is realized in the Epistle of James, I will use the term "echo" as it has been defined by Stanley E. Porter (see below) to indicate how a New Testament text can relate to the Old Testament and other Jewish writings. However, before any analysis can be done, there are several terms that first need to be defined.

First, a theme is constituted by means of an association of words, pattern of language, or any other pattern of meaning making that articulates a particular notion that recurs in the discursive practices of a culture. Therefore, it is at or beyond the sentence-level in which themes are formulated (in accordance with the context of situation). By contrast, conceptual meanings refer to the semantic ranges of lexical items that are constrained by their linguistic context (i.e., co-text).[14] A text, however, contains more abstract notions or complex ideas than what a single word can convey. Only if lexical items are grouped together could these notions be expressed. When certain combinations of words or patterns of thought are reiterated in the texts of a community, they can be recognized according to their thematic meaning. For example, the thematic meaning of "lamb" as a sacrificial agent can only be understood when it is contextually associated with Passover, whether textually or intertextually. Over time, as themes recur in texts of the same social and literary environment, they become recognized as tradition by the language community.

A tradition, then, is understood as the recurrent semantic combinations of words, phrases, or other patterns of thought in a particular language community and its texts, which, in turn, are located at the level of the context of culture.[15] Porter defines tradition as "wordings or larger patterns of thought recorded in writings venerated by various peoples and appropriated and reappropriated by later writers in their own interpretations and applications of these in new contexts and situations."[16]

13. Porter, *Sacred Tradition*, 4.

14. In SFL, there are three strata of context: (1) co-text (intra-linguistic context), context of situation (immediate environment of the text), and context of culture (the total cultural background of the text). See Halliday in Halliday and Hasan, *Language, Context, and Text*, 6.

15. My definition of tradition conflates Jay L. Lemke's thematic formations and intertextual thematic formations. See Lemke, "Text Structure," 165; Dawson, "Books of Acts," 21–22. See also Lemke, "Discourse in Conflict," 30.

16. Porter, *Sacred Tradition*, 3.

When a certain period of time passes, the tradition becomes a cultural norm or value in a certain community or society. Thus, a tradition can be defined as a reservoir for the history of thoughts and the system of culture from which a text in a certain community is read, perceived, interpreted, and repeated.

Next, Porter's formulation of echo enables us to link the New Testament texts to themes or traditions in the Old Testament.[17] The term echo, however, has often been conflated with allusion in literary studies.[18] This has been the case in biblical studies as well. Richard Hays's conflation of allusion and echo is widely accepted and practiced.[19] However, Porter separates echo from allusion by restrictively using the notion of echo to trace the sacred Old Testament themes or traditions that are used in the New Testament.[20]

There are two major differences between allusion and echo in Porter's view. The first distinguishing feature concerns whether the meaning of a text retains the meaning of its original context. As far as allusion is concerned, the original context can become blurred for the sake of adjustment for the new context. That is to say, thematic similarity is not required for an allusion, whereas an echo is concerned with thematic parallels between texts. Second, allusions and echoes are different in their references. Through allusion, a particular person, incident, location, and

---

17. Ibid., 45 n. 67. Porter criticizes discussions of the Old Testament in the New Testament that are too atomistic because they are constrained to "smaller units of text and often their individual wordings" ("Further Comments," 10). For instance, in the early stage, according to Christopher Beetham, scholars' interests revolved around "textual matters (e.g., textual variants), comparison with rabbinic modes of interpretation, and the problems associated with the question of what version or text the New Testament authors depended upon for their quotations" (*Echoes of Scripture*, 1).

18. In literary studies, Hollander, *Figure of Echo*, adds the subtitle "A Mode of Allusion in Milton and After." This shows his understanding of echo as a "mode of allusion."

19. In biblical studies, see Hays, *Echoes of Scripture*, 18–21; Beetham, *Echoes of Scripture*, 20–24; Dunn, "Jesus Tradition," 159; Wagner, *Heralds of the Good News*, 9–13. For Porter's thorough criticism of Hays's formulation of echo using seven criteria, see Porter, *Sacred Tradition*, 9–10; see also Shaw, "Reception," 238–41.

20. Porter's use of the term echo is best understood on the continuum of five categories: "formulaic quotation, direct quotation, paraphrase, allusion, and echo" (*Sacred Tradition*, 34). For further definition, Porter groups these five categories into three groups: direct quotation (*Formulaic Quotation* and *Direct Quotation*), indirect quotation (*Paraphrase* and *Allusion*), and echo.

the like are indirectly indicated, whereas through echo, a more abstract concept or theme is evoked.[21]

For the sake of linguistic method, it is helpful to clarify how Porter defines echo in relationship to the other intertextual categories he identifies—paraphrase, allusion, and quotation. In contrast to paraphrase and allusion "echo may be consciously intentional or unintentional, involving not paraphrase of a specific passage nor allusion to a person, place, literary work etc., but by means of *thematically related language* invoking some more general notion or concept."[22] Echo is also distinct from quotation in that echo, while containing similarity of language, does not contain word-for-word matching.[23] And though echo does contain similarity of language, it is distinguishable in that the similarity realizes a paraphrase, which is "typified by the use of words in the same semantic domain, or similar words in differing syntax, as a recognizable passage."[24] As far as echo is concerned, what matters is not structure, but thematic relations between related texts. In short, echo is not bound to the repetition of the same words (quotation) or lexical items in the same semantic domain (paraphrase). Instead, particular language conveying a particular theme is the clue for determining an echo.

SEMANTIC DOMAINS AND CHAIN ANALYSIS IN SEARCH FOR THEME

As discussed above, an echo is identified by the occurence of thematically related language between texts. Identification of intertextual thematic relations, as defined in this essay, begins with the identification of a theme. In search for a theme, I will bring the theory of semantic domains developed by Johannes P. Louw and Eugene A. Nida into association with chain analysis as informed by SFL.[25]

21. Porter, *Sacred Tradition*, 45.

22. Ibid., emphasis added.

23. In Porter's five categories of intertextual references, formulaic quotations are recognized by their introductory formula whereas direct quotations are identified by an at-least-three-identical-words criterion. The concurrence of two words can be seen as a coincidence, Porter argues, but "the three form a minimal unit of determinable syntax and conceptual relation." See ibid., 35.

24. Ibid., 36.

25. This methodology is indebted to Cynthia Westfall. See Westfall, *Discourse Analysis*, 47–52; Westfall, "Blessed Be the Ties," 201–9.

It is now widely acknowledged that any attempt to delve into the semantic range of words should be based on the semantic domain and the semantic field approach. As D. A. Carson rightly puts it, "linguistically, meaning is not an intrinsic possession of a word."[26] From a corpus-driven lexicological standpoint, words "are considered as nodes of semantic relationships."[27] With this understanding, Louw and Nida's lexicon utilizes the concept of semantic domains, which are made up of semantically related words.[28] Therefore, the meaning of a certain word is examined in a systemic way—that is, through comparison with other words that belong to the same semantic field, not through finding a translational equivalent or equivalents.[29] For this reason, Louw and Nida's lexicon will be utilized in this study. In addition, meanings of words in text are also revealed not in isolation but by the way they constrain one another. Louw and Nida stress this point when they state: "the correct meaning of a word within any context is the meaning which fits the context best."[30]

Next, two lingusitic concepts, cohesion and coherence, are in need of consideration. Cohesion refers to the textual property of *connectedness* through linguistic means (e.g., reference, substitution, ellipsis, conjunction, and the like) in language.[31] Therefore, cohesion is what "make[s] a sequence of sentences a text."[32] This implies that the interpretation of what follows is constrained by what goes before. Louw and Nida's lexicon based on semantic domains contributes to the recognition of semantic associations among lexcial items.

Coherence is what makes a text make sense to its readers or hearers. Our understanding as readers of a text is not exclusively bound to the text itself. Rather, we bring shared cultural or special knowledge into our reading so as to understand it. Therefore, when parts of a text hang together well and it is relevant to its immediate context of situation, we will easily

---

26. Carson, *Exegetical Fallacies*, 31.

27. Almela and Sánchez, "Words as 'Lexical Units,'" 21.

28. Jeffrey Reed defines a semantic domain as "words grouped according to their shared, distinctive, and supplementary (i.e., contextually relevant) semantic features" (*Discourse Analysis*, 297). See also Louw and Nida, *Greek-English Lexicon*, 1:1; Nida and Louw, *Lexical Semantics*; Porter, "On the Shoulders," 47–60.

29. Poythress, "Greek Lexicography," 286.

30. Nida and Louw, *Lexical Semantics*, 12.

31. Halliday and Hasan define cohesion as "the range of possibilities that exist for linking something with what has gone before" (*Cohesion in English*, 10).

32. Fitzgerald and Spiegel, "Textual Cohesion," 263.

understand the meaning of the text.[33] If a text is not coherent, a reader will be unable to understand the text.[34] In everyday life, we encounter *more* coherent texts and *less* coherent texts, be it intentional or unintentional on part of the speaker/writer; it may be a language user's intent to be unintelligible. Taking these linguistic concepts into consideration, the conceptual meaning of any lexical items would be best interpreted, to use Porter's terms, in a context of "continuity of textual structure" (cohesion) and "continuity of thought" (coherence).[35]

Chain analysis is a tool for the mapping of diverse relations among lexical items. When related words co-occur, we can draw a line between them. The line that is spread across a given unit is called a chain. There are three types of chains: lexical chains, "formed by various occurrences of repetition"; semantic chains, "formed by lexis that share the same semantic domains"; and participant chains, "formed by noun phrases, pronouns, and verbs that refer to the same person."[36] Once these lines are drawn, relations, be they lexical, semantic, or participant, existing among words are revealed. In this way, each lexical item can be analyzed in relation to other connected terms at the multi-sentence level.

Of particular interest is the identification of a theme that is found through a particular association of lexical items serving to present a particular notion or idea. In search of a theme, I will particularly pay attention to participant chains and their interactions with other chains. Hasan underscores the significant role of participant chains, which are synonymous with her identity chains: "the construction of the text because of the entities, events, [and] circumstances that one is talking about need to be made specific if there is to be repeated mention of the same."[37] Hasan's chain analysis centers around participant chains as the backbone of discourses and their interactions with other chains. For this reason, it is presumed that the relations, actions, attitudes, and descriptions of participants in text serve to constitute a more detailed notion—i.e., theme.

33. Halliday and Hasan, *Cohesion in English*, 23. See also Reed, "Cohesive Ties," 133–34.

34. Westfall, "Blessed Be the Ties," 206.

35. Porter, "Cohesion in James," 46.

36. Westfall, "Blessed Be the Ties," 208.

37. Hasan, "Cohesive Harmony," 205–6.

TRACKING THE ORIGIN OF DOUBLE-MINDEDNESS LANGUAGE IN JAMES

In this section, semantic domain theory and chain analysis will be applied to Jas 1:5–8, 4:1–10, Deut 6:4–5 LXX, and Hos 10:2 LXX. In so doing, I will show how these texts are thematically related.

Δίψυχος *in James 1:8 and 4:8*

The overall structure of the Epistle of James has been heavily debated with little agreement among scholars.[38] Bauckham pessimistically notes that "there seems to be not even the beginnings of a consensus."[39] However, it is not impossible to identify small units. Thus, I will analyze verses 1:8 and 4:8 containing δίψυχος in light of their co-texts, 1:5–8 and 4:1–10 respectively.[40]

In Jas 1:5–8, there are two primary participant chains: God and the recipients of the letter as referred to in the phrase τις ὑμῶν ("anyone among you [pl.]," v. 5).[41] Lexical items pointing to God appear three times (vv. 5, 6, 7), including the ellipsis of τοῦ διδόντος θεοῦ ("[God] who gives") in v. 6 as the object of αἰτείτω ("ask"). The word order (τοῦ διδόντος θεοῦ πᾶσιν ἁπλῶς καὶ μὴ ὀνειδίζοντος, "God who gives to everyone in a generous and not disparaging manner," v. 5) appears to be emphasizing the character of God as provider.[42] There is no limitation

38. Dibelius argued that due to the parenetic nature of the letter of James we cannot expect a coherent flow of thoughts and themes (*Epistle of James*, 2). Many scholars have endeavored to provide a counter argument to Dibelius. See Elliott, "James," 71–72; Wall, *Community of the Wise*, 34–38. As a result, Taylor acknowledges the emergence of a scholarly consensus in some areas. See Taylor, "Recent Scholarship," 112. For a comprehensive discussion, see McKnight, *Letter of James*, 47–55; Taylor, "Recent Scholarship," 90–111.

39. Bauckham, *Wisdom of James*, 61.

40. I will follow Bauckham's identification (see ibid., 70, 64). Luke Timothy Johnson makes Jas 3:13—4:10 one section that can be divided in two subsections: 3:13—4:6 and 4:7–10. He argues that the former section becomes the ground of exhortation of the latter and the connective οὖν links them ("Jas 3:13-4:10," 332–33). In my view, Jas 3:13—4:10 has a similar thematic structure to Jas 1:5–8 with some elaboration and advancement of ideas. However, this study limits its scope to 4:1–10 for the sake of brevity.

41. Unless otherwise noted, translations of Greek texts are mine.

42. The author places the participle διδόντος ("giving") in front of θεοῦ ("God") and puts the object (πᾶσιν, "all") of the participle and adverbial phrase after θεοῦ ("God").

indicated to what God can give. The adverbial phrase (ἁπλῶς καὶ μὴ ὀνειδίζοντος) illustrates the manner of God's provision.

Lexical items referring to an unspecified person among the recipients are spread across the participant chain of God.[43] The process chains of asking (αἰτείτω, vv. 5, 6), giving (διδόντος, v. 5), and receiving (λήμψεταί, v. 7) relate these two participant chains. Any member of the recipients who lacks (λείπεται, v. 5) in wisdom is encouraged to *ask* God who *gives* freely and abundantly. They must ask in faith. Otherwise, they will *receive* nothing from God.

5 Εἰ δέ τις ὑμῶν ~~λείπεται σοφίας,~~ αἰτείτω παρὰ τοῦ διδόντος θεοῦ πᾶσιν ἁπλῶς καὶ μὴ ὀνειδίζοντος, καὶ δοθήσεται αὐτῷ. 6 αἰτείτω ~~δὲ ἐν πίστει μηδὲν~~ διακρινόμενος· ὁ γὰρ διακρινόμενος ἔοικεν κλύδωνι θαλάσσης ἀνεμιζομένῳ καὶ ῥιπιζομένῳ. 7 μὴ γὰρ οἰέσθω ὁ ἄνθρωπος ἐκεῖνος ~~ὅτι~~ λήμψεταί τι παρὰ τοῦ κυρίου, 8 ἀνὴρ δίψυχος, ~~ἀκατάστατος ἐν πάσαις ταῖς ὁδοῖς~~ αὐτοῦ.

Figure 1: Participant Chain of τις ὑμῶν in Jas 1:5–8

The meaning of διακρινόμενος (v. 6) deserves consideration since it modifies one of the primary participants, an unspecified member among the recipients. The meaning of διακρίνομαι is disputed, however.[44] Most translations (e.g., NRSV, NIV, NASB) render it as "doubting" or "doubt," while the KJV translates it as "wavering." Porter suggests that it is better translated as "divided" or "at variance with oneself."[45] The consideration of semantic domains can help clarify its meaning in this co-text.

Διακρινόμενος in v. 6 is closely tied to δίψυχος in v. 8 in three ways. First, διακρινόμενος (31.37) and δίψυχος (31.38) both belong to semantic domain 31, "Hold a View, Believe, Trust."[46] Second, they constitute the participant chain of an unspecified member among the recipients.

43. According to Westfall, identity chains are recognized by "identification, pronouns (anaphoric or cataphoric), and the inclusion of the participants in the person and number of verbs or participles" (*Discourse Analysis*, 50).

44. Peter Spitaler rejects the "NT meaning" of διακρίνομαι ("doubt") in James 1:8. Instead, he advocates "a Classical/Hellenistic Greek meaning" ("contest/dispute/quarrel") ("Dispute with God," 560–64, 79).

45. Porter, "Is *dipsuchos* a 'Christian' Word," 479.

46. Louw and Nida, *Greek-English Lexicon*, 1:370.

Third, metaphorical expressions of instability are utilized to elaborate the meanings of διακρινόμενος (v. 6) and δίψυχος (v. 8): Ὁ . . . διακρινόμενος is the one like "a wave of the sea, moved and tossed back and forth by the wind," and δίψυχος is the one who is "unstable in every aspect of one's ways."[47] James, therefore, makes an intentional correlation between διακρινόμενος and δίψυχος, the nature and scheme of which is depicted in the figure below. Given the linearity of a written text, as the flow of argument unfolds, the meaning of διακρινόμενος becomes clearer, especially when the flow ends with δίψυχος. Therefore, Porter's rendering of διακρινόμενος as "divided" or "at variance with oneself"[48] is reaffirmed in light of and in connection to δίψυχος ("divided- or double-souled"), the meaning of which is transparent according to its morphological components.

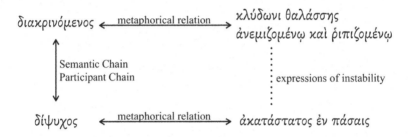

Figure 2: The Relation between διακρινόνμενος and δίψυχος

Two observations have been made so far. The first is the comparison between God and a hypothetical member among the recipients. God gives everything single-mindedly and non-disparagingly to his people. Since his wholeness is intact, those asking for divine help for wisdom must correspond to the quality of his single-mindedness. Given that the hypothetical situation is prayer, a believer's attitude is directed to God alone. Second, δίψυχος can be used to infer the meaning of διακρινόμενος through its transparent meaning (i.e., *morphological* make-up). In Jas 1:5–8, the sense of δίψυχος has not been fully developed on its own beyond its morphology.

47. Dan McCartney, *James*, 94. The relation between δίψυχος and ἀκατάστατος could be consequential (Hort, *James*, 13) or synonymous (Allison, *Epistle of James*, 190).

48. Porter, "Is *dipsuchos* a 'Christian' Word," 479.

It is possible to further tease out the thematic meaning of δίψυχος in 4:8 within its co-text (4:1–10). Like the previous unit, there are two primary participants in this unit: God and the direct addressees of the Epistle of James. Again, the most prominent feature of this unit is the participant chain of the recipients in the second-person plural. From 4:1 (ὑμῖν, "you") to 4:5 (δοκεῖτε, "you assume"), a series of second-person plural pronouns and indicative verb-forms form the participant chain. After the quotation in vv. 5–6, this chain is reconnected by means of nine successive second-person plural imperatives. The chain is illustrated in the figure below.

1 Πόθεν πόλεμοι καὶ πόθεν μάχαι ἐν ὑμῖν; οὐκ ἐντεῦθεν, ἐκ τῶν ἡδονῶν ὑμῶν τῶν στρατευομένων ἐν τοῖς μέλεσιν ὑμῶν; 2 ἐπιθυμεῖτε καὶ οὐκ ἔχετε, φονεύετε καὶ ζηλοῦτε καὶ οὐ δύνασθε ἐπιτυχεῖν, μάχεσθε καὶ πολεμεῖτε, οὐκ ἔχετε διὰ τὸ μὴ αἰτεῖσθαι ὑμᾶς, 3 αἰτεῖτε καὶ οὐ λαμβάνετε, διότι κακῶς αἰτεῖσθε, ἵνα ἐν ταῖς ἡδοναῖς ὑμῶν δαπανήσητε. 4 μοιχαλίδες, οὐκ οἴδατε ὅτι ἡ φιλία τοῦ κόσμου ἔχθρα τοῦ θεοῦ ἐστιν; ὃς ἐὰν οὖν βουληθῇ φίλος εἶναι τοῦ κόσμου, ἐχθρὸς τοῦ θεοῦ καθίσταται. 5 ἢ δοκεῖτε ὅτι κενῶς ἡ γραφὴ λέγει· πρὸς φθόνον ἐπιποθεῖ τὸ πνεῦμα ὃ κατῴκισεν ἐν ἡμῖν, 6 μείζονα δὲ δίδωσιν χάριν; διὸ λέγει·

ὁ θεὸς ὑπερηφάνοις ἀντιτάσσεται,
ταπεινοῖς δὲ δίδωσιν χάριν.

7 ὑποτάγητε οὖν τῷ θεῷ, ἀντίστητε δὲ τῷ διαβόλῳ, καὶ φεύξεται ἀφ' ὑμῶν· 8 ἐγγίσατε τῷ θεῷ καὶ ἐγγιεῖ ὑμῖν. καθαρίσατε χεῖρας, ἁμαρτωλοί, καὶ ἁγνίσατε καρδίας, δίψυχοι. 9 ταλαιπωρήσατε καὶ πενθήσατε καὶ κλαύσατε. ὁ γέλως ὑμῶν εἰς πένθος μετατραπήτω καὶ ἡ χαρὰ εἰς κατήφειαν. 10 ταπεινώθητε ἐνώπιον τοῦ κυρίου καὶ ὑψώσει ὑμᾶς.

Figure 3: The Second Person Plural Participant Chain in Jas 4:1–10

In the midst of the ties of this participant chain, three words are used for directly addressing this participant: μοιχαλίδες ("adulteresses," v. 4), ἁμαρτωλοί ("sinners," v. 8), and δίψυχοι ("the double-minded," v.

8). The author refers to the addressees as adulteresses[49] because of their wrong motivation for prayer. They have a craving for the friendship with the world.[50] This leads them to enmity with God, which has already been made known (οἴδατε, v. 4) to them. In v. 8 these people are called "sinners" and "double-minded ones" in the midst of a series of commands.[51] It is obvious that, on the one hand, μοιχαλίδες constrains the meaning of ἁμαρτωλοί and δίψυχοι, and, on the other hand, δίψυχοι sharpens and complements the sense of the preceding two. Thus, that an "adulteress" attempts to love both the world and God simultaneously is best communicated by the word δίψυχοι.

The participant chain of God first appears in v. 4 and then continues until v. 10. However, the process chains of asking (αἰτέω, vv. 2–3) and receiving (λαμβάνω, v. 3) presume God as the one who hears prayers. God is the God who is jealous (Jas 4:5; cf. Exod 20:5; 43:14; Deut 4:24; 5:9; 6:15; 32:21; Ezek 16:38; Nah 1:2)[52]—that is, God does not allow an unfaithful attitude toward himself. In Jas 1:5 God is depicted as a willing giver who gives without reproach. In Jas 4:5, however, another side of God's character is emphasized: God is angry at religious infidelity and double-minded loyalties.

49. The NRSV renders μοιχαλίδες as "adulterers." This translation is unsatisfactory due to the mistranslation of the gender of the word. In this paper, the feminine gender ("adulteresses") is of significance since it is one of the signals indicating the link between double-mindedness in James and Hos 10:1–2. This will be discussed in detail later.

50. According to McKnight, "Friendship involves commitment to one another, fidelity, and the expectation of mutual instruction from mutual moral development" in the ancient world (*Letter of James*, 333).

51. The author makes a series of commands directly addressed to those pursuing this world, encouraging them to go back to God. These commands illustrate the proper single-minded attitude toward God: ὑποτάγητε ("submit yourselves [to God]"), ἀντίστητε ("resist [the devil]"), ἐγγίσατε ("draw near [to God]"), καθαρίσατε ("cleanse [hand]"), ἁγνίσατε ("purify [heart]"), ταλαιπωρήσατε ("lament"), πενθήσατε ("mourn"), κλαύσατε ("weep"), and ταπεινώθητε ("humble yourselves"). There is one third-person singular imperative in v. 9: μετατραπήτω ("let your merriment be turned into grief"). Through all these imperatives in Jas 4:7–10, the author proceeds to call for the repentance of the addressees by turning their back on the world and returning to God.

52. According to Porter's category, a formulaic direct quotation (v. 5) is in view. For the detailed discussion of possible Old Testament references, see McKnight, *Letter of James*, 336–38. In my opinion, the Old Testament theme of God's jealousy toward the Israelites' idolatry is relevant to James 4:1–10. See Johnson, *Letter of James*, 268–69.

The theme that the double-minded language in Jas 1:8; 4:8 serves to formulate can be characterized as follows. First of all, both texts have two primary participants: God and the addressees (whether directly addressed or not). Second, these two participant chains interact through the process chains of asking and receiving. Thus, the primary participants' roles can be defined as the giver and the petitioner respectively. Third, the acceptance of a request is contingent upon the attitude of the beneficiary toward God. Fourth, the improper attitude is described as divided affection for earthly desire and God.

In light of these characteristics, I will make two points with regard to the thematic contribution of the double-minded language in Jas 1:5–8 and 4:1–10. First, the double-minded language pertains to the relationship between God and the petitioner. Second, James associates it with a lack of allegiance and an ambivalent attitude toward God. If we extend our scope, dividedness of mind is in stark contrast with the theme that "God is one" (εἷς ἐστιν ὁ θεός) in 2:19. This is further connected to the topic of the entire Epistle of James as acknowledged and contended by Bauckham:

> The overarching theme of James is "perfection" or "wholeness" (1:4). Wholeness requires wholehearted and single-minded devotion to God, and its opposite is that half-heartedness in devotion to God and that divided loyalty, vacillating between God and the world, which James calls double-mindedness (1:8; 4:8). Also part of this complex of thought in James is the cultic language of purity and defilement (1:27; 4:8). The unblemished wholeness of the sacrifice suggests the image of the pure heart as the state of integrity before God or entire devotedness to God that is, again, the opposite of double-mindedness (4:8).[53]

THE TRAJECTORY OF THE SHEMA TRADITION

Scholars have appealed to Jewish tradition, in particular the *Shema*,[54] as the potential source that leads to the birth of double-minded language.

53. Bauckham, *Wisdom of James*, 165. See also Elliott, "Epistle of James," 71–81. Along the same lines, Moo contends that "Basic to all James says in his letter is his concern that his readers stop compromising with worldly values and behavior and give themselves wholly to the Lord" (*Letter of James*, 46).

54. According to Joseph Fitzmyer, "the three (or four) faculties (heart, soul, might [and mind]) were meant to sum up the totality of undivided dedication to him [God]" in Deut 6:5 (*Gospel according to Luke*, 878).

McKnight contends that "the word, literally 'two-souled,' grows out of Jewish soil, especially Old Testament language of the 'double-hearted' person. Daily recital of the *Shema* makes a 'whole heart' devoted to love of God a moral preoccupation, thus setting a divided heart into the context of covenantal fidelity with respect to *Torah* observance."[55] Since the *Shema* tradition is based on Deut 6:4–5, I will examine these verses according to the methodology outlined above.[56]

Deuteronomy 6:4–5 LXX is concerned with the relationship between God and Israel (i.e., the projected audience) and the latter's attitude to the former. There are two primary participant chains: God (κύριος → ὁ θεός → κύριος → ἐστιν → κύριον τὸν θεόν) and Israel (Ἰσραήλ → ἡμῶν → ἀγαπήσεις → σου [4x]). The first half talks about the nature of God: "God is one."[57] In addition, God is portrayed as a giver of "a land flowing with milk and honey" in its preceding co-text (v. 3). The remaining half talks about the proper attitude toward this monotheistic God. The process chain of loving (ἀγαπήσεις, v. 5) relates the two participant chains. The semantic domain of ἀγαπάω ("love") is "Attitudes and Emotions," and the subdomain is "Love, Affection, Compassion."[58] The lexical repetition of ὅλης ("whole") emphasizes the importance of totality, which is the conceptual opposite of something being divided. According to Louw and Nida's lexicon, the semantic tie between καρδία (26.3) and ψυχή (26.4) is also in view.[59]

In Deut 6:4–5, however, oneness and wholeness are emphasized, and this stands in contrast to the fact that the divided nature of believers comes to the fore in Jas 1:8 and 4:8. The absence of double-minded language precludes us from claiming a *direct* connection between Deut 6:4–5 and Jas 1:8 and 4:8. Nevertheless, what these texts emphasize is that whole and undivided devotion to the one God is what is good and right, though expressed in opposite ways. Thematically, both the *Shema* and δίψυχος connote an absolute commitment to God.

---

55. McKnight, *Letter of James*, 91–92. See also Moo, *Letter of James*, 63.

56. Deuteronomy 6:4–5 LXX: Ἄκουε, Ἰσραηλ· κύριος ὁ θεὸς ἡμῶν κύριος εἷς ἐστιν· καὶ ἀγαπήσεις κύριον τὸν θεόν σου ἐξ ὅλης τῆς καρδίας σου καὶ ἐξ ὅλης τῆς ψυχῆς σου καὶ ἐξ ὅλης τῆς δυνάμεώς σου. The presumption of this study is that the "Bible" for the author of James was the Greek version of the Old Testament (LXX). See Swete, *Old Testament in Greek*, 392; Stamps, "Use of the Old Testament," 10–11.

57. Gerhardsson, *Shema in the New Testament*, 302.

58. Louw and Nida, *Greek-English Lexicon*, 1:293.

59. Ibid., 1:321.

Since communal traditions are dynamic and progressive in nature, it is appropriate to trace the development of the *Shema* tradition as a means of inquiring into the intertextual significance of δίψυχος in the sections of the Epistle of James under consideration. The *Shema* is the quintessential statement of the Jewish belief system[60] developed in the course of religious history up to the period of Second Temple Judaism and even into early Christianity[61] It has been continually recited, taught, cultivated, developed, reinterpreted, and reaffirmed.

The *Shema* tradition seems to have developed in two strands. The first strand is concerned with the theme of undivided loyalty to Yahweh. It is not difficult to find Old Testament references appealing to whole-hearted devotion: Deut 11:13; Ps 101:2; 1 Chr 28:9; 2 Chr 31:21; and Ezek 11:19. All these verses emphasize the integrity of heart toward God, and thus directly follow the *Shema* tradition. Jesus also recites the *Shema* tradition (Matt 22:37; Mark 12:29–30; Luke 10:27).

Another strand is concerned with a divided mind. This shows that the *Shema* command in Deut 6:4–5 has developed in an antithetical way by expressing the concept of a dividedness of the mind. There are three references (Ps 12:2, 1 Chr 12:33 and Sir 1:28) that have often been referred to as the origin of δίψυχος in James.[62]

Ps 11:3 LXX (12:2 MT)	1 Chr 12:34 LXX (12:33 MT)	Sir 1:28
μάταια ἐλάλησεν ἕκαστος πρὸς τὸν πλησίον αὐτοῦ, χείλη δόλια ἐν καρδίᾳ καὶ ἐν καρδίᾳ ἐλάλησαν.	καὶ ἀπὸ Ζαβουλων ἐκπορευόμενοι εἰς παράταξιν πολέμου ἐν πᾶσιν σκεύεσιν πολεμικοῖς πεντήκοντα χιλιάδες βοηθῆσαι τῷ Δαυιδ οὐχ ἑτεροκλινῶς.	μὴ ἀπειθήσῃς φόβῳ κυρίου καὶ μὴ προσέλθῃς αὐτῷ ἐν καρδίᾳ δισσῇ.

The Hebrew בלב ולב (Ps 12:2) is translated in the LXX as ἐν καρδίᾳ καὶ ἐν καρδίᾳ (Ps 11:3). Psalm 11:3 LXX states, "Each spoke vanities to his fellow; lips are deceitful, in the heart and in the heart they spoke" (NETS). The double-minded language is used, but this is concerned with

60. Tan, "Shema," 198.

61. Ruzer, *Mapping the New Testament*, 76–90.

62. Wolverton, "Double-Minded Man," 167–68; Martin, *James*, 20; Bauckham, *Wisdom of James*, 145; Porter, "Is *dipsuchos* a 'Christian' Word," 477.

the attitude toward human beings, not God. Thus, no thematic relationship is found between Jas 1:8 and 4:8 and Ps 11:3 LXX (12:2 MT).

In 1 Chr 12:34 LXX, we can find the word ἑτεροκλινῶς ("unwaveringly"). This expression indicates an undivided mind towards the idea of crowning David as the king of Israel (1 Chr 12:23, 38). Therefore, this verse is not related thematically with δίψυχος in James either.

Δίψυχος in James could be a paraphrase of Sir 1:28 (ἐν καρδίᾳ δισσῇ, "with a double heart") on the basis of the use of words in the same semantic domain (καρδίας–ψυχή)[63] but with different syntax. In addition, Sir 1:28 is in a co-text in which the wise author shares his wisdom, saying that God is the source of all wisdom (Sir 1:1) and that the beginning of wisdom is to fear the Lord (Sir 1:14). These statements certainly share similarities with the co-text of Jas 1:8. However, the phrase μὴ προσέλθῃς αὐτῷ ἐν καρδίᾳ δισσῇ is ambiguous; that is, the referent of αὐτῷ is not completely clear. The NETS renders αὐτῷ as "him," indicating the Lord in v. 28a. The reference of αὐτῷ, however, could arguably be φόβῳ κυρίου ("the fear of the Lord"). This reading is more plausible since in v. 30 a similar construction using the same predicator has "the fear of the Lord" (οὐ προσῆλθες φόβῳ κυρίου) as its complement (i.e., object).[64] Not only that, the meaning of ἐν καρδίᾳ δισσῇ is further elaborated in v. 30 as ἡ καρδία σου πλήρης δόλου ("your heart full of treachery"). Here a double mind refers to a deceitful mind in relation to the fear of the Lord. In this sense, although ἐν καρδίᾳ δισσῇ in Sir 1:28 has morphological, lexical, and semantic ingredients for δίψυχος, the thematic similarity of Sir 1:28 to Jas 1:8 and 4:8 is absent.

---

63. In Deut 6:5 LXX, καρδίας and ψυχή are used to render the Hebrew לבב and נפש, respectively. There is an intention to make a distinction between the two. However, Louw and Nida place καρδία and ψυχή in the domain of "Psychological Faculties"—§26.3 and §26.4, respectively (Louw and Nida, *Greek-English Lexicon*, 1:321–22). Keep in mind that these two words have diverse meanings according to their use in context. But it seems to me that their usage in James and Hosea reflect the inner self, which belongs to the domain indicated above. Davies and Allison also put them in the same category in terms of "internal components of a human personality" (*Gospel according to Saint Matthew*, 3:241).

64. I take φόβῳ κυρίου as an object in the dative case of οὐ προσῆλθες, though one could make the case that this word group functions as an adjunct. In either case, my point stands.

DOUBLE-MINDEDNESS IN HOS 10:2 LXX

Hosea 10:2 has been neglected by commentators on James as noted above. In this section I will demonstrate that Hos 10:2 LXX shares both lexical and thematic parallels with Jas 1:8 and 4:8. Upon this ground, it will be argued that Hos 10:2 LXX is a bridge linking double-mindedness to the *Shema* tradition.[65]

First, Hos 10:2 LXX has lexical and morphological resources that could possibly lead to the coinage of δίψυχος. The first conceptual similarity is found in the use of ἐμέρισαν ("they divided") in 10:2. This conceptual parallel is found in Jas 1:8 and 4:8 through the use of the prefix δι, since it is a common choice in Greek to make a compound word with the meaning of being divided or double.[66] Hosea 10:2 LXX refers to a divided καρδία, while James refers to a double ψυχή. Though καρδία and ψυχή may not be interchangeable, they are grouped in the same semantic domain as noted above. In fact, καρδία and ψυχή share more similarities than dissimilarities in meaning, and in Jas 4:8, we see that καρδίας occurs along with δίψυχοι, both of which refer to a person's inner state of mind.

---

65. The temporal priority between Deuteronomy and Hosea is disputed. It is assumed by most Old Testament scholars that Hosea predates Deuteronomy. See Wolff, *Book of the Prophet Hosea*, xxxi; Zobel, *Prophetie und Deuteronomium*, 49. Carsten Vang, however, attempts to determine the direction of dependency between the two books by comparing the thematic similarities and discrepancies. As opposed to the majority opinion on this topic, he concludes that "The surprising complete lack of marriage and adultery metaphors in Deuteronomy compared with the book of Hosea suggests that Hosea is reusing the 'divine' theme from an older Deuteronomy tradition" ("God's Love," 193). For those advocating for Deuteronomistic priority, see Rooker, "Book of Hosea," 62; Gisin, *Hosea*, 299. Further discussion is beyond the scope of this study. However, the most important point relevant to the present study is that they are closely correlated in terms of the theme of Yahweh's love, be it Hoseanic priority or Deuteronomistic priority.

66. Porter, "Is *dipsuchos* a 'Christian' Word," 474.

Hos 10:1–2 (NETS)	Hos 10:1–2 LXX	Jas 1:8; 4:8	Jas 1:8; 4:8 (NRSV)
Israel is a well-growing vine; fruit thrives on it. According to the multitude of its fruits, he increased altars; according to the good things of his land, they built steles. It divided their hearts. Now they will be annihilated; he will break down their altars; their steles will suffer distress.	Ἄμπελος εὐκληματοῦσα Ισραηλ, ὁ καρπὸς αὐτῆς εὐθηνῶν· κατὰ τὸ πλῆθος τῶν καρπῶν αὐτοῦ ἐπλήθυνεν τὰ θυσιαστήρια, κατὰ τὰ ἀγαθὰ τῆς γῆς αὐτοῦ ᾠκοδόμησεν στήλας. ἐμέρισαν καρδίας αὐτῶν, νῦν ἀφανισθήσονται· αὐτὸς κατασκάψει τὰ θυσιαστήρια αὐτῶν, ταλαιπωρήσουσιν αἱ στῆλαι αὐτῶν.	(1:8) ἀνὴρ δίψυχος, ἀκατάστατος ἐν πάσαις ταῖς ὁδοῖς αὐτοῦ. (4:8) ἐγγίσατε τῷ θεῷ καὶ ἐγγιεῖ ὑμῖν. καθαρίσατε χεῖρας, ἁμαρτωλοί, καὶ ἁγνίσατε καρδίας, δίψυχοι.	(1:8) being double-minded and unstable in every way (4:8) Draw near to God, and he will draw near to you. Cleanse your hands, you sinners, and purify your hearts, you double-minded.

Second, Hos 10:2 thematically relates to Jas 1:8 and 4:8. In Hos 10:1, the writer metaphorically describes the prosperity of Israel as a luscious vine.[67] The result of Israel's "agro-economic" success, however, results in an unexpected outcome. People invested their economic surplus into building more altars. Sacred steles were also built. In light of Hos 8:11, the increase of altars and standing stones, whether they were for YHWH or Canaanite gods, are the indicators of Israel's increasing "estrangement from YHWH."[68] If they were for YHWH, the Israelites misunderstood God who demands their hearts rather than heartless cultic services. If they worship deities, in particular Baal, they violate the covenant with YHWH. The latter is more convincing when co-texts like Hos 2:8, 9:10, and 11:2 are taken into consideration.[69] Andrew Dearman rightly notes

67. According to Vang, "The divine love will show up in much blessing and prosperity (7:12–13)" ("God's Love," 188).

68. Dearman, *Book of Hosea*, 260.

69. Laurie J. Braaten's interpretation of Hos 2 sheds light on the interpretation of Hos 10:1. Braaten argues that "The people commit whoredom by worshipping Baal as their provider god instead of Yahweh, thereby 'wedding' the land to Baal (Hos 2:10b[8b]). The bride land 'commits' whoredom due to the people's action, resulting in the land's being allied to 'lovers.' The bride—like her children—attributes her gifts to these lovers rather than to her real husband Yahweh (2:7–10a[5–8a])" ("God Sows," 108–9).

that "the issue at hand is a matter collectively of Israel's heart, not the matter of cultic worship per se."[70]

In Hos 10:2, material prosperity divides the heart of Israel. Its inner being is distorted due to the adulterous intention to love both YHWH and Baal, the god of prosperity. The prophet accuses Israel of committing sins against the command in Deut 6:5.[71] Israel's sin causes the anger of God and his judgment in 10:2b. In this way, Hos 10:2 issues an indictment against Israel's inner state of mind because it is divided on the basis of the *Shema* tradition. The essence of their sin is the divided mind that serves both false gods and YHWH simultaneously. This theme significantly overlaps with what we have seen in Jas 1:8 and 4:8.

The two arguments given above are convincing enough to claim that there is an intertextual thematic connection between Hos 10:2 and Jas 1:8 and 4:8. However, peripheral evidence is also available in favor of my argument. First, James calls those who desire to be friends of the world "adulteresses" in Jas 4:4. According to Bauckham, "James uses the image of marriage and adultery in the manner of the OT prophets: God's people who compromise with worldly values are adulterous women, attempting the impossible task of combining marriage to God their husband, who requires exclusive loyalty, and liaison with another partner, the world."[72] In fact, the theme of harlotry permeates Hosea.[73] God commanded the prophet to marry adulterous Gomer (1:2). Hosea's broken marriage is analogous to the covenant between God and Israel, which is interrupted by the misbehavior of the latter. However, as Dwight Daniels rightly spells out, "not the slightest trace of the marriage imagery which Hosea associates with the covenant is to be found in Deuteronomy."[74] This observation provides substantiation that James is to be appropriately connected to Deuteronomy through Hosea.

Second, Deut 6:4–5 and Hosea, the first book of the "single collection titled 'The Book of the Twelve,'"[75] were available to the writers of the New Testament.[76] According to Craig Evans, "Deuteronomy 6:4–5

70. Dearman, *Book of Hosea*, 260.

71. Ibid., 261.

72. Bauckham, *Wisdom of James*, 179.

73. See Ortlund, *Whoredom*, 47–75.

74. Daniels, *Hosea and Salvation History*, 121.

75. Braaten, "God Sows," 104.

76. Availability to the author and/or the audience is the first criterion to identify

was part of the *Shema* that an observant Jew was to recite twice daily (cf. Mishnah Berakot 1:1–4)."[77] And since Christianity stems from Judaism, the significance of the *Shema* for early Christians can be assumed. Historical facts also support that "in the ancient synagogue, the Torah was read sequentially each Sabbath in a continuous cycle, accompanied by a reading from the prophets called a *haftarah*."[78] According to Charles Perrot, the four books that were "most in use" in the ancient synagogues were the Torah, Isaiah, the Twelve Prophets, and the Psalms.[79] Moreover, first-century Judaism accorded authoritative status to the interpretation of the Torah by the prophets.[80] Thus, it is a plausible hypothesis that the *Shema* tradition was also understood with the aid of the prophetic books, which must have been familiar to New Testament writers and probably the audience as well.

CONCLUSION

In this study, it has been argued that δίψυχος in Jas 1:8 and 4:8 echoes the double-minded language in Hos 10:2 through which it is linked to the *Shema* tradition. To use a contemporary analogy, when one clicks on the hyperlink "δίψυχος," one is not immediately directed to Deut 6:5, but rather to Hos 10:2 where the prophetic understanding of the *Shema* is expressed. Porter's notion of echo is used to refer to the underlying thematic connections between sacred traditions and the New Testament texts. Then, the theory of semantic domains and chain analysis were applied as a methodology in order to analyze the thematic features of the double-minded language in James.

In the case of δίψυχος in James, many commentators tend to relate it to the *Shema* tradition, and this relation has been demonstrated convincingly through the linguistic analysis in this paper as well. However, the

---

echo in Hays's model, and this is followed by Beale's. See Hays, *Echoes of Scripture*; Beale, *Handbook*. Porter criticizes this model for the fact that availability to the original reader has nothing to do with determining echo. It is the author who makes the echo irrespective of the knowledge of the audience about the source material. Porter, *Sacred Tradition*, 9. Agreeing with Porter, I present the availability of the *Shema* passages and Hosea to the author of James as the secondary evidence.

77. Evans, "New Testament Use of the Old Testament," 73. See also Gerhardsson, *Shema in the New Testament*, 301.

78. Heine, "Early Christian Reception of the Prophets," 408.

79. Perrot, "Reading of the Bible," 154–55.

80. Foster, *Renaming Abraham's Children*, 34–35.

antithetical relationship between the double-minded concept in James and the single-minded loyalty to YHWH in Deut 6:4–5 led me to find a missing piece of the puzzle that completes the whole picture. Finally, I identified Hos 10:2 LXX as the bridge linking the *Shema* to James. Double-mindedness language in James echoes the developed theme of the *Shema* in Hosea. In conclusion, James may *own* the intellectual property of the Christian neologism δίψυχος, but he *owes* the theme of double-mindedness to Hosea's interpretation of the *Shema* tradition in Hos 10:1–2.

This study can move forward the discussions of James in three ways. First, it is widely perceived that Old Testament texts such as Lev 19, Deut 6, and Prov 3:34 play a key role in the overall arguments of James.[81] Therefore, the term "echo" as defined by Porter holds promise for examining further intertextual thematic relations between the Old Testament and the Epistle of James. Second, the identification of a theme with linguistically informed and rigorous methods is crucial in the study of James since the thematic coherence among units with different themes such as perfections, law, faith, speech, and deeds is closely tied to the discussion of the structure of James.[82] Third, this study can shed light on how the sacred traditions in Old Testament were received and appropriated in the New Testament. Rather than focusing on one text in the Old Testament in order to trace the origin of a theme in any given text, this study proposes the possibility of the development of sacred traditions through a series of texts over time.

BIBLIOGRAPHY

Adamson, James B. *The Epistle of James*. NICNT. Grand Rapids: Eerdmans, 1976.

Allison, Dale C., Jr. *A Critical and Exegetical Commentary on the Epistle of James*. ICC. New York: Bloomsbury T. & T. Clark, 2013.

Almela, Moisés, and Aquilino Sánchez. "Words as 'Lexical Units' in Learning/Teaching Vocabulary." *IJES* 7 (2007) 21–40.

Bauckham, Richard. *James: Wisdom of James, Disciple of Jesus the Sage*. London: Routledge, 1999.

Beale, G. K. *Handbook on the New Testament Use of the Old Testament: Exegesis and Interpretation*. Grand Rapids: Baker Academic, 2012.

Beetham, Christopher A. *Echoes of Scripture in the Letter of Paul to the Colossians*. BibInt 96. Leiden: Brill, 2008.

81. Taylor, "Recent Scholarship," 109–11. See also Johnson, "Use of Leviticus 19," 399.

82. Taylor, "Recent Scholarship," 95–103.

Braaten, Laurie J. "God Sows: Hosea's Land Theme in the Book of the Twelve." In *Thematic Threads in the Book of the Twelve*, edited by Paul L. Redditt and Aaron Schart, 104–32. BZAW 325. Berlin: de Gruyter, 2003.

Carson, D. A. *Exegetical Fallacies*. Grand Rapids: Baker, 1984.

Daniels, Dwight R. *Hosea and Salvation History: The Early Traditions of Israel in the Prophecy of Hosea*. BZAW 191. Berlin: de Gruyter, 1990.

Davids, Peter H. *The Epistle of James: A Commentary on the Greek Text*. NIGTC. Grand Rapids: Eerdmans, 1982.

Davies, W. D. *Paul and Rabbinic Judaism: Some Rabbinic Elements in Pauline Theology*. Philadelphia: Fortress, 1980.

Davies, W. D., and Dale C. Allison. *A Critical and Exegetical Commentary on the Gospel according to Saint Matthew*. 3 vols. Edinburgh: T. & T. Clark, 1991.

Dawson, Zachary K. "The Books of Acts and *Jubilees* in Dialogue: A Literary-Intertextual Analysis of the Noahide Laws in Acts 15 and 21." *JGRChJ* 13 (2017) 9–40.

Dearman, J. Andrew. *The Book of Hosea*. NICOT. Grand Rapids: Eerdmans, 2010.

Dibelius, Martin. *James: A Commentary on the Epistle of James*. Revised by Henrich Greeven. Translated by Michael A. Williams. Hermeneia. Minneapolis: Fortress, 1976.

Dunn, James D. G. "Jesus Tradition in Paul." In *Studying the Historical Jesus: Evaluations of the State of Current Research*, edited by Bruce D. Chilton and Craig A. Evans, 155–78. NTTS 19. Leiden: Brill, 1994.

Elliott, John H. "The Epistle of James in Rhetorical and Social Scientific Perspective: Holiness–Wholeness and Patterns of Replication." *BTB* 23 (1993) 71–81.

Emadi, Samuel. "Intertextuality in New Testament Scholarship: Significance, Criteria, and the Art of Intertextual Reading." *CurBS* 14 (2015) 8–23.

Evans, Craig A. "New Testament Use of the Old Testament." In *New Dictionary of Biblical Theology: Exploring the Unity and Diversity of Scripture*, edited by T. Desmond Alexander et al., 72–80. IVP Reference Collection. Leicester: IVP, 2000.

Fitzgerald, Jill, and Dixie L. Spiegel. "Textual Cohesion and Coherence in Children's Writing." *Research in the Teaching of English* 20 (1986) 263–80.

Fitzmyer, Joseph A. *The Gospel according to Luke X–XXIV: Introduction, Translation, and Notes*. AB 28A. Garden City: Doubleday, 1985.

Foster, Robert B. *Renaming Abraham's Children: Election, Ethnicity, and the Interpretation of Scripture in Romans 9*. WUNT 2.421. Tübingen: Mohr Siebeck, 2016.

Gerhardsson, Birger. *The Shema in the New Testament: Deut 6:4–5 in Significant Passages*. Lund: Novapress, 1996.

Gisin, Walter. *Hosea: Ein Literarisches Netzwerk beweist seine Authentizität*. BBB 139. Berlin: Philo, 2002.

Halliday, M. A. K. *Explorations in the Functions of Language*. Explorations in Language Studies. London: Hodder, 1973.

Halliday, M. A. K., and Ruqaiya Hasan. *Cohesion in English*. ELS 9. London: Longman, 1976.

———. *Language, Context, and Text: Aspects of Language in a Social-Semiotic Perspective*. 2nd ed. Oxford: Oxford University Press, 1989.

———. "Text and Context: Aspects of Language in a Social-Semiotic Perspective." *Sophia Linguistica: Working Papers in Linguistics* 6 (1980) 4–90.

Hasan, Ruqaiya. "Coherence and Cohesive Harmony." In *Understanding Reading Comprehension: Cognition, Language, and the Structure of Prose*, edited by James Flood, 181–219. Newark, DE: International Reading Association, 1984.

Hatina, Thomas R. "Intertextuality and Historical Criticism in New Testament Studies: Is There a Relationship?" *BibInt* 7 (1999) 28–43.

Hays, Richard B. *Echoes of Scripture in the Letters of Paul.* New Haven, CT: Yale University Press, 1989.

Heine, Ronald E. "Early Christian Reception of the Prophets." In *The Oxford Handbook of the Prophets*, edited by Carolyn J. Sharp, 407–22. Oxford: Oxford University Press, 2016.

Hollander, John. *The Figure of Echo: A Mode of Allusion in Milton and After.* Quantum Books. Berkeley: University of California Press, 1981.

Hort, F. J. A. *The Epistle of St James.* London: Macmillan, 1909.

Johnson, Luke Timothy. "Jas 3:13–4:10 and the *Topos* περὶ φθόνου." *NovT* 25 (1983) 327–47.

———. *The Letter of James: A New Translation with Introduction and Commentary.* AB 37A. New York: Doubleday, 1996.

———. "The Use of Leviticus 19 in the Letter of James." *JBL* 101 (1982) 391–401.

Kristeva, Julia. "Word, Dialogue and Novel." In *The Kristeva Reader*, edited by Toril Moi, 34–61. New York: Columbia University Press, 1986.

Laws, Sophie. *A Commentary on the Epistle of James.* BNTC. San Francisco: HarperCollins, 1980.

Lemke, Jay L. "Discourses in Conflict: Heteroglossia and Text Semantics." In *Systemic Functional Approaches to Discourse: Selected Papers from the 12th International Systemic Workshop*, edited by James D. Benson and William S. Greaves, 29–50. Norwood, NJ: Ablex, 1988.

———. "Intertextuality and Educational Research." In *Uses of Intertextuality in Classroom and Educational Research*, edited by Nora Shuart-Faris and David Bloome, 3–15. Greenwich: IAP, 2004.

———. "Intertextuality and Text Semantics." In *Discourse in Society: Systemic Functional Perspective: Meaning and Choice in Language: Studies for Michael Halliday*, 85–114. London: Ablex, 1995.

———. "Text Structure and Text Semantics." In *Pragmatics, Discourse and Text: Some Systemically Inspired Approaches*, edited by Erich H. Steiner and Robert Veltman, 158–70. Advances in Discourse Processes 37. London: Pinter, 1988.

Louw, Johannes P., and Eugene A. Nida. *A Greek-English Lexicon of the New Testament: Based on Semantic Domains.* 2 vols. New York: United Bible Societies, 1988.

Marshall, S. S. C. "Δίψυχος: A Local Term?" *SE* 6 (1973) 348–51.

Martin, Ralph P. *James.* WBC 48. Waco, TX: Thomas Nelson, 1988.

McCartney, Dan G. *James.* BECNT. Grand Rapids: Baker Academic, 2009.

McKnight, Scot. *The Letter of James.* NICNT. Grand Rapids: Eerdmans, 2011.

Moo, Douglas J. *The Letter of James.* PNTC. Grand Rapids: Eerdmans, 2000.

Moyise, Steve. "Intertextuality and the Study of the Old Testament in the New Testament." In *The Old Testament in the New Testament: Essays in Honour of J. L. North*, edited by Steve Moyise and J. L. North, 14–41. JSNTSup 189. Sheffield: Sheffield Academic, 2000.

Nida, Eugene A., and Johannes P. Louw. *Lexical Semantics of the Greek New Testament: A Supplement to the Greek-English Lexicon of the New Testament Based on Semantic Domains.* SBLRBS. Atlanta: Scholars Press, 1988.

Orr, Mary. *Intertextuality: Debates and Contexts.* Malden, MA: Blackwell, 2003.

Ortlund, Raymond C., Jr. *Whoredom: God's Unfaithful Wife in Biblical Theology.* New Studies in Biblical Theology. Grand Rapids: Eerdmans, 1996.

Perrot, Charles. "The Reading of the Bible in the Ancient Synagogue." In *Mikra: Text, Translation, Reading, and Interpretation of the Hebrew Bible in Ancient Judaism and Early Christianity*, edited by M. J. Mulder and Harry Sysling, 137–59. Philadelphia: Fortress, 1988.

Porter, Stanley E. "Cohesion in James: A Response to Martin Dibelius." In *The Epistle of James: Linguistic Exegesis of an Early Christian Letter*, edited by James D. Dvorak and Zachary K. Dawson, 45–68. LENT 1. Eugene, OR: Pickwick, 2019.

———. "Further Comments on the Use of the Old Testament in the New Testament." In *The Intertextuality of the Epistles*, edited by Thomas L. Brodie et al., 1–13. Sheffield: Sheffield Phoenix, 2006.

———. "Is dipsuchos (James 1:8, 4:8) a 'Christian' Word?" *Biblica* 71 (1990) 469–98.

———. "'On the Shoulders of Giants': The Expansion and Application of the Louw-Nida Lexicon." In *Linguistic Analysis of the Greek New Testament: Studies in Tools, Methods, and Practice*, 47–60. Grand Rapids: Baker Academic, 2015.

———. *Sacred Tradition in the New Testament: Tracing Old Testament Themes in the Gospels and Epistles.* Grand Rapids: Baker Academic, 2016.

———. "The Use of the Old Testament in the New Testament: A Brief Comment on Method and Terminology." In *Early Christian Interpretation of the Scriptures of Israel: Investigations and Proposals*, edited by Craig A. Evans and James A. Sanders, 79–96. JSNTSup 14. Sheffield: Sheffield Academic, 1997.

Poythress, Vern S. "Greek Lexicography and Translation: Comparing Bauer's and Louw-Nida's Lexicons." *JETS* 44 (2001) 285–96.

Reed, Jeffrey T. "Cohesive Ties in 1 Timothy: In Defense of the Epistle's Unity." *Neot* 26 (1992) 131–47.

———. *A Discourse Analysis of Philippians: Method and Rhetoric in the Debate over Literary Integrity.* JSNTSup 136. Sheffield: Sheffield Academic, 1997.

Rooker, Mark F. "The Use of the Old Testament in the Book of Hosea." *CTR* 7 (1993) 51–66.

Ropes, James H. *A Critical and Exegetical Commentary on the Epistle of St. James.* ICC. Edinburgh: T. & T. Clark, 1916.

Ruzer, Serge. *Mapping the New Testament: Early Christian Writings as a Witness for Jewish Biblical Exegesis.* JCPS 13. Leiden: Brill, 2007.

Seitz, Oscar Jacob F. "Afterthoughts on the Term 'Dipsychos'." *NTS* 4 (1958) 327–34.

———. "Antecedents and Signification of the Term ΔΙΨΥΧΟΣ." *JBL* 66 (1947) 211–19.

———. "Two Spirits in Man: An Essay in Biblical Exegesis." *NTS* 6 (1959) 82–95.

Shaw, David A. "Converted Imaginations? The Reception of Richard Hays's Intertextual Method." *CurBS* 11 (2013) 234–45.

Spitaler, Peter. "James 1:5–8: A Dispute with God." *CBQ* 71 (2009) 560–79.

Stamps, Dennis L. "The Use of the Old Testament in the New Testament as a Rhetorical Device: A Methodological Proposal." In *Hearing the Old Testament in the New Testament*, edited by Stanley E. Porter, 9–37. McMaster New Testament Studies. Grand Rapids: Eerdmans, 2006.

Swete, Henry B. *An Introduction to the Old Testament in Greek*. Cambridge: Cambridge University Press, 1902.

Tan, Kim Huat. "The Shema and Early Christianity." *TynBul* 59 (2008) 181–206.

Taylor, Mark E. "Recent Scholarship on the Structure of James." *CurBS* 3 (2004) 86–115.

Vang, Carsten. "God's Love according to Hosea and Deuteronomy: A Prophetic Reworking of a Deuteronomic Concept?" *TynBul* 62 (2011) 173–94.

Wagner, J. Ross. *Heralds of the Good News: Isaiah and Paul "In Concert" in the Letter to the Romans*. NovTSup 101. Leiden: Brill, 2002.

Wall, Robert W. *Community of the Wise: The Letter of James*. The New Testament in Context. Valley Forge: Trinity Press International, 1997.

Westfall, Cynthia Long. "Blessed Be the Ties that Bind: Semantic Domains and Cohesive Chains in Hebrews 1.1–24 and 12.5–8." *JGRChJ* 6 (2009) 199–216.

———. *A Discourse Analysis of the Letter to the Hebrews: The Relationship between Form and Meaning*. LNTS 297. London: T. & T. Clark, 2005.

Wolff, Hans Walter. *A Commentary on the Book of the Prophet Hosea*. Translated by G. Stansell. Hermeneia. Philadelphia: Fortress, 1974.

Wolverton, Wallace I. "Double-Minded Man in the Light of Essene Psychology." *ATR* 38 (1956) 166–75.

Yoon, David. "The Ideological Inception of Intertextuality and its Dissonance in Current Biblical Studies." *CurBS* 12 (2013) 58–76.

Zobel, Konstantin. *Prophetie und Deuteronomium: Die Rezeption prophetischer Theologie durch das Deuteronomium*. BZAW 199. Berlin: de Gruyter, 1992.

6

An Analysis of James 2:14–26 with Special Reference to the Intertextual Reading of Abraham and Rahab

XIAXIA E. XUE

INTRODUCTION

SEVERAL IMPORTANT ISSUES PLAGUE the text of Jas 2:14–26. A perennially difficult issue concerns the author's handling of the relationship between faith and works in comparison with how Paul dealt with these two concepts in his letters.[1] Some scholars argue that James and Paul held conflicting positions,[2] while others propose that James and Paul address different issues (wherein Paul addresses unbelievers' salvation, and James deals with the issue of believers' sanctification), and so their views should not be set at odds with each other.[3] Still others argue that James and Paul

1. See Jenkins, "Faith and Works," 62–78; Bauckham, *James*, 120–40; Dowd, "Faith That Works," 195–205; Rakestraw, "James 2:14–26," 31–50; McKnight, *Letter of James*, 260–61.

2. See Dibelius, *James*, 165; Wall and Lemcio implied the contradiction between Paul and James in saying that the "Pauline corpus followed by the non-Pauline corpus . . . indicates that the non-Pauline letters play a subordinate role, keeping Pauline letters in proper check-and-balance . . . God's message 'begins' with Paul and then moves to the other apostolic witnesses to correct any interpretations of Paul which might lead to dangerous results for faith and practice" (*New Testament as Canon*, 176–77); Cf. Bauckham, *James*, 113–20; Limberis in his paper argues that James responds to and argues against Paul, particularly in the Abraham passage ("Provenance of the Caliphate Church," 397–420; see also Cheung, *Genre*, 194–96).

3. See Rainbow, *Way of Salvation*, 213–23, where he proposes that Paul and James address different audiences and make complementary points; see also Dunn, *Beginning from Jerusalem*, 1142–44, who argues, "James was remembered as responding

use the same terms (e.g., δικαιόω, ἔργον, and πίστις), but they have different connotations in their writings.[4] Other ways of dealing with this question have been proposed, but the views represented here show this issue to be far from resolved. In my view, if this discussion is to see progress in the future, then more attention needs to be given to understanding Paul and James in their respective contexts. Therefore, I maintain that the Epistle of James must be read on its own terms and within its contextual situation, instead of being hijacked by Paul's understanding of faith and works.

Rather than letting a Pauline understanding of faith and works affect the interpretation of James, some scholars examine Jas 2:14–26 through the lens of rhetoric, especially the diatribe form.[5] Many different approaches have been applied to James's text, and even some intertextual studies focus on James's relationship with the Jesus tradition, particularly the Gospel of Matthew and the so-called Q document.[6] However, little attention has been paid to the intertextuality in Jas 2:14–26 regarding Scripture.[7] Even in the few works offering an intertextual analysis of this passage, the major focus has been on James's intertextual relationships with Paul, or on the use of Abraham and the parts of Scripture associated with him.[8] Many of these studies have either downplayed or ignored the

---

in some sense and in some degree to what he had heard of Paul's teaching on Abraham's faith . . . what he [James] is emphasizing is the importance of faith coming to expression in obedience to God ([Jas] 2.21–23) and in active concern for the welfare of others (2.15–16, 25). Concerns for ritual purity or the purity of table-fellowship are not in view. It is almost as though James deflects the sort of criticism of Paul represented in Acts 21.21, not by refuting Paul, but rather by emphasizing what Paul also emphasized—the importance of faith coming to expression in love-motivated, love-expressing action (Gal. 5.6), the importance of those baptized into Christ continuing to live lives commanded by and expressive of righteousness (Romans 6)." See also, Michaelis, *Introduction*, 302–6.

4. See McKnight, *James*, 259–63; Rakestraw, "James 2:14–26," 36–42; Ward, "James and Paul," 162–63; Maxwell, "Justified by Works," 375–78.

5. Van der Westhuizen, "Stylistic Techniques," 89–107; McKnight, "James 2:18a," 355–64; Watson, "James 2," 94–121.

6. Batten, "Jesus Tradition," 381–90; Batten, *What Are They Saying*, 72–83; Hartin, *James and the Q Sayings of Jesus*; Bauckham, *James*, 29–111; Deppe, "Sayings of Jesus."

7. Exceptions include Wall, "Intertextuality of Scripture," 217–36; Popkes, "The Composition of James and Intertextuality," 91–112.

8. See Instone-Brewer, "James as a Sermon," 250–68, who compares the structure of James to some parts of Jubilees, focusing on the trials of Abraham. See also

important role of Rahab in this passage and how she is associated with Abraham. Since the importance that James has given to this marginalized "harlot" has yet to be satisfactorily accounted for, I will attempt to fill in this gap by using an intertextual thematic analysis that I have adapted from the works of Jay Lemke. This analysis will demonstrate that James links the patriarchal father Abraham with the Canaanite prostitute Rahab for a particular social purpose. Specifically, I will argue that the author's use of scriptural references serves to identify himself with the socially vulnerable and marginalized groups within his audience.

A METHODOLOGY FOR INTERTEXTUAL ANALYSIS[9]

Many biblical scholars employ the term "intertextuality" to describe the relationship created when an Old Testament text is used in a New Testament text.[10] Traditionally, when speaking of biblical intertextual relationships, the focus has been upon the wording found within the texts. Thus, the treatment of textual adaptation involves an analysis of such phenomena as verbatim copying, near-verbatim copying, explicit or near-explicit reference, paraphrase, and allusion in the host text in relation to previous texts.[11] Jay Lemke, as a social semiotician,[12] however,

---

Soards, "Early Christian Interpretation of Abraham," 18–26.

9. This methodology in part shares similar ideas with my previous article; see Xue, "Intertextual Discourse Analysis," 277–308.

10. Biblical scholars have used many terms to describe the connection between previous texts and later texts, and intertextuality is one of them (see Boda, "Quotation and Allusion," 296). For instance, see Hays, *Echoes*; Moyise, *Old Testament in the Book of Revelation*; Moyise, *Paul and Scripture*; Watts, *Isaiah's New Exodus*; Beale, *John's Use of the Old Testament*; Pao, *Acts and the Isaianic New Exodus*; Manning, *Echoes*; Watson, *Paul and the Hermeneutics of Faith*. It is worth noting that the use of the term is not restricted to New Testament studies, and it is used in Old Testament studies as well. According to Thomas Hatina, "Historically oriented Old Testament scholars generally use the term in much the same way as their New Testament counterparts, namely as a designation for the appropriation of prior texts by later texts" ("Intertextuality and Historical Criticism," 28 n. 2).

11. See Brodie et al., "Conclusion," 288–90.

12. Lemke's research interests cover broad fields, particularly in social theory and social semiotics, discourse analysis, and others. He is now professor emeritus, and as explained on his personal website, he "was active for many years in the International Systemic Linguistics Association and its annual congresses on functional linguistics and has served as co-editor of the journals *Linguistics and Education and Critical Discourse Studies*" (http://www.jaylemke.com/short-biography/ [cited 18 January, 2016]).

considers intertextual relationships in a more profound way.[13] He places intertextuality on the level of a system of social meaning-making practices that are characteristic of the community.[14] Thus, intertextuality refers to a principle that is at home in the context of social semiotics, which holds that all meanings are made within communities and that the analysis of meaning should not be separated from the social, historical, cultural, and political dimensions of such communities.[15] Lemke defines the system of intertextuality in terms of social dynamics; he writes, "Diverse social interests and points-of-view speak with distinct voices that proclaim different thematic propositions, assign differing valuations, and may even make use of different characteristic genres and speech-activities."[16] When this definition of intertextuality is applied to a biblical text, specifically in order to understand the meaning of James's references to Old Testament characters, we need to consider the other dimensions and viewpoints of talking about the characters of Abraham and Rahab in the recurrent textual formations known in the community in which James wrote his letter. This will enable us to construct intertextual relationships among these particular texts to locate James's viewpoint in the diverse textual data.

Lemke's theory of intertextuality relates to his view of the nature of texts. First, Lemke states, "The primary function of language, and of all semiosis, is to create, sustain and change social reality."[17] As a result, he views instances of language use, or texts, as the "arenas where we may hear the conflicts being fought out, or being contained."[18] He proceeds to develop a way of examining intertextual relationships that locates a text's

13. He has indicated that, two texts that "share only one or a few key words is not enough, and may be quite irrelevant if those words are being used with different thematic meanings in the different texts," and in addition, he points out that "the texts may not share words, but use thematically equivalent synonyms or even figurative expressions. It is semantic patterns that the texts must share" ("Intertextuality and Text Semantics," 91).

14. Ibid., 85.

15. Lemke, *Textual Politics*, 8.

16. Lemke, "Discourses in Conflict," 30.

17. Lemke, "Interpersonal Meaning," 86.

18. Lemke, "Discourses in Conflict," 39. Lemke also states, "Every text combines ITFs [Intertextual Thematic Formations] whose thematic and actional intertextual ties enmesh it in the social heteroglossia of the community" ("Discourses in Conflict," 39). For Lemke's concept of ITFs, see Xue, "Intertextual Discourse Analysis," 281. See also, Lemke, "Intertextuality and the Project of Text Linguistics," 223; Lemke, "Discourses in Conflict," 30–31.

meaning, where "meaning" is viewed "differently from different social positions within the community."[19] In other words, the meaning of a text is found within its intertextual relationships, since meaning is made in a community. As he states, "The notion of intertextuality grounds text semantics because meanings are made in a community through the relations of texts that may nowhere be made explicitly in any one text, and because every text makes its meanings against the background of the regular, recurrent, recognizable discourse-types of a community."[20]

Also, in Lemke's theory of intertextuality the concept of heteroglossia is foundational. This concept, pertaining to the nature of language, was first postulated by Mikhail Bakhtin, who said that, "language is heteroglot from top to bottom: it represents the co-existence of socio-ideological contradictions between the present and the past, between differing epochs of the past, between tendencies, schools, circles and so forth."[21] Lemke thus developed his method for intertextual analysis around the notion of heteroglossia in order to understand different social voices and their relationships. He explains the reason for approaching intertextuality in this way: "In a more fully developed social theory of the role of language and discourse in society . . . we need to understand these different discourse voices are not simply different; they are also systematically related to one another, and related in ways that depend on the wider social relations between the subcommunities that use them."[22] An intertextual analysis thus seeks to identify the various voices that a text relates to in some way—where the term "voices" is understood as the social and ideological positions represented by the textual formations in a text. But, more than this, Lemke's intertextual analysis also seeks to ascertain from where the positions derived, including different social classes, professions, age groups, philosophical and religious views, political opinions, and so on.[23]

This paper will utilize related literature in order to hear the voice of the social class that James seeks to articulate through his use of Scripture,

19. Lemke, "Discourses in Conflict," 33.

20. Ibid., 29–30.

21. Bakhtin, "Discourse in the Novel," 291. Pam Morris comments that for Bakhtin, language "is perceived as stratified through and through into multiple social discourses each representing a specific ideological-belief system, a way of seeing the world: heteroglossia" (*Bakhtin Reader*, 73).

22. Lemke, *Textual Politics*, 38.

23. Lemke, "Discourses in Conflict," 30.

and to compare James's voice to the voices of his contemporaries in the Jewish and Christian literature.

SITUATING THE SOCIAL CONTEXT OF JAMES

Multiple theories have been offered regarding the social milieu of the Epistle of James. Some scholars believe James was composed in the middle of the second century in order to counter Marcion.[24] Others argue for the authenticity of the epistle as written by James, the brother of Jesus, and situate it in the middle of the first century during the first decades of the Jesus movement.[25] Still others consider James to have been composed in the last quarter of the first century,[26] the author likely having knowledge of Paul's Letter to the Romans. In addition, the epistle has been regarded as "a relatively structureless compendium of wisdom traditions with no specific reference to time or place."[27] However, some of these views have incurred much criticism in recent scholarship. For instance, it has been argued that James should not be simply considered a collection of moral precepts, since social issues are implied in the text itself.[28] Neither should James be understood as a reaction to Paul or to post-70 CE Paulinism, since the contrast in wording between James and Paul is insufficient to explain the alleged conceptual conflict between them (cf. Jas 2:21–25 vs. Gal 2:15–21; Rom 3:21–31; 4:1–8).[29] Rather, a

24. Nienhuis, *Not by Paul Alone*, 22–28.

25. For scholars who put James at this early date, see Johnson, "Social World of James," 178–97; Verseput, "Genre and Story," 104–10; Martin, "Life-Setting of the Epistle of James," 97–100.

26. Stephen Wilson argues that the discussion of faith and works in Jas 2:14–26 shows James has Paul as his target in mind and the epistle "was composed sometime in the last quarter of the first century" (*Related Strangers*, 152–55).

27. Johnson, "Social World of James," 193. Dibelius represents this type of view and has had a great impact on Jacobean scholarship since the publication of his commentary on James; see Dibelius, *James*, 21–50. Allison lists various hypotheses of the *Sitz im Leben* of the epistle in his commentary; see Allison, *James*, 32–50.

28. See Maynard-Reid, *Poverty and Wealth in James*, who explores the epistle and demonstrates James's deep concern with social issues, especially for social justice. See also Edgar, *Has God Not Chosen the Poor*, 30–43.

29. Robert Rakestraw indicates "that there is a difference in the emphasis put upon 'faith' by Paul and James. To each, faith is good and necessary for salvation, but James emphasizes the intellectual-objective aspect of faith," which describes what faith should look like for those who have already been justified, and Paul the volitional-subjective aspect which actually *includes* the former and which should *follow* it. A person

proper understanding of James requires an understanding of the social milieu of the mid-first century when the epistle was probably written.

First-century Greco-Roman society was highly structured and stratified.[30] People's resources depended on their position in the social order.[31] The steep pyramid of social power correspondingly affected morality and ethics.[32] In a society in which the poor had no voice, James challenges the social hierarchy by identifying with the marginalized and seeking to arouse his audience's compassion toward them.

Several indicators suggest that the life setting of the audience of the epistle is both socio-economic and religious.[33] First, in the opening, the author refers to the readers as "the twelve tribes in the Diaspora" (1:1). Although many commentators over the centuries have interpreted διασπορά as a literal geographical place,[34] today many scholars posit a figurative meaning, identifying διασπορά with "true Israel" (the Christians),[35] or with religiously and socially marginalized groups in the Diaspora, particularly those experiencing affliction.[36] By comparing similar types of extant texts—Jer 29:1–23; the Epistle of Jeremiah; 2 Macc 1:1–19, 1:10–2:28, 2 Bar. 78–86, Verseput convincingly argues that "the diasporic existence of the addressees is associated with affliction."[37] Therefore, the designation διασπορά in the epistle's opening probably refers to Jewish Christian groups undergoing suffering.

Second, the author addresses the audience as "brothers" fifteen different times (Jas 1:2, 9; 2:1, 14–15; 3:1, 10, 12; 4:11; 5:7, 9, 10, 12, 19),

---

must believe what is true and then act from the heart upon that truth and personally trust the object of his or her faith" ("James 2:14–26," 37). Richard Bauckham has also rightly pointed out that the striking coincidences of language do not indicate James's reference to the Pauline discussions of faith and works (*James*, 127–40).

30. According to Meeks, "Even slaves within a household ranked themselves" (*Moral World*, 34).

31. Ibid., 37.

32. See ibid., 32–39.

33. See Martin, "Life-Setting," 99, who considers the focus of the epistle to be more socio-economic than religious.

34. For this view, see Bauckham, *James*, 16; Moo, *Letter of James*, 23–24; Hartin, *James*, 25–27; Adamson, *Epistle of James*, 49–50.

35. Ropes, *Epistle of St. James*, 118–27; Allison, *James*, 116; Dibelius, *James*, 66–67; Cargal, *Restoring the Diaspora*, 45–49, who, in view of Jas 5:19–20, suggests those in the διασπορά refer to those wandering from the truth.

36. Verseput, "Genre and Story," 101.

37. Ibid., 101.

rather than as "sons" or "children" as in Paul.[38] This egalitarian language suggests that he was expecting his addressees, whether rich or poor, to treat each other equally, in the same way that he addresses them.[39] After encouraging those who are facing trials and affliction in 1:2–8, the author argues on behalf of the poor by reversing the status of rich and poor (1:9–11). The brother who is lowly shall boast (καυχάσθω in 1:9 vs. πᾶσαν χαρὰν ἡγήσασθε in 1:2) in his exaltation (ὁ ἀδελφὸς ὁ ταπεινὸς ἐν τῷ ὕψει αὐτου), and the rich in his lowliness (ὁ δὲ πλούσιος ἐν τῇ ταπεινώσει αὐτοῦ). The explanation of this reversal in 1:10b–11 reflects the language of Isa 40:2–9,[40] the theme of which is that the wicked shall perish, and God's people, who are afflicted, shall be comforted. This exaltation of the poor and debasement of the rich permeates the body of the epistle (Jas 1:2—5:11). In the closing (5:1–11), this reversal is even more remarkable: "You rich people, weep and wail for the miseries . . . Your riches have rotted, and your clothes are moth-eaten. Your gold and silver have rusted . . . be patient, brothers, until the coming of the Lord. The farmer waits for the precious crop from the earth." This theme of the reversal of status between rich and poor was not uncommon in the first century Greco-Roman world.[41] In the New Testament Gospel tradition, there are also socially marginal people who are significant in the ministry of Jesus; some are without possessions, others are in a devalued status, homeless, or despised.[42]

38. Some scholars share this view. See Johnson, "Social World of James," 196; Edgar, *Has God Not Chosen the Poor*, 101–2.

39. Johnson, "Social World of James," 196.

40. Allison, *James*, 197.

41. For example, in the apocalyptic writing of 1 Enoch, the concept of judgment against the rich is remarkable. In 94:8—97:10, it reads, "Woe to you, ye rich, for ye have trusted in your riches, and from your riches shall ye depart. . . . Woe unto you, ye sinners, for your riches make you appear like the righteous, but your hearts convict you of being sinners . . . and tread under foot the lowly with your might. . . . Woe to you who acquire silver and gold in unrighteousness . . ." See also Sir 8:2; 10:31; 11:19; 13:3–7, 19–23. According to Aune, the apocalyptic worldview believes that the present world order is both evil and oppressive, under the temporary control of evil powers, but God will soon destroy this present evil world order and replace it with a new and perfect order corresponding to Eden. There are a number of major aspects of apocalyptic eschatology with scholarly agreement, e.g., the temporal dualism of the two ages, the radical discontinuity between this age and the new world, the expectation of the imminent arrival of the reign of God, the cataclysmic intervention of God resulting in salvation for the righteous, etc. (Aune, "Apocalypticism," 27).

42. Edgar, *Has God Not Chosen the Poor*, 108. See also Maynard-Reid, *Poverty*

Third, besides the positive designation of the audience as "brothers," Jas 4:1–12 also addresses some as "adulteresses" (μοιχαλίδες), "sinners" (ἁμαρτωλοί), and "double-minded" (δίψυχοι), designations that signify status in relationship to God.[43] The address μοιχαλίδες should be understood metaphorically to describe believers' unfaithful behavior regarding their relationship with God,[44] which is clarified in the next verse as the author remarks, "friendship with the world is enmity with God" (4:4). Likewise, the designations "sinners" and "double-minded" are employed to portray the addressees negatively, the former accusing them of "having breached the standards of God's order," and the latter without "being whole in commitment to God."[45] It is probable that the author associates these addressees with the rich. Firstly, the repeated uses of ἐκ τῶν ἡδονῶν ὑμῶν, ἐν ταῖς ἡδοναῖς ὑμῶν and ἐπιθυμεῖτε indicate that the pleasure "you" are seeking probably is about the luxuries of life.[46] Second, though the verb δαπανάω, which connects with ἡδονή, is uncommon in the New Testament, according to BDAG, the meaning is "to use up or pay out material or physical resources, spend, spend freely."[47] In other words, the author states in 4:3 that the rich ("you") ask or pray wrongly in order to spend freely for their own pleasures (ἵνα ἐν ταῖς ἡδοναῖς ὑμῶν δαπανήσητε). Third, in accordance with the way James speaks of the rich elsewhere, it is very possible that the "you" in Jas 4:1–12 refers to the rich.[48]

---

and Wealth in James, 32–37.

43. Edgar, *Has God Not Chosen the Poor*, 105.

44. According to Raymond C. Ortlund, the covenant community's relationship with God is of a marital nature, so failure to live out the union with God would be considered as whoredom. The Pentateuch and the prophetic books demonstrate that Israel commits whoredom, for they turned to idols, other than worshipping YHWH. James takes on the similar concept of μοιχαλίδες (*Whoredom*, 8–11, 137–43); see also Allison, *James*, 607; Edgar, *Has God Not Chosen the Poor*, 103.

45. Edgar, *Has God Not Chosen the Poor*, 103–4.

46. Josephus used ἐπιθυμιῶν and ἡδονῆς as synonyms (see *Ant.* 18.340); James refutes "you" who desire but do not have or satisfy (Jas 4:2); a similar idea to this is found in Philo, *Leg.* 3.149: ἡ δέ ἐπιθυμία πληροῦται μέν οὐδέποτε ("the desire is never filled up"), in which context Philo blamed those people who had rushed with eagerness to wine and other luxuries.

47. BDAG, "δαπανάω," 171.

48. Allison also implies that the "you" here must refer to the rich, as he indicates: "Given what James has to say about the rich elsewhere, the reader may think of the well-to-do spending money on themselves" (*James*, 607).

Finally, the "you" whom the author addresses throughout 4:13—5:6 are the rich. He argues against the rich with a series of imperatives ("you rich people, weep and wail for the miseries"). The author criticizes the rich for being double-minded, unfaithful to God ("adulteresses"), and committing sins. The sin of the rich is that "they know the good thing to do, but they fail to do it" (4:17). This corresponds to 1:27, where the pure and undefiled before God care for orphans and widows in their distress. In short, the author's critique of the rich is based on their ethical behavior, whether they show love toward the poor. In other words, their behavior is evaluated on the basis of religious fidelity—their relationships with God and the world.

In conclusion, the author's designations for his audience show that he has at least two groups in his mind—the poor, who are afflicted and mistreated, and the rich, who do the mistreating. It can also be inferred that there is a group within the audience whose sympathy toward the poor the author seeks to gain.[49]

A TEXTUAL ANALYSIS OF JAMES 2:14–26

A dominant concern of 2:14–26 is the suffering of the socially marginalized. Just as James was remembered as a man living a life of poverty and having suffered greatly,[50] the Epistle of James is filled with encouragement for those who suffer (1:2–4, 12; 5:7–11), and pleads for the poor while criticizing the rich (1:9–11, 26–27; 2:1–13; 4:13—5:6). In the opening clause, the author addresses the audience as "my brothers," and proceeds to encourage them to remain joyful with patient endurance amidst their difficult circumstances of testing (Jas 1:2–8). If these brothers in testing are paralleled with the brother who is in lowly circumstances (ὁ ἀδελφὸς ὁ ταπεινὸς), then vv. 9–11 echo the previous instruction to the brothers in temptation.[51] The reversal of the antithesis between lowly and exalted and rich and lowly encourages the audience to view low status positively

---

49. See ibid., 45–46, where he argues that three groups of the community are implied in the text. First, the community must be filled with poor who are under oppression. Secondly, the rich in the community seem not to show mercy to those in need. Thirdly, it can be inferred that there is a group of the audience that the author attempts to affect and seeks to gain their sympathy toward the mistreated, the poor.

50. Refer to the discussion on James as the brother of Jesus in ibid., 30.

51. Edgar, *Has God Not Chosen the Poor*, 147.

by showing the downfall of the rich,[52] since "the rich will disappear like
a flower in the field" (v. 10). Verse 12 offers positive encouragement to
those in difficult circumstances, for those who stand the test will receive
the crown of life in the Lord.

The pericope of Jas 2:14–26 shares the concern for the marginalized
found in the previous parts of the book. In his address "my brothers"
(ἀδελφοί μου), the author demonstrates the proper attitude toward the
rich and the socially marginal poor in 2:1–13. They are not to treat the
poor with discrimination, but in a way that fulfills the royal law, which is
to "love your neighbor as yourself" (2:8–9). The neighbor here can refer
to the brothers or sisters in 2:15–16. Moreover, the author reverses the
status of the rich and the poor in terms of their religious faith in God's eschatological order. Instead of choosing the rich, God chose the poor to be
rich in faith and to inherit the kingdom (2:5). It is in this literary context
that the issue of faith and works is introduced (2:14–26). A concluding
indicator of the author's attitude toward rich and poor is his attack on
the rich (4:13—5:6). Hence the whole section of 2:14–26 is permeated by
the theme that God has reversed the status of the poor, and it is the poor
whom God has chosen.

It might seem that the epistle argues against Paul on the relationship between faith and works. However, reading Jas 2:14–26 in its literary
context indicates that it is a sub-section even within ch. 2. Clearly for the
author, "work" is about caring for the poor or the marginalized, as the
following analysis will demonstrate.

An Analysis of James 2:14–17: Faith Alone (Mere Words)
without Works

The direct address "my brothers" in Jas 2:14 indicates a new topic. The
section begins with a rhetorical question, τί τὸ ὄφελος (what good is it?).
From the table below, it can be seen that the structure of 2:14a is parallel to that of 2:15–16. Both structures are governed by the interrogative
clause τί τὸ ὄφελος ("What good is it?"), modified by complex ἐάν conditional clauses. In 2:14a, the ἐάν conditional clause, "if one says to have
faith but does not have works," is illustrated by the example in 2:15–16
where a brother or sister is naked and lacks daily food, and nothing is
done but to say to him/her, "go in peace, keep warm, and eat to the full."
"Faith" (πίστις), that is, the one claiming faith, carries a negative tone,

52. Ibid., 146–49; Maynard-Reid, *Poverty and Wealth in James*, 38–47.

because this faith is not accompanied by corresponding deeds. It is note-worthy that the brother or sister depicted here is clearly identified with the socially marginal poor.[53] The person dramatically lacks clothing to the point of being naked (γυμνοί), and also lacks daily food (ἐφημέρου τροφή). The author addresses these persons as "brother or sister" (v. 15), thereby showing his tender concern for the marginalized class. Mean-while the author addresses the audience as "my brothers" (2:14; cf. 2:1),[54] and appeals to them not to respond to the poor with a peace-greeting without any material support. It can be inferred that this audience be-longs to the group whose sympathy toward the poor the author attempts to arouse. He argues that the one who claims to have faith cannot save himself (2:14b μὴ δύναται . . . σῶσαι αὐτόν). The phrase μὴ δύναται . . . σῶσαι involves the eschatological salvation envisaged in 1:21, 2:13, and 4:12.[55] In other words, the author connects religious piety/faith with merciful deeds toward the marginalized (cf. 1:27). He then concludes in v. 17 that "faith without works is dead."

2:14a	2:15–16
Τί τὸ ὄφελος,	τί τὸ ὄφελος;
ἀδελφοί μου,	
ἐὰν πίστιν λέγῃ τις ἔχειν	ἐὰν ἀδελφὸς ἢ ἀδελφὴ γυμνοὶ ὑπάρχωσιν καὶ λειπόμενοι τῆς ἐφημέρου τροφῆς εἴπῃ δέ τις αὐτοῖς ἐξ ὑμῶν· ὑπάγετε ἐν εἰρήνῃ, θερμαίνεσθε καὶ χορτάζεσθε,
ἔργα δὲ μὴ ἔχῃ;	μὴ δῶτε δὲ αὐτοῖς τὰ ἐπιτήδεια τοῦ σώματος,
2:14b	**2:17**
μὴ δύναται ἡ πίστις σῶσαι αὐτόν;	οὕτως καὶ ἡ πίστις, ἐὰν μὴ ἔχῃ ἔργα, νεκρά ἐστιν καθ᾽ ἑαυτήν.

This critique of the separation of faith from works occurs repeatedly. Early on, the author contrasts the doer of the word with the mere hearer (1:22). The chains "to say to have faith," "to say good things without do-ing," and "to be only hearers" appear in opposite semantic relationship with "works" or "doings." The former is valued negatively, e.g., "deceiv-ing," "dead," or "useless." The latter is valued positively, stressing concern

---

53. Ibid., 169.

54. In Jas 2:1 the author obviously persuades "my brother" not to show partially.

55. McKnight, *Letter of James*, 229; Allison, *James*, 461–62.

for the poor (Jas 2:1–7; cf. Lev 19:15–18), love of the neighbor (Jas 2:8; cf. Lev 19:15), care for orphans and widows in their distress (Jas 1:27), and being a doer of the word (1:25). Hence, for the author, non-dead faith (living faith) is demonstrated through the concern for the needy and the socially marginalized.

An Analysis of James 2:18–26

With the adversative conjunction ἀλλά, the author advances his argument that faith without works is invalid or useless. This section shares a similar pattern with Jas 2:14–17. It begins with a critique of the separation of faith from works (2:18a vs. 2:14a), and then provides a theological-creedal argument (2:18b–19 vs. 2:14b). This is followed by positive and negative examples to reinforce the point of the ineffectiveness of faith without works (2:21–25 vs. 2:15–16), finally concluding with the statement, "faith without works is dead" (2:26 vs. 2:17). Although similar in pattern to vv. 14–17, the argument of this section is clearly more detailed.

In vv. 18–19, the author employs the speech pattern of an interlocutor. There has been much controversy over the identity of the speaker (who τις refers to), and where the projected speech introduced with ἐρεῖ ends. Numerous scholarly interpretations have been postulated.[56] This paper agrees with the view that the punctuation falls after κἀγὼ ἔργα ἔχω (and I have works). That is, the τις of v. 18 is the same as that in v. 14, the opponent of James, who separates faith from work. The author opposes this separation by arguing that "if you show me your faith without works, I will show you my faith by my works" (v. 18b).[57] Therefore, v. 18 would read as follows: "Someone will say, 'you have faith, I have works,'" to which James responds, "Show me your faith without works, and I will show you my faith from my works." In v. 19, the author provides a further theological argument. Faith or belief is allied with the Jewish *Shema*, "God is one."[58] Here James's concept of faith refers to mental agreement—that is, intellectual belief rather than personal commitment. The author assesses this creedal-only faith negatively. First, he points out that

---

56. See Allison, *James*, 468–71, where he summarized twelve explanations for these. See also McKnight, "James 2:18a," 355–64.

57. Ropes, *Epistle of St. James*, 208–14; Hartin, *James*, 151–52; Johnson, *Letter of James*, 239–40; Moo, *James*, 126–30.

58. The monotheistic confession alludes to Deut 6:4, "The Lord is our God, the Lord alone," or "The Lord our God, the Lord is one."

the demons share a similar confessional faith, albeit with fear (v. 19b). Second, he evaluates faith without works as "barrenness" (ἀργή), echoing the rhetorical question in v. 14b—"Is mere faith able to save you?" Again, the author argues that true faith is accompanied by works, and vv. 18–20 strengthens his refutation of separation of faith and works in v. 14.

In contrast to vv. 15–16, vv. 21–25 provide two positive examples of faith combining with works. The exemplar Abraham is the first example in vv. 21–24. He is designated as "our father," who, as the basis for membership in the people of God,[59] was justified by works (v. 21b). It has been noted that the phrase "justified by works" (ἐξ ἔργων ἐδικαιώθη) uses the plural form, whereas the aorist participle clause ἀνενέγκας Ἰσαὰκ τὸν υἱὸν αὐτοῦ ἐπὶ τὸ θυσιαστήριον ("when he offered his son Isaac on the altar") describes only one event. Following Ward, some scholars have argued that the sacrifice of Isaac is only one instance of a larger collection of deeds.[60] In the words of McKnight, it "sums up all the other works in the testing of Abraham's faith,"[61] which is a common theme in the Jewish tradition (Jub. 19, Philo, Abr. 167).[62] In v. 22, the author refers twice to plural works, i.e., faith working together with works and faith being completed by works. The plural "works" could refer to a series of works, or tests, of Abraham's faith. This is explained in v. 23 by the alliance of the quotation of Gen 15:6 with a reference to Abraham as God's friend (2 Chr 20:7; Isa 41:8; cf. Gen 18:7; Philo, Sobr. 56).[63] Philo has connected the concept of Abraham as "God's friend" with Gen 18:7. In this perspective, the author links Gen 15:6 with the sacrifice of Isaac (Gen 22) and also with Gen 18:7. He implies that "works" refer to the series of tests of Abraham's faith, including Abraham's hospitality to the three travelers in Gen 18. Also, a Jewish tradition views the Aqedah as the apex of the series of

---

59. Allison, *James*, 481–82.

60. Ward, "Works of Abraham," 283–90; McKnight, *Letter of James*, 245–51.

61. McKnight, *Letter of James*, 250.

62. McKnight has argued that the Aqedah is the primordial or preeminent act of faith (ibid., 250). Prior to the Aqedah was Abraham's hospitable receiving of the three travelers, and it is this incident that led to the birth of Isaac (Gen 18). It is worthy of noticing that in Gen 18, Abraham's welcoming the three travelers includes washing their feet and providing them food and rest, which is in contrast to the example in Jas 2:15–16.

63. According to Philo, *Sobr.* 56, God speaks in the case of Abraham, μὴ ἐπικαλύψω ἐγὼ ἀπὸ Ἀβραὰμ τοῦ φίλου μου; ("I should not hide from Abraham my friend, should I?"), which is close to Gen 18:7 LXX: "I should not hide from Abraham what I am about to do, should I?"

Abraham's tests.[64] Verse 23 is the central focus of vv. 22–24 in the middle of the two projection clauses (v. 22 and v. 24) that are governed by "you see" in the present tense form (βλέπεις, ὁρᾶτε):

Verse 22: βλέπεις ὅτι ἡ πίστις συνήργει . . . ἐκ τῶν ἔργων

Verse 24: ὁρᾶτε ὅτι ἐξ ἔργων δικαιοῦται ἄνθρωπος καὶ οὐκ ἐκ πίστεως μόνον

Therefore, it is apparent that the significance of v. 23 is to link Abraham's faith with a series of his works, particularly his hospitality, and that this combination illustrates the statement that faith is completed by works (v. 22) and that a person is justified by works and not by faith alone (v. 24). In addition, in vv. 21–24 the implied theme of the hospitality of Abraham corresponds with the hospitality of the second exemplar, Rahab.

With the connective καί and the adverb ὁμοίως (likewise), Rahab is introduced. The structures of v. 21 and v. 25 are parallel:

	2:21	2:25
Introduction	Ἀβραὰμ ὁ πατὴρ ἡμῶν	Ῥαὰβ ἡ πόρνη
About justification	οὐκ ἐξ ἔργων ἐδικαιώθη;	οὐκ ἐξ ἔργων ἐδικαιώθη;
About deed(s)	ἀνενέγκας Ἰσαὰκ τὸν υἱὸν αὐτοῦ ἐπὶ τὸ θυσιαστήριον	ὑποδεξαμένη τοὺς ἀγγέλους καὶ ἑτέρᾳ ὁδῷ ἐκβαλοῦσα

An intriguing question is why the author juxtaposes the patriarchal father Abraham with the prostitute Rahab. Allison says the answer is "unknown."[65] The medieval theologian John Calvin, in his commentary on James, states the question directly: "This seems a strange procedure, to link such dissimilar characters. Why not select someone from the great number of the noble Patriarchs, to cite along with Abraham?"[66] Others view the association as "deliberate and provocative,"[67] while some even think that the author fails in his argument by contrasting Abraham with the extreme example of Rahab.[68]

64. The Jewish concept of viewing the Aqedah as the apex of Abraham's ten tests will be further discussed in the next section.

65. Allison, *James*, 501.

66. Calvin, *Calvin's Commentaries*, 286–87.

67. Adamson, *James*, 133.

68. Ropes, *Epistle of St. James*, 224–25.

Scholars have offered numerous explanations for the juxtaposition with Rahab, and I will list the significant ones with some comments. First, both figures were identified as proselytes.[69] However, there are many other proselytes in Jewish history, so why in particular was Rahab chosen, since she was paid scant attention before the Common Era?[70] Second, the author includes both sexes (male and female) in order to be gender inclusive.[71] However, Rahab is not the only female in scripture to be noted for good deeds. Third, Rahab was chosen because she was famous for her faith.[72] Fourth, in contrast with the third option, Rahab was chosen because she was an example of justification by deeds instead of faith.[73] Fifth, both Rahab and Abraham were representatives of hospitality.[74] Sixth, the author includes contrasting social classes of rich and poor—thus, the honorable patriarch and the poor marginal prostitute.[75]

While I do not find any one of these suggestions wholly convincing, the last two merit further attention. Abraham's hospitality was well known in Jewish literature.[76] In addition, as I have argued earlier, the plural "works" implies a series of tests of faith that Abraham encoun-

69. According to Pheme Perkins, "The combination of Abraham and Rahab as figures may have been based on their appeal to proselytes" (*First and Second Peter*, 114). Abraham was remembered as the convert to monotheism (Jub. 11:16–17; 12:1–8, 16–21; Philo, *Abr.* 69–71); Rahab's conversion is recorded in Josh 2.

70. Rahab appears in the Hebrew Bible only in Joshua and almost disappears in the intertestamental literature. According to Allison, "Neither the Apocrypha nor the Pseudepigrapha mention her. The two spies of Josh 2 can even be introduced in LAB 20.6–7 without intimation of her role. She is also missing from the Dead Sea Scrolls and Philo. Between Joshua and the Melkilta, the only extant Jewish work to comment on the woman is Josephus, who tells her story in *Ant.* 5.5–15, 26, 28–30" (*James*, 500).

71. According to Johnson, the use of a female is striking, and it is not accidental, since the figures of Abraham and Rahab correspond to "brother and sister" who are in need in 2:15 (*Letter of James*, 245).

72. Bauckham, *James*, 124–25. In Josh 2:12, Rahab asks the spies to give her "a sign of faith," by which she can know she and her family will be spared.

73. Popkes, *Brief des Jakobus*, 186. See also Allison, *James*, 504.

74. Ward, "Works of Abraham," 283–90; Hartin, *James*, 161.

75. Wall, "Intertextuality of Scripture," 221; Baker and Ellsworth, *Preaching James*, 72.

76. According to Ward, Abraham "appears as the paradigm of the hospitable man. Thus in *Avot of Rabbi Nathan* I, ch. 7, Abraham surpassed even Job in showing hospitality to the poor. The same view of Abraham appears in the *T. Abr.* The title 'friend' appears to be given Abraham especially because of his hospitality, and this hospitality deters the Angel of Death from touching Abraham" ("Works of Abraham," 286).

tered, so his welcoming of the three messengers in Gen 18 is implied in Jas 2:21–24. Rahab's hospitality is elaborated in Jas 2:25—ὑποδεξαμένη τοὺς ἀγγέλους (welcoming the messengers) and ἑτέρᾳ ὁδῷ ἐκβαλοῦσα (sending them the other way)—and the similar wording ὑποδεξαμένη and ἀγγέλους also occurs in Abraham's welcoming of the three travelers in Gen 18. While hospitality could be a reason for the linking of the two figures, this commonality does not completely explain why the writer of James chose to invoke these particular figures in this context. Wall has observed the opposing social classes that could be represented by Abraham and Rahab,[77] but their combination is not intended to simply contrast social classes. Instead, it is more likely that the author correlates the patriarch with the socially marginalized prostitute Rahab in a way that highlights their faithful similarities *despite* their social differences in order to elicit the audience's compassion and identification with the poor. This explains why Jas 2:14–26 is surrounded by texts related to the reversal status of rich and poor.

In sum, both sections of Jas 2:14–26 (vv. 14–17 and vv. 18–26) are concerned with the poor in the kingdom of God. Each uses examples in order to arouse the audience's compassion toward the marginalized class.

AN INTERTEXTUAL THEMATIC ANALYSIS: READING JAMES 2:14–26 WITH OTHER VOICES

Heteroglossic voices remain to be examined for a synoptic reading of Jas 2:14–26. Biblical texts are not produced on an island, since they are always in relationship with texts from wider Jewish literature and tradition. Listening to the voices of other texts can clarify, deepen, and extend the meaning of James's text. In the following, references to Abraham and Rahab in Jewish literature will be made in order to hear the voices that the text interacts with in some way.

Abraham in the Context of Early Jewish and Christian Literature

ABRAHAM'S FAITH AND WORKS IN EARLY JEWISH LITERATURE

Second Temple Jewish literature contains numerous accounts of Abraham's faith and works. God's promise of innumerable descendants (Gen 15) and Abraham's sacrifice of Isaac (the Aqedah, Gen 22) are well-known (e.g., 1 Macc 2; Wis 44; Jub. 17–18; Philo, *Virt.* 216, *Abr.* 167; Josephus,

---

77. Wall, "Intertextuality of Scripture," 230–31.

Ant. 1.223–33, etc.), and are recounted in greatest detail in the book of Jubilees.

Jubilees is believed to have been written in 170–150 BCE,[78] and likely was popular among Jews of the first century CE in Palestine.[79] The book retells the material in Genesis and the first half of Exodus. The story of Abraham plays an important role in Genesis (11:26—25:10), and has been rewritten in Jubilees in 11:14—23:8. According to James VanderKam, the purpose of this book's retelling of the earliest biblical stories is to critique the author's contemporaries' association with non-Jews by emphasizing the ancient covenant that separated Jews from the Gentiles.[80] In Jubilees, Abraham is depicted as a nearly perfect man, knowing and doing well God's will. In his last speech, he calls upon the Israelites to separate themselves from the Gentiles and to no longer associate with them (Jub. 22:16–19).

Jubilees omits Gen 12:11–15 from the sojourn in Egypt, in which Abram instructs Sarai not to tell the Pharaoh that she is his sister. Also omitted are depictions of Abram that may have created negative impressions, e.g., Abram's fear of being killed (Gen 12:12) and his attempt to save his own life.[81]

Abraham's works and faith are depicted in Jub. 13–18. After restoring booty to the king of Sodom, he receives nothing for the sake of the Lord's name. The Lord then makes a covenant of seed with him in his dream: "And he looked at the heavens and he saw the stars. And he said to him, 'Thus shall your seed be.' And he believed the Lord and it was counted for him as righteousness" (Jub. 14:5–6). After a portrayal of Abraham's deeds, the author summarizes:

> Now the Lord was aware that Abraham was faithful in every difficulty which he had told him. For he had tested him through his land and the famine; he had tested him through the wealth of kings; he had tested him again through his wife when she was taken forcibly, and through circumcision; and he had tested him through Ishmael and his servant girl Hagar when he sent them

78. VanderKam, *Jubilees: A Critical Text*, vi; see also Wintermute, "Jubilees," 2:44.

79. Instone-Brewer, "James as a Sermon," 252.

80. VanderKam, *Book of Jubilees*, 139–41. The author is probably a priest, who advocated that the Jews, as God's chosen people, were to be separated from the Gentiles. During the rule of Antiochus (175–64 BCE), there were Jews who wanted to make a covenant with the Gentiles and wished to join closely with non-Jews.

81. Van Ruiten, *Abraham in the Book of Jubilees*, 77.

away. In everything through which he tested him he was found faithful (Jub. 17:17–18).

For the writer of Jubilees, Abraham's faithfulness to God was not completed with one single act, but characterized his whole life.

Abraham's faithfulness reached its apex in his sacrifice of Isaac. After the sacrifice,

> He said, "I have sworn by myself," says the Lord: "because you have performed this command and have not refused me your first-born son whom you love, I will indeed bless you and will indeed multiply your descendants like the stars in the sky and like the sands on the seashore. Your descendants will possess the cities of their enemies. All the nations of the earth will be blessed through your descendants because of the fact that you have obeyed my command. I have made known to everyone that you are faithful to me in everything that I have told you. Go in peace" (Jub. 18:15–16).

These words echo Abraham's dream of the Lord's promise of the seed in Jub. 14. They also repeat that Abraham was faithful in every test. There is no separation of Abraham's faith from what he did in front of the Lord. Therefore, the author of Jubilees views Abraham's faith as a series of deeds, with no chronological distance between Abraham's belief in God's promise (Gen 15) and the Aqedah (Gen 22). As Richard Bauckham has pointed out, it is not new in Jewish tradition to regard "the Aqedah as the supreme instance of Abraham's faith working along with his works."[82]

Wisdom of Ben Sira and 1 Maccabees share a similar view of Abraham's faith and works.[83] Both state that Abraham was found faithful when tested, which can refer to the series of tests that Abraham encountered as recounted in Jubilees (Jub. 17:17–18; cf. 1 Macc 2:52; Sir 44:20). Consistent with Jubilees, both Wisdom of Ben Sira and 1 Maccabees argue for separation of the Gentiles in order to safeguard Israel's identity as God's chosen people. If the Aqedah is considered the climax of the

---

82. Bauckham, *James*, 123.

83. The apocryphal book Wisdom of Ben Sira was likely compiled sometime in the first quarter of the second century BCE, which is before the Maccabean crisis under Antiochus IV. It is noted that the teaching of Ben Sira, as a series of aphorisms and reflections on Israel's Scriptures, is not systematic, but it covers broad subjects concerning the Scriptures, such as God, the election of Israel, retribution, repentance, faith, good works, and fear of the Lord. See Skehan and Di Lella, *Wisdom of Ben Sira*, 9, 75, 131.

tests, the plural ἔργον in Jas 2:21–23 can refer to the same series of tests of Abraham as in the Jewish tradition.[84]

It has been noted that Jewish tradition depicts Abraham as a nearly perfect man and aims to remind the Israelites to separate themselves from the impure Gentile nations in order to safeguard their identity as his seed. James, however, places the most noble patriarchal father with a socially despised woman, setting him side by side with the impure Canaanite prostitute Rahab in order to identify with the marginalized in his community. Therefore, when Jas 2:21–25 is read intertextually with the Jewish tradition, it is apparent that the epistle's interweaving of faith with works, though similar in lauding Abraham as a faithful man of good deeds, diverges from that tradition by coupling the Patriarch Abraham indiscriminately with the harlot Rahab. James's allying of Abraham's faith and works with Rahab's is unprecedented in Second Temple Jewish literature.

Abraham's Faith and Works in Paul and Hebrews

Paul's teaching on Abraham's faith and works concentrates in Rom 4 and Gal 2, and may appear to contradict the view of James. In Rom 4:2–3, Paul argues that Abraham was not justified by works, but by his faith in God, which was reckoned to him as righteousness. Paul uses chronological distance to argue that Abraham's faith, not works, was the basis for God reckoning him righteous, since Abraham was considered to be righteous before he was circumcised. "Work" for Paul refers to circumcision, one of the identity markers of God's chosen people. Hence it is faith—wholehearted trust in God—and not works that certifies Abraham as God's chosen. Paul also ties works to the law; for example, in Gal 2:16 Paul wrote, "Yet we know that a person is not justified by works of the law but through faith in Jesus Christ." But does this mean that James contradicts Paul's claim that trust in God establishes and maintains one in the people of God? By no means. Paul's separation of faith from works of law does not contradict James because the two writers emphasize different aspects of faith and works. As we saw, faith for James refers to intellectual

---

84. Instone-Brewer shares a similar view. For him, the reference to the works of Abraham implies that James was thinking of other incidents in Abraham's life, other tests that demonstrated his faith, ("James as a Sermon," 255). Also, Wall holds this view as well; see "Intertextuality of Scripture," 224–26. Ward, however, argues that the works refer to the story of Abraham's reception of the three travelers (Gen 18), indicating his hospitality ("Works of Abraham," 286).

assent, and works refer to deeds of charity. Paul, however, views faith as full trust and dependence on God and his Son sent in the fullness of time.

In Heb 11:17–19, the author associates faith with Abraham's sacrifice of Isaac—πίστει προσενήνοχεν Ἀβραὰμ τὸν Ἰσαὰκ πειραζόμενος καὶ τὸν μονογενῆ προσέφερεν ("by faith Abraham, when put to the *test*, offered up Isaac, his only son")—making it seem that Abraham's faith is expressed through the Aqedah. But it is Abraham's trust in God's power to bring back the dead (λογισάμενος ὅτι καὶ ἐκ νεκρῶν ἐγείρειν δυνατὸς ὁ θεός) that actually constitutes his faith. Thus Hebrews aligns more closely with Paul than with James.

In conclusion, as an apostle for the Gentiles, Paul is concerned with justification by faith because of his Gentile mission and because of attempts by his opponents to impose the Mosaic Law on his converts. Paul separates faith from the works of the law as the means to the blessings of salvation for both Jews and Gentiles. James addresses different issues. Although his wording about justification differs from Paul, it cannot be concluded that James argues against Paul or Paulinism.

Rahab in the Context of Early Jewish and Christian Literature

RAHAB IN EARLY JEWISH LITERATURE

Before discussing Rahab in early Jewish literature, it will be helpful to recall how her story is depicted in the Hebrew Bible (Josh 2 and 6:15–25). Before the Israelites enter Canaan, Joshua sends two spies to view Jericho. A prostitute named Rahab receives them and then helps them escape from the king of Jericho because she has heard of the great wonders done by Yahweh for Israel during their exodus from Egypt. Believing that this God will help the Israelites to conquer Canaan as well, Rahab asks the spies to keep her and her family safe when they attack Jericho. When Jericho is taken, Joshua protects Rahab and her family as promised.

This story raises several interesting issues. For example, the prostitute is named, but the two spies are not. The name Rahab and the label "prostitute" are mentioned five times. The name goes with the label almost every time it appears except in Josh 2:3, and the label without the name is spoken once when Joshua asks the two spies to go into the prostitute's house and bring the family out (Josh 6:22). It seems that Rahab's identity as a prostitute is well known in Jericho.[85] In the book of Joshua,

85. In a Jewish tradition, pre-conversion Rahab has been depicted as faithless "in terms of her relationships with men and her spiritual allegiances"; also, Rahab's beauty

however, there is an absence of any moral comment about her being a prostitute, although prostitution was regarded as a shameful profession in Jewish culture.[86]

Although little is said about Rahab in early Jewish literature, there are a few references to her. It seems that Rahab's acceptance of Jewish beliefs made her the archetypal Gentile proselyte.[87] For this exegetical tradition, Rahab's pre-conversion life as a prostitute contrasts with her repentant life, which emphasizes that one can convert to the Jewish faith.[88] A second way the account of Rahab has been sanitized is to portray her as a woman of faith who has left her prostitution, married Joshua, and bore children from whom the prophets descended.[89]

Another way to make Rahab a respectable figure is to replace the label prostitute with "innkeeper," as in Josephus's account of her in the *Jewish Antiquities* (5.2–15, 28–30). In contrast with Josh 2, Josephus's portrayal of Rahab has several notable features not found in the biblical Joshua story. First, after a detailed search of the city, the spies go to an "inn" for their supper and then plan to depart (*Ant.* 5.5–7). In other words, Josephus presents Rahab's house as a true inn instead of a brothel, and the spies do not aim to sleep there; Rahab is merely a suitable hostess for them. Second, Rahab's testimony to God's wonders performed for the Israelites has been generalized into one statement: "[F]or so far she [Rahab] said she had been assured by those divine miracles of which she had been informed" (*Ant.* 5.12b). It seems that Josephus downplays Rahab's religious faith or knowledge.[90] Finally, in view of the exchange between Rahab and the two spies (and Joshua), it is Rahab's sheltering of the spies that preserves her and her family. Not only do they remain intact when the Israelite army kills the Canaanites and destroys Jericho, but Rahab is also repaid with lands and esteem.[91] Therefore, in Josephus's account,

---

(as one of the four beauties alongside Sarah, Abigail and Esther) made men unable to resist having sexual relations with her, including every king and tribal leader in the region (Foster, *Significance of Exemplars*, 108).

86. Ibid., 109.

87. Ibid.

88. Charles, "Rahab," 208. See also Foster, *Significance of Exemplars*, 109.

89. Charles, "Rahab," 208.

90. Cf. Begg, "Rahab Story in Josephus," 129.

91. It reads, "So these spies acknowledged that they owed her thanks for *what she had done* already, and nonetheless swore to *repay* her *kindness*, not only in words, but in *deeds*" (*Ant.* 5.13a). Again when the Israelites conquered the city, it reads, "And

Rahab becomes a moral figure, and it is her kind deed of sheltering and preserving the spies that saves her. James's reading of Rahab seems closer to Josephus's Rahab account in its emphasis on Rahab's hospitality over her faith. However, James does not sanitize Rahab, but retains her identity as a marginalized prostitute.

RAHAB IN EARLY CHRISTIAN CIRCLES

The New Testament writers who mention Rahab (and who are contemporaries of Josephus) are James, Matthew, and the author of Hebrews. Besides Jas 2:25, Rahab is mentioned in Heb 11:31 and Matt 1:5. In Hebrews, Rahab is labeled as a prostitute (ἡ πόρνη) as in Josh 2, and is lauded as an example of faith and hospitality by receiving the spies (δεξαμένη τοὺς κατασκόπους) in peace (11:31). James's depiction of Rahab is close to that of Hebrews, since both speak of her receiving the spies/messengers (ὑποδεξαμένη τοὺς ἀγγέλους). Hebrews, however, casts Rahab's deeds as an act of faith, while James stresses her works—receiving the messengers and sending them out by another way.

Matthew places Rahab in the Messiah's genealogy (1:5),[92] where she is identified as the foremother of Boaz, from whose branch King David comes. It is clear, therefore, that Rahab's status in Jewish tradition had been accepted by the time of the New Testament in some Christian communities.[93] In early Christian literature, the book of 1 Clement (12:1–8) praises Rahab as the harlot of faith and hospitality. Her faith is not considered different from Christian faith: "[T]hat she should hang out from her house a scarlet thread, thereby showing beforehand that through the blood of the Lord there shall be redemption unto all them that believe and hope on God" (1 Clem. 12:7). In Origen's *Homilies on Joshua*, Rahab is portrayed as the prostitute who received Joshua's messengers (the two spies) by faith and was filled with the Holy Spirit: "[T]he prostitute who

---

when she [Rahab] was brought to him, Joshua owned to her that they owed her thanks for her preservation of the spies; so he said he would not appear less than she in his *kindness* to her; whereupon he gave her certain lands immediately, and had her in great esteem ever afterwards" (*Ant.* 5.30b–c [emphasis mine]).

92. For discussion on whether Rahab, the wife of Salma, is the same Rahab in Josh 2, see Bauckham, "Tamar's Ancestry and Rahab's Marriage," 320–29. Bauckham pursues the basis of Rahab's marriage to Salma to 1 Chron 2:54–55; Salma's father Nahshon is identified as having lived in the same generation as Joshua, and is a contemporary of Rahab. This would indicate that Boaz's father Salma would refer to Boaz's forefather. "Father" in Matt 1:5 is not limited to a one-generation distance.

93. Foster, *Significance of Exemplars*, 112.

receives them [two spies] becomes, instead of a prostitute, a prophet. For she says, 'I know that the Lord your God has delivered this land to you.' You see how that one who was once a prostitute and impious and unclean, is now filled with the Holy Spirit" (*Homilies* 3.4). Hence in one branch of the early Christian circle, Rahab was portrayed as holy, playing a role in the Messiah's genealogy, even becoming a prophet filled with the Holy Spirit. By contrast, James's depiction of Rahab preserves her identity as the prostitute and emphasizes her hospitable deeds of receiving the spies, but does not attempt to upgrade her social or religious status.

Weaving Abraham into Rahab: James's Intertextual Voices

By employing Abraham as an exemplar, James does not follow Jewish tradition in showing Abraham's perfection, nor does he ask his audience to separate from the Gentiles as in Jubilees, Wisdom of Ben Sira, and 1 Maccabees. Otherwise he would not have paralleled Abraham with the Gentile prostitute Rahab. Also, James is not interested in Rahab's faith in God's salvation as in some early Christian circles. He describes Rahab as (1) a prostitute, (2) justified by works, and (3) the one who welcomed the messengers and hospitably sent them off. But the question is why James interweaves the patriarchal father with the prostitute Rahab, describing both their works as resulting in justification and combining them as two equal exemplars by the connective phrase ὁμοίως ... καὶ. Based on the preceding analysis, this paper postulates that the alliance of the respectable patriarchal father Abraham with the prostitute Rahab seeks to lead the audience to identify with the marginalized social class and to elicit their compassion, mercy, and help toward the poor and needy, the least, in their community.

This understanding fits the argumentation of Jas 2. After warning against bias favoring the rich and after appealing for equal treatment of rich and poor (2:1–7), James asks his audience to do according to the Scripture—that is, to "love your neighbor as yourself," because the royal law demands care for the poor. Otherwise, judgment will come (2:8–13). James 2:14–26 is set in this literary context. It continues to ask the audience to show mercy toward the destitute (2:15–16), because one's living faith must be accompanied with merciful deeds. In addition, in Jas 1 and 2 nearly all deeds refer to acts of mercy toward the poor, the oppressed, and the weak. Abraham and Rahab as two exemplars sustain the appeal to love neighbors as those who are in need. Abraham, the noblest patriarchal father, is placed in the same context as the marginalized prostitute. Thus, it is not right to be prejudiced against the poor and to favor the rich (cf. 2:1–4). What matters is not the social status of the audience, but how the audience treats the lowly class.

CONCLUSION

This paper has examined the social context of James through the language used in the text, and has analyzed Jas 2:14–26 in detail to discern its structure and meaning in its literary context. Intertextual texts from the related Second Temple Jewish and early Christian literature have been utilized to compare James's use of the scriptural figures Abraham and Rahab. An intertextual methodology has been employed to examine Jas 2:14–26 in order to explore the author's viewpoint on the social classes of his community. The investigation found that James allies with the socially marginalized through his close association of the noble patriarchal father Abraham with the despised prostitute Rahab. James also diverges from Jewish tradition and literature in his assessment of Abraham and Rahab. He neither tries to argue for the perfection of Abraham, nor to sanitize Rahab as a faithful person filled with the Holy Spirit. Rather, he identifies himself with the socially marginalized in order to arouse his audience to show compassion toward the needy. His epistle to his community addresses an audience consisting of those who are rich and those who are poor, and he attempts to move them toward being a community of caring people who reach across barriers of social status. He urges them to understand that "the wisdom that comes from above is first of all pure; then peace-loving, considerate, submissive, full of mercy and good fruit, impartial, and sincere" (Jas 3:17).

BIBLIOGRAPHY

Adamson, James B. *The Epistle of James*. NICNT. Grand Rapids: Eerdmans, 1976.

Allison, Dale C., Jr. *A Critical and Exegetical Commentary on the Epistle of James*. ICC. New York: Bloomsbury T. & T. Clark, 2013.

Aune, David E. "Apocalypticism." In *Dictionary of Paul and His Letters*, edited by Gerald F. Hawthorne et al., 25–35. Downers Grove, IL: InterVarsity, 1993.

Baker, William R., and Thomas D. Ellsworth. *Preaching James*. St. Louis: Chalice, 2004.

Bakhtin, Mikhail M. "Discourse in the Novel." In *The Dialogic Imagination: Four Essays*, edited by Michael Holquist, 259–422. Translated by Caryl Emerson and Michael Holquist. Austin: University of Texas Press, 1981.

Batten, Alicia J. "The Jesus Tradition and the Letter of James." *RevExp* 108 (2011) 381–90.

————. *What Are They Saying about the Letter of James?* WATSA. New York: Paulist, 2009.

Bauckham, Richard J. "Tamar's Ancestry and Rahab's Marriage: Two Problems in the Matthean Genealogy." *NovT* 37 (1995) 320–29.

————. *James: Wisdom of James, Disciple of Jesus the Sage.* London: Routledge, 1999.

Beale, G. K. *John's Use of the Old Testament in Revelation.* JSNTSup 166. Sheffield: Sheffield Academic, 1998.

Begg, Christopher T. "The Rahab Story in Josephus." *LASBF* 55 (2005) 113–30.

Boda, Mark J. "Quotation and Allusion." In *Dictionary of Biblical Criticism and Interpretation*, edited by Stanley E. Porter, 296–97. London: Routledge, 2007.

Brodie, Thomas L., et al. "Conclusion: Problems of Method." In *The Intertextuality of the Epistles: Explorations of Theory and Practice*, edited by Thomas L. Brodie et al., 284–96. NTM 10. Sheffield: Sheffield Phoenix, 2006.

Calvin, John. *Calvin's Commentaries: A Harmony of the Gospels Matthew, Mark and Luke, and the Epistles of James and Jude*, edited by David W. Torrance and Thomas F. Torrance. Translated by A. W. Morrison. Grand Rapids: Eerdmans, 1972.

Cargal, Timothy B. *Restoring the Diaspora: Discursive Structure and Purpose in the Epistle of James.* SBLDS 144. Atlanta: Scholars, 1993.

Charles, Ronald. "Rahab: A Righteous Whore in James." *Neot* 45 (2011) 206–20.

Cheung, Luke L. *The Genre, Composition and Hermeneutics of the Epistle of James.* Carlisle, Cumbria, UK: Paternoster, 2003.

Deppe, Dean B. "The Sayings of Jesus in the Epistle of James." PhD diss., Free University of Amsterdam, 1989.

Dibelius, Martin. *James: Commentary on the Epistle of James*, edited by H. Koester. Revised by H. Greeven. Translated by M. Williams. Hermeneia. Philadelphia: Fortress, 1976.

Dowd, Sharyn E. "Faith That Works: James 2:14–26." *RevExp* 97 (2000) 195–205.

Dunn, James D. G. *Christianity in the Making.* Vol. 2, *Beginning from Jerusalem.* Grand Rapids: Eerdmans, 2009.

Edgar, David Hutchinson. *Has God Not Chosen the Poor? The Social Setting of the Epistle of James.* LNTS 206. Sheffield: Sheffield Academic, 2001.

Foster, Robert J. *The Significance of Exemplars for the Interpretation of the Letter of James.* WUNT 2.376. Tübingen: Mohr Siebeck, 2014.

Hartin, Patrick J. *James.* Sacra Pagina 14. Collegeville, MN: Liturgical, 2003.

————. *James and the Q Sayings of Jesus.* JSNTSup 47. Sheffield: Sheffield Academic, 1991.

Hatina, Thomas R. "Intertextuality and Historical Criticism in New Testament Studies: Is There a Relationship?" *BibInt* 7 (1997) 28–43.

Hays, Richard B. *Echoes of Scripture in the Letters of Paul.* New Haven: Yale University Press, 1989.

Instone-Brewer, David. "James as a Sermon on the Trials of Abraham." In *The New Testament in Its First Century Setting: Essays on Context and Background in Honour of B. W. Winter on His 65th Birthday*, edited by P. J. Williams et al., 250–68. Grand Rapids: Eerdmans, 2004.

Jenkins, C. Ryan. "Faith and Works in Paul and James." *BSac* 159 (2002) 62–78.

Johnson, Luke Timothy. *The Letter of James: A New Translation with Introduction and Commentary.* AB 37A. New York: Doubleday, 1995.

————. "The Social World of James: Literary Analysis and Historical Reconstruction." In *The Social World of the First Christians: Essays in Honor of Wayne A. Meeks*, edited by L. Michael White and O. Larry Yarbrough, 178–97. Minneapolis: Fortress, 1995.

Lemke, Jay L. "Discourses in Conflict: Heteroglossia and Text Semantics." In *Systemic Functional Approaches to Discourse: Selected Papers from the 12th International Systemic Workshop*, edited by James D. Benson and William S. Greaves, 29–50. Norwood, NJ: Ablex, 1988.

————. "Interpersonal Meaning in Discourse: Value Orientations." In *Advances in Systemic Linguistics: Recent Theory and Practice*, edited by Martin Davies and Louise Ravelli, 82–104. OLS. London: Pinter, 1992.

————. "Intertextuality and Text Semantics." In *Discourse in Society: Systemic Functional Perspectives: Meaning and Choice: Studies for Michael Halliday*, edited by Peter H. Fries and Michael Gregory, 85–114. Norwood, NJ: Ablex, 1995.

————. "Intertextuality and the Project of Text Linguistics: A Response to de Beaugrande." *Text* 20 (2000) 221–25.

————. *Textual Politics: Discourse and Social Dynamics*. Critical Perspectives on Literacy and Education. London: Taylor & Francis, 1995.

Limberis, Vasilikj. "The Provenance of the Caliphate Church: James 2.17–26 and Galatians 3 Reconsidered." In *Early Christian Interpretation of the Scriptures of Israel: Investigations and Proposals*, edited by Craig A. Evans and James A. Sanders, 397–420. JSNTSup 148. Sheffield: Sheffield Academic, 1997.

Manning, Gary T., Jr. *Echoes of a Prophet: The Use of Ezekiel in the Gospel of John and in Literature of the Second Temple Period*. LNTS 270. London: T. & T. Clark, 2004.

Martin, Ralph P. "The Life-Setting of the Epistle of James in the Light of Jewish History." In *Biblical and Near Eastern Studies: Essays in Honor of William Sanford LaSor*, edited by Gary A. Tuttle, 97–103. Grand Rapids: Eerdmans, 1978.

Maxwell, David R. "Justified by Works and Not by Faith Alone: Reconciling Paul and James." *ConJ* 33 (2007) 375–78.

Maynard-Reid, Pedrito U. *Poverty and Wealth in James*. Maryknoll, NY: Orbis, 1987.

McKnight, Scot. "James 2:18a: The Unidentifiable Interlocutor." *WTJ* 52 (1990) 355–64.

————. *The Letter of James*. NICNT. Grand Rapids: Eerdmans, 2011.

Meeks, Wayne A. *The Moral World of the First Christians*. LEC 6. Philadelphia: Westminster, 1986.

Michaelis, Johann D. *Introduction to the New Testament*. Translated by Herbert Marsh. Vol. 4. 2nd ed. London: Luke Hanfard, 1802.

Moo, Douglas J. *The Letter of James*. PNTC. Grand Rapids: Eerdmans, 2000.

Morris, Pam, ed. *The Bakhtin Reader: Selected Writings of Bakhtin, Medvedev, Voloshinov*. London: Edward Arnold, 1994.

Moyise, Steve. *The Old Testament in the Book of Revelation*. JSNTSup 115. Sheffield: Sheffield Academic, 1995.

————. *Paul and Scripture*. Grand Rapids: Baker Academic, 2010.

Nienhuis, David R. *Not by Paul Alone: The Formation of the Catholic Epistle Collection and the Christian Canon*. Waco, TX: Baylor University Press, 2007.

Ortlund, Raymond C., Jr., *Whoredom: God's Unfaithful Wife in Biblical Theology*. NSBT. Grand Rapids: Eerdmans, 1996.

Pao, David, W. *Acts and the Isaianic New Exodus*. WUNT 2.130. Tübingen: Mohr Siebeck, 2000.

Perkins, Pheme. *First and Second Peter, James, and Jude*. IBC. Louisville: John Knox, 1995.

Popkes, Wiard. "The Composition of James and Intertextuality: An Exercise in Methodology." *ST* 51 (1997) 91–112.

———. *Der Brief des Jakobus*. THKNT 14. Leipzig: Evangelische, 2001.

Rainbow, Paul A. *The Way of Salvation: The Role of Christian Obedience in Justification*. Waynesboro, GA: Paternoster, 2005.

Rakestraw, Robert V. "James 2:14–26: Does James Contradict the Pauline Soteriology?" *CTR* 1 (1986) 31–50.

Ropes, James H. *A Critical and Exegetical Commentary on the Epistle of St. James*. ICC. Edinburgh: T. & T. Clark, 1916.

Skehan, Patrick W., and Alexander A. Di Lella. *The Wisdom of Ben Sira: A New Translation with Notes*. AB 39. New York: Doubleday, 1987.

Soards, Marion L. "The Early Christian Interpretation of Abraham and the Place of James within that Context." *IBS* 9 (1987) 18–26.

Van der Westhuizen, J. D. N. "Stylistic Techniques and Their Functions in James 2.14–26." *Neot* 25 (1991) 89–107.

Van Ruiten, Jacques T. G. A. M. *Abraham in the Book of Jubilees: The Rewriting of Genesis 11:26—25:10 in the Book of Jubilees 11:14—23:8*. JSJSup 161. Leiden: Brill, 2012.

VanderKam, James C. *The Book of Jubilees: A Critical Text*. CSCO 88. Leuven: Peeters, 1989.

———. *The Book of Jubilees*. GAP. Sheffield: Sheffield Academic, 2001.

Verseput, Donald J. "Genre and Story: The Community Setting of the Epistle of James." *CBQ* 62 (2000) 96–110.

Wall, Robert W. "The Intertextuality of Scripture: the Example of Rahab (James 2:25)." In *Bible at Qumran: Text, Shape, and Interpretation*, edited by Peter W. Flint, 217–36. Grand Rapids: Eerdmans, 2001.

Wall, Robert W., and Eugene E. Lemcio. *The New Testament as Canon: A Reader in Canonical Criticism*. JSNTSup 76. Sheffield: Sheffield Academic, 1992.

Ward, Roy B. "James and Paul: Critical Review." *ResQ* 7 (1963) 159–64.

———. "The Works of Abraham: James 2:14–26." *HTR* 61 (1968) 283–90.

Watson, Duane F. "James 2 in Light of Greco-Roman Schemes of Argumentation." *NTS* 39 (1993) 94–121.

Watson, Francis. *Paul and the Hermeneutics of Faith*. Edinburgh: T. & T. Clark, 2004.

Watts, Rikki E. *Isaiah's New Exodus and Mark*. WUNT 2.88. Tübingen: Mohr Siebeck, 1997.

Wilson, Stephen G. *Related Strangers: Jews and Christians, 70–170 C.E.* Minneapolis: Augsburg Fortress, 1995.

Wintermute, O. S. "Jubilees (Second Century B.C.)." In *The Old Testament Pseudepigrapha*, edited by James H. Charlesworth, 35–142. Vol. 2. Garden City: Doubleday, 1985.

Xue, Xiaxia. "An Intertextual Discourse Analysis of Romans 9:30—10:13." In *Modeling Biblical Language: Selected Papers from the McMaster Divinity College Linguistics Circle*, edited by Stanley E. Porter et al., 277–308. LBS 13. Leiden: Brill, 2016.

7

The Rules of "Engagement"

Assessing the Function of the Diatribe in James 2:14–26 Using Critical Discourse Analysis

ZACHARY K. DAWSON

INTRODUCTION

THE PAST GENERATION HAS seen a substantial influx of rhetorical analyses in biblical studies, many of which have focused on the letter of James. These analyses range in methods from those strictly addressing the conventions of ancient Greco-Roman rhetoric to those primarily concerned with employing modern rhetorical categories, while still others have used methods that incorporate both sets of categories to various extents.[1] All together they have created enough contradictory conclusions

---

1. For studies that employ ancient rhetorical categories to the Epistle of James see van der Westhuizen, "Stylistic Techniques," 89–107; Baasland, *Jakobsbrevet,* 177–78; Watson, "James 2," 94–121; Watson, "Rhetoric of James 3.1–12," 48–64. For studies that take a modern rhetorical approach see Wuellner, "Der Jakobusbrief," 5–66; Elliott, "The Epistle of James," 71–81. For one study that makes exceptional use of both ancient and modern categories of rhetoric see Batten, "Ideological Strategies," 6–26. Batten relies on modern rhetorical categories to facilitate discussion about the structure of the letter but makes use of ancient categories when discussing particular instantiations of ideological/rhetorical strategies. It is also appropriate to include here Thurén, "Risky Rhetoric," 262–84, who argues that the letter's effectiveness is contingent upon the audience's ability to follow the writer's rhetorical scheme. Although his study appeals to ancient categories of rhetoric, his approach is much more pragmatically executed with one of his primary focuses being to call into question Wuellner's generally accepted rhetorical structure of James.

to declare this area in New Testament studies far from unified.[2] A prime example of this is the multitude of suggested outlines of the rhetorical structure of the letter of James. A survey of the work of Ernst Baasland, Hubert Frankenmölle, and Wilhelm Wuellner typifies the field where, apart from their assessments that Jas 5:7–20 makes up the *peroratio*, there is no agreement on any of the rhetorical sections in the letter.[3] Moreover, most scholars classify James in the deliberative rhetoric species, but even the consensus with this most general of rhetorical categories eludes unanimity.[4] Lauri Thurén argues that James is a letter exemplifying epideictic rhetoric, despite the numerous exhortations characteristic of the deliberative species, because the text promotes already existing social values.[5] The larger problem concerning Thurén's conclusions, and those of Baasland, Frankenmölle, Wuellner, and others, is that they bring into Jacobean studies that which is a pervasive issue within the discipline of rhetorical criticism as a whole—the failure for scholars to agree how to identify and describe ancient categorical phenomena.[6]

To be sure, a reliable rhetorical criticism will account for ancient categories that a writer may have employed. Thus, the work of George A. Kennedy, which demonstrates a rhetorical criticism based upon classical categories described in the ancient Greek and Latin handbooks,[7] remains useful (though various problems with using this form of rhetorical criticism have been identified). However, while it has been well attested that biblical writers, including James, employed ancient rhetorical practices in their writings, identifying these practices is limited insofar as they mainly display a writer's competence to utilize a discourse form

2. See Martín-Asensio, "Hallidayan Functional Grammar," 84, who makes this same claim with reference to rhetorical criticism in biblical studies as a whole. Jacobean studies are no exception. For works assessing the landscape of Jacobean rhetorical analysis in recent scholarship see Watson, "Assessment of the Rhetoric," 99–120; Watson, "Rhetorical Criticism," 187–90; Batten, *What Are They Saying*, 16–26.

3. See Baasland, *Jakobsbrevet*, 177–78; Frankenmölle, "Das semantische Netz des Jakobusbriefes," 161–97; Wuellner, "Jacobusbrief," 5–66.

4. See van der Westhuizen, "Stylistic Techniques," 91–92; Watson, "James 2," 94–121; Watson, "Rhetoric of James 3.1–12," 48–64.

5. See Thurén, "Risky Rhetoric," 276–77.

6. See Di Marco, "Rhetoric and Hermeneutic," 479. See also Martín-Asensio, "Hallidayan Functional Grammar," 87 n. 17, who offers a concise discussion of this issue.

7. See Kennedy, *New Testament Interpretation*.

to exercise power as a socially adept agent.[8] In other words, identifying instantiated conventions shows why a text would not have been a rhetorical failure per se, but not how a writer navigates social relations in such a way to maximize compliance from the audience—that is, what rhetoric aims to accomplish. Norman Fairclough, a prominent Critical Discourse Analysis (CDA) theorist, insightfully comments on this particular limiting factor:

> The 'structure' option . . . has the virtue of showing events, actual discoursal practice, to be constrained by social conventions, norms, histories. It has the disadvantage of tending to defocus the event on the assumption that events are mere instantiations of structures, whereas the relationship of events to structures would appear to be less neat and less compliant. This privileges the perspective of reproduction rather than that of transformation, and the ideological conventionality and repetitiveness of events.[9]

Rhetorical criticism has tended to overemphasize how writers reduplicated conventional practices of argumentation, which in turn has inhibited progress because analyses to date have not accounted for certain important aspects of interpersonal relations in discourse. Certainly, discursive practices function ideologically as "identity kits" to obtain social goods,[10] and so they are indispensable for comprehensive analyses of

---

8. A number of other scholars who account for ancient categories in their rhetorical models have voiced objections against strictly adopting Kennedy's method. For example, Snyman, "Persuasion in Philippians 4.1–20," 325–37, who affirms Kennedy's contention that the categories of pathos, ethos, and logos are fundamental to ancient rhetoric, writes, "Classical rhetoric with all of its categories can be of help in understanding any written document, provided that it is not followed rigidly but rather used as a frame of reference for empirical study" (335). See also, Basevi and Chapa, "Rhetorical Function of a Pauline 'Hymn,'" 350, where they explain that Paul's rhetoric contains aspects of Jewish tradition, which affects the Greco-Roman persuasive tools he employs.

9. Fairclough, "Language and Ideology," 57. The use of the term "structure" in this context refers to societal structures, such as institutions and the social relationships within them. It should not be confused with "rhetorical structure" as used by biblical scholars, which refers to textual structures.

10. Lemke, *Textual Politics*, 12–13. The term "identity kit," taken from James Paul Gee's understanding of the ideological functionality of discourse, refers to the social habits that people embody (both verbally and nonverbally) that are characteristic of patterns of discourse. "Social goods" refers to those things that are considered to be good to have or bad to lose by a person, group, or society; one apparently universal

rhetoric, but issuing forth from them is the struggle to somehow reshape such practices for another social group to achieve a transformation of relations of power and solidarity[11]—a reorienting of a group of people to assume the writer's ideology. Because of this I suggest that a more productive way forward is not with the rhetorical critical method that grew to popularity in response to H. D. Betz's commentary on Galatians,[12] but with the analytic potential that sociolinguistic models can bring to bear on rhetorical features of New Testament documents.

One of the distinguishing features of rhetorical criticism is its basic assumption that a text must reveal its context; however, scholars who have couched the concept of "context" in various critical theories have produced an increasingly diverse and disunified discipline.[13] Wuellner summarizes the different directions rhetorical critics have gone in accounting for context in their work, ranging from the theory of intertextuality,[14] to the notion of the rhetorical situation, to the precepts that condition the writer's and reader's evaluative stances, and ideology.[15] While each theory of context for which Wuellner accounts brings its own explanatory potential to bear on texts, an ideal analysis would bring the diverse strengths of these theories into a proper balance and focus. It is my contention that Systemic Functional Linguistics provides a paradigm whereby this ideal can be achieved. I suggest that two major components are necessary for an improved descriptive method of rhetorical analysis. First is a social theory of discourse that accounts for how language functions in relation to social structures, practices, events, and tenor relations. This provides the necessary backdrop for interpreters to evaluate a writer's attempt to persuade an audience with persuasion being understood as the principal goal of rhetoric. Second is a theory of language that understands language as a semiotic system that mediates social activity, and that is equipped with the tools available to describe the linguistic phenomena of that system and how they correlate with social realities. While there are multiple

---

example is respect (a notion that varies, of course, depending upon one's context of culture). See Gee, *Social Linguistics and Literacies*, 18.

11. Fairclough, *Discourse and Social Change*, 87–88.

12. Betz, *Galatians*. See also Betz, "Literary Composition," 353–79.

13. Wuellner, "Where Is Rhetorical Criticism Taking Us," 449–50.

14. On intertextuality, Wuellner refers explicitly to Jonathan Culler's view. See Culler, *On Deconstruction*, 130–31, 135.

15. Wuellner, "Where Is Rhetorical Criticism Taking Us," 449–50.

prospects that demonstrate methodologies geared toward analyzing language in this way,[16] the present work will make use of the social theory of discourse espoused by Norman Fairclough (CDA) with particular attention given to ideology, Gramscian hegemony, and Bakhtinian dialogism.[17] These theoretical concepts in turn will be mediated through Hallidayan functional grammar by means of the system of Engagement developed by J. R. Martin and P. R. R. White. Oriented to be both socially and linguistically sensitive, this linguistic method will yield results that challenge common assumptions concerning the social environment and the role of the diatribe in James. The goal of this approach is not to promote an unbridled tongue for rhetorical analysis, but hopefully to propel a small rudder to begin redirecting the course of a much larger ship, the way we talk about the rhetoric of discourse in New Testament studies.

TOWARD A SOCIAL THEORY OF DISCOURSE

Drawing on the work of John Frow, Fairclough states that the ideology of a particular discourse needs to be understood as the appropriation of its function in use:

> Rather than particular types of discourse having inherent political or ideological values . . . different types of discourse in different social domains or institutional settings may come to be politically or ideologically 'invested' in particular ways. This implies that types of discourse may also come to be invested in different ways—they may come to be 'reinvested.'[18]

---

16. For an article assessing several potential linguistic approaches to analyzing the relationship between language and social activity, see Fewster, "Symbolizing Identity," 87–96.

17. The potential for exegesis that CDA holds for biblical studies has been relatively unexplored. However, see Porter "Is Critical Discourse Analysis Critical," 47–70, who concludes that when CDA is shed of its ideological commitments, it provides a helpful method for describing social relations in discursive context, among other strengths. For concise overviews of CDA as a method, see Locke, *Critical Discourse Analysis*; Fairclough et al., "Critical Discourse Analysis," 258–84.

18. Fairclough, *Discourse and Social Change*, 67. Cf. Frow, "Discourse and Power," 193–214. Fairclough uses the term "discourse" in a broader sense to refer to forms of social practice, which implies two things: (1) people can use language as a mode to act upon the world and each other, and as a mode of representation; and (2) a dialectical relationship exists between discourse (social practice) and social structure (*Discourse and Social Change*, 62–64).

This notion for the present study suggests that the diatribe as a type of discourse in the letter of James does not necessarily function as it did in other contexts.[19] Whereas diatribes were first used by philosophers as didactic tools in classroom settings, and then were later used in the preaching styles of Cynics and Stoics,[20] James writes from a different social domain entirely, namely first-century Christianity, which would guarantee some variability in how the diatribe is used in his letter.[21] James does not automatically take on the persona of a lecturer; the use of diatribe does not necessarily invoke the pedagogical activity of a classroom if in fact this discourse formation has been reinvested.[22] Might James have borrowed a type of discourse familiar to his audience, but utilized it to accomplish an unconventional end? If so, how then might we account for how new contexts constrain old practices? To begin, this section will account for aspects of social realities that constrain meaning in text and how a text can possibly function rhetorically to any success. By accounting for these constraints in play, the ways in which discourse types get reinvested becomes observable, which in turn paves a way for new rhetorical sensitivities.

19. See Olbricht, "Rhetorical Criticism," 327, who makes the similar point that, "While analyzing biblical documents according to the dictates of classical rhetoric may be of some help, even more helpful may be approaching the biblical documents as a separate genre, since it makes as much sense to declare a separate genre for these religious discourses as it does a separate genre for political assemblies, courts, and occasional discourses of praise and blame. The rhetoric of the 'biblical' genre will be generated through scrutiny of biblical texts and their unique features."

20. See Aune, *Literary Environment*, 200.

21. See Ropes, *Epistle of St. James*, 13–16, who notes a number of these differences. See also Stowers, *Diatribe*, 76, who, summarizing the goal of this discourse type states, "The instruction was not simply to impart knowledge, but to transform the students, to point out error and to cure it. Our review of the sources suggests that the dialogical element of the diatribe was an important part of this pedagogical approach." I concur with this assessment of the function of the diatribe as it developed in its secular contexts. What the present work seeks to show is that while the goal of the diatribe remains relatively static, the way in which it functions in context varies depending on social domain and context of situation. Cf. Watson, "James 2," 120, who notes how James shows the adaptability of diatribal features for rhetorical argumentative schemes.

22. Contra Stowers, "Diatribe," 74.

Ideology: Views and Strategies

Recent scholarship in biblical studies has tried to bring the slippery notion of ideology into clearer focus. Alicia Batten for one, whose article on ideological strategies in James has been a great help for writing this chapter, follows the works of Raymond Guess and Terry Eagleton in explaining the range of contemporary meanings that ideology assumes.[23] While I would encourage others to refer to Batten's article, it is necessary here to describe again Guess's categories of ideological criticism.

The development of the early Christian movement resulted from a process of resocialization; small "post-Jesus groups" assumed a revised identity and an ideology that served for members to understand the boundary markers of their "in-group."[24] Using the helpful insights of social-scientific criticism, Bruce Malina explains that the resocialization process includes the resolving of early conflicts while the negotiations of establishing normative guidelines for group behavior solidify.[25] This description pairs well with the multidisciplinary orientation of CDA that treats discourse analysis as a discipline extending beyond "how linguistics has traditionally written about 'language use', 'parole' or 'performance.'"[26] While linguistics is a prerequisite for discourse analysis, other backgrounds such as sociology, cultural-anthropology, (social-)psychology, and politics are also taken into account to show how "discourse is shaped by structures, but also contributes to shaping and reshaping them, to reproducing and transforming them."[27] The term "discourse" is defined here to refer to a form of social practice that contributes to the construction of social identities, social relationships, and systems of knowledge and belief.[28] While there are other forms of social practice, the term "discursive

23. Batten, "Ideological Strategies," 6–26. See Guess, *Idea of a Critical Theory*; Eagleton, *Ideology*.

24. Meeks, *First Urban Christians*, 86; Meeks, *Origins of Christian Morality*, 8, 18–36. See Dvorak, "Ask and Ye Shall Position the Readers" in this volume; Hartin, *James*, 13, who explains the purpose of the letter of James to be "socialization," defined synonymously with Meeks's term "resocialization." See also McCartney, *James*, 38, who endorses this same view.

25. Malina, *New Testament World*, 209.

26. Fairclough, *Discourse and Social Change*, 62.

27. Fairclough, "Language and Ideology," 59. See also, Fairclough, *Discourse as Social Change*, 66, where he states that this concept is a necessary criticism of the deterministic character of structuralism.

28. Fairclough, *Discourse and Social Change*, 63–64.

practice" is used to refer to those practices that explicitly use language, as well as the processes of production, distribution, and consumption.[29] The term "text" is reserved to refer to manifestations of discursive practice, a particular linguistic instance of social practice.[30]

In the discursive practice of established groups are beliefs, desires, values, motives, rituals, etc. Identifying ideological features such as these focuses on the descriptive sense of ideology: a non-evaluative, neutral approach that describes both discursive aspects (e.g., concepts, ideas, beliefs) and non-discursive aspects (e.g., gestures, attitudes, rituals),[31] and thereby acknowledges that every human group has an ideology. However, not *every* individual in a group will have the same beliefs, values, attitudes, and so on. Individuals, and even sub-groups within larger groups, contain variety and display diversity, which often leads to conflict.[32] Conflict can result in the undesirable consequence of group faction, which in turn prompts the production of discourse that seeks to achieve cohesion under a common ideology. Ideological criticism seeks to show how writers take up this task to construct social boundaries by promoting the ideological markers that are found in a particular group, to evaluate them as good, desirable, and necessary. This is ideology in the positive sense, where the definable feature is the idea of *constructing* ideology.[33] Conversely, ideology can be understood in a pejorative sense to describe how beliefs or behaviors can have a false or tainted origin that can even lead to legitimating reprehensible behavior. The pejorative sense identifies where agents in society are deluded in some way, either about themselves, their stances, their society, their values, etc.[34] The advantage of incorporating this view into an analysis is that it highlights the ways

---

29. Ibid., 71–72.

30. Ibid., 71.

31. Guess, *Idea of a Critical Theory*, 5–6. This sense of ideology is consonant with the view commonly used in biblical studies set forth by Elliott, *What Is Social-Scientific Criticism*, 130: "An integrated system of beliefs, perspectives, assumptions, and values, not necessarily true or false, that reflect the perceived needs and interests of a group or class at a particular time in history," who quotes from Davis, *Problem of Slavery*, 14. See Batten, "Ideological Strategies," 8, who makes this observation.

32. Guess, *Idea of a Critical Theory*, 5.

33. Ibid., 22–23.

34. Ibid., 12.

writers try to persuade in the sense of correcting the worldview, thought patterns, and behavior patterns of the addressees.[35]

The sense commonly applied by biblical scholars, according to Batten, is the descriptive sense.[36] However, because ideology in each sense has interpretive value, and because these views are not mutually exclusive, it is unnecessary to limit an approach to describing ideology in discourse to only one sense. Ideologies represent aspects of the world in texts that affect social relations that "contribute to establishing, maintaining or changing social relations of power, domination and exploitation."[37] Accounting for how texts effect change in social relations is paramount for rhetorical analysis and goes beyond the purely descriptive sense as explained above. Therefore, only by incorporating the positive and pejorative views of ideology with the descriptive view can rhetorical analyses be framed in such a way to account for how discourse effects social relations, the very type of analysis that CDA is equipped to do.

Drawing on Althusser, Fairclough makes the important claim that ideology has "material existence in the practices of institutions, which opens up the way to investigating discursive practices as material forms of ideology."[38] This raises the question: At what level of discourse is ideology located? Addressing this, Fairclough answers, "Ideology invests language in various ways at various levels, and . . . we don't have to choose between different possible 'locations' of ideology, all of which seem partly justified and none of which seems entirely satisfactory. The key issue is whether ideology is a property of structures or a property of events, and the answer is 'both.'"[39] To go further, systemic functional linguists J. R. Martin and David Rose explain in their model of social context that

35. Ibid. The way in which I have divided up the perspectives on analyzing ideology in discourse, following Guess, and bringing these views together is not novel. See Martin, *English Text*, 507–8, who divides up a multifaceted perspective of ideology into what he calls the *synoptic* and the *dynamic* views, where the *synoptic* view shares similarities to the descriptive view, and the *dynamic* view shares similarities to the pejorative and positive views. However, with as little of description that is provided, using Guess's fuller description is more helpful for this article. For one study that considers Martin's contextual model of ideology, see Dvorak, "Interpersonal Metafunction," 38–44.

36. See Batten, "Ideological Strategies," 8.

37. Fairclough, *Analysing Discourse*, 9.

38. Fairclough, *Discourse and Social Change*, 87. See Althusser, "Ideology and Ideological State Apparatuses," 39–44.

39. Fairclough, "Language and Ideology," 57.

ideology undergirds all levels of semiosis with respect to social relations.[40] Therefore, since ideology permeates social interaction it proves self-limiting to conduct rhetorical analyses that privilege one aspect of discourse over others, though such studies can be enlightening and do not necessarily warrant negative criticism. For instance, when addressing the organization of James as a coherent and cohesive letter, a structural analysis proves most helpful. This type of analysis, if viewed through the SFL lens, addresses the textual metafunction of language as it relates to rhetoric. Several studies of James attend to the so-called rhetorical situation, which describes the situation a text addresses; these analyses would relate readily to rhetoric as it is constrained by the ideational metafunction of language. While important, neither of these approaches can sufficiently attend to the notion that ideologies produce textual variants in structures when writers exploit the fluidity of structures to transform discourse, the term "structure" here not referring to textual organization, but institutional and societal organization.[41] This means that rhetorical analysis also needs to account for how writers subjectively utilize and alter structures for their own ends; here, an analysis attending primarily to the interpersonal metafunction of language becomes necessary. I will focus this analysis at the level of semantics, dealing with meaning at the level of clause and clause-complex.

It is important to recognize that at work in these levels of meaning are "ideological strategies," which, through the linear progression of a discourse, navigate the audience toward adopting a certain set of beliefs and behaviors. Since ideological strategies function in many ways they need now be explained in terms of what they intend to *do*.

In simple terms, this is a study of how James uses ideological formations to effect change in his audience. Such formations derive from the group's set of beliefs and values and are instantiated to promote the particular interests of a group. One of these interests is group cohesion—that those within the group maintain solidarity and a specific sense of identity. Thus, the intended function of many ideological strategies is to *unify*. This strategy can be observed in James's employment of language of belonging, particularly with his repetitive use of ἀδελφοί μου/ἀδελφοί μου

40. Martin and Rose, *Genre Relations*, 17–18. See also Lemke, "Interpersonal Meaning in Discourse," 86, where he states, "The primary function of language, and all of semiosis, is to create, sustain and change social reality."

41. See Fairclough, "Language and Ideology," 59.

ἀγαπητοί/ἀδελφοί (1:2, 16, 19; 2:1, 5, 14; 3:1; 4:11; 5:7, 10, 12, 19). Meeks explains that special terms such as these play a role in the resocialization process "by which an individual's identity is revised and knit together with the identity of the group."[42] In addition to this, I would include the inverse strategy that other ideological formations *disunify* by castigating certain forms of "otherness" that are opposed to, or otherwise incompatible with, the values and beliefs of a group. The drawing of boundaries with regard to behavior and beliefs can be observed throughout the letter of James with regard to doubting (1:6–8), favoritism (2:1–11), in-fighting (4:1–3; 5:9), friendship with the world (4:4), and more. Those who would display such behavior are charged as being double-minded (1:8; 4:8), law-breakers (2:9), adulteresses (4:1), and sinners (4:8). These address only some of the ways that solidarity and separation are accomplished in the letter.[43]

Ideological strategies are also *action-oriented*; they translate theoretical ideas into a practical state furnishing a group with certain behaviors and practical activities.[44] In texts oriented to elicit compliance, this feature of ideology gets realized heavily at the level of semantics through the verbal mood system. James's emphasis on behavior has received much attention throughout history (admittedly, this has largely been due to the interpretive controversy concerning faith and works that has driven much of the scholarship on this letter). Such discussion regardless of the tone, however, should be expected not least because James contains such a high frequency of imperative verb forms, 55 of 264 (20.8 per cent) finite forms.[45] This concentration reflects the emphasis of the writer's preoccupation with outward expressions of the group's ideology.

Third, when ideological strategies take form in discourse they do not simply express social interests in a neutral sense; they *rationalize*

---

42. Meeks, *First Urban Christians*, 85–86.

43. For a recent article from a SFL perspective that explores how writers try to persuade their addressees to conform to patterns of solidarity and separation, see Dvorak, "Prodding with Prosody," 85–120.

44. Eagleton, *Ideology*, 47–48.

45. See Varner, *Book of James*, 50–51, who presents the statistical data that James contains the highest frequency of imperative verbs to total words among New Testament books. However, one should take note that James does not contain the highest frequency of imperative forms in the New Testament when only finite verbs are considered.

them.[46] Rationalized positions imply that they are easily contested or discreditable and thus must be defended in a way that makes counter-intuitive positions seem standard, ethical, or necessary.[47] The makarism, for example, found in Jas 1:12, which emulates the Jesus tradition,[48] rationalizes through an assertive causal clause the value of occupying low social standings in the eyes of the wider society—one who endures under trial is blessed *because* he will receive the crown of life promised by the Lord. This displays the characteristic meant by "rationalize" because it "attempts to provide plausible explanations and justifications for social behavior which might otherwise be the object of criticism."[49]

A fourth ideological strategy is to *legitimate* social interests, which is necessary if a group is to adhere to an ideology, accept the authority of those who assume power, and evaluate their behavior according to the criteria set forth by their leaders.[50] Put simply, legitimating ideological strategies are moves to rule by consent. Prime examples of these moves in James are his usages of rhetorical/leading questions by which he extends to his audience junctures to concede to value positions; e.g., οὐ διεκρίθητε ἐν ἑαυτοῖς καὶ ἐγένεσθε κριταὶ διαλογισμῶν πονηρῶν (Jas 2:4). In this question is James's invitation for the audience to evaluate their behavior by his standards. By means of the question type,[51] the expected answer is "yes," which functionally serves as a legitimating ideological strategy in a monologic discourse.[52]

---

46. Eagleton, *Ideology*, 51. Note that Fairclough sees rationalization as a form of legitimation; see his *Analysing Discourse*, 98–100.

47. On the nature of rationalizing ideological strategies I do not share the more pessimistic views expressed by Eagleton, who states, "[Ideologies] try to defend the indefensible, cloaking some disreputable motive in high-sounding ethical terms" (ibid.). While this may be accurate for interpreting other texts, and even for the arguments of the opponents of the biblical writers, there remains an element attached to Eagleton's description of rationalizing ideological strategies that is incompatible with the nature of Scripture. When affirming a high view of Scripture, rationalizing ideologies employed by the biblical writers are best explained as defending *seemingly* absurd value positions.

48. See Kloppenborg, "Emulation of the Jesus Tradition," 121–50.

49. Eagleton, *Ideology*, 52.

50. Ibid., 54–55.

51. See Porter, *Idioms*, 278, where he makes the important point that, while questions of fact negated with οὐ expect a positive answer, it is the writer who decides that the question expects a positive answer, not the objective facts themselves.

52. See Dawson, "Language as Negotiation," 384–85. See also Dvorak, "Ask and

Fifth, ideological strategies *naturalize*; beliefs are construed as natural, a result of the world being as it is, commonsensical.[53] This kind of strategy attempts to generate an irrefutable consistency between itself and social reality, where reality is first redefined by the group's ideology.[54] This creates an interpretive circle where the group's idea of social reality is self-confirmed by their ideology, and where the ideology functions to establish the "common sense" that makes the idea of social reality self-evident. With this concept, a prevailing belief or expected behavior is not necessarily combatted by an opposing viewpoint as much as it is "thrust beyond the very bounds of the thinkable."[55] With a new way of understanding the world, events such as the social struggles mentioned in Jas 1:2 become understood through a new interpretive lens; facing trials (πειρασμοῖς) accompanies the guarantee of future perfection, which functions to change the audience's attitude toward present on-goings. Having joy amidst suffering is a paradox that *makes sense*. Where rationalization addresses the act of persuading where a claim might be readily contested, naturalization deals with persuasion from the angle where addressees would already find themselves positioned. In this respect, naturalization can serve the task of comforting and encouraging, knowing, like in the situation of James's letter, that the present state of things is the way they are supposed to be in light of the present social reality. It might be the case that certain ideological strategies could be interpreted by different recipients as either *rationalizing* or *naturalizing* based on their current predisposition toward the ideology of the group.

Gramscian Hegemony

Batten addressed a crucial point when she stated that the dominant ideology of James's context must be accounted for before one can analyze James's attempts to uphold and/or challenge that ideology.[56] Also important is to consider James's social location with regards to the group(s) he addresses, as best can be recovered from his language. This is because James's social location determines whether and how James was socially "allowed" to uphold and/or challenge the dominant ideology of his day,

---

Ye Shall Position the Readers" in this volume.

53. Eagleton, *Ideology*, 58. See also Fairclough, *Discourse and Social Change*, 92.

54. Eagleton, *Ideology*, 58.

55. Ibid.

56. Batten, "Ideological Strategies," 9.

given that meaning is always selectively available depending upon one's social status and relations. Thus, a theory of power, where power is understood as the ability to gain compliance or exercise control over another,[57] must accompany a theory of ideology; these two notions are inextricably linked for individuals in society. Concerning this assertion Martin and Rose comment, "There is no meaning outside of power. Even in everyday contexts within our local kin and peer groups, our relative power and control in a context may be conditioned by age, gender and other status markers . . . Within specific situations, these register variables translate into our options to dominate or defer, to assert or concede authority, and to command attention or pay attention to others."[58] Provided this codependent relationship, a framework for analyzing discursive practices needs to contain a theory of power. The present work adapts the Gramscian theory of hegemony for this criterion and relies on the elaboration of this theory by Fairclough given his extensive integration of hegemony into the analysis of discursive practices. It is appropriate to begin with a definition:

> Hegemony is leadership as much as domination across the economic, political, cultural and ideological domains of a society. Hegemony is the power over society as a whole of one of the fundamental economically-defined classes in alliance with other social forces, but it is never achieved more than partially and temporarily, as an 'unstable equilibrium'. Hegemony is about constructing alliances, and integrating rather than simply dominating subordinate classes, through concessions or through constant struggle around points of greatest instability between classes and blocs, to construct or sustain or fracture alliances and relations of domination/subordination, which takes economic, political and ideological forms.[59]

This description of hegemony addresses its activity in a broad-scale societal view. Fairclough, however, has shown that hegemonic struggle extends beyond the socio-economic context that constrained Gramsci's theorizing. The notion of negotiating power relations and eliciting consent from subordinates also takes place within institutions of civil society,

---

57. See Dvorak, "Prodding with Prosody," 88.

58. Martin and Rose, *Genre Relations*, 17–18.

59. Fairclough, *Discourse and Social Change*, 92. See also Fairclough, "Language and Ideology," 61.

such as familial, educational, and religious institutions, whereby there exists various uneven relationships in these domains.[60] Gramscian hegemony then serves as a model for describing the levels of instability and struggle in individual institutions, such as the family, schools, courts of law, and the like.[61] In more general terms then, hegemony can be defined as "a kind of negotiating process in a conflict of interests,"[62] where conflicts occur in various social domains, and not necessarily to the ends of the dominant ideology of a society.[63] This leaves room for this concept to operate within factions and counter-cultural movements, but where relations to the dominant power remain observable through the concept of dialogism, which I discuss below.[64] As ideologies intersect in various ways, the composite result for individuals and groups is a struggle of facing contradictions, such as the early church's struggle of whether or not to adhere to the Mosaic Law, or whether or not to allow eating food sacrificed to idols. Examples such as these demonstrate how hegemony serves as a model for institutional domains, and not only for the dominant societal power (e.g., Rome in the first century) because early Christians underwent struggles around points of instability by which alliances were formed, identities were shaped, and power relations were established and maintained.

Discourse functions as an instrument in the struggle for social change and the constant establishing and reestablishing of social relations. Fairclough's comment sets the appropriate agenda: "Discoursal change, and its relationship to ideological change and to social struggle and change in a broader sense, is where the emphasis must be placed, and where the language/ideology problem should be confronted."[65] As a result, this warrants for the focus to be placed on the types and content of

60. Fairclough, "Language and Ideology," 61–62.

61. Fairclough, *Discourse and Social Change*, 94.

62. Mikinori, "Concept of Hegemony," 20.

63. This is contrary to the original conception of hegemony according to Gramsci where the daily activities of the working class are subtly and pervasively infused with the ideology of the dominant power. See Eagleton, *Ideology*, 113–14.

64. See Gramsci, *Selections*, 194–95, where he observes the unevenness of the field of ideologies that conflict or come together to form a restructured and rearticulated "ideological complex" by means of continuous ideological struggle, though his discussion is limited to the contexts of historical political movements. See also Fairclough, "Language and Ideology," 62.

65. Fairclough, "Language and Ideology," 64.

ideological strategies that James employs, as well as the semantic features used to construe them, since identifying the kinds of opposition James faced is a step in uncovering the social relations at play and being negotiated in the letter.

Regarding change in the event—that is the writing and sending of the letter in a particular way and under a set of social circumstances— what receives attention is how the writer goes outside conventional expectations. What sort of innovations does the writer make that seem to suggest conflicting domains of experience? James, in his letter, addresses his audience as beloved brothers and sisters, sinners, adulteresses, and double-minded. Such contradictory vocabulary when seen in context suggests a struggle in how the writer positions his audience; these terms both supply an immediate motivation for change on the part of the audience and a means by which the writer attempts to accomplish it.[66]

Structural change takes into account variations in types of discourse—that is, the shifts in how a type of discourse manages power relations.[67] These variations will be observed in James's use of the diatribe whereby, in addition to it invoking an unequal relationship characteristic of its conventional mode, it also was transformed to serve a new hegemonic purpose by which the audience could be ideologically positioned before they had a reason to become defensive against James's judgments.

Bakhtinian Dialogism and the Principle of Heteroglossia

Two important concepts for analyzing interpersonal meaning in discourse are *dialogism* and *heteroglossia*, theoretical principles of discourse developed by Mikhail Bakhtin. For Bakhtin, the starting point of language as a social phenomenon is the utterance, "a moment of discourse, as a *social event*, as an act that contributes to the social activity of discourse."[68] Accordingly, when a language user makes an utterance, he or she goes through a process of selecting words, and these words are not taken from their system in their neutral dictionary form, but are usually taken from other utterances similar to them in theme, composition, and style.[69] All

66. Ibid.

67. Ibid., 65.

68. Lemke, *Textual Politics*, 22, emphasis original.

69. Bakhtin, "Problem with Speech Genres," 87. For clarification of Bakhtin's point see Holquist, *Dialogism*, 49, where he writes, "Meaning comes about in both the individual psyche and in shared social experience through the medium of the sign, for

utterances, then, are somehow shaped and developed by constant interaction with other utterances whether the language user writes with awareness of or detachment from this interaction.[70] This is the Bakhtinian notion of *dialogism*, whereby a language user makes use (consciously or unconsciously) of the polyphony of discursive and social forces that comprise the meaning potential available amidst a heteroglossic backdrop, where there is literally a multitude of other voices interacting with the writer's utterance in some way.[71] Jay Lemke states this simply: "The utterance always originates in and functions as part of a social *dialogue* (whether the other participants in this dialogue are considered to be actually present or are only implied)."[72]

During the development of this social theory of discourse Bakhtin realized that utterances *mean* against a background of utterances that contain different ideologies of other social groups, what he calls "bounded verbal-ideological belief systems" and "social languages of heteroglossia" in other places.[73] Explicating this concept, Bakhtin writes,

> All the languages of heteroglossia, whatever the principle underlying them and making each unique, are specific points of view on the world, forms for conceptualizing the world in words, specific world views, each characterized by its own objects, meanings and values. As such they all may be juxtaposed to one another, mutually supplement one another, contradict one another and be interrelated dialogically. As such they encounter one another and co-exist in the consciousness of real people.[74]

In this theory, every utterance principally acts as a reaction to other utterances, whether former or potential, in a way that "refutes, affirms, supplements, and relies upon the others, presupposes them to be known, and somehow takes them into account."[75] Upon the making of an utterance there arises a unique meaning with relation to both the present context and the heteroglossic backdrop whereby the language

---

in both spheres understanding comes about as a response to a sign with signs."

70. Bakhtin, "Problem with Speech Genres," 89.

71. Holquist, *Dialogism*, 69. See also Bakhtin, "Problem with Speech Genres," 87–96.

72. Lemke, *Textual Politics*, 23.

73. See ibid., 24. See also Dvorak, "Not Like Cain," 4–6.

74. Bakhtin, "Discourse in the Novel," 289–90.

75. Bakhtin, "Problem with Speech Genres," 91.

user anticipates their addressee's response. Accounting for this Bakhtin again writes, "The word in living conversation is directly, blatantly, oriented toward a future answer-word: it provokes an answer, anticipates it and structures itself in the answer's direction."[76] This means that when a writer chooses a discourse type (e.g., diatribe), its structure will assume social voices—that is, socially instituted ways of speaking and acting—to relate sociologically to an audience.[77] Concerning this Lemke explains, "We speak with the voices of our communities, and to the extent that we have individual voices, we fashion these out of the social voices already available to us, appropriating the words of others to speak a word of our own."[78] Therefore, when one can describe how one utterance as a social event struggles against the heteroglossic backdrop of similar discourse formations then the one's-own-ness of an instantiated discourse type is unearthed.[79] This brings the social theory of discourse heretofore described full circle: language users can make particular utterances according to a discourse type, but they can incorporate new elements into the discourse type from a different group's ideology, such as their own, which produces new meanings and new uses for utterances; this creates a new social language, or *discourse formation*, which then when adopted by other social agents can produce social change.[80] Such a process does not happen overnight; it has to be tried and rejected and tried again, being accepted by others over time until it eventually becomes a socially acceptable discourse formation.

One who promotes an ideology needs to understand that his or her addressees are a potential disruptive force to the language user's desired

76. Bakhtin, "Discourse in the Novel," 280; see also Lemke, *Textual Politics*, 19, who clarifies the point that the significance of an utterance is its understanding against past utterances, but also against future utterances regardless if the writer knows about them. While it is sometimes absent from his work, Bakhtin does account for the finer point that "the utterance is constructed while taking into account possible responsive reactions, for whose sake, in essence, it is actually created" ("Problem with Speech Genres," 94). For example, see Bakhtin, "Discourse in the Novel," 281.

77. Lemke, *Textual Politics*, 24.

78. Ibid., 24–25.

79. See Lemke, "Discourses in Conflict," 30.

80. Ibid., 25. See also Bakhtin, "Discourse in the Novel," 358–59, where he refers to this process as *hybridization*: "We may even say that language and languages change historically primarily by means of hybridization, by means of mixing of various [social] 'languages' co-existing within the boundaries of a single dialect . . . but the crucible for this mixing always remains the utterance."

governing ideology. As a result, to be rhetorically successful—that is, effectually persuasive—the voices of others must be taken into account. Martin and White's system of Engagement, which operates on the level of Discourse Semantics,[81] and of which dialogism and heteroglossia play a formational role, provides a model that isolates the interpersonal semantic resources of language that functionally take into account others' voices in the social context for the purpose of fashioning rhetorically successful ideological strategies. This work now turns its attention to this system.

THE SYSTEM OF ENGAGEMENT

The system of Engagement maps the semantic choices available to a language user to either dialogically expand or contract a text with regard to inter-subjective functionality.[82] This means that a writer engages in some way with the voices of the heteroglossic backdrop, either by acknowledging or ignoring them, conceding to or denying them in various ways. In addition to engaging with the polyphony of voices that make up this backdrop, language users also engage with the voices of their audiences according to the dialogic principle of Bakhtin and Vološinov; when a language user makes an utterance it "responds to something, affirms something, anticipates possible responses and objections, seeks support, and so on."[83] Thus, language users can be assumed to take into account other ideological stances that will either impede or supplement their goals whether they are from the surrounding culture or the writer's audience. In this respect, language users assume their audiences to be either in alignment or disalignment with the value positions they construe, and so writers will depict for themselves an "ideal" audience more or less aligned with certain value positions so that they can negotiate with their

81. Porter identifies a problem with Martin's model in that the stratum of Discourse Semantics lacks criteria linking it to the lexicogrammatical stratum (Porter, "Systemic Functional Linguistics," 40–41). Martin means something different by Discourse Semantics than Halliday does by his stratum of Semantics, but this is not the place to join in the debate on the relationship between them. I wish only to show that the semantic patterns of engagement strategies identifiable at the clause and clause-complex levels in Jas 2 serve as the basis for understanding the role of the diatribe in the letter and yield enough linguistic data to postulate the tenor relations influencing the writer's language.

82. Martin and White, *Language of Evaluation*, 102.

83. Vološinov, *Marxism*, 139. See also White, "Beyond Modality," 261.

addressees according to this inter-subjective positioning.[84] On this point, Martin and White write, "Thus one of our central concerns is with the ways in which these resources act to 'write the reader into the text' by presenting the speaker/writer as, for example, taking it for granted that the addressee shares with them a particular viewpoint, or as anticipating that a given proposition will be problematic (or unproblematic) for the putative reader, or as assuming that the reader may need to be won over to a particular viewpoint, and so on."[85] In this work's analysis of Jas 2, I will refer to these negotiations as "engagement strategies," which in turn function as ideological strategies.

The framework of this system is directed towards showing how inter-subjective positioning is accomplished through linguistic means. It characterizes the language user's interpersonal style according to how he or she engages with alternative voices.[86] Martin and White describe these engagement strategies based on expansive and contractive semantics that become realized in texts by means of the Engagement system network.[87] Dialogically expansive texts allow for other voices to be brought into a text to support the writer's own ideological position in some way. Dialogically contractive texts restrict other voices from intruding into the text, even to the point of fending off all other voices in monoglossic, or "single-voiced," texts.[88] Not all dialogically contractive texts are monoglossic; contraction is accomplished by controlling certain voices in the text to do specific tasks. For example, a leading question (i.e., a question that rhetorically prompts a specific kind of answer) is inherently heteroglossic because it invites the addressee to respond, but to respond in a certain way, the way in which the writer leads. In a monologic text (i.e., a text that only has one-way communication), such as with a letter, questions do not run the same risk they do when addressees have the immediate opportunity to contest how they are being prompted to answer. Since monologic texts are privileged in that they can put words in their recipients' mouths so to speak, writers must consider their audiences' (potential) stances so as not lose their compliance along the way. If this is a risk a writer is aware of, and he or she is struggling to establish

84. Martin and White, *Language of Evaluation*, 95.
85. Ibid.
86. Ibid., 93.
87. Ibid., 102.
88. Ibid., 99.

secure social relations with a group, could not diatribe be a useful tool in creating solidarity early on in a text?

All utterances can be categorized according to one of the dialogic options discussed above. Thus, to map the ways in which language users dialogically expand and contract texts, J. R. Martin and David Rose develop a system indicating that there are at least three categories of semantic resources that need to be accounted for: "Projection," "Modality," and "Concession."[89] These same three resources also function in the system of Engagement as adapted for New Testament Greek, which I show in the following sections.[90]

Projection

One way that language users may engage with other voices is to report directly or indirectly some speech, thought, or feeling of a source.[91] Direct and indirect discourse are grammaticalized in a variety of ways in Greek. Quite often, direct quotations must be deduced by context, and other quotations are introduced by the conjunction ὅτι or verbs of saying or thinking such as λέγω.[92] Indirect discourse can be realized through several constructions; K. L. McKay organizes them according to the infinitive construction, the ὅτι construction, and the participle construction.[93] James 2:16 provides an example: εἴπῃ δέ τις αὐτοῖς ἐξ ὑμῶν, ὑπάγετε ἐν εἰρήνῃ, θερμαίνεσθε καὶ χορτάζεσθε, (*But someone from among you might say to them, "Go in peace, be warmed and be filled"*). Here, the writer projects the voice of a hypothetical person who acts a certain way toward a poor person. This projected speech, which dialogically expands the text, introduces a potential stance that another voice might assume within the audience's social environment. However, not all projected speech expands a text for the sake of expanding dialogic space. For example, the rest of the Jas 2:16 reads: μὴ δῶτε δὲ αὐτοῖς τὰ ἐπιτήδεια τοῦ

89. Martin and Rose, *Working with Discourse*, 48–59. This is a variation of the fuller explanation of Engagement first developed in Martin and White, *Language of Evaluation*, 92–135.

90. For a fuller sketch of how I have begun to model these categories for Greek, see Dawson, "Language as Negotiation," 371–82.

91. Martin and Rose, *Working with Discourse*, 49. The term "projection" is taken from Halliday, *Introduction to Functional Grammar*, 547–49.

92. See McKay, *New Syntax* 97–99, who gives a concise explanation of the various formations for direct quotation in New Testament Greek.

93. See ibid., 99–105.

σώματος, τί τὸ ὄφελος; (*yet you do not give to them that which is necessary for the body. What good is that?*). This demonstrates the confluence of dialogic expansion and contraction; a writer dialogically expands a text with the purpose of making some value judgment concerning it, which dialogically contracts the text having refuted an opposing voice.[94]

Modality

Another semantic resource for engaging with other voices is modality. Critical for this discussion is Halliday's explanation that all dialogue is characterized by negotiation; all communicative participants use language for the purpose of exchanging either goods-&-services or information.[95] Thus, a writer of a monologic text, such as a letter, usually assumes the role(s) of a *giver* of information and/or a *demander* of goods-&-services, where all such instantiations encode the writer's ideology in some way. As follows, there are two forms of negotiation: Modalization refers to the negotiation of information (i.e., propositions) and Modulation refers to the negotiation of goods-&-services (i.e., proposals).[96] Modality functions as a cline between positive and negative polarity, the semantic space between "yes" and "no";[97] the poles stand for monoglossic zones and the space between them display varying levels of dialogic space.

F. R. Palmer states, "Modality could . . . be defined as the grammaticalization of speakers' (subjective) attitudes and opinions."[98] Since the Greek mood system is fundamentally characterized by subjectivity, and because it also constitutes the most pervasive linguistic resource for negotiating social relations, it will presently suffice for analyzing modality with reference to engagement strategies.[99]

94. On the confluence of dialogical expansion and contraction see Dvorak, "Interpersonal Metafunction," 90–92. Dialogic confluence is a prevalent feature of conditionals in Greek.

95. Halliday, *Introduction to Functional Grammar*, 135–39. See also J. R. Martin, *English Text*, 31–35.

96. For a fuller description of "Modalization" and "Modulation" see Halliday, *Introduction to Functional Grammar*, 176–83, 686–98.

97. Martin and Rose, *Working with Discourse*, 53.

98. Palmer, *Mood and Modality*, 16. See also Porter, *Verbal Aspect*, 321.

99. See Lemke, "Interpersonal Meaning in Discourse," 85–86.

The Modalization scale categorizes statements of information based upon a writer's portrayed sense of certainty;[100] it operates on a scale from "it is" to "it is not" separated by varying degrees of probability. Statements of fact, or bare assertions, in Greek are realized by indicative mood-forms, which grammaticalize the semantic feature of assertive attitude, or [+assertion].[101] These statements are monoglossic in function; they do not usually recognize other voices in their communicative context.[102] However, one twist is accounted for by Martin and White: "One key distinction within monoglossic assertions turns on whether the disposition of the text is such that the proposition is presented as taken-for-granted, or whether, alternatively, it is presented as currently at issue or up for discussion."[103] Language users can have multiple reasons for stating propositions as factual; they might believe the proposition to be true, or they might be lying, or invoking sarcasm, condescension, or contempt where the assertive attitude creates the necessary tone for rhetorical purposes. They might also be opinions that are no longer at issue with the audience (or at least thought to be), or they might be stated with the knowledge that further argumentation will be needed for the audience to accept them.[104]

There are also a number of reasons why a writer might use a non-indicative mood-form to negotiate information. These reasons could range from a writer being uncertain about the truth of a proposition to the writer opting to employ conventions of politeness or to be sensitive to other features of tenor relations. Whatever the reason, non-indicative mood-forms function to dialogically expand a text. Thus, the subjunctive mood and the optative mood, which grammaticalize the semantic features of [+projection] and [+projection, +contingency] respectively,[105]

100. The present study assumes the position of Jan Gonda's refined description of the Greek moods, whereby the main distinction from the traditional view of Greek mood-forms is that statements, for instance, are subjectively asserted as true regardless of whether they are true or not; attitude indicates how the writer wants the audience to understand how the writer views the action. See Gonda, *The Character of Indo-European Moods*, 164–65.

101. Porter, *Verbal Aspect*, 165–66.

102. Martin and White, *Language of Evaluation*, 99.

103. Ibid., 100.

104. Ibid., 100–102.

105. Porter, *Verbal Aspect*, 322. See also Porter, *Idioms*, 56–61. Note: the term "projection" is used in two different ways in this essay. When referring to configurations

function to allow other voices into a text; they situate between the poles of "it is" and "it is not" to construe probability.

Modulation refers to the scale of modality pertaining to obligation and thus sets up a scale from "do" to "don't do."[106] The imperative mood, which grammaticalizes the semantic feature of [+direction] occupies both ends of this scale as positive and negative commanding. The directive attitude is monoglossic in function; the only voice present is that of the one commanding, and thus the addressees are not afforded dialogic space by which they could argue against the writer's orders. However, this does not suggest that actual compliance on part of the addressees is automatic, but in terms of the text itself they are positioned in such a way where they are negotiated to comply. Subjunctive and optative mood-forms in proposals function dialogically the same as they do in propositions.

Modality is also extended through interpersonal grammatical metaphor.[107] Metaphors of mood expand the meaning potential of propositions and proposals. This is illustrated easily enough in the English sentence, "I urge you to change your mind!" Taken at its lexicogrammatical level the speech function realized here is a statement. However, metaphors of mood allow for propositions and proposals to be further elaborated in delicacy, the purpose of which is to expand the system of negotiation with metaphorical realizations that show more discretion as writers attempt to secure compliance and agreement from their addressees.[108] The statement above would appropriately be interpreted by an addressee as a command, but in a way that increases the chance of compliance more than the obligatory imperative, "Change your mind!" would have given the consideration of tenor variables. Indicative mood-forms in Greek can function in this way as well. Also, of particular relevance for the present

---

that introduce reported speech I use a capital "P" to differentiate from referring to the semantic feature of the Subjunctive mood, for which I use the lowercase.

106. Halliday, *Introduction to Functional Grammar*, 177.

107. For a recent work that takes up the issues of the Greek speech functions and interpersonal grammatical metaphor, see Porter, "Systemic Functional Linguistics," 9–47. Though no other work has modeled the Greek speech functions as fully as Porter does in this article, I would call attention to the absence of the future form in his systematizing of the Greek speech functions, which I believe needs to be included. However, perhaps more needs to be known about future form in Greek before one can confidently situate it within this system network. See also Dawson, "Language as Negotiation," 373–80, where discussion on where the future form situates within this system is explored.

108. Halliday, *Introduction to Functional Grammar*, 704–5.

study, so can future tense-forms. Future tense-forms, though compli-
cated to situate in the Greek verbal system,[109] produce monoglossic texts
that function on both scales of modality via interpersonal grammatical
metaphor and have their own unique potential for navigating tenor relations because they grammaticalize the specific feature of [+expectation].[110]

Concession

In SFL a full multidimensional model of conjunction has been developed
for English, which shows how conjunctive relations are mapped across
all three metafunctions; these are categorized as "external" and "internal"
conjunction.[111] External conjunction corresponds to the ideational (ex-
periential) metafunction; conjunction functions to construe experience
of sequences and events.[112] Internal conjunction, on the other hand, is
necessarily divided up into two kinds depending on how it performs in
text.[113] Martin and Rose describe one type of internal relations as primarily functioning to organize texts, and thus classify "internal" conjunction
as textual meaning.[114] Expanding on Halliday and Hasan's account of
"internal" conjunction, Martin and Rose show these relations function
to negotiate claims, and thus are interpersonal.[115] They refer broadly to
the category of interpersonal conjunction as "Concession" because it pertains to the notion of "counter-expectancy" and how language users track
the expectations of their audiences and adjust them as the text unfolds.[116]
Monitoring expectations is a pervasive feature of conjunctions and can
also be realized by adverbs, prepositions, and various other constructions
in Greek (e.g., παρά as a preposition can function to mark a contrary
expectation).[117] In Greek, common resources for tracking, then adjust-

109. See Porter, *Verbal Aspect*, 414, where he explains that the future form is not
fully modal, but that it shares similarities to attitude.

110. Porter, *Verbal Aspect*, 403.

111. Halliday and Hasan, *Cohesion in English*, 238–41.

112. Martin and Rose, *Working with Discourse*, 116.

113. See Thompson, "But Me Some Buts," 763–91, who distinguishes these categories and demonstrates how they function across each metafunction in English.

114. Martin and Rose, *Working with Discourse*, 204–5.

115. Ibid., 56–57; Halliday and Hasan, *Cohesion in English*, 238–71.

116. Martin and Rose, *Working with Discourse*, 56–58.

117. See ibid., 57–58, where they illustrate this feature in English adverbs, again
following Halliday and Hasan, *Cohesion in English*, 230–31, who also include prepositional phrases in the conjunctive adjunct category.

ing, managing, or developing audience expectations are conjunctions such as ἀλλά, δέ, μέν, and πλήν, and the like.[118] Following Martin and Rose, I will use the term "Concession" as the semantic category to refer to these conjunctions, though this term is misleadingly narrow when a fuller consideration of the interpersonal semantics of conjunctions is in view.[119] Other resources of Concession pertain to temporality, particles called "continuatives," used to introduce events occurring either sooner or later than expected, which get formulated in Greek by deictic indicators such as ἔτι, τὸ λοιπόν, and οὔπω, and the like.[120] This briefly sketches how the category of interpersonal conjunction is a category in the Greek language, and a semantic resource utilized for the purpose of positioning readers to adopt certain beliefs and behaviors. It will be shown that the social theory of discourse developed above informs how "internal" conjunction constrains the meaning of text, dialogically contracting and expanding it, and factors as junctures of navigating the writer's audience to his or her promoted value position.

ANALYSIS OF JAMES 2:14–26

Duane Watson states, "James 2.14–26 is particularly diatribal."[121] While stylistic features of the diatribe can be identified throughout the whole of ch. 2, they are most heavily concentrated in the latter half of the chapter. Because I have offered a dialogical analysis of Jas 2:1–13 in a previous article, I will summarize the ideological strategies that I found operative in that work as they contribute to the linear progression of how James navigates various social relations. This will be helpful in assessing the significance of similar and different semantic resources employed in 2:14–26. I have identified nine ideological strategies at work in Jas 2:1–13, determined from the semantic resources of Projection, Modality, and Concession, realizing all of the different types of ideological strategies described above (except *unifying*, but which is still accounted for by the ἀδελφοί μου address in 2:1). I believe that it is with this continued work that the significance of my previous analysis will be brought to bear for

118. For a full list of these particles, see Louw and Nida, *Greek-English Lexicon*, 1:794.

119. Martin and Rose, *Working with Discourse*, 52.

120. Again, see Louw and Nida, *Greek-English Lexicon*, 1:646.

121. Watson, "James 2," 119.

insights into the social relations at play in the letter, and consequently with the diatribe.

I offer here a summarized analysis of the dialogicality of 2:1–13 as it relates to the interpersonal positioning of the addressees. A key feature of this section of text is how dialogically expanded James keeps this part of his letter as he establishes beliefs and values concerning the partiality of the rich. There are three primary semantic means by which James accomplishes this: subjunctive mood-forms in the setting up of the assembly situation (vv. 2–4, 10), the use of both first- and third-class conditions (vv. 2–4, 8–9, 11), and the use of leading questions (vv. 4, 5, 6, 7). The heteroglossic features of this section do not preclude James's intent on establishing a firm, even non-negotiable stance towards partiality. Much to the contrary: despite the dialogical space for the audience to combat James's argument, he still makes the well-placed judgment that the audience dishonors the poor person (v. 6). Also, James concludes this paragraph by cancelling out all other voices by means of imperative and indicative mood-forms. James shows that he is very much concerned with the behavior of the addressees (οὕτως λαλεῖτε καὶ οὕτως ποιεῖτε ὡς διὰ νόμου ἐλευθερίας μέλλοντες κρίνεσθαι), and so by what means does James attempt to be effectual in his value positioning? He projects the situation where partiality is shown to the rich man, he crafts his ideological stances with conditional statements, and he invites his audience to comply along the way by asking leading questions. James's words are the rudder gently redirecting the ship as the audience is brought progressively on board. Rhetorically it is not time to call his addressees μοιχαλίδες (4:4), ἁμαρτωλοί (4:8), or δίψυχοι (4:8), or to charge them with numerous moral judgments (4:1–3), or to compound them with (re)directives (4:7–11). Such moves too early would start an uncontrollable fire. The ship is sailing in that direction, but as will be apparent in vv. 14–26, James has not yet docked his passengers in his ideological port.

James 2:14–17

[14] Τί τὸ ὄφελος ἀδελφοί μου ἐὰν πίστιν λέγῃ τις ἔχειν ἔργα δὲ μὴ ἔχῃ μὴ δύναται ἡ πίστις σῶσαι αὐτόν [15] ἐὰν ἀδελφὸς ἢ ἀδελφὴ γυμνοὶ ὑπάρχωσιν καὶ λειπόμενοι τῆς ἐφημέρου τροφῆς [16] εἴπῃ δέ τις αὐτοῖς ἐξ ὑμῶν ὑπάγετε ἐν εἰρήνῃ, θερμαίνεσθε καὶ χορτάζεσθε μὴ δῶτε δὲ αὐτοῖς τὰ ἐπιτήδεια τοῦ σώματος τί τὸ ὄφελος [17] οὕτως καὶ ἡ πίστις ἐὰν μὴ ἔχῃ ἔργα νεκρά ἐστιν καθ᾽ ἑαυτήν

[14]What benefit is it, my brothers and sisters, if someone happens to say to have faith but should not have actions? That faith is not able to rescue them is it? [15]If a brother or sister is without clothing and lacking in food for the day, [16]and someone among you should say, "Depart in peace. Warm yourself and be filled." And yet you do not give to them what is necessary for the body, what benefit is that? [17]In like manner also, the faith, if it is without actions, is dead being by itself.

Verse 14 begins a new paragraph with the reiterated unifying address ἀδελφοί μου. The first sentence is a leading question, making this verse heteroglossic, but dialogically contractive as a certain answer is expected. However, the subjunctive verb λέγῃ also contributes to expanding the text with the resources of Modality and Projection as it introduces indirect discourse. The projected speech brings into the text the voice who says, "I have faith, and that's sufficient." James's leading question functions to negotiate information with his audience, whereby he positions them to answer, "Faith without works is *not* beneficial." This is a *legitimating* strategy that allows the writer to establish stances without imposing obligatory behaviors on his audience; steps are first taken to position them by consent to adopt certain beliefs and values. The second question in v. 14 serves as a follow-up question to reinforce the stance that faith without works is useless; it, too, is a *legitimating* ideological strategy.

Verses 15–16 introduce a third-class condition, a construction necessarily heteroglossic because it employs subjunctive mood-forms. The protasis holds up for consideration the hypothetical situation where a brother or sister is without clothing and lacking in food. Additionally, dialogic expansion occurs with an engagement strategy of Projection realized in the attributing of speech to a potential voice by means of direct discourse. The words of the voice grammaticalize direction towards the poor person, commanding the poor person to have his or her needs met. This mode of behavior is then followed by a question directed toward the audience: "What good is that?" which is the apodosis of the condition. Thus, the same *legitimating* ideological strategy is accomplished in v. 15 as was made in v. 14, but this time with a different configuration of semantic resources, which work to create a concrete situation whereby the uselessness of faith minus works is exemplified.

Following this strand of questions and conditions, the writer moves to further manage the addressees' expectations by drawing an inference, οὕτως καὶ ἡ πίστις ἐὰν μὴ ἔχῃ ἔργα νεκρά ἐστιν καθ᾽ ἑαυτήν (v. 17), an engagement strategy realized by Concession. This value statement, functions as a *naturalizing* ideological strategy as it makes a commonsensical conclusion concerning the foregoing hypothetical situation. The writer does this while including an embedded third class condition, ἐὰν μὴ ἔχῃ ἔργα, in the primary clause, which serves to hedge any persistent voice that might challenge this value statement.

James 2:18–19

18 Ἀλλ᾽ ἐρεῖ τις σὺ πίστιν ἔχεις κἀγὼ ἔργα ἔχω δεῖξόν μοι τὴν πίστιν σου χωρὶς τῶν ἔργων κἀγώ σοι δείξω ἐκ τῶν ἔργων μου τὴν πίστιν 19 σὺ πιστεύεις ὅτι εἷς ἐστιν ὁ θεός, καλῶς ποιεῖς καὶ τὰ δαιμόνια πιστεύουσιν καὶ φρίσσουσιν

18*But it can be expected that someone among you will say, "One has faith and one has actions." [James responds,] "Show to me your faith without actions, and I will show to you faith from my actions.* 19*You believe that God is one. You do well; the demons also believe, and they shudder."*

Though James has naturalized the value position that "faith minus works equals death" and navigated his audience to his conclusion statement on this value position, which has been fleshed-out and solidified over the past seventeen verses, and whereas it would be logically expected to move to new subject matter, he instead counters their expectations by means of the concessive resource ἀλλά and introduces an opposing voice into the text. For this reason v. 18 serves as a significant juncture of counter-expectancy. Since James already naturalized this value position, the new voice is placed in immediate opposition to "the way things are." A belief that opposes an ideological position on such grounds is necessarily viewed as nonsensical, intolerable. James has primed his audience to see the ideological flaws present in the imaginary interlocutor's position, thus maximizing the potential for their agreement.

The rest of Jas 2 has been attested to display traditional diatribe style,[122] and so the preceding analysis will begin to shed light on how the writer has reinvested this type of discourse. Verse 18 introduces an opponent's voice by means of a future form (ἐρεῖ), making this a monoglossic formulation of introducing direct discourse (Projection); the direct discourse itself is dialogically expansive. This divergence from the subjunctive form

122. See McKnight, *Letter of James*, 237.

introducing other voices may be an indication that the writer is engaging with a known position that opposes the foregoing value statement that faith minus actions is worthless. The semantic feature of the future form certainly points in this direction, but more importantly for this analysis, James engages an opposing voice more directly by introducing this opposing voice via a monoglossic formulation (i.e. a future tense-form) over against the previous pericope's dialogically expansive subjunctive forms. This is exegetically significant because in engaging an imaginary interlocutor, James imports a new configuration of tenor relations into the text, the relations (purportedly) between him and this constructed opponent. Already with the future verb ἐρεῖ James shows a different disposition towards their relationship than he has heretofore with his real addressees. In here lies the rhetorical value of the diatribe; James can negotiate values and beliefs by any means he sees fit without the immediate concern of compromising the tenor relations he has established with his addressees because he is not directly addressing them. The addressees get to look on at the dialogue between James and this imaginary interlocutor and evaluate it for themselves without being put on the defensive.

The writer also employs the semantic resource of Concession by means of the adversative conjunction ἀλλά, which directs the audience toward considering the ensuing argument via "counter-expectancy." The reason why this argument may not be expected from the audience's perspective is because it takes up the same issue raised in the previous paragraph, but instead of repeating a hypothetical scenario, it engages a *specific* voice, a voice that consists of an actual belief, and thus is more vital and more contextually relevant for the audience's present situation.

The translation of v. 18 above reflects the belief taken by the imaginary interlocutor, that one can have faith and another can have actions, and both are legitimate means of fulfilling God's covenant with his people. The translation above allows the first and second person pronouns to be more general; instead of "You (James) have faith, and I (the opponent) have actions," which does not logically flow with the argument, the logical problem is solved by taking the pronouns more generally with the translation: "One has faith and one has actions."[123] Thus, the opponent's

---

123. The need for adjusting this translation has been identified by Jacobean scholars. The majority of scholars agree that the pronouns should be taken more generally. See Mayor, *Epistle of James*, 100; Ropes, *Epistle of St. James*, 208, who proposes: "One has pre-eminently faith, another has pre-eminently works" as a translation; Dibelius, *James*, 154–55; McKnight, "Unidentifiable Interlocutor," 355–64; McKnight, *Letter of*

speech, which only consists of this one sentence, contests James's previous value position for its legitimacy. James then responds to this opponent's argument, as portrayed by James himself, in good diatribe fashion. The response continues through the end of v. 23, and so the whole response should be interpreted as dialogically contractive as a whole, refuting the opponent's position. However, the present model is built to be more linguistically sensitive for a clause-by-clause analysis, which allows for a closer look at the intricacies of this response. Further, it should be kept in mind that this text functions as a means of positioning the audience; by addressing the imaginary interlocutor the writer negotiates information with the audience—he is "coming at them from the side" so to speak, or what one might call "rhetorical flanking."

The beginning of the writer's response to his opponent begins with the command, "You show (δεῖξόν) your faith without actions." This monoglossic formation bypasses any conventions of politeness; the goal is to refute the opponent, to leave this position completely rejected. The next clause functions as the writer's turn in this exchange; he will then show his faith accompanied with actions. The semantic feature of expectation in the verb δείξω functions to keep this clause monoglossic. The exchange "you show to me . . . and I will show to you . . . " makes a qualitative contrast between "expressions of faith." The implication is that the writer's faith is superior to the opponent's because it possesses supporting evidence concerning its validity.

The first clause of v. 19 contains a "thinking" verb, πιστεύεις, which produces dialogic confluence as it grammaticalizes the assertive attitude (Modality) as well as assigns content of "believing" to the opponent (Projection). Since the source of "believing" is not the author, the clause σὺ πιστεύεις ὅτι εἷς ἐστιν ὁ θεός must be said to be heteroglossic, but it is still dialogically contractive due to the attitude of the clause.

The second clause of v. 19 is a two-word bare assertion, καλῶς ποιεῖς, a value statement positively evaluating the opponent's belief that there is one God. These two clauses together serve as what could be a *unifying* engagement strategy, attributing a belief to the interlocutor followed by a commendation for having that belief. However, the same verb of thinking appears in the next clause, a repeated use of attribution, but this time belief is assigned to demons, which indicates that the previous positive evaluation of the opponent's belief was sarcastic in retrospect,

---

James, 238; Martin, *James*, 86–87; Moo, *Letter of James*, 129.

reversing the unifying effect of the engagement strategy. The writer also has a monoglossic statement to make about demons and their belief: they shudder (φρίσσουσιν). Therefore, twice in four clauses the writer's strategy of negotiating information with the imaginary interlocutor has been to assign belief, and then to make a statement concerning that belief. When taken together, there occurs a comparison between the opponent and demons—they both only have belief, but also implicit in the contrast, the demons behave appropriately while the opponent deludes him- or herself into thinking that faith alone is sufficient.

James 2:20–23

20 Θέλεις δὲ γνῶναι ὦ ἄνθρωπε κενέ ὅτι ἡ πίστις χωρὶς τῶν ἔργων ἀργή ἐστιν 21 Ἀβραὰμ ὁ πατὴρ ἡμῶν οὐκ ἐξ ἔργων ἐδικαιώθη ἀνενέγκας Ἰσαὰκ τὸν υἱὸν αὐτοῦ ἐπὶ τὸ θυσιαστήριον 22 βλέπεις ὅτι ἡ πίστις συνήργει τοῖς ἔργοις αὐτοῦ καὶ ἐκ τῶν ἔργων ἡ πίστις ἐτελειώθη 23 καὶ ἐπληρώθη ἡ γραφὴ ἡ λέγουσα ἐπίστευσεν δὲ Ἀβραὰμ τῷ θεῷ καὶ ἐλογίσθη αὐτῷ εἰς δικαιοσύνην καὶ φίλος θεοῦ ἐκλήθη

20"Now are you willing to recognize, you empty-headed fool, that faith without actions is useless? 21 Was not Abraham, our father, justified by actions when he offered up Isaac his son on the altar? 22 You see that faith was working with his actions and from his actions his faith was made complete. 23 And the Scripture was fulfilled, which says, 'And Abraham believed in God and it was credited to him as righteousness,' and he was called a friend of God."

Verse 20 is a rhetorical question and thus is heteroglossic, but dialogically contractive. The connective δέ realizes Concession, where the question posed develops the expectation of the imaginary interlocutor. After the comparison of the opponent's and the demons' beliefs, the writer demands information from the opponent. At this point the writer portrays his opponent as a fool; the explanation of the demons' belief in God should be enough to indicate the falsehood of the opponent's ideological stance; indeed, faith without actions is worthless. This ideological strategy, unlike other prior questions, is not *legitimating* because the writer is not directly asking his recipients to concede to this belief. Instead, this question functions as a *naturalizing* ideological strategy; it attempts to create consistency with the belief that faith and actions must go together because demons, who by definition are against God, practice belief without works.

An important element in v. 20 that falls outside the purview of the system of Engagement is the use of social name-calling, ὦ ἄνθρωπε κενέ. Social name-calling serves as a way of designating where one situates with reference to the group. By calling this imaginary interlocutor an empty-headed fool, the writer attempts to distance his audience from the type of person that embodies the opponent's ideology. This instance of social name-calling should then be interpreted as a *unifying* ideological strategy; by attempting to distance the audience from the interlocutor's view, James draws lines in the proverbial sand that indicate which beliefs must be castigated so that the group can consistently conform to its identity and behavioral norms.

The writer continues with a leading question in v. 21 directed at his interlocutor. This question, like the last, functions to *naturalize* the writer's ideology for his real audience. The dialogical space is opened for the opponent to concede that Abraham was indeed justified by his actions, which consistently connects historical Jewish teaching with the writer's value position. Moreover, that all one needs to do is invoke the narrative of the father of the Jewish people to illustrate the absurdity of the interlocutor's idea shows the shallowness of it. The interpersonal features, namely the outright shaming, accompanying the dialogical expansion of the two questions in vv. 20 and 21 create an important contrast to how James dialogically expanded the text for his addressees' voices earlier in 2:1–17. The conventions of the diatribe allow James to engage forcefully with the social positions at risk in the social environment, even using language that would be humiliating and alienating if directed at the addressees themselves.

Next in v. 22, the writer makes a bare assertion, βλέπεις ὅτι ἡ πίστις συνήργει τοῖς ἔργοις αὐτοῦ καὶ ἐκ τῶν ἔργων ἡ πίστις ἐτελειώθη, closing all dialogical space. In terms of exchange, the position of the writer is depicted as apparent to the opponent, glaringly obvious, and there is no room for negotiation. Continuing to use Abraham as argumentative support, the writer in v. 23 introduces the voice of Torah in a quotation, which affirms that it was due to Abraham's belief, worked out in his willingness to sacrifice his son, Isaac, that righteousness was credited to him. This use of Projection dialogically expands the text to allow the voice of Torah to come into dialogue with the text, a voice that the recipients would consider authoritative. Because of its authority, a value position supported by Torah can be easily reasoned to be standard, ethical, and necessary, and so this projected speech functions as a *rationalizing* ideological strategy.

James 2:24–26

ὁρᾶτε ὅτι ἐξ ἔργων δικαιοῦται ἄνθρωπος καὶ οὐκ ἐκ πίστεως μόνον ὁμοίως δὲ καὶ Ῥαὰβ ἡ πόρνη οὐκ ἐξ ἔργων ἐδικαιώθη ὑποδεξαμένη τοὺς ἀγγέλους καὶ ἑτέρᾳ ὁδῷ ἐκβαλοῦσα ὥσπερ γὰρ τὸ σῶμα χωρὶς πνεύματος νεκρόν ἐστιν, οὕτως καὶ ἡ πίστις χωρὶς ἔργων νεκρά ἐστιν

You see that a man is justified by actions and not by faith alone. And also was not Rahab the prostitute also justified by actions when she received the messengers and sent them out another way? For just as the body without the spirit is dead, so too faith without works is dead.

In this section the writer turns his attention back to his audience; this is made clear by the shift in person from second person singular to second person plural in the verb ὁρᾶτε. In like manner as the bare assertion above that the opponent saw faith working with actions, the writer now makes the same monoglossic statement to his audience. Further, just as the writer dialogically expanded the text with his opponent to acknowledge the voice of Torah, he does the same here asking the question about Rahab's actions. Was not she, too, justified by actions? The dialogic space is opened for the purpose of allowing the audience to concede to the writer's value position. The writer, even after the use of the diatribe in vv. 18–23, still attempts to position by consent, *legitimating* his value position, which is the predominant ideological strategy in ch. 2 when the audience is directly addressed.

The conjunction γάρ in v. 26 realizes internal consequence; the writer has navigated his audience to the point where the logical conclusion that faith without actions is dead. This use of Concession accompanied by the assertive attitude realized in the auxiliary verb ἐστίν ends this section of text with a monoglossic formation expressed as a conclusion. The writer's value position has been constructed and defended against competing voices, and the audience is construed as being aligned with the writer's ideological stance.

CONCLUSION

As has been brought to light by this analysis, the engagement strategies used in the diatribe differ markedly from the sections of text that directly address the writer's audience. As a whole, the text before and after the diatribe is more heteroglossic. The shift from the subjunctive mood forms in 2:14–17 to the future forms thereafter is a key marker of this. Also, by asking multiple leading questions, the writer's rhetoric works to make the audience position themselves; he strategically directs them while avoiding squelching their dialogic involvement in the text. The diatribe, on the other hand, does not follow the same engagement strategy. Instead of being dialogically expansive, the diatribe is characterized predominantly by dialogic contraction. The imaginary interlocutor's position is expressed in a short quotation, but then the writer's voice stifles the opponent, only briefly allowing it to intrude to concede to the writer's questions. However, even in this brief heteroglossic moment, the writer calls the imaginary interlocutor an empty-headed fool. Not only was his faith-minus-actions stance logically ridiculous—just consider the demons for example—but more, the opponent's position does not even align with their father of faith, Abraham. In the tearing down of the opponent's position the writer carefully controls the dialogicality of the text, which indicates that the writer's value position is essential and non-negotiable for the Christian community. Linguistically, when insult meets monogloss there is little room left for negotiating stances; there is, however, overt shaming and adamant demanding.

In ch. 2 of the letter, James is unwilling to address his audience in the manner that he interacts with his imaginary interlocutor, though he does so later in ch. 4. But why not here? The linguistic findings of the Engagement model suggest that hegemonic struggle is the answer. While the context of situation cannot be fully recovered, an SFL model allows for some recovery of context given that language necessarily redounds with context.[124] Thus, the voices that James brings into the text to contest redound with the context of situation.[125] That James does not confront

124. See Hasan, "Place of Context," 166–89; Martin, "Discourse Studies," 158–60; "Modelling Context" 25–61.

125. Several studies have affirmed, though not by using a SFL framework, that the situations projected in James indicate that the audience was becoming reliant upon a rich patron who embodied a conflicting ideological construct to that of the audience. See Batten, "Asceticism of Resistance in James," 355–70; "God in the Letter of James," 257–72; Edgar, *Has God Not Chosen the Poor*, 113–36; Kloppenborg, "Patronage

his audience directly concerning their duplicity reflects features of tenor relations. By keeping the text dialogically expanded in vv. 1–17 James works to reestablish behavioral norms and Christian identity without causing the audience to raise their defenses to become hostile toward James himself. If his audience will adopt these components of James's ideology, then he can more effectively address the contradictions of his audience's ideological complex at a later point in the text.

The diatribe in ch. 2 follows this same rhetorical strategy. Diatribe produces a different dialogical pathway, and by addressing an imaginary interlocutor James can say what he wills without reservation of distancing his audience from him or the ideological stances he promotes. James can be assertive, sarcastic, and condemning, as he is, while keeping the text dialogically closed off from his audience, and he will not detract from his goal to reshape his audience's behavior. Further, James also reestablishes the social alliances that are grounded in assuming James's ideology. These social relations are strengthened by James's ideological strategies, and foremost by his *legitimating* strategies—namely his use of leading questions where he positions the audience by their own consent, and also by *unifying* their group by familial addresses. Together these ideological strategies combat the issues of ideological struggle within the group in a rhetorically effectual manner so that James can proceed as an authority figure having re-solidified relations of power.

In short, the diatribe is implemented and ideologically reinvested to allow the writer to reestablish solidarity and power relations, along with behavioral norms, Christian identity, and beliefs in a way that is forthright and forceful, yet does not raise the defenses of the addressees. The use of diatribe does not simply "amplify the argument" as some have suggested;[126] it functions to provide James with the linguistic leg-room to kick out those adverse views that were mutually incompatible with the identity of the group, and to reestablish necessary social relations, both with his audience and his audience's disposition to "empty-headed fools," so that James can elicit compliance from his addressees and accomplish social change.

Avoidance in James," 755–94; Wachob, *Voice of Jesus*, 178–85. See McKnight, *Letter of James*, 181, who acknowledges the semantic feature of the subjunctive mood-form and suggests the dialogues in James potentially reflect the audience's situation, but further adds that their depictions are not merely hypothetical, but "rhetorically" hypothetical.

126. Contra Watson, "James 2," 120.

BIBLIOGRAPHY

Althusser, Louis. "Ideology and Ideological State Apparatuses (Notes towards an Investigation)." In *Essays on Ideology*, 1–60. London: Verso, 1984.

Aune, David E. *The New Testament in Its Literary Environment*. LEC 8. Philadelphia: Westminster, 1987.

Baasland, Ernst. *Jakobsbrevet*. KNT 16. Uppsala: EFS, 1992.

Bakhtin, Mikhail M. "Discourse in the Novel." In *The Dialogic Imagination: Four Essays*, edited by Michael Holquist, 259–422. Translated by Caryl Emerson and Michael Holquist. Austin: University of Texas Press, 1981.

———. "The Problem of Speech Genres." In *Speech Genres & Other Late Essays*, edited by Caryl Emerson and Michael Holquist, 60–102. Translated by Vern W. McGee. Austin: University of Texas Press, 1986.

Basevi, Claudio, and Juan Chapa. "Philippians 2.6–11: The Rhetorical Function of a Pauline 'Hymn.'" In *Rhetoric and the New Testament: Essays from the 1992 Heidelberg Conference*, edited by Stanley E. Porter and Thomas H. Olbricht, 338–56. JSNTSup 90. Sheffield: Sheffield Academic, 1993.

Batten, Alicia J. "An Asceticism of Resistance in James." In *Asceticism and the New Testament*, edited by L. E. Vaage and V. L. Wimbush, 355–70. London: Routledge, 1999.

———. "God in the Letter of James: Patron or Benefactor?" *NTS* 50 (2004) 257–72.

———. "Ideological Strategies in the Letter of James." In *Reading James with New Eyes: Methodological Reassessments of the Letter of James*, edited by Robert L. Webb and John S. Kloppenborg, 6–26. LNTS 342. London: T. & T. Clark International, 2007.

———. *What Are They Saying about the Letter of James?* WATSA. New York: Paulist, 2009.

Betz, Hans Dieter. *Galatians*. Hermeneia. Philadelphia: Fortress, 1979.

———. "The Literary Composition and Function of Paul's Letter to the Galatians." *NTS* 21 (1975) 353–79.

Culler, Jonathan. *On Deconstruction: Theory and Criticism after Structuralism*. Ithaca, NY: Cornell University Press, 1982.

Davis, David Brion. *The Problem of Slavery in the Age of Revolution 1770–1823*. Ithaca, NY: Cornell University Press, 1975.

Dawson, Zachary K. "Language as Negotiation: Toward a Systemic Functional Model for Ideological Criticism with Application to James 2:1–13." In *Modeling Biblical Language: Selected Papers from the McMaster Divinity College Linguistics Circle*, edited by Stanley E. Porter et al., 362–90. LBS 13. Leiden: Brill, 2016.

Di Marco, Angelico-Salvatore. "Rhetoric and Hermeneutic—on a Rhetorical Pattern: Chiasmus and Circularity." In *Rhetoric and the New Testament: Essays from the 1992 Heidelberg Conference*, edited by Stanley E. Porter and Thomas H. Olbricht, 479–491. JSNTSup 90. Sheffield: Sheffield Academic, 1993.

Dibelius, Martin. *James: Commentary on the Epistle of James*, edited by H. Koester. Revised by H. Greeven. Translated by M. Williams. Hermeneia. Philadelphia: Fortress, 1976.

Dvorak, James D. "Ask and Ye Shall Reposition the Readers: James's Use of Questions to (Re-) Align His Readers." In *The Epistle of James: Linguistic Exegesis of an Early Christian Letter*, edited by James D. Dvorak and Zachary K. Dawson, 196–245. LENT 1. Eugene, OR: Pickwick, 2019.

————. "'Not Like Cain': Marking Moral Boundaries through Vilification of the Other in 1 John 3:1–18." *Dialogismos* 1 (2016) 1–19.

————. "The Interpersonal Metafunction in 1 Corinthians 1–4: The Tenor of Toughness." PhD diss., McMaster Divinity College, 2012.

————. "'Prodding with Prosody': Persuasion and Social Influence through the Lens of Appraisal Theory." *BAGL* 4 (2015) 85–120.

Eagleton, Terry. *Ideology: An Introduction.* New York: Verso, 1991.

Edgar, David H. *Has God Not Chosen the Poor? The Social Setting of the Epistle of James.* JSNTSup 206. Sheffield: Sheffield Academic, 2001.

Elliott, John H. "The Epistle of James in Rhetorical Social Scientific Perspective: Holiness-Wholeness and Patterns of Replication." *BTB* 23 (1993) 71–81.

————. *What Is Social-Scientific Criticism?* GBS. Minneapolis: Fortress, 1993.

Fairclough, Norman. *Analysing Discourse: Textual Analysis for Social Research.* Abingdon: Routledge, 2003.

————. *Discourse and Social Change.* Cambridge: Polity, 1992.

————. "Language and Ideology." In *Critical Discourse Analysis: The Critical Study of Language,* 56–68. 2nd ed. Harlow, UK: Pearson, 2010.

Fairclough, Norman, et al. "Critical Discourse Analysis." In *Discourse Studies: A Multidisciplinary Introduction,* edited by Teun A. van Dijk, 357–84. 2nd ed. London: Sage, 1997.

Fewster, Gregory P. "Symbolizing Identity and the Role of Texts: Proposals, Prospects, and Some Comments on the Eucharist Meal." *BAGL* 2 (2013) 81–108.

Frankenmölle, Hubert. "Das semantische Netz des Jakobusbriefes: Zur Einheit eines umstrittenen Briefes." *BZ* 34 (1990) 161–97.

Frow, John. "Discourse and Power." *ES* 14 (1985) 193–214.

Gee, James Paul. *Social Linguistics and Literacies: Ideologies in Discourses.* 5th ed. New York: Routledge, 2015.

Gonda, Jan. *The Character of Indo-European Moods, with Special Reference to Greek and Sanskrit.* Wiesbaden: Harrassowitz, 1956.

Gramsci, Antonio. *Selections from the Prison Notebooks.* Edited and translated by Quintin Hoare and Geoffrey Nowell Smith. New York: International, 1971.

Guess, Raymond. *The Idea of a Critical Theory: Habermas and the Frankfurt School.* New York: Cambridge University Press, 1981.

Halliday, M. A. K. *Halliday's Introduction to Function Grammar.* Revised by Christian M. I. M. Matthiessen. 4th ed. London: Routledge, 2014.

Halliday, M. A. K., and Ruqaiya Hasan. *Cohesion in English.* ELS 9. London: Longman, 1976.

Hartin, Patrick J. *James.* Sacra Pagina 14. Collegeville, MN: Liturgical, 2003.

Hasan, Ruqaiya. "The Place of Context in a Systemic Functional Model." In *Continuum Companion to Systemic Functional Linguistics,* edited by M. A. K. Halliday and Jonathan J. Webster, 166–89. London: Continuum, 2009.

Holquist, Michael. *Dialogism: Bakhtin and His World.* London: Routledge, 1990.

Kennedy, George A. *New Testament Interpretation through Rhetorical Criticism.* Chapel Hill: University of North Carolina Press, 1984.

Kloppenborg, John S. "The Emulation of the Jesus Tradition in the Letter of James." In *Reading James with New Eyes: Methodological Reassessments of the Letter of James,* edited by Robert L. Webb and John S. Kloppenborg, 121–50. LNTS 342. London: T. & T. Clark International, 2007.

————. "Patronage Avoidance in James." *HTS* 55 (1999) 755–94.

Lemke, Jay L. "Discourses in Conflict: Heteroglossia and Text Semantics." In *Systemic Functional Approaches to Discourse: Selected Papers from the 12th International Systemic Workshop*, edited by James D. Benson and William S. Greaves, 29–50. Norwood, NJ: Ablex, 1988.

————. "Interpersonal Meaning in Discourse: Value Orientations." In *Advances in Systemic Linguistics: Recent Theory and Practice*, edited by Martin Davies and Louise Ravelli, 82–104. London: Pinter, 1992.

————. *Textual Politics: Discourse and Social Dynamics.* Critical Perspectives on Literacy and Education. Abingdon: Taylor & Francis, 1995.

Locke, Terry. *Critical Discourse Analysis.* London: Continuum International, 2004.

Louw, Johannes P., and Eugene A. Nida. *Greek-English Lexicon of the New Testament Based on Semantic Domains.* 2 vols. 2nd ed. New York: United Bible Societies, 1988.

Malina, Bruce J. *The New Testament World: Insights from Cultural Anthropology.* 3rd ed. Louisville: Westminster John Knox, 2001.

Martin, J. R. "Discourse Studies." In *Continuum Companion to Systemic Functional Linguistics*, edited by M. A. K. Halliday and Jonathan J. Webster, 154–165. London: Continuum, 2009.

————. *English Text: System and Structure.* Amsterdam: Benjamins, 1992.

————. "Modelling Context: A Crooked Path of Progress in Contextual Linguistics." In *Text and Context in Functional Linguistics*, edited by Mohsen Ghadessy, 25–61. Amsterdam: Benjamins, 1999.

Martin, J. R., and David Rose. *Genre Relations: Mapping Culture.* London: Equinox, 2008.

————. *Working with Discourse: Meaning Beyond the Clause.* 2nd ed. New York: Continuum, 2007.

Martin, J. R., and P. R. R. White. *The Language of Evaluation: Appraisal in English.* New York: Palgrave Macmillan, 2005.

Martin, Ralph P. *James.* WBC 48. Waco, TX: Word, 1988.

Martín-Asensio, Gustavo. "Hallidayan Functional Grammar as Heir to New Testament Rhetorical Criticism." In *The Rhetorical Interpretation of Scripture: Essays from the 1996 Malibu Conference*, edited by Stanley E. Porter and Dennis L. Stamps, 84–107. JSNTSup 180. Sheffield: Sheffield Academic, 1999.

Mayor, Joseph. B. *The Epistle of James: The Greek Text with Introduction Notes and Comments.* 3rd ed. London: Macmillan, 1910.

McCartney, Dan G. *James.* BECNT. Grand Rapids: Baker Academic, 2009.

McKay, K. L. *A New Syntax of the Verb in New Testament Greek: An Aspectual Approach.* SBG 5. New York: Peter Lang, 1994.

McKnight, Scot. "James 2:18a: The Unidentifiable Interlocutor." *WTJ* 52 (1990) 355–64.

————. *The Letter of James.* NICNT. Grand Rapids: Eerdmans, 2011.

Meeks, Wayne A. *The First Urban Christians: The Social World of the Apostle Paul.* New Haven: Yale University Press, 1983.

————. *The Origins of Christian Morality: The First Two Centuries.* New Haven: Yale University Press, 1993.

Mikinori, Nakanishi. "A Consideration of the Concept of Hegemony in Terms of Critical Discourse Analysis Focusing on Intertextuality and Assumptions." *GCWCRB* 59 (2009) 15–21.

Moo, Douglas J. *The Letter of James*. PNTC. Grand Rapids: Eerdmans, 2000.

Olbricht, Thomas H. "Rhetorical Criticism." In *Dictionary of Biblical Criticism and Interpretation*, edited by Stanley E. Porter, 325–27. London: Routledge, 2007.

Palmer, F. R. *Mood and Modality*. Cambridge: Cambridge University Press, 1986.

Porter, Stanley E. *Idioms of the Greek New Testament*. 2nd ed. BLG 2. Sheffield: Sheffield Academic, 1994.

———. "Is Critical Discourse Analysis Critical? An Evaluation Using Philemon as a Test Case." In *Discourse Analysis and the New Testament: Approaches and Results*, edited by Stanley E. Porter and Jeffrey T. Reed, 47–70. JSNTSup 170. Sheffield: Sheffield Academic, 1999.

———. "Systemic Functional Linguistics and the Greek Language: The Need for Further Modeling." In *Modeling Biblical Language: Selected Papers from the McMaster Divinity College Linguistics Circle*, edited by Stanley E. Porter et al., 9–47. LBS 13. Leiden: Brill, 2016.

———. *Verbal Aspect in the Greek of the New Testament with Reference to Tense and Mood*. SBG 1. New York: Peter Lang, 1989.

Ropes, James Hardy. *A Critical and Exegetical Commentary on the Epistle of St. James*. ICC. Edinburgh: T. & T. Clark, 1916.

Snyman, A. H. "Persuasion in Philippians 4.1–20." In *Rhetoric and the New Testament: Essays from the 1992 Heidelberg Conference*, edited by Stanley E. Porter and Thomas H. Olbricht, 325–37. JSNTSup 90. Sheffield: Sheffield Academic, 1993.

Stowers, Stanley K. "The Diatribe." In *Greco-Roman Literature and the New Testament*, edited by David E. Aune, 71–83. SBLSBS 21. Atlanta: Scholars, 1988.

———. *The Diatribe and Paul's Letter to the Romans*. SBLDS 57. Chico, CA: Scholars, 1981.

Thompson, Geoff. "But Me Some Buts: A Multidimensional View of Conjunction." *Text* 25 (2005) 763–91.

Thurén, Lauri. "Risky Rhetoric in James?" *NovT* 37 (1995) 262–84.

van der Westhuizen, J. D. N. "Stylistic Techniques and Their Functions in James 2.14–26." *Neot* 25 (1991) 89–107.

Varner, William. *The Book of James: A New Perspective: A Linguistic Commentary Applying Discourse Analysis*. The Woodlands, TX: Kress Biblical Resources, 2010.

Vološinov, Valentin N. *Marxism and the Philosophy of Language*. Translated by Ladislav Matejka and I. R. Titunik. London: Routledge, 1995.

Wachob, Wesley H. *The Voice of Jesus in the Social Rhetoric of James*. SNTSMS 106. Cambridge: Cambridge University Press, 2000.

Watson, Duane F. "An Assessment of the Rhetoric and Rhetorical Analysis of the Letter of James." In *Reading James with New Eyes: Methodological Reassessments of the Letter of James*, edited by Robert L. Webb and John S. Kloppenborg, 99–120. LNTS 342. New York: T. & T. Clark International, 2007.

———. "James 2 in Light of Greco-Roman Schemes of Argumentation." *NTS* 39 (1993) 94–121.

———. "The Rhetoric of James 3.1–12 and a Classical Pattern of Argumentation." *NovT* 35 (1993) 48–64.

———. "Rhetorical Criticism of Hebrews and the Catholic Epistles Since 1978." *CurBS* 5 (1997) 175–207.

White, P. R. R. "Beyond Modality and Hedging: A Dialogic View of the Language of Intersubjective Stance." *Text* 23 (2003) 259–84.

Wuellner, Wilhelm. "Der Jakobusbrief im Licht der Rhetorik und Textpragmatik." *LB* 43 (1978) 5–66.

———. "Where Is Rhetorical Criticism Taking Us?" *CBQ* 49 (1987) 448–63.

8

Ask and Ye Shall Position the Readers

James's Use of Questions to (Re-)Align His Readers

JAMES D. DVORAK

INTRODUCTION

THAT AN ENTIRE CHAPTER of this book is dedicated to James's use of questions might seem a bit odd or perhaps even surprising, given that the letter of James is not exactly brimming with questions. In fact, by my count, there are only eighteen questions in the Greek text of the letter (see Appendix).[1] However, as the title suggests, the scope of this chapter is broader than merely identifying and counting the questions that appear in the letter. The thesis of this article is that James used questions as a means of positioning (or re-positioning) his readers, or at least attempting to do so, such that they would adopt (or adopt again) a particular theological (ideological) perspective and its attendant values. In arguing for this thesis, I will make three moves.

First, I will describe the ideological purpose of the letter of James. An important part of this move is to define key terminology (e.g., "values" and "ideology") and to create the theoretical context for why and how I will proceed to read the letter critically. In the second move, I will

1. James 2:2–4, 5, 6, 7, 14, 16, 20, 21, 25; 3:11, 12, 13; 4:1 (2x), 4, 5–6, 12. Note that, following NA28, I do not read Jas 2:1 as a question (contra NRSV). Also, following Dibelius (*James*, 252) and Johnson (*Letter of James*, 329), I read Jas 5:13–14 neither as conditionals (*If anyone among you is sick/cheerful*) nor as questions (*Is anyone among you sick/cheerful?*) (contra Davids [*Commentary on James*, 191], Varner [*Book of James*, 190], Martin [*James*, 205], NRSV, NASB, NIV, NET and other popular contemporary English versions).

lay out a two-part sociolinguistic model for analyzing questions. The first part lays out the basic grammar and syntax of questions, paying particular attention to how questions are identified as open or closed. The second part, utilizing a functional linguistic model known as Appraisal Theory, establishes the connection between James's grammatical, syntactical, and lexical choices and the interpersonal meaning(s) realized by those choices that would, at least potentially, position his readers to take up or to give up one or another value position. I zero in on a model of Engagement that describes how questions function in values negotiation and paraenesis/resocialization. The final move in the chapter will be to analyze a number of the questions that James uses in his letter and to offer an interpretation of each from the perspective of the theory and model that I have put forward.

THE LETTER OF JAMES AS RENEGOTIATION OF CORE GROUP VALUES AND IDEOLOGY

The Negotiation of Ideology and Values as "Struggle"

Although there is widespread disagreement among scholars regarding the precise identity of the recipients[2] and the specific details of the purpose of the letter of James,[3] there appears to be relatively little disagreement over the letter's hortatory nature, that is, its intent to be *per*suasive in regards to some issues and behaviors and *dis*suasive in regards to others.[4] There is a growing trend among Jacobean scholars in asking "what the text intends to do" to its readers rather than asking the more historical and literary-critical question of what the letter "is."[5] These scholars have

---

2. Wall's comment ("James, Letter of," 548) is typical: "The precise identity of the first readers of James is indeterminate and opinion remains divided. Lacking specific details of the readers' identity, most exegetes are content to locate them in either of two places: post-Pauline Diaspora or in prewar (AD 66–70) Palestine-Syria." See also Davids, *Commentary on James*, 28–34.

3. Throughout this essay, I use the somewhat cumbersome "letter of James" to refer to the document itself; I reserve "James" to refer to the writer of the letter and not the colloquial shorthand name for the letter. For a recent discussion regarding which James might be the actual writer of the letter, see McKnight, *Letter of James*, 13–38; see also Batten, *What Are They Saying*, 28–46.

4. For example, Köstenberger et al., *Lion and the Lamb*, 315, speak of the hortatory nature of the letter as a "given."

5. Wachob, *Voice of Jesus*, 3.

begun to focus their attention on the letter's *ideological purpose,*[6] and this is demonstrable in how they describe the letter's intent. For example, deSilva points out that, like the Greco–Roman ethical philosophers, James employs diatribe *"to promote a particular set of behaviors and attitudes while calling contrary behaviors and attitudes into question . . ."*[7] Cargal argues that James's intent appears to have been "to *convince* the implied reader[s] to adopt a certain *'system of convictions'* . . . regarding *how to perceive and order the realm of human experience."*[8] Wachob claims that the letter was intended to fulfill a "social function," namely "to *constrain the thought and behavior of its audience"*[9] and "to effect a particular kind of community by remolding the thought and behavior of its addressees to conform with a particular understanding of God's truth."[10] Batten asserts that the letter "deliberately seeks to *convince* its audience about *what to think and what to do,* and this *persuasion* clearly involves consideration of material concerns, as well as the relationship between ideas and practices."[11] In short, these scholars take the letter of James to be an example of paraenesis—not in the same way that Dibelius understood it (i.e., as a literary form consisting of a loose collection of sayings and traditions) but as a social purpose, namely the strengthening or adoption of a certain set of values.[12]

One may abstract from this what scholars tend to think are the main features of the letter's ideological purpose:

1. How James portrayed the implied readers in terms of their beliefs, perspectives, and assumptions about God

2. How James portrayed the readers' understanding of what it meant to be a group of Jesus followers

6. See Batten, "Ideological Strategies," 6–26.

7. deSilva, *Introduction to the New Testament,* 821 (italics added). See also Dawson, "Rules of 'Engagement,'" in this volume.

8. Cargal, *Restoring the Diaspora,* 40 (italics added).

9. Wachob, *Voice of Jesus,* 22 (italics added).

10. Ibid., 187.

11. Batten, "Ideological Strategies," 16 (italics added).

12. Penner, "Epistle of James in Current Research," 270. See also Perdue, "The Social Character of Paraenesis," 5–39; Perdue, "Paraenesis and the Epistle of James," 241–56.

3. How and to what extent, in James's view, these things shaped the ethos[13] of the group[14]

This purpose becomes more perceptible through a careful examination of the positive, negative, and/or (seemingly) neutral evaluations that James makes in relation to each of these features.[15] Equally important is an examination of the engagement strategies James employs in order to present himself "as recognizing, answering, ignoring, challenging, rejecting, fending off, anticipating or accommodating actual or potential interlocutors and the value positions they represent."[16] These two types of analysis, which make up the two major axes of appraisal analysis,[17] provide a way to perceive and to describe the *ideological struggle* reflected and acted out in the text. "Ideological struggle" is shorthand for the negotiation of values and the ideological stance(s) that those values reify. This negotiation is generally referred to as a "struggle" because, typically, the participants involved in the negotiation vie to privilege certain value positions over others through various expressions of power.[18] This social process is commonly referred to as persuasion (or, negatively, dissuasion), which is an inexorable part of resocialization. I will return to this topic, but first it is necessary to define the somewhat plastic terms "ideology" and "value."

13. I.e., the generally fixed patterns of behavior (see Louw and Nida, *Greek-English Lexicon*, 2:507).

14. It is important to make clear that James and the intended recipients of his letter lived in a group-oriented/collectivist rather than individualistic society (Malina, *New Testament World*, 60–66). I take "group" to refer to a "collection of individuals who perceive themselves to be members of the same social category [and] share some emotional involvement in this common definition of themselves" (Tajfel and Turner, "Integrated Theory of Intergroup Conflict," 40). This stands over against a collectivity, which is a random gathering of people (Malina, *New Testament World*, 198–220).

15. "Evaluation" refers to one's attitude or stance towards, perspective upon, or feelings about entities, propositions, or subject matter under discussion (Dvorak, "To Incline Another's Heart," 606; Hunston and Thompson, *Evaluation in Text*, 5).

16. Martin and White, *Language of Evaluation*, 2. See also Dvorak, "Interpersonal Metafunction," 5.

17. See now Dvorak, "Interpersonal Metafunction," 50–108; Dvorak, "To Incline Another's Heart," 607–15; Dvorak, "Prodding with Prosody," 93–103.

18. I define "power" as "one's ability to exercise control over and to gain compliance from another with regard to the other's beliefs, attitudes, behaviors, etc." (Dvorak, "Prodding with Prosody," 87–90). See also Pilch, "Power," 137–39; McVann, "Compliance," 30.

Of these two terms, "ideology" is the more abstract and encompassing notion. I find Elliott's definition to be the most serviceable:

> [Ideology is] an integrated system of beliefs, perspectives, assumptions, and values, not necessarily true or false, that reflect the perceived needs and interests of a group or class at a particular time in history; that contain the chief criteria for interpreting social reality; and that serve to define, explain, and legitimate collective wants and needs, interests, values, norms, and organizational goals in a continuous interaction with the material forces of history.[19]

In short, ideology is a conglomeration of a group's value preferences or orientations[20] that gives meaning to the group's activities and that distinguishes that group from other groups.[21]

What I find satisfying about Elliott's formulation is that it respects and holds in balance the notion that ideology is to be understood as both *system* and *process*. The system perspective, which is very similar to what some call "world view,"[22] portrays ideology somewhat neutrally as a kind of "map" by which a social group constructs a more or less ordered ethos or, as Cargal puts it, a "system of convictions." Yet, Elliott's definition also suggests that ideology is not merely a monolithic, "static" representation of the way a group views the world. It is also a dynamic process by which a group's members, through the enactment and articulation of their beliefs, perspectives, assumptions, and values, concomitantly *perpetuate*, *protect*, and *promote* those beliefs, perspectives, assumptions, and values.[23] This implies engagement with other groups' ideologies, and if, for whatever reason, the others' points of view are appraised as "less favorable" than the ideology of one's own group, group members will promote the ideology of their own group and demote the others' ideologies.[24] In other

---

19. Elliott, *What Is Social-Scientific Criticism*, 130.

20. See Pilch, "Interpreting the Bible," 92–99; Kluckhohn and Strodtbeck, *Variations in Value Orientations*, 4.

21. Malina, *Christian Origins*, 112; Hodge and Kress, *Social Semiotics*, 3.

22. Gregory Elliott refers to this as the "socially relative" view of ideology (Elliott, "Ideology," 340). Compare with Sire's definition of "world view" (*Universe Next Door*, 17): "A world view is a set of presuppositions (assumptions which may be true, partially true, or entirely false) which we hold (consciously or subconsciously, consistently or inconsistently) about the basic make-up of our world."

23. Malina, *Christian Origins*, 178–79.

24. See ibid., 178–79. See also Hodge and Kress, *Social Semiotics*, 123, where they

words, different groups interpret "the way things are" (or are not) and "the way things ought to be" (or ought not to be) in different ways, and the result is tension and struggle.[25] Most of the time, this tension goes relatively unnoticed; occasionally, however, some issue arises that foregrounds ideological difference, which then results in "clashing and (re-)hashing" of values.[26]

"Values" (or "value positions") are shared ideas or standards about what constitutes the worthwhile goals and directions in life for members of a group.[27] Although values are typically described abstractly as "ideas," it cannot be overstated that values can only be recognized through the semogenic (i.e., meaning-making) *behaviors* or *social actions* of the group and its members. Pilch and Malina appropriately emphasize this connection in the multiple ways as they define "value": (1) "a general quality and direction in life that human beings are *expected to embody in their behavior*"; (2) "a general, normative *orientation of action* in a social system"; and (3) "an emotionally anchored *commitment to pursue and support certain directions or types of actions*."[28]

At a finer level of delicacy, values may be divided into three categories: core, peripheral, and means.[29] Core values (also called ends values) are the more general, yet most important, expressions of a group's ends or goals.[30] Because they are the most important, it is expected that group members will, to a greater or lesser degree, realize them in every human interaction.[31] Means values (also called instrumental values) are the values that are acted out in order to facilitate the realization of core and peripheral values.[32] Peripheral values (also called secondary values)

---

discuss modality as an expression of "affinity" (or lack thereof).

25. Dvorak, "To Incline Another's Heart," 605.

26. See Martin, *English Text*, 581–82.

27. See Peoples and Bailey, *Humanity*, 31. Malina (*Christian Origins*, 112) describes a value as "[t]he ordinary name for the general direction of the flow of action, a direction socially expected and usually pursued in the group."

28. Pilch and Malina, "Introduction," xix (italics added). Berger and Luckmann, *Social Construction of Reality*, 93–94.

29. See Pilch and Malina, "Introduction," xxii–xxiv.

30. Malina, *Christian Origins*, 112.

31. Pilch and Malina, "Introduction," xxii–xxiii.

32. Ibid.

are values that are expected to be realized only in specific situations and specific kinds of interaction.[33]

Perhaps an example will help to make this more concrete. Social-scientific critics[34] have demonstrated nearly unequivocally that honor—i.e., the public claim to social worth and the public acknowledgement of it—was the central core value of the ancient circum-Mediterranean world, which includes the world portrayed in the Bible.[35] As such, honor was the primary goal towards which people "channeled the flow of action" of their lives.[36] In the social institution of kinship, the peripheral yet still exceedingly important value of family-centeredness derived from the core value of honor.[37] In fact, the relationship between honor and family-centeredness is so interdependent that at birth a person inherited the honor status of the family into which they were born.[38] It then was their lot in life to maintain that status, and doing so required adopting and contributing to a certain ethos within the kin group. One means value enacted to fulfill the value of family-centeredness is "love" (ἀγάπη) or "sibling love" (φιλαδελφία), which, in social terms, refers to attachment to the group/family, bonding, belonging, or commitment.[39] Family members could demonstrate love for each other in a number of different ways, but in essence loving was accomplished through various other means values such as harmony, concord, unity, generosity, and the like.[40] By contrast, whereas in contemporary US society "sibling rivalry" and other forms of dysfunction are considered a "normal" feature of kinship, in the world of the Bible, such rivalries and dysfunctions, although they

---

33. Ibid.

34. See Esler, "Social-Scientific Approaches," 337–40; Dvorak, "John H. Elliott's Social-Scientific Criticism," 251–78; Dvorak, "Edwin Judge," 179–203.

35. Meeks, *Moral World*, 12; Malina, "Honor and Shame," 89–90; Malina, *New Testament World*, 27–53; Neyrey, "Loss of Wealth, Loss of Family and Loss of Honour," 140–41; deSilva, *Honor, Patronage, Kinship & Purity*, 23–27; Rohrbaugh, "Honor," 109–25. Although it is more appropriate to refer to both honor and *positive* shame (positive shame refers to one's concern about and protection of honor), as core values, here, for the sake of brevity, I am focusing on honor.

36. Malina, *Christian Origins*, 112–13.

37. See McVann, "Family-Centeredness," 64–67.

38. deSilva, *Honor, Patronage, Kinship & Purity*, 158.

39. Malina, "Love," 106–9.

40. See deSilva, *Honor, Patronage, Kinship & Purity*, 165–73.

certainly existed and are described in the Bible,[41] were considered potentially shameful and could put a family in a socially precarious position.

There are two further properties of values that Pilch and Malina mention that are important for the current study. First, values and the behaviors through which they are acted out are *emotionally anchored*. This becomes especially apparent in lived experience when core values differ between groups (or individuals) and conflict arises. To be sure, the four main social institutions of contemporary US society—politics, economics, religion, and kinship[42]—are rife with examples, but to keep from getting too far afield, consider the following example from the realm of kinship. Imagine a situation in which a thirteen-year-old boy spends the night with one of his schoolmates. While there, the friend's parents allow both boys to watch an R-rated movie even though they know that the parents of the thirteen-year-old do not allow him to watch movies with such a rating.[43] When the parents of the thirteen-year-old discover what has happened, the sense of difference between themselves and the parents of their son's friend becomes salient. Further, they feel a threat to solidarity, perhaps even a breach of trust, which may further lead to feelings of anger or disappointment. These feelings may result in any number of social actions such as placing limits on when, where, and how much time their son spends with his friend; speaking negatively about the friend's parents and their actions; or even confronting the other teenager's parents and engaging in a potentially heated debate about "shoulds" and "oughts."[44]

41. Consider the Joseph novella (Gen 37–50) as just one example. See also the Testaments of the Twelve Patriarchs, esp. the Testament of Simeon, behind which, ostensibly, looms the legend of Joseph and his envious brothers. See also Elliott, *Beware the Evil Eye*, 183–84.

42. "Briefly, *kinship* is about naturing and nurturing people; it is held together by commitment (also called loyalty or solidarity) and forms a structure of human belonging. *Economics* is about provisioning a group of people; it is held together by inducement, that is, the exchange of goods and services, and forms the adaptive structure of society. *Politics* looks to effective collective action; it is held together by power and forms the vertical organizational structure of a society. Finally, *religion* deals with the overarching order of existence, with meaning; it is held together by influence; it provides reasons for what exists and the models that generate those reasons" (Malina, *Social Gospel of Jesus*, 16).

43. One can see already that all four social institutions are interrelated and complementary; rarely (if ever) does social behavior occur that reifies values from only one of these areas. In this example, the two salient institutions are kinship and, likely, religion.

44. See now Malina and Neyrey, "Conflict in Luke–Acts," 97–122; Malina and

Second, because values are *shared* ideas or standards, the members
of the group sharing them *expect* everyone who belongs to the group to
live up to or in accordance with them, especially if they are core values of
the group. These expectations play a significant role in marking out the
social boundaries of the group. If someone in the group does not live up
to or in line with the group's values, or if they behave in a way that overtly
contradicts the group's values, then that person is considered to be "out
of bounds" and in need of correction. If they do not respond to the correction, change their behavior, and move back "within bounds" (via some
sort of ritual), they run the risk of being shunned by their groupmates or
expelled from the group. An example of this, albeit on the extreme end
of the spectrum, is Paul's charge to the Corinthians to expel from their
group the man who was involved in an illicit, adulterous, and possibly
incestuous relationship with his stepmother (1 Cor 5:1–5).[45] The apostle
even goes so far as to make the following charge, which boldly draws a
very clear social boundary around the group (5:11):[46]

> [11] νῦν δὲ ἔγραψα ὑμῖν μὴ συναναμίγνυσθαι ἐάν τις ἀδελφὸς
> ὀνομαζόμενος ἢ πόρνος ἢ πλεονέκτης ἢ εἰδωλολάτρης ἢ
> λοίδορος ἢ μέθυσος ἢ ἅρπαξ, τῷ τοιούτῳ μηδὲ συνεσθίειν.

> [11] *But now I write to you, if anyone who is called a brother or
> sister would be a sexually deviant person or a greedy person or an
> idolater or a slanderer or a drunkard or a robber, not to associate
> with that person, not even to eat with such a one.*

The Struggle is Real: James as Resocialization

Hopefully, the discussion so far has demonstrated that at its most basic
level the struggle over ideology and values is really the struggle to form
and to maintain groups—communities of character, as Hauerwas calls
them[47]—that are shaped by and that behave in certain ways on the basis
of shared ideology and core values. As with all groups, these communi-

---

Neyrey, *Calling Jesus Names*.

45. For discussion, see Fitzmyer, *First Corinthians*, 233–34; Thiselton, *First Epistle
to the Corinthians*, 384–87.

46. All translations throughout this chapter are my own unless otherwise noted.
For further discussion of this verse, see Fitzmyer, *First Corinthians*, 243–44; Thiselton,
First Epistle to the Corinthians, 413–14.

47. See Hauerwas, *Community of Character*, 129–52. See also Meeks, *Moral
World*, 12.

ties derive from some person or persons who see the need for change "in the way things are."[48] Jesus envisioned and promoted the return of a theocracy,[49] and the post-Jesus groups, which includes the writers and recipients of letters collated in the New Testament, sought redemption (i.e., restoration of honor to God's people) and salvation (i.e., rescue from the present evil age) for those who are the people of God/YHWH.[50] Becoming a member of the Christian community required a "conversion"[51] or, in sociological terms, a "resocialization."[52] Those with whom the message proclaimed by Jesus or about Jesus resonated were compelled to set aside or to alter willingly any ideological stance or values orientation that did not align with those of the Christian community and to adopt those that did.[53]

At the risk of oversimplifying, it appears that at a very basic level, both the Jesus and post-Jesus groups generated solidarity around a view of God/YHWH as benefactor and patron who, through the mediator (savior) Jesus, provides all that is necessary for an ordered life, and who in return expects honor (praise, worship) and the extension of his generous benefaction to others.[54] Accordingly, Theissen argues that this ideological edifice was constructed upon two central values: (1) love of neighbor and (2) renunciation of status.[55] These core values shaped and found expression in many peripheral and means values that constituted the "habitus" of the followers of Jesus.[56] They constrain one's responses to the myriad unpredictable contingencies of the moment, and shape

48. Malina, *New Testament World*, 202; Malina, "Early Christian Groups," 99.

49. This is referred to in the gospels as "the kingdom of God" and "the kingdom of the heavens." See now Malina, *Social Gospel of Jesus*, 113–39, 141–61.

50. See Malina, *Social Gospel of Jesus*, 141–61; Malina, *New Testament World*, 198–219; Malina, "Early Christian Groups," 100–110. See also Aune, *Apocalypticism, Prophecy, and Magic*, 4–12.

51. See Nock, *Conversion*, 1–16.

52. Meeks, *Moral World*, 13–17; Dvorak, "To Incline Another's Heart," 600 n. 10. See also Meeks, *Origins of Christian Morality*, 8; Dvorak, "Edwin Judge," 193–98; Schaefer and Lamb, *Sociology*, 113; Brim, "Adult Socialization," 556.

53. See Dvorak, "Prodding with Prosody," 88. See also Gass and Seiter, *Persuasion*, 34.

54. See now Neyrey, "God, Benefactor and Patron," 465–92.

55. Theissen, *Theory of a Primitive Christian Religion*, 63–80. See Jas 2:1, 8–13.

56. "Habitus" is Bourdieu's designation for the embodied system of socially structured and structuring dispositions that guide one's moment-by-moment responses to life events (Bourdieu, *Outline of a Theory of Practice*, 72–95).

them in such a way that, on the whole, regardless of the crises that may arise, things tend to eventuate in fairly typical ways in the community of believers.[57] As one gradually assimilates this ideology and attendant core values, she or he comes to align their own ways of being and doing with those of the group to which they have converted.[58]

Logically, all of this seems rather straightforward, but resocialization is really a quite complex process, and its success is fraught with difficulty. One challenge is presented by competing ideologies and value positions. Bakhtin refers to these as the social voices of *heteroglossia*, the "specific points of view on the world, forms for conceptualizing the world in words, specific worldview, each characterized by its own objects, meanings, and values. As such they may all be juxtaposed to one another, mutually supplement one another, contradict one another, and be interrelated dialogically."[59] Similar to Bourdieu's "habitus," heteroglossia denotes the many persistent habits of thinking, doing, believing, and feeling that are characteristic of the many different groups in one's social world.[60] Yet, in Bakhtin's view, these diverse social voices, in Althusserian fashion, clamor after people's adherence, hailing and "interpellating"—even recruiting—them, compelling them to (re-)consider whether or not the values of their group are the "right" ones with which to identify and by which to fashion one's life.[61] Despite living well before the advent of such

---

57. Lemke, *Textual Politics*, 33.

58. There are various terms used in the New Testament to refer to one's general direction or "way of life"; see, e.g., ἔθος or ἀναστροφή (see Louw and Nida, *Greek–English Lexicon*, 2:505–11 ["Behavior and Related States"]). Although Louw and Nida do not include the term in domain 41 of their lexicon, it seems that James uses ἔργα ("deeds") in this way (rather than referring to individual, discrete deeds/works) in ch. 2 of the letter. See Moo, *Letter of James*, 123: "James uses 'works' in a general sense to refer to actions done in obedience to God."

59. Bakhtin, "Discourse in the Novel," 291–92. See also Dvorak, "Not Like Cain," 5; Lemke, *Textual Politics*, 24. Compare to VanGemeren's use of *vox populi* in *Interpreting the Prophetic Word*, 26–27.

60. Lemke, *Textual Politics*, 24–25; Dvorak, "Not Like Cain," 5–6.

61. See Althusser, "Ideology and Ideological State Apparatuses," 1–60, esp. 44–51. VanGemeren, in discussing ancient Israel, frames this same notion around the concepts of *Realpolitik* and *vox populi* (*Interpreting the Prophetic Word*, 26), both of which hail and interpellate members of a society. He defines *Realpolitik* in its more pejorative sense as "power politics," which he further unpacks as the "pragmatic application of any technique by which an individual or a group can maintain or enhance life. . . . It is manipulative, works at the expense of others, and undermines the essential nature of [prophetic] revelation" (*Interpreting the Prophetic Voice*, 26). *Vox populi* ("the voice of

technologies as television, the Internet, email, and the smartphone, the ancients nevertheless endured the barrage of heteroglossia often through the ever active channels of gossip networks. In fact, as Rohrbaugh points out, gossip was often the means by which group ideology and values (and, thus, group boundaries) were clarified, challenged, maintained, and/or erased.[62] Thus, conversion from one group to a different group, even if some overlap in beliefs and values existed, could result in the convert becoming the target of sharp-tongued busybodies. Differences between the groups' beliefs would be made salient, and much of the gossip, likely a concentrated dose of shame, would be focused on getting the convert to withdraw from the new group and to return to the original group. In such a situation, the convert would experience considerable social pressure to retract her or his acceptance of the "novel" ideas of the new group and to return to the safe tradition of the original group.[63]

A second challenge to resocialization is the fact that the process "is never complete and the contents it internalizes face continuing threats . . . [from] the marginal situations of human experience that cannot be completely bracketed in everyday activity."[64] To be sure, the "continuing threats" mentioned here are presented by the social voices of heteroglossia just discussed, but something potentially more insidious is in view here, namely, those moments of disorienting crisis that arise repeatedly throughout the life of a person or group. Imagine a scenario in which a person has become part of the Christian community. Such a conversion at the very least necessitates the adoption of the core values of faith(fulness) (i.e., loyalty, commitment), hope (i.e., allegiance, trust), and love (i.e.,

---

the people") is a form of *Realpolitik*. As VanGemeren uses the term, *vox populi* refers to what society or "the world" (κόσμος as a "world system," i.e., "the practices and standards of secular society" [see Louw and Nida, *Greek-English Lexicon*, 2:508–9]) considers to be "common sense" (see Fairclough, *Discourse and Social Change*, 92; Fairclough, *Language and Power*, 106–8). When people succumb to the hailing of *vox populi*, they "establish a sacred alliance of relative values" with the world, and they are typically rewarded with some form of social capital. However, when people align with the "prophetic word" that is so often anti-societal or opposed to societal values and norms, they are often persecuted in some way, not only by withholding social capital, but also in ways that at least attempts to strip them of any social capital they may already have had.

62. Rohrbaugh, "Gossip in the New Testament," 251–53.

63. See now McVann, "Change/Novelty Orientation," 14–16.

64. Berger and Luckmann, *Social Construction of Reality*, 147.

personal and group attachment),[65] and it is expected that these will be expressed both towards God and towards the others in the group. Now imagine that a crisis arises in which, perhaps, the continued existence of the group suddenly becomes uncertain. How might this new convert respond to this threat? Pilch correctly observes that "crisis always causes one's basic values to stand out rather starkly."[66] Moreover, in moments of crisis, people have a tendency to revert to the "first choice" responses of their primary socialization or of a previous resocialization in which they learned and experienced some level of "success" in dealing with the same or a similar crisis.[67] Thus, that person or some subset of people in the group begins to act in ways that are not consonant with the group's ideological stance or value orientation. When this happens, an authoritative figure presiding over the group will likely point out that the behavior is inconsistent with the ideology and values of the group. In extreme cases, the leader may also call out a subset of the group (see, e.g., Jude) or even individual group members (see, e.g., 3 John), labeling them as deviants.

I join most other Jacobean scholars in pointing out the extreme difficulty if not impossibility of determining the precise historical *Sitz im Leben* of the letter of James or the specific identity of its intended readers. However, I do think the letter provides sufficient information for at least a sketch of the situation James addresses. First, by calling himself "slave/servant of God and of the Lord Jesus Christ" (θεοῦ καὶ κυρίου Ἰησοῦ Χριστοῦ δοῦλος [1:1]) and by addressing the letter to "the twelve tribes in the dispersion" (ταῖς δώδεκα φυλαῖς ταῖς ἐν τῇ διασπορᾷ [1:1]), whether or not this nomenclature ought to be understood literally (i.e., to Jewish Christians living outside Judea/Palestine) or metaphorically (i.e., referring to all Christians who live as "strangers and aliens in the world"),[68] James enacts a relationship between himself and the readers

65. See now Malina, "Faith/Faithfulness," 61–63; Malina, "Love," 106–9; Pilch, "Trust (Personal and Group)," 173–75.

66. Pilch, *Cultural Context of the New Testament*, 121.

67. See ibid., where Pilch suggests that even Jesus, having urged his followers to "do the will of God" and to "keep the commandments" (a value orientation of "doing") reverted to the orientation of "being" that was more typical of the non-elite in the circum-Mediterranean world in which he lived. See also Pilch and Malina, "Introduction," xxiv–xl.

68. See the discussions in Wall, "James, Letter of," 548–49; deSilva, *Introduction to the New Testament*, 817–18; Cargal, *Restoring the Diaspora*, 47–49; McKnight, *Letter of James*, 65–68; Davids, *Commentary on James*, 63–64; Moo, *Letter of James*, 24, and most other major New Testament introductions and commentaries on the letter of

that he deems necessary if he is to make a claim on their lives. He is the stable, authoritative "voice from the center," filling the role of the wise teacher who resides in the "homeland," the ideal community where it is imagined that "all is right in the world" and from which it is appropriate to receive correction (even rebuke), instruction, and encouragement.[69] On the other hand, the readers, as James casts them, existed at the "subaltern sidelines"[70] as people plagued by ambiguity and "doubleness."[71] They needed to be reminded of the theology (ideology) and values that they had accepted upon their conversion to the Christian movement, and James determines to complete this task. Demonstrably, the first major section of the letter (1:2–12) proves this in that James, with uses of τέλειος/τελειόω and ὁλόκληρος (vv. 2–4), introduces and emphasizes the value of wholeness/completeness over against lack/deficiency (λείπω [v. 4, 5]) and forms of doubleness (διακρίνω [v. 6] and δίψυχος [v. 8]).[72]

Second, as one reads through the letter, it becomes increasingly apparent that, like diasporic communities in general, the addressees' communal life (again, as James saw it) was characterized by ill-defined and porous social boundaries; ambiguous/double or hybrid identity; tension or outright misunderstanding regarding how tradition (i.e., the "presentness" of group ideology and values established in the past and passed on to each generation)[73] ought to be interpreted and put into practice; and a high susceptibility to cultural assimilation.[74] Like an accelerant poured onto a fire, the "various kinds of trials" (πειρασμοῖς ποικίλοις [1:2]) experienced by the group intensified the group's diasporic characteristics,

---

James.

69. See now Coker, "Calling on the Diaspora," 442–46.

70. Ibid., 446–49.

71. Ibid., 444; Elliott, "Holiness-Wholeness," 71–80. See also Wuellner, "Der Jakobusbrief," 5–66; Penner, "Epistle of James in Current Research," 294; Lockett, "Wholeness in Intertextual Perspective," 92–106. On wholeness as a biblical social value, see Neyrey, "Wholeness," 175–78; deSilva, *Honor, Patronage, Kinship, & Purity*, 241–315 (esp. 279–315).

72. Elliott, "Holiness-Wholeness," 72.

73. This is a wordplay based on Malina's description of tradition as "the presentness of the past" (Malina, *Christian Origins*, 35).

74. See Coker, "Calling the Diaspora," 449–53. VanGemeren shows how Israel, living in a pagan context, struggled with the same diasporic characteristics (see *Interpreting the Prophetic Word*, 25–27).

especially ambiguity/doubleness. The disequilibrium wrought by the trials exacerbated a number of toxic behaviors, including the following:[75]

- discrimination among the group members and currying favor from wealthy and powerful patrons outside the community (2:1–14)

- dishonoring the poor via litigation and neglect (2:6–7, 13, 14–16)

- defrauding others (4:13—5:6)

- pursuit of one's own selfish interests (1:14–15; 4:1–10)

- slandering and passing judgment against fellow group members (4:11–12; 5:9)

- personal doubt and lack of commitment to the group and to God (1:6–8; 4:8)

- duplicity of speech (3:1–12)

- inconsistency between words and deeds (1:22–24; 2:1–26; 5:12)

- loss of patience and hope (1:2, 12–15; 5:7–11)

- defection from the group (5:19–20)

Elliott rather alliteratively summarizes the situation well:

> As the author describes the scene, ethnic, economic, and social differences had led to social division; and divisions, to personal doubt, dissimulation, despair, and defection. Factiousness and fission within the community were accompanied by a split in the attitudes and actions of individuals themselves. The community and its members were undergoing an erosion of integrity and cohesion at both the personal and the social levels of life.[76]

James understands that this kind of doubleness packs a doubly negative punch: not only does it threaten the solidarity and integrity of the group by challenging the group's ideology and core values, it also presents a fierce challenge to the honor of God and of his son Jesus. For this reason, armed with the insightfulness of wisdom, the tradition, and a prophetic frankness of speech, James takes up his stylus and puts to papyrus his attempt at resocializing the readers.

---

75. See Elliott, "Holiness–Wholeness," 75.

76. Ibid.

"DO YOU NOT KNOW?" THE DISCURSIVE FUNCTIONS OF QUESTIONS IN RESOCIALIZATION[77]

Grammar and Syntax

As a discourse analyst, I prefer to start textual analysis "at the bottom," beginning the process by identifying the grammatical, syntactical, and lexical realizations of the meanings the writers are attempting to make, and then working "upwards" to determine what those meanings may be. Of course, the first step in this process, as it pertains to questions, is to determine whether or not the clause or clause complex being analyzed is, indeed, a question. Although below I will mention two generally agreed upon rules of thumb for making this determination, the analysis I present below proceeds from the point of already having made this determination. There are, however, two further bits of grammatico-syntactical information that an analyst must gather in order to determine the meaning (i.e., social function) of any given question. One is to determine whether the question is an open question, a closed question, or a τ-question and the other is to determine the effect of the questioner's verbal attitude (or, modality) on the semantics of the question.

OPEN QUESTIONS, CLOSED QUESTIONS, AND τ-QUESTIONS

Like most Greek grammars, I distinguish among three broad categories of questions as they appear in the Greek of the New Testament, and these categories are defined on the basis of grammatical and syntactical indicators, namely the presence or absence of negative particles in the question—and if present, which negative particles are actually put to use by the writer. The three broad categories are open questions, closed questions, and τ-questions.[78]

Moule says that open questions are "those which give no indication of the answer expected";[79] Porter sharpens this by adding that such questions give "no *grammatical* indication *whether a positive or negative answer* is expected."[80] It is sometimes difficult to distinguish between an

---

77. The contents of this section are from Dvorak, "'Why Would Anyone Want to Do That?' The Function of Questions in the Negotiation of Values," an unpublished paper presented at the annual meeting of the SBL in Boston, MA, November 2017. I have modified and corrected the content prior to using it here.

78. See Porter, *Idioms*, 276–80; Moule, *Idiom Book*, 158–59.

79. Moule, *Idiom Book*, 158.

80. Porter, *Idioms*, 276 (italics added).

open question and a statement because this must be determined on the basis of context.[81] Two of the most useful rules of thumb in making this decision are:[82] (1) if the structure read as a statement would contradict the clear statements of the text, then it may be a question; and (2) if the structure read as a statement would pose a set of alternatives, then it may be a question. So, for example, at Gal 3:2b Paul writes, ἐξ ἔργων νόμου τὸ πνεῦμα ἐλάβετε ἢ ἐξ ἀκοῆς πίστεως ("you received the Spirit by works of law or by obedience of faith"), which the NA28 editors mark as a question. In this case, both rules of thumb apply and support the editors' decision. The two choices offered in the text—reception of the Spirit by works of law or reception of the Spirit by obedience of faith—represent *opposing* value positions rather than a choice between two equally positive points of view. Also, when read as a statement, not only does it become syntactically problematic, it also contradicts the main trajectory of Paul's argument in Galatians. Moreover, if that is not enough, the preceding clause, τοῦτο μόνον θέλω μαθεῖν ἀφ᾽ ὑμῶν ("Only this do I want to learn from you"), is best understood as a kind of "setup" for a question, and thus provides further support for reading it as an open question.

Closed questions, sometimes called polar questions, are those that generate an expectation for either a positive or a negative answer.[83] This distinction hinges on which negative particle is used in the question: questions in which a form of οὐ (or cognates) appears expect a positive response; questions in which a form of μή (or cognates) appears expect a negative response. For example, at 1 Cor 3:16, Paul enquires οὐκ οἴδατε ὅτι ναὸς θεοῦ ἐστε καὶ τὸ πνεῦμα τοῦ θεοῦ οἰκεῖ ἐν ὑμῖν; ("Do you not understand that you are God's temple and the Spirit of God dwells among you?"). The οὐκ in this question signals that the readers—insofar as Paul portrays them in the text (i.e., the "readers-in-the-text")—are expected to supply an affirmative answer, namely that, indeed, they do not understand that they are God's temple and that the Spirit of God dwells among them. At 1 Cor 12:30, Paul asks three rapid-fire questions, each of which contains the negative particle μή: μὴ πάντες χαρίσματα ἔχουσιν ἰαμάτων; μὴ πάντες γλώσσαις λαλοῦσιν; μὴ πάντες διερμηνεύουσιν; ("All do not

---

81. Ibid. Porter also notes that the Greek question mark (;) used in the Greek New Testament is inserted by the editors, thus making them open for debate (277). Robertson says that the question mark began to appear in about the ninth century (cf. Robertson, *Grammar*, 242).

82. These are from Porter, *Idioms*, 276.

83. Ibid., 277–79; Moule, *Idiom Book*, 159.

have gifts of healing, do they? All do not speak in tongues, do they? All do not interpret, do they?"). The use of μή in each of these questions creates the expectation that the readers-in-the-text will respond with a negative response: no, not all have gifts of healing; no, not all speak in tongues; and no, not all interpret.

It is worth mentioning that there are three instances in the New Testament where the compound negative μή οὐ appears in questions: at Rom 10:18, at 1 Cor 9:4, and at 1 Cor 9:5. These constructions, like those in which only μή appears, create the expectation for a negative response from the readers.[84] Moule says that in these cases the οὐ negates the verb, but the μή negates the clause and, thus, creates the expectation for a negative answer.[85] So, 1 Cor 9:4, μὴ οὐκ ἔχομεν ἐξουσίαν φαγεῖν καὶ πεῖν; may be glossed "It is not that we do not have the authority to eat and drink, is it?" where the tag question in English communicates the expectation of a negative response. When the compound negative οὐ μή appears in questions, like those where only οὐ appears, it creates the expectation of an affirmative answer, as at John 18:11: τὸ ποτήριον ὃ δέδωκέν μοι ὁ πατὴρ οὐ μὴ πίω αὐτό; ("The cup that the father has given to me, shall I not drink it?") expects the affirmative answer, "Yes, I shall drink it."[86]

T-questions are those that are introduced by interrogative pronouns (e.g., τίς, τί) or various other particles, including some adverbs (e.g., ποῦ, πόθεν).[87] These kinds of questions have discursive effects that are similar to both open and closed questions. In a manner of speaking, τ-questions are "fill-in-the-blank" questions; they prompt the interrogated person(s) to supply the appropriate referent to, say, an interrogative pronoun (τίς ["Who?"]) or interrogative adverb (πόθεν ["Whence?"]). Thus, on the one hand they are like closed questions in that the potential answers are limited by context. Yet, on the other hand they are like open questions in that they typically generate among the interrogated person(s) some sort of engagement with other people or value positions.

---

84. Porter, *Idioms*, 279.

85. Moule, *Idiom Book*, 156. Porter agrees (*Idioms*, 279).

86. Porter, *Idioms*, 279.

87. Ibid.; Moule, *Idiom Book*, 158. Estes (*Questions and Rhetoric*, 50–51) refers to these as π-questions; Porter, "Systemic Functional Linguistics," 29, calls them τ-questions. I follow Porter's convention.

VERBAL MOOD AND MODALITY

Another area of grammar and syntax that impacts the way questions are to be interpreted is that of verbal mood and modality. Traditionally, verbal mood has been defined in the grammars as the morphologically signaled grammaticalization of a language user's subjective perspective on or attitude toward the relation of the verbal action to reality,[88] where "reality" refers to the language user's *values-shaped and values-constrained perception of how things are (or are not) or how things ought to be (or ought not be)*.[89] Porter puts these mood forms into two modal categories.[90] The first category, which he calls "assertive," includes only the indicative mood, since it is the only verbal mood form that grammaticalizes assertions of the language user's opinion of the verbal process as being actual or factual (or not).[91] The second group, which he labels "non-assertive," includes the imperative, subjunctive, and optative moods, and these are subdivided further. The imperative grammaticalizes directive attitude, while the subjunctive and optative both grammaticalize projective attitude, but

88. Porter, *Idioms*, 50. See also Porter, *Verbal Aspect*, 164–65; Mathewson and Emig, *Intermediate Greek Grammar*, 160. Young describes verbal mood as how a speaker/writer views what s/he is saying/writing with respect to its "factuality" (see *Intermediate New Testament Greek*, 136).

89. Porter, *Idioms*, 51. Mathewson and Emig, *Intermediate Greek Grammar*, 161: "The primary use of the indicative mood in NT Greek is to make assertions about reality from the perspective of the writer or speaker, irrespective of objective reality," which assumes that such a thing as "objective reality" (a reality unaffected by context?) actually exists. Berger and Luckmann (*Social Construction of Reality*, 53–67) remind us, that reality is a social construct comprised of the countless habitualized processes, as well as the attitudes and expectations that are attached to those processes, that have been crystallized into social institutions or, in Malina's terms, value structures (Malina, *Christian Origins*, 114–15). These value structures find their institutional realization in the norms and standards of various groups (the conglomeration of which groups is called "society"). As people are born into and socialized in these groups, these values become internalized such that they define the group members' social identity, as well as their notion of what constitutes reality (Malina, *Christian Origins*, 115; Berger and Luckmann, *Social Construction of Reality*, 67–183). Thus, as regards the definition of verbal mood, it is probably more appropriate to say that verbal mood signals the language user's subjective attitude regarding the relationship of the verbal action to her or his representation of reality as it is constrained (both in the sense of restricted and compelled) by the composite values of the group or groups to which she or he belongs (see Fairclough, *Analysing Discourse*, 165–67).

90. Porter, *Verbal Aspect*, 165–66. See also Porter, "Systemic Functional Linguistics," 26–32.

91. Porter, *Verbal Aspect*, 165–66.

with slight variation in that the subjunctive grammaticalizes projection "with no expectation of fulfillment," while the optative grammaticalizes projection "with contingent expectation of fulfillment."[92] In his tome on verbal aspect, Porter correlates assertive and non-assertive with epistemic and deontic modality, respectively.[93] Epistemic modality refers to the linguistic expression of a language user's level of commitment to or confidence in the assertions or propositions they make with respect to what they perceive to be "reality."[94] Deontic modality is concerned with the linguistic expression of a language user's commitment to the realization of some action or event.[95]

As it pertains to questions, only three of the mood forms are used— indicative, subjunctive, and optative—and grammars tend to describe these uses as follows:

- The indicative mood form is employed in a question when the question is really just a statement that is "dressed up" as a question,[96] or when a language user wants to elicit from others the degree of their commitment to an assertion about the "reality" they have presented.[97]

- The subjunctive mood form in a question, often labeled "deliberative," is employed when a language user wishes to ask for some sort of decision regarding the projected verbal idea.[98]

- The optative mood form in a question, often labeled "deliberative" or "potential," is employed when a person is pondering the meaning

92. Ibid., 170. See also Porter, "Systemic Functional Linguistics," 26–32.

93. Porter, *Verbal Aspect*, 165–66.

94. See Palmer, *Mood and Modality*, 8–9; Fairclough, *Analysing Discourse*, 167.

95. See Palmer, *Mood and Modality*, 9–10.

96. Often this is couched in the lingo of transformative grammar, as with Young, *Intermediate New Testament Greek*, 137: "An interrogative indicative is used in questions. It is basically a statement that has undergone a transformation. Thus the question 'Is John here?' has at the deep structure level the statement 'John is here.'" On the difference between systemic–functional and transformational grammatical approaches, see Halliday, "Language as Code," 3–7; Halliday, *Language as Social Semiotic*, 8–35 (esp. 12–18). See also, Dvorak, "To Incline Another's Heart," 602–7.

97. See Young, *Intermediate New Testament Greek*, 221.

98. See Mathewson and Emig, *Intermediate Greek Grammar*, 167. See also Young, *Intermediate New Testament Greek*, 139.

of something, the identity of someone, or what should be done in a given situation.[99]

These are all appropriate descriptions so far as they go, but one persistent shortcoming inherent in all three descriptions is the apparent assumption that the sole function of verbal mood and modality is to reveal a *writer's* attitudinal stance toward the propositions or proposals *they* make, as if the most significant point of interpretation is how the writers perceive *their own* information and action exchanges.[100] Hodge and Kress offer a more sensible perspective. They argue that modality expresses affinity—i.e., solidarity—between a speaker or writer and the hearer or reader.[101] As people engage one another in the negotiation of values, as I described above, they present certain perspectives of reality or what they consider to be "truth," and as they do so, other participants in the dialogue will show greater or lesser degrees of affinity or alignment with the reality that is portrayed. This occurs in every text and, indeed, every utterance. The higher the degree of affinity or alignment (i.e., the higher the acceptance of the reality that is represented), the more that portrayed reality becomes the basis for judgment and action.[102] Thus, "Whoever controls modality can control which version of reality will be selected out as the valid version in that semiosic process."[103] This would have been especially true in the agonistic honor/shame culture of the first-century circum-Mediterranean world, where questions were often employed as a means of challenging one's view of reality/truth, as well as one's honor, for the purpose of (re-)positioning them back within some set of social boundaries.[104]

This view aligns more closely with the relatively recent work done in SFL Appraisal Theory that extends modality by incorporating Bakhtin's

---

99. Young, *Intermediate New Testament Greek*, 141.

100. White, "Beyond Modality," 261.

101. Hodge and Kress, *Social Semiotics*, 123.

102. Ibid., 147.

103. Ibid.

104. See Neyrey, "Questions," 657–81.

notions of heteroglossia and dialogism.[105] Bakhtin, as well as Halliday,[106] presumes that the basic reality and purpose of language is social interaction or dialogue.[107] As Vološinov put it, "The actual reality of language-speech is not the abstract system of linguistic forms, not the isolated monologic utterance, and not the psychological act of its implementation, but the social event of verbal interaction implemented in an utterance or utterances."[108] The resulting model, referred to as Engagement, extends the traditional approach to modality "by attending not only to writer certainty, commitment, and knowledge . . . but also to the matter of how the writer or speaker engages and positions her or his own voice vis-à-vis other voices and value positions . . . ."[109] An analysis of modality, thus, includes an investigation into whether or not a writer's propositions or proposals are dialogically expansive or dialogically contractive, and this distinction is made on the basis of whether and to what extent an utterance actively allows semiotic space for alternative voices or, alternatively, acts to challenge, fend off, or restrict the scope of these voices.[110] With this model one not only asks, "What is the writer's knowledge about and degree of commitment to the information being exchanged?" or "What is the writer's level of commitment to necessity or to action regarding the activity being exchanged?" but also "In what way does the writer's commitment to these things position their perspective in relation to alternative points of view?" and "How does the writer's modality function to *position the readers* to take up the same stance or point of view they are promoting?" The full model of Engagement is fairly extensive and, thus, cannot be fully detailed here; however, for the purpose of this chapter, I

105. See Martin and White, *Language of Evaluation*; White, "Beyond Modality," 259–84; Dvorak, "Interpersonal Metafunction"; Dvorak, "Prodding with Prosody," 99–102; Dvorak, "Not Like Cain," 1–19; Dvorak, "To Incline Another's Heart," 599–620 (esp., 611–14).

106. Halliday and Matthiessen, *Introduction to Functional Grammar*, 135. See Dvorak, "Not Like Cain," 3–6; Dawson, "Language as Negotiation," 373.

107. See Vološinov, *Marxism and the Philosophy of Language*, 139. White, "Beyond Modality," 261.

108. Vološinov, *Marxism and the Philosophy of Language*, 139. White, "Beyond Modality," 261.

109. Dvorak, "Prodding with Prosody," 99; see also Martin and White, *Language of Evaluation*, 2.

110. Martin and White, *Language of Evaluation*, 102; Dvorak, "Interpersonal Metafunction," 77.

will zero in on how questions function in the expansion or contraction of dialogic space in the negotiation of values.[111]

The Interpersonal Semantics of Questions

As outlined above, questions in the New Testament are either open, closed, or a hybrid (τ-questions); that is, they either make no grammatical indication as to whether they expect an affirmative or negative answer, or, if a negative particle is used, they do create this expectation. In the expanded notion of modality just described, open questions are dialogically *expansive* simply because they do not, in the way they are structured, assume or expect an answer, even if the writer goes on to supply an answer (e.g., "Should we continue to sin that grace may abound? Absolutely not!" [Rom 6:1]). Closed questions, however, are dialogically *contractive* because, in the way that they are asked, they presume or expect either a positive or negative answer. In the Engagement model, open questions are called *expository questions*, because these are often used to introduce alternative points of view or values into a discourse, so that they may be discussed further (often these are uncritically referred to as "rhetorical questions," even though, technically, they are not).[112] Closed questions are labeled *leading questions* because they are asked for the purpose of leading the readers to a certain conclusion about what is asked (these are, technically, rhetorical questions).[113]

In terms of social function, expository questions expand dialogic space by making allowances for, and sometimes explicitly reference, alternative value positions in the colloquy.[114] In regards to interpersonal meaning, this increases the potential for solidarity between the writer and the implied reader(s) who may hold to the alternative position that is referenced, at least to the extent to which alternative points of view and their proponents are recognized as real or potential participants in the colloquy.

Leading questions, on the other hand, contract dialogue because they already presume or expect an answer. As a result, little to no semiotic

---

111. See now Dvorak, "Interpersonal Metafunction," 75–93; Martin and White, *Language of Evaluation*, 92–135; Hart, *Discourse, Grammar and Ideology*, 52–56. See also Dawson, "Language as Negotiation," 363–82.

112. See Goatly, *Critical Reading and Writing*, 89.

113. Ibid.

114. Martin and White, *Language of Evaluation*, 108.

space is opened up for the consideration of other points of view or value positions. Closed "rhetorical" questions project an audience that already knows the answer—or, from the questioner's point of view, *should* already know the answer—thus an answer need not be supplied. This is known as *contraction by concurrence*,[115] which is often used to signal a value position that is or should be taken for granted as a presupposition (i.e., an agreement between the writer and reader exists or is portrayed to exist).[116] Thus, leading questions are ideologically powerful insofar as they project certain value positions as "universal" and as "common sense," with the result that any other point of view that does not align with the one being represented by the presumed answer to the question is illegitimate and should be rejected.[117] Occasionally, a writer asks a leading question and subsequently provides an explicit answer for it. When this happens, the question–answer pair is to be interpreted as emphatic.

"WHAT IS THE BENEFIT . . . ?" ANALYZING QUESTIONS IN THE LETTER OF JAMES

Having now outlined the underlying sociolinguistic theory and constructed an interpretive model, in this section I will apply it to a number of questions that occur in the letter of James in order to demonstrate its heuristic benefit. In the appendix to this chapter, I have supplied a basic analysis of all of the questions that, by my reckoning, appear in the letter of James. In what follows I will provide a more detailed analysis of questions that appear in two stretches of text in the letter: 2:14–17 (three questions) and 3:13—4:6 (five questions). In each case, I will place the text in the broader structural and ideological context of the letter so as to honor both the semantic constraints of surrounding co-text and the overarching social and ideological purpose of the letter. Then, I will analyze each question with regard to its grammatical type (open or closed) and its discourse function (expository or leading). Finally, I will conclude each section with comments on how each question functions to position the intended readers vis-à-vis the value position(s) that are put at risk at those moments in the letter.

115. Ibid., 123

116. See ibid., 100–101, 121, 122–23.

117. See Fairclough, *Language and Power*, 64; Fairclough, *Analysing Discourse*, 55–61; Fairclough, *Discourse and Social Change*, 92–93.

James 2:14–17: The Inseparability of Faith and Deeds

¹⁴ Τί τὸ ὄφελος, ἀδελφοί μου; ἐὰν πίστιν λέγῃ τις ἔχειν, ἔργα δὲ μὴ ἔχῃ, μὴ δύναται ἡ πίστις σῶσαι αὐτόν; ¹⁵ ἐὰν ἀδελφὸς ἢ ἀδελφὴ γυμνοὶ ὑπάρχωσιν καὶ λειπόμενοι ὦσιν τῆς ἐφημέρου τροφῆς, ¹⁶ εἴπῃ δέ τις αὐτοῖς ἐξ ὑμῶν· ὑπάγετε ἐν εἰρήνῃ, θερμαίνεσθε καὶ χορτάζεσθε, μὴ δῶτε δὲ αὐτοῖς τὰ ἐπιτήδεια τοῦ σώματος, τί τὸ ὄφελος; ¹⁷ οὕτως καὶ ἡ πίστις, ἐὰν μὴ ἔχῃ ἔργα, νεκρά ἐστιν καθ' ἑαυτήν.

¹⁴ *What is the benefit, my brothers and sisters, if someone would claim¹¹⁸ to have faith, but would not have deeds? That faith is not able to save¹¹⁹ that person, is it? ¹⁵ If a brother or a sister is naked and happens to be lacking daily food, ¹⁶ but someone among you would say to them, "Go in peace, warm yourself and fill yourself,"¹²⁰ but that person does not give to them the things necessary for the body, what is the benefit? ¹⁷ So also faith, if it does not have deeds, is dead by itself.*

In terms of structure, by using the OpenText.org model, Varner concludes that Jas 2:14–26 is the second main unit in Jas 2.¹²¹ The beginning of the unit is marked by the address formula ἀδελφοί μου ("my brothers and sisters"), the question τί τὸ ὄφελος . . . ἐὰν . . . ("What is the benefit . . . if . . .?"), and a change of topic from the problem of partiality discussed in the first unit (2:1–13) to the inseparability of faith and deeds.¹²² The unit ends at v. 26 with a summary statement regarding the inseparability of faith and deeds (ὥσπερ γὰρ τὸ σῶμα χωρὶς πνεύματος νεκρόν ἐστιν, οὕτως καὶ ἡ πίστις χωρὶς ἔργων νεκρά ἐστιν ["For just as the body

118. The gloss of λέγῃ as "claim" is not intended necessarily to suggest that James thinks the subject does not really have a genuine faith. See Cargal, *Restoring the Diaspora*, 121.

119. See the discussion of σῴζω in McKnight, *Letter of James*, 229; Moo, *Letter of James*, 123–24; Adamson, *James*, 399–404; Martin, *James*, 81–82; Davids, *Commentary on James*, 120. All of these interpret the term to refer to eschatological salvation. For an alternative view, see Hodges, *Gospel Under Siege*, 26–27.

120. I read both θερμαίνεσθε καὶ χορτάζεσθε as second person present middle imperatives. NASB glosses them as passives.

121. Varner, *Book of James*, 102.

122. Ibid., 102, 104. I will not enter here into a discussion as to whether or not James intentionally engages Paul's teaching of salvation by faith alone. See the following and sources they cite for discussion: Penner, "Epistle of James in Current Research," 287–93; Johnson, *Letter of James*, 58–64; Moo, *Letter of James*, 37–42; Davids, *Commentary on James*, 19–21 and 120–34; Davids, "James and Paul," 457–61.

apart from the spirit is dead, so also faith apart from deeds is dead"]),
and another new unit begins at 3:1, which takes up the topic of speech.[123]
Verses 14–17 constitute the first of three sub-units that make up the unit;
the other two are vv. 18–19 and vv. 20–26.[124] Although held together by
the interacting semantic chains realized by lexemes built on the πιστ- and
εργ- stems,[125] each sub-unit is distinctive. From a dialogic perspective,
the first sub-unit (vv. 14–17) introduces the topic of the larger unit;[126] the
second sub-unit (vv. 18–19) introduces into the colloquy the alternative
value position with which James wished to engage; and the third sub-unit
(vv. 20–26) contains James's response to that value position.[127]

As alluded to earlier, Elliott has demonstrated that the major problem James perceived among the putative readers was a fundamental lack
of wholeness.[128] The readers, from James's point of view, were exhibiting "doubleness" in many areas of personal and congregational life, such
as showing partiality (2:1–4, 9) or teachers who inappropriately utter
both blessings and curses (3:1–12). Keenly, Elliott observes that James
deals with the different manifestations of doubleness by first stating the
negative condition and then following up with what to do about it, the
positive response, that is, how the readers ought to think and act in those
situations.[129] Thus, for example, privileging the rich to the neglect of the
poor is to be replaced with justice (2:1);[130] so-called teachers who exhibit
doubleness in their speech either should no longer be teachers (3:1) or
they need to replace their boasting with wisdom and meekness (3:13).[131]
James 2:14–17, the unit of text under investigation here, addresses a negative condition in which the assumed readers lack "faith-in-action toward
the needy," in response to which James demands that the readers *dem-*

---

123. Varner, *Book of James*, 116. See also Davids, *Commentary on James*, 133–34.

124. See Varner, *Book of James*, 103–4.

125. Notably, 14 of the 19 occurrences of the πιστ- root lexemes appear in these
13 verses, and 12 of the 17 occurrences of the εργ- root lexemes appear in this unit.

126. Davids, *Commentary on James*, 120.

127. Varner, *Book of James*, 108–16.

128. Elliott, "Holiness–Wholeness," 71–81.

129. Ibid., 75–78.

130. "Within a kinship group, 'justice' means enduring loyalty to one's kin" (Malina, "Patronage," 133).

131. Elliott, "Holiness–Wholeness," 76. Meekness "refers to the value of humility
when coupled with gentleness or non-violence" (Malina, "Meekness," 109). See also
Malina, "Humility," 99–100.

onstrate their faith through generous, gracious treatment of the poor.[132]
Thus, the ideological purpose in the current stretch of text is to convince
the readers that faith in God is not a status that gains a person privilege;
it is, rather, a status that constrains—both in the sense of compelling and
restraining—one's direction in life, including how one interacts with both
the wealthy and the poor. It is exhibited in complete reliance upon God,
which, in line with the axiom "like parent like children," should result in
the people of God being fully reliable towards one another.[133] Thus faith
(πίστις), as a value, may be defined as follows:

> Faith/faithfulness refers to the value of reliability. . . . Relative to
> persons, faith is reliability in interpersonal relations; it thus takes
> on the value of enduring personal loyalty, of personal faithful-
> ness. The nouns "faith," "belief," "fidelity," "faithfulness"—as well
> as the verbs "to have faith" and "to believe"—refer to the social
> glue that binds one person to another. This bond is the social,
> externally manifested, emotionally rooted behavior of loyalty,
> commitment, and solidarity. As a social bond, it works along
> with the value of (personal and group) attachment (translated
> "love") and the value of (personal and group) allegiance or trust
> (translated "hope").[134]

The questions in this sub-unit play a significant role in positioning the readers[135] to take up the same value position regarding faith that
James maintains.[136] There are three questions in this short span of text;

132. Ibid., 76.

133. On the "like parent like children" value, see deSilva, *Honor, Patronage, Kinship & Purity*, 187–88 (see also 169–71, on being reliable to others in the [fictive] kin
group).

134. Malina, "Faith/Faithfulness," 61–62.

135. Many commentators (e.g., Nystrom, *James*, 147; Martin, *James*, 79) view the
text here as a form of diatribe, although it may be best to follow Davids (*Commentary
on James*, 120 and Dawson, "Rules of Engagement" [in this volume]) and simply refer
to it as "dialogical," since, in fact, the text also fits the shape of a sermon or homily (see
Dibelius, *James*, 2 n. 6; Wachob, *Voice of Jesus*, 59–60). Regardless, Nystrom, Martin,
and others picture James as debating with some assumed or even fictional person (e.g.,
Nystrom, *James*, 147). However, I do not believe that James addresses an unknown
or fictional someone. Rather, he casts his assumed readers in the role of the dialogue
partner. Although he does not explicitly qualify τις with ἐξ ὑμῶν in v. 14, he does do so
in v. 16, and he does shift to the second person plural δῶτε in v. 16. Thus, it seems that
he considers the readers or some subset of them as his dialogue partner, despite the use
of the third person singular verbs and the use of the indefinite pronoun.

136. The use of the lexeme ὄφελος (benefit) confirms that James is engaged in

the first two appear in v. 14 and the third in v. 16. The first question is a τ-question: τί τὸ ὄφελος . . . ἐὰν πίστιν λέγῃ τις ἔχειν, ἔργα δὲ μὴ ἔχῃ ("What is the benefit . . . If someone claims to have faith but does not have deeds?"). Davids argues that "τί τὸ ὄφελος is a regularly occurring phrase . . . always expecting a negative answer: it is no use at all."[137] This interpretation results from comparing a number of instances of this question across multiple texts that are also considered to be dialogical or "diatribal," and, therefore, comparable to James. I will not take time here to critique the methodology employed in such a reading, except to point out that it does not appear to take into account the linguistic features of the question; therefore, such a view illegitimately reads an assumption—viz. that the question presumes a negative response—into the text of James. Grammatically, the question is an *open question* and, therefore, neither presumes nor expects a negative or positive response. Relative to the functional model outlined above, as an open question it is *expository*, and as such it is heteroglossic and, thus, expands the dialogue in the text.

Exactly how the question expands dialogue requires taking into account the structure of the third class condition.[138] There are two possible ways to read the conditional structure. The first, following OpenText.org, interprets the protasis (ἐὰν πίστιν λέγῃ τις ἔχειν, ἔργα δὲ μὴ ἔχῃ ["if someone claims to have faith but does not have deeds"]) as being dependent upon the clause that follows it (μὴ δύναται ἡ πίστις σῶσαι αὐτόν; ["That faith[139] is not able to save that person, is it?"]), the second question in this stretch of text. This leaves the first question to stand independently, as follows:

> *What is the benefit?*
> ↓ *If someone claims to have faith but does not have deeds,*
> *then that faith is not able to save that person, is it?*

Structurally, this makes sense, since in the Greek of the New Testament, protases tend to precede apodoses in any class of condition.[140]

---

values negotiation.

137. Davids, *Commentary on James*, 120.

138. See Estes, *Questions and Rhetoric*, 135–41 on what he calls "conditional questions."

139. The article (ἡ) specifying πίστις functions anaphorically, pointing back to πίστιν in v. 14, hence "that faith" (see McKnight, *Letter of James*, 229 n. 14). On the anaphoric use of the article in Greek, see Porter, *Idioms*, 106.

140. Porter, *Idioms*, 254.

However, such is not always the case (see, e.g., Matt 4:9; 18:28; Acts 5:8; Col 1:22–23; 1 John 2:3; 3:13; 4:1),[141] and there are good reasons for reading the opening question as the apodosis upon which the third class protasis is dependent, as follows:

> What is the benefit
>> ↑ if someone claims to have faith but does not have deeds?
> That faith is not able to save that person, is it?

This second interpretation of the structure makes sense for a couple of reasons. Note that the sub-unit closes with the same question that opened it (. . . what is the benefit?), and in this second instance the question functions as the apodosis to a condition. Thus, reading the first question as an apodosis reveals a chiastic symmetry:

> What is the benefit
>> ↑ if someone claims to have faith but does not have deeds?
> That faith is not able to save that person, is it?
>> ↓ If a brother or a sister is naked and happens to be lacking daily food, but one from among you would say to them, "Go in peace, warm yourself and fill yourself," but that person does not give to them the things necessary for the body,
> what is the benefit?

From this stems a second reason this interpretation makes sense, namely that it makes the second question (μὴ δύναται ἡ πίστις σῶσαι αὐτόν ["This faith is not able to save that person, is it?"]) the focal point of the sub-unit. According to grammar, this is a closed, negative question,[142] and because it is negated with μή, it presumes a negative response: "No, such a [deed-less][143] faith cannot save that person." In terms of discourse semantics, this is a *leading question*; the presumed answer creates a moment of *concurrence* in the colloquy where James and the putative readers are depicted as being in agreement with one another on a value position that is to be understood as "common sense." On this point, dialogue is

---

141. One could also count the instances of εἰ/ἐάν + μή and other such structures, which tend to follow their apodoses (see, e.g., Rom 10:15).

142. I.e., the question realizes assertive attitude, interrogative mood, and denial (schematically, [+assertive: +interrogative: +denial]). For realization schemes, see Porter, "Systemic Functional Linguistics," 45–46.

143. McKnight, *Letter of James*, 229 rightly reads the question as follows: "Can [that kind of workless] faith save you?"

squelched; there is no dialogic space in the text to take the positive alternative that such a faith could or is able to save the person who claims to have faith but who does not demonstrate that faith with deeds.

It is also worth noting that the negative prosody generated by the negative answer presumed in the central question radiates backwards and forwards,[144] so that the readers are more likely to answer the first and last questions pessimistically: there is no benefit that comes from a "deed-less" faith. Moreover, the protasis of the final question constitutes a sort of comic *reductio ad absurdum* argument.[145] If faith (πίστις) is concerned with the "social, externally manifested, emotionally rooted behavior of loyalty, commitment, and solidarity" as noted above, it would be ridiculous for a person to say that they have faith and then not act like it. Behaving in such a way would certainly *not* constitute "common sense" from James's perspective.

In summary, then, the questions in this sub-unit engage the readers in dialogue, first opening up dialogic space by introducing the notion of benefit and tying it directly to the social value of faith. The second question is central both structurally and thematically, and it serves as James's main tool in re-positioning the readers, primarily by creating in the text a moment at which both he and the readers concur that a "deed-less" faith does not and cannot "save."

James 3:13—4:6 Why Divisions Exist Among You

13 Τίς σοφὸς καὶ ἐπιστήμων ἐν ὑμῖν; δειξάτω ἐκ τῆς καλῆς ἀναστροφῆς τὰ ἔργα αὐτοῦ ἐν πραΰτητι σοφίας. 14 εἰ δὲ ζῆλον πικρὸν ἔχετε καὶ ἐριθείαν ἐν τῇ καρδίᾳ ὑμῶν, μὴ κατακαυχᾶσθε καὶ ψεύδεσθε κατὰ τῆς ἀληθείας. 15 οὐκ ἔστιν αὕτη ἡ σοφία ἄνωθεν κατερχομένη ἀλλ᾽ ἐπίγειος, ψυχική, δαιμονιώδης. 16 ὅπου γὰρ ζῆλος καὶ ἐριθεία, ἐκεῖ ἀκαταστασία καὶ πᾶν φαῦλον πρᾶγμα. 17 ἡ δὲ ἄνωθεν σοφία πρῶτον μὲν ἁγνή ἐστιν, ἔπειτα εἰρηνική, ἐπιεικής, εὐπειθής, μεστὴ ἐλέους καὶ καρπῶν ἀγαθῶν, ἀδιάκριτος, ἀνυπόκριτος. 18 καρπὸς δὲ δικαιοσύνης ἐν εἰρήνῃ σπείρεται τοῖς ποιοῦσιν εἰρήνην. 1 Πόθεν πόλεμοι καὶ πόθεν μάχαι ἐν ὑμῖν; οὐκ ἐντεῦθεν, ἐκ τῶν ἡδονῶν ὑμῶν τῶν στρατευομένων ἐν τοῖς μέλεσιν ὑμῶν; 2 ἐπιθυμεῖτε καὶ οὐκ

144. See Dvorak, "Prodding with Prosody," 103–7; Hood, "Persuasive Power of Prosodies," 37–49.

145. McKnight, *Letter of James*, 229: "James now offers a comic example, and it would be humorous if it were not so tragic."

ἔχετε, φονεύετε καὶ ζηλοῦτε καὶ οὐ δύνασθε ἐπιτυχεῖν, μάχεσθε
καὶ πολεμεῖτε, οὐκ ἔχετε διὰ τὸ μὴ αἰτεῖσθαι ὑμᾶς, ³ αἰτεῖτε καὶ
οὐ λαμβάνετε, διότι κακῶς αἰτεῖσθε, ἵνα ἐν ταῖς ἡδοναῖς ὑμῶν
δαπανήσητε. ⁴ μοιχαλίδες, οὐκ οἴδατε ὅτι ἡ φιλία τοῦ κόσμου
ἔχθρα τοῦ θεοῦ ἐστιν; ὃς ἐὰν οὖν βουληθῇ φίλος εἶναι τοῦ
κόσμου, ἐχθρὸς τοῦ θεοῦ καθίσταται. ⁵ ἢ δοκεῖτε ὅτι κενῶς ἡ
γραφὴ λέγει· πρὸς φθόνον ἐπιποθεῖ τὸ πνεῦμα ὃ κατῴκισεν ἐν
ἡμῖν, ⁶ μείζονα δὲ δίδωσιν χάριν; διὸ λέγει· ὁ θεὸς ὑπερηφάνοις
ἀντιτάσσεται, ταπεινοῖς δὲ δίδωσιν χάριν.

¹³ *Who is wise and understanding among you? That person is to
make known through good conduct their deeds done in meekness
produced by wisdom.*[146] ¹⁴ *But if you have bitter envy*[147] *and selfish
ambition in your heart,*[148] *do not boast against and lie against the
truth.* ¹⁵ *This is not wisdom that has come down from above, but is
earthly,*[149] *world-oriented,*[150] *demonic.* ¹⁶ *For where envy and selfish ambition exist, there is disorder*[151] *and every evil deed.* ¹⁷ *But
wisdom from above is first pure then peaceable, gentle, compliant,
full of mercy and good fruit, unwavering, without hypocrisy.* ¹⁸
*Now the fruit of justice is sown in peace through the ones making
peace.* ¹ *Whence the battles and whence the fights among you? Are
they not from your passions that wage war among your members?*
² *You want yet you do not have; you murder and you envy yet you
are not able to obtain; you fight and you battle; you do not have
because you do not ask;* ³ *you ask yet you do not receive, because
you ask with wrong motives, in order to waste them on your own
passions.* ⁴ *Adulteresses, do you not understand that friendship*

---

146. I have interpreted the genitive form σοφίας as a subjective genitive (see Porter, *Idioms*, 94–95). Compare to Moo's "genitive of source" (*Letter of James*, 170).

147. On reading ζῆλος as "envy" rather than "jealous," see Johnson, *Brother of Jesus*, 189–95. See also Elliott, "Envy," 344–64; Seeman, "Zeal/Jealousy," 180–82.

148. Note the *singular* form of καρδία, which, in a collectivist culture, likely referred to their collective heart, not individual hearts (contra NRSV). See Malina, "Collectivism in Mediterranean Culture," 17–28.

149. See Johnson, *Letter of James*, 272: "earthbound."

150. On glossing ψυχική as "world-oriented," see Greek-English Lexicon, *Greek-
English Lexicon*, 2:509 ("worldly-minded") and Thiselton, *First Epistle to the Corinthians*, 267–70 on Paul's use of the term in 1 Cor 2:14.

151. See Osiek, "Ordering," 124–25.

*with the world[152] is enmity with God?[153] Thus, whoever wants
to be a friend of the world becomes an enemy of God. [5] Or do
you think that the scripture speaks in vain? The spirit that dwells
among you desires for envy, [6] but he gives greater grace, therefore
it says, "God opposes the proud but gives grace to the humble."*

Scholars generally agree that a new unit begins at Jas 3:1, as signaled
by the restated address formula ("my brothers and sisters" [ἀδελφοί
μου]), the shift away from the use of faith (πίστις) and deeds (ἔργα), and
the prohibition that many of the readers are not to be(come) teachers
(μὴ πολλοὶ διδάσκαλοι γίνεσθε). However, where the unit ends has been
debated.[154] McKnight argues that Jas 3:1—4:12 makes up the full unit—a
unit that, to be sure, discusses multiple themes, all of which are aimed
at those among the readership who would be teachers (διδάσκαλοι):[155]
teachers and the tongue (3:1–12); teachers and wisdom (3:13–18); teachers and dissensions (4:1–10); teachers, the community, and the tongue
(4:11–12).[156] Dibelius maintained that 3:1–12 and 3:13—4:12 were each
distinct units, and that the latter should be further sub-divided into three
sub-units: 3:13–17, 4:1–6 (which links to the previous sub-unit by the
"isolated saying" in 3:18), and 4:7–12.[157] Varner seems to treat 3:1–12,
3:13–18, 4:1–10, and 4:11–12 as individual units or "sections" as he calls
them.[158] Yet, being strongly influenced by Johnson, Varner points out the
strong thematic connection between 3:13–18 and 4:1–10 and maintains
that, although there are significant linguistic reasons for taking 3:13–18
and 4:1–10 as separate units, they serve as the "thematic peak" and "hortatory peak," respectively, of the entire letter.[159]

---

152. The genitive τοῦ κόσμου is objective ("friendship with the world"), as noted
by McKnight (*Letter of James*, 332 n. 274) and Johnson (*Brother of Jesus*, 209). It should
be noted that the term φιλία likely refers to a patron/benefactor-client relationship
(see Batten, "God in the Letter of James," 50, 52, 58; see also Elliott, "Patronage and
Clientage," 144–56).

153. This is another objective genitive.

154. See Johnson, "James 3:13—4:10," 332–34.

155. Although, McKnight adds, James may not have teachers exclusively in mind
past 3:12 (*Letter of James*, 266).

156. See McKnight, *Letter of James*, 265–68, 298, 320, 331, 359. Compare with
Moo, *Letter of James*, 145–46.

157. Dibelius, *James*, 207–8.

158. See Varner, *Book of James*, 35. He also calls them "paragraphs."

159. Varner, *Book of James*, 143. It should be noted that Johnson sees 4:4–10 as the

I tend to agree with McKnight and others who take 3:1—4:12 as forming a complete unit; however, rather than seeing an address to teachers as the organizing principle as McKnight does,[160] I follow Moo who argues that "3:1—4:12 exhibits a general unity of thought, centered on the problem of community divisiveness and extending to its cause—selfish, envious attitudes—and its manifestation—sinful, critical speech."[161] This makes more sense in light of the problem of doubleness that, as we have seen, James is most interested in curbing.

In regards to sub-units, like most commentators I take 3:1–12 as a distinct chunk of text, focusing as it does on the tongue/speech. Like Dibelius, I take 3:13—4:12 together, but unlike him, I do not see any reason to break apart 3:13—4:6.[162] Rather, in this stretch of text, James seems concerned to point out that the addressees are behaving as though they are controlled by "wisdom from below" rather than "wisdom from above." This manifests in the envy-motivated fights and battles that exist among them. Additionally, while I, like Dibelius, think 3:18 is an axiom or proverb that likely was common among the early group of believers, it makes no discursive sense to take it as an isolated saying as Dibelius does.[163] Instead, as reported speech, this axiom/proverb functions as an integral part of James's argument in that it exemplifies behavior guided by "wisdom from above," which is then set over against the "earthly, world-oriented, demonic wisdom" that is manifest in the self-aggrandizing, envy-induced fighting and quarreling exhibited by the readers.[164] Finally,

---

thematic center of the entire letter (Johnson, *Letter of James*, 84). See also Johnson, *Brother of Jesus*, 187–89.

160. I am not convinced by McKnight's argument, which is essentially, "[I]t should be noticed that the word 'teacher' occurs only in 3:1 and never again. So, when James turns in 4:11 to 'brothers,' we can either assume that the brother is the teacher (as in 3:1) or we can conclude that James has expanded his audience from teachers to all males or, more generically, to anyone in the community" (*Letter of James*, 266). He treats διδάσκαλοι in 3:1 as if it is an address, but it is not. Actually, ἀδελφοί ("siblings") is the address in 3:1, not to mention the imperative is second person plural "you" (γίνεσθε ["be(come)"]).

161. Moo, *Letter of James*, 200.

162. See Johnson, *Brother of Jesus*, 187.

163. Dibelius, *James*, 208, 214–15.

164. See Moyise's discussion of how quotations (i.e., reported speech) function in his "Quotations," 17–18. On the function and importance of intertextuality and reported speech in discourse, see Fairclough, *Analysing Discourse*, 39–61; also Wortham and Reyes, *Discourse Analysis*, 49–51.

4:7–12 forms a sub-unit that is saturated with directive attitude realized through both commands and prohibitions; moreover, these commands, which appear to "flow directly from the quotation of Prov. 3:34 in v. 6,"[165] give this stretch of text a clear interpersonal aim by calling the readers to repentance and submission to God. In sum, then, I see 3:1—4:12 as a complete unit, which may be subdivided as follows: 3:1–12 (controlling tongue/speech); 3:13—4:6 (accusation/indictment of envy-motivated fighting and living by "wisdom from below" rather than "wisdom from above"); 4:7–12 (call to repentance).[166]

The unit commences with the first of five questions it contains: Τίς σοφὸς καὶ ἐπιστήμων ἐν ὑμῖν; ("Who is wise and understanding among you?"). In terms of functional grammar, this is an identifying relational clause in the form of a τ-question.[167] This becomes more visible when the clause is reframed as a statement: "the wise and understanding [person] among you is whom" or "the wise and understanding [person] is played by whom." The interrogative pronoun τίς functions here as a predicate nominative and, thus, serves as the complement to the absent but implied predicator ἐστίν.[168] The adjectives σοφός and ἐπιστήμων are to be read not as predicated qualities but as substantivized adjectives. Thus, in terms of functional grammar, the "wise and understanding [person]" group functions as Token and, in this case, also the Identifier; the "whom" group functions as Value and Identified.[169] The social purpose of this question is to invite the readers to consider who among them, if anyone, might fittingly be the referent of τίς—to "fill in the blank" so to speak. Thus, this question is on the one hand like an open, expository question in that it is dialogically expansive, opening space for this sort of consideration. On the other hand, the question is like a closed question in that the interrogative pronoun τίς has a limited number of possible referents. Regardless, James does not allow the readers to fill in the blank. Instead, he closes up the dialogic space by providing the "right" answer for them: the wise and understanding person among them is the one who proves it (δείκνυμι)

165. Moo, *Letter of James*, 192.

166. See Lockett, "Wholeness in Intertextual Perspective," 103.

167. On identifying relational clauses, see Halliday, *Introduction to Functional Grammar*, 122–28; Reed, *Discourse Analysis of Philippians*, 65–69.

168. See the OpenText.org clause annotation at http://www.opentext.org/texts/NT/Jas/view/clause-ch3.vo.html#Jam.c3_44.

169. See Halliday, *Introduction to Functional Grammar*, 124–28 on the functional labels Token and Value and Identifier and Identified.

through her or his good conduct and deeds done in the meekness that is produced by wisdom (3:13b).[170] In so doing, James once again invites the readers to share with him the value position that deeds (ἔργα) and a good or appropriate way of life (καλῆς ἀναστροφῆς) in general are the key indicators of a life guided by wisdom.[171] From James's point of view, however, the readers are neither guided by nor seeking wisdom; rather, their fighting, division, and doubleness prove that they are driven by envy and selfish ambition (3:14–17).

This brings us to the next two questions in this sub-unit, both of which occur at 4:1, and these two questions interact with one another in essentially the same way as the questions occurring at 2:14 (see discussion above). The first question (4:1a) is an open, expository question: πόθεν πόλεμοι καὶ πόθεν μάχαι ἐν ὑμῖν; ("Whence the battles and whence the fights among you?"). Note that the interrogative adverb "whence" (πόθεν) signals James's existential assumption that battles and fights do, indeed, exist among the group of believers he is addressing.[172] It also implies that the battles and fights have a cause—they do not "just happen." The readers are positioned to accept these implicit assumptions. Further, as Malina has pointed out, because James and his readers lived in a strong group society, it was assumed that every effect was caused by some personal agency, whether divine or human.[173] Here, then, the social purpose of the question is two-pronged. First, it makes salient *that* battles and fights do exist among the readers.[174] Second, perhaps more importantly, it opens a way for James to place the blame for the battles and fights squarely on the readers themselves.

This is where the next question comes into play (4:1b). James asks οὐκ ἐντεῦθεν, ἐκ τῶν ἡδονῶν ὑμῶν τῶν στρατευομένων ἐν τοῖς μέλεσιν

---

170. This and surrounding text align with the Jesus tradition expressed in Matt 7:15–20. See Stanton, "Jesus Traditions," 568.

171. See Wall, "James, Letter of," 552–53.

172. On assumptions, including existential assumptions, see Fairclough, *Analysing Discourse*, 55–58.

173. See Malina, *Christian Origins*, 87–89 (esp. 89); Malina, *New Testament World*, 100–104.

174. Note, too, the force that is added to the point through repetition. James essentially asks the same question twice in a row ("Whence . . . and whence . . . ?") and, although not the same word for battles and fights, he uses two words that overlap semantically (both are placed in domain 39 by Louw and Nida, *Greek-English Lexicon*, 2:496 [πόλεμος] and 2:495–96 [μάχη]).

ὑμῶν ("They come from the passions that wage war among your members, don't they?"). Note that this is a closed, leading question. Because James uses the negator οὐκ ("not"), an affirmative answer is expected. The preceding question ("Whence . . . ?") was dialogically expansive in that it opened semiotic space in which other voices could have supplied answers. However, by means of this leading question, James supplies the answer that he is looking for. This immediately collapses any dialogic space that he had opened with the previous expository question. Just like the closed, leading question at 2:14 (μὴ δύναται ἡ πίστις σῶσαι αὐτόν ["This faith is not able to save him/her, is it?"]), this question creates a moment in the colloquy when both James and the readers concur: "Yes, the battles and fights do come from the passions that wage war among us." It should be no surprise to them, then, that they desire (ἐπιθυμέω) but do not have; they covet (ζηλόω) but cannot obtain; they ask and do not receive because they ask with "wrong motives" (NIV [κακῶς])—and this results in disputes and conflict (4:1, 3).

The fourth question in this sub-unit occurs at a point where "James breaks off from an analysis of the situation and begins preaching a word of rebuke."[175] Rather pointedly, even accusatorially,[176] James inquires οὐκ οἴδατε ὅτι ἡ φιλία τοῦ κόσμου ἔχθρα τοῦ θεοῦ ἐστιν; ("Do you not understand that friendship with the world is enmity from God?" or "You do not understand that friendship with the world is enmity with God, do you?"). Johnson notes that

> οὐκ οἴδατε is a stock phrase in parenesis, in which the point is remembering traditional ethical standards, not learning new ones. This is the only time it occurs in James, though it is an expression familiar to us from Paul's letters, where it introduces elements of traditional Christian understanding, or even proverbial sayings. The phrase not only reminds the reader of what they already know; its negative phrasing suggests a rebuke as well—they should not need reminding.[177]

---

175. Martin, *James*, 148.

176. The use of the address μοιχαλίδες ("adulteresses"), especially in contrast with his more typical ἀδελφοί ("brothers and sisters" [1:2, 16; 2:1, 5, 14; 3:1, 10, 12; 4:11; 5:7, 9, 10, 12, 19]), is a very strong clue that James is now being very direct with the putative readers. "This scornful epithet is calculated to awaken them to the dangerous sin into which they have fallen and the clarity of the choice they must make" (Ortlund, Jr., *Whoredom*, 140–41). See Hunt, "Brothers, Sisters—Adulteresses" in this volume.

177. Johnson, *Brother of Jesus*, 208–9. See also McKnight, *Letter of James*, 332.

Moreover, since the question is of the closed variety, and the use of οὐκ creates the expectation of an affirmative answer ("Yes, we do not understand . . . " or, in more common English parlance, "No, we do not understand . . . "), it is, thus, dialogically contractive. It creates a concurrence or "a ground of shared understanding"[178] between James and the readers-in-the-text by squelching the heteroglossic polyphony so that what remains is a single discernible voice, and that voice pronounces friendship with the world as hostility with God.[179] In fact, the statement immediately following seems to indicate that James truly believes that, indeed, the readers do *not* actually understand what they should understand. Thus, he explicitly tells them that whoever would desire to be a friend of the world becomes an enemy of God.

The fifth and final question in this sub-unit and in our discussion is located at 4:5 (or, as some read it, 4:5–6a), a segment of text that is notoriously convoluted. As Johnson has put it, "This tangle involves questions of punctuation, the determination of grammatical subject and object, and the relation of the explicit scriptural citation in 4:6 to the ostensible citation (or allusion) in 4:5."[180] Much of the disagreement is tied up with establishing the boundaries of the question. NA28 extends the question to include 4:6a on the assumption that 4:5b–6a is the full scriptural quotation that James includes. Westcott and Hort and Tischendorf cut the question off at the end of 4:5. Laws seems to follow the latter, but she then reads πρὸς φθόνον ἐπιποθεῖ τὸ πνεῦμα ὃ κατῴκισεν ἐν ἡμῖν as a second question ("Does the spirit which he made to dwell in us long enviously?").[181] However, all of these approaches have problems, the main ones being that (a) no text exists in the form that James quotes, so it is difficult to extend the question past the verb λέγει in v. 5 (at this point, one can only speculate that James is alluding to or paraphrasing

---

178. Johnson, *Brother of Jesus*, 209.

179. See McKnight, *Letter of James*, 332–35; Johnson, *Brother of Jesus*, 213–14.

180. Johnson, *Brother of Jesus*, 185. He also says, "Not only are the problems many and difficult; they have also been dissected so many times that a quiet despair falls over any investigator sufficiently unwary to poke about in the area at all" (ibid., 182). See also Laws, "Does Scripture Speak in Vain?" 210–15; Laws, *Epistle of James*, 174–79; Allison, *Epistle of James*, 610–22.

181. See Laws, *Epistle of James*, 167, 174–79.

but not directly quoting scripture);[182] and (b) the grammar does not really support two questions as Laws has suggested.[183]

Perhaps a way forward is to step back from the bark in order to view the trees. A broader view may allow us to perceive a pattern in the discursive moves that James makes in 4:4–6 and may also give us a better clue as to what James is trying to accomplish with this text. Davids keenly observes the parallel structure between vv. 4 and 5: οὐκ οἴδατε ὅτι . . . ἢ δοκεῖτε ὅτι.[184] I am inclined to read the conjunction ἢ as connecting the two questions, seeing that both questions are instantiated with verbs representing mental processes (knowing/thinking). Additionally, there is a balance between the two questions in terms of polarity, the first being negative but the second positive. After each question, James gives a declaration that tells the readers what they ought to understand (οἶδα) or think (δοκέω). Finally, in v. 6b he concludes (διό) and brings the accusation to a close with scriptural warrant (Prov 3:34), which also sets up for the call to repentance in 4:7–12 with the actual scriptural quotation. The pattern of moves is as follows:

> *Question*: Do you not know that friendship with the world is hostility with God?[185]
>
> *Response*: Thus, whoever would desire to be a friend of the world makes him-/herself an enemy of God.
>
> *Question*: Or do you think that the scripture speaks in vain/emptily/meaninglessly?
>
> *Response*: The spirit[186] that dwells among us desires toward envy but he gives greater grace.

182. See Davids, *Commentary on James*, 162–63; McKnight, *Letter of James*, 336–37, 340–41.

183. See McKnight, *Letter of James*, 336 n. 286.

184. Davids, *Commentary on James*, 162.

185. See previous discussion where it was noted that this question already expects the answer, "No, we do not know . . ." Thus, the stated answer adds tremendous force to James's point.

186. It is best to take πνεῦμα in this text to refer not to the Holy Spirit but to the human spirit. This makes the most sense because (a) as Laws points out, "if this is seen to refer to the Holy Spirit, it would be the only reference in the epistle" (*Epistle of James*, 176) (see also Johnson, *Letter of James*, 280–81; Varner, *Book of James*, 151); (b) as McKnight notes, seeing it as a reference to the human spirit "has the advantage of picking up the theme of human zeal, ambition, and envy/jealousy from 3:14, 16; 4:2" (*Letter of James*, 337); and (c) it is grammatically suitable to take τὸ πνεῦμα as nominative and, thus, the grammatical subject of the verb ἐπιποθεῖ and eliminate the

Warrant: Therefore, it says, "God opposes the proud, but gives grace to the humble."

So then, given this discursive pattern, the fifth question is ἢ δοκεῖτε ὅτι κενῶς ἡ γραφὴ λέγει ("Or, do you think that scripture speaks emptily/ meaninglessly?"). Grammatically, this is an open question and as such has the effect of expanding dialogue in the text by introducing the notion that, from James's point of view, the readers appeared to think that scripture speaks emptily or meaninglessly. Generally speaking, scholars assume that the question is "rhetorical" and that the implied answer "must be, surely not!"[187] However, because the question is open, it does *not* create an expectation for either a negative or positive response. Moreover, as in the first question–response pair, the response here seems to betray James's belief that the readers, on the basis of their envy-fueled fighting, do not actually take the scripture to be meaningful and, thus, applicable to the life of the group and the lives of its members.

CONCLUSION

As stated at the outset, the thesis of this article is that James used questions as a means of positioning (or re-positioning) his readers (or at least attempting to do so) such that they would adopt (or adopt again) a particular theological/ideological perspective and its attendant values. I argued that James, from what he had heard about the group of believers to whom he addressed his letter, perceived that they were succumbing to the social mores of the world with the result that they lacked wholeness and, thus, holiness. As stated most clearly in 3:13—4:6, the addressees were rejecting God in favor of friendship with the world, and this was made clearly manifest in their divided, even hostile behavior toward one another. To James's way of thinking, they needed rebuke, correction, and a clear call to repentance (see esp. 4:7–12).

It should be clear from the above analyses that James's use of questions played an extremely important role in enacting resocialization through the text of the letter, especially in the obvious negotiation of values. We have seen that persuading others to leave behind certain value positions and to replace them with others is in essence an exercise in generating a particular representation of reality ([re-]presentational

---

need to assume an elided θεός.

187. Davids, *Commentary on James*, 162.

meaning) and then attempting to guide and to position others to accept that reality (interpersonal meaning).[188] In addition to positive and negative appraisals,[189] James adroitly harnesses the interpersonal power of questions as a key means of guiding and positioning the readers. The model of Engagement confirmed this. As Neyrey pointed out, questions, especially those asked in paraenetic writings like James, are not typically asked merely to gain information (although sometimes they are); instead, questions in this genre are often asked in order "to achieve a special rhetorical effect,"[190] and this "special effect" is centrally concerned with positioning readers to align with the writer's value positions.

It was shown how closed questions, depending upon which negator (οὐ or μή and related forms) James used, create in the text a sense of concurrence or agreement between the writer and the implied readers. Thus, for example, at Jas 2:14 by asking the closed question with μή as the negator "That faith is not able to save you, is it?" James positions his readers by naturalizing the response "No, it is not able to save."[191] Inherent in this response is a negative evaluation of faith that is disconnected from deeds, which is intended to point the readers away from such a faith if it can even be called "faith." This is why in the model these kinds of questions are called *leading questions* and are considered dialogically *contractive*. They limit the possible "right" answers. By contrast, James used open questions to introduce other points of view into the text in order to engage with them, even if only briefly. At 4:5, for example, James asked "Or do you think that scripture speaks emptily/meaninglessly?" Through the use of this open question, he makes salient what he believes to be the readers' evaluation of the scripture, viz., that they *do* think it speaks emptily/meaninglessly. He follows this question both with a statement and a scriptural warrant (Prov 3:34) as a means of reorienting the readers' take on not only what the scriptures say but also how they ought to be understood in relation to the groups' values. As described above, τ-questions require the readers to "fill in the blank" and, thus, function somewhere

188. See Hodge and Kress, *Social Semiotics*, 121–25. Also see again Dvorak, "Prodding with Prosody," 85–120; Dvorak, "To Incline Another's Heart," 599–624.

189. See Dvorak, "Interpersonal Metafunction"; Dvorak, "To Incline Another's Heart," 607–11.

190. Neyrey, "Questions," 659.

191. Note again that the actual readers of the letter may actually have resisted such a reading, but the point is that James naturalizes a reading in which they agree with him.

between closed and open questions. At 3:13 James asked "Who among you is wise and understanding?" On the one hand, the question is open and dialogically expansive because it challenges the putative readers to evaluate themselves and other members of the group and to supply a name or names to fill in the blank. On the other hand, the question is not entirely open, since the interrogative pronoun τίς has a limited number of possible referents. Regardless, James goes on to provide the "right" answer for them, viz., that the "who" is the person who demonstrates wisdom and understanding through their deeds. In the end, then, James again naturalizes a reading position for the readers to assume, and it is one that would align with his point of view. This is how James (and other biblical writers) used questions for the social purpose of paraenesis or resocialization.

APPENDIX

Questions in the Letter of James

KEY:

OQ Open question (no grammatical indication of positive or negative answer)

τ-Q Question with interrogative word; the interrogative word acts as a sort of placeholder for what the questioner wants to know.

PQ Positive question (with οὐ/οὐκ/οὐχ [including forms such as οὔπω]) expecting affirmative answer

NQ Negative question (with μή) expecting negative answer

LQ Leading ("Rhetorical") Question (dialogically contractive)

EQ Expository Question (dialogically expansive)

Ref.	Text	Grammar: OQ/PQ/ NQ	Discourse Function: LQ/EQ
2:2–4	[[ἐὰν γὰρ εἰσέλθῃ εἰς συναγωγὴν ὑμῶν ἀνὴρ χρυσοδακτύλιος ἐν ἐσθῆτι λαμπρᾷ, εἰσέλθῃ δὲ καὶ πτωχὸς ἐν ῥυπαρᾷ ἐσθῆτι, ἐπιβλέψητε δὲ ἐπὶ τὸν φοροῦντα τὴν ἐσθῆτα τὴν λαμπρὰν καὶ εἴπητε, Σὺ κάθου ὧδε καλῶς, καὶ τῷ πτωχῷ εἴπητε, Σὺ στῆθι ἐκεῖ ἢ κάθου ὑπὸ τὸ ὑποπόδιόν μου,]] οὐ διεκρίθητε ἐν ἑαυτοῖς καὶ ἐγένεσθε κριταὶ διαλογισμῶν πονηρῶν;	PQ [+assertion: +interroga- tive: +affir- mative]	LQ
2:5	οὐχ ὁ θεὸς ἐξελέξατο τοὺς πτωχοὺς τῷ κόσμῳ πλουσίους ἐν πίστει καὶ κληρονόμους τῆς βασιλείας ἧς ἐπηγγείλατο τοῖς ἀγαπῶσιν αὐτόν;	PQ [+assertion: +interroga- tive: +affir- mative]	LQ
2:6	οὐχ οἱ πλούσιοι καταδυναστεύουσιν ὑμῶν καὶ αὐτοὶ ἕλκουσιν ὑμᾶς εἰς κριτήρια;	PQ [+assertion: +interroga- tive: +affir- mative]	LQ
2:7	οὐκ αὐτοὶ βλασφημοῦσιν τὸ καλὸν ὄνομα τὸ ἐπικληθὲν ἐφ᾽ ὑμᾶς;	PQ [+assertion: +interroga- tive: +affir- mative]	LQ
2:14	Τί τὸ ὄφελος, ἀδελφοί μου [[ἐὰν πίστιν λέγῃ τις ἔχειν ἔργα δὲ μὴ ἔχῃ]];	τ-Q [+assertion (implied): +inter- rogative: +elemental]	EQ
2:14	μὴ δύναται ἡ πίστις σῶσαι αὐτόν;	NQ [+assertive: +inter- rogative: +denial]	LQ

2:16	[[εἴπῃ δέ τις αὐτοῖς ἐξ ὑμῶν ὑπάγετε ἐν εἰρήνῃ, θερμαίνεσθε καὶ χορτάζεσθε, μὴ δῶτε δὲ αὐτοῖς τὰ ἐπιτήδεια τοῦ σώματος,]] τί τὸ ὄφελος;	τ-Q [+assertion (implied): +interrogative: +elemental]	EQ
2:20	Θέλεις δὲ γνῶναι, ὦ ἄνθρωπε κενέ, ὅτι ἡ πίστις χωρὶς τῶν ἔργων ἀργή ἐστιν;	OQ [+assertive: +interrogative: +tonal]	EQ
2:21	Ἀβραὰμ ὁ πατὴρ ἡμῶν οὐκ ἐξ ἔργων ἐδικαιώθη ἀνενέγκας Ἰσαὰκ τὸν υἱὸν αὐτοῦ ἐπὶ τὸ θυσιαστήριον;	PQ [+assertion: +interrogative: +affirmative]	LQ
2:25	ὁμοίως δὲ καὶ Ῥαὰβ ἡ πόρνη οὐκ ἐξ ἔργων ἐδικαιώθη ὑποδεξαμένη τοὺς ἀγγέλους καὶ ἑτέρᾳ ὁδῷ ἐκβαλοῦσα;	PQ [+assertion: +interrogative: +affirmative]	LQ
3:11	μήτι ἡ πηγὴ ἐκ τῆς αὐτῆς ὀπῆς βρύει τὸ γλυκὺ καὶ τὸ πικρόν;	NQ [+assertive: +interrogative: +denial]	LQ
3:12	μὴ δύναται, ἀδελφοί μου, συκῆ ἐλαίας ποιῆσαι ἢ ἄμπελος σῦκα;	NQ [+assertive: +interrogative: +denial]	LQ
3:13	Τίς σοφὸς καὶ ἐπιστήμων ἐν ὑμῖν;	τ-Q [+assertive: +interrogative: +elemental]	EQ

4:1	Πόθεν πόλεμοι καὶ πόθεν μάχαι ἐν ὑμῖν;	τ-Q [+assertive: +inter- rogative: +elemental]	EQ
4:1	οὐκ ἐντεῦθεν, ἐκ τῶν ἡδονῶν ὑμῶν τῶν στρατευομένων ἐν τοῖς μέλεσιν ὑμῶν;	PQ [+assertion: +interroga- tive: +affir- mative]	LQ
4:4	μοιχαλίδες, οὐκ οἴδατε ὅτι ἡ φιλία τοῦ κόσμου ἔχθρα τοῦ θεοῦ ἐστιν;	PQ [+assertion: +interroga- tive: +affir- mative]	LQ
4:5	ἢ δοκεῖτε ὅτι κενῶς ἡ γραφὴ λέγει;	OQ [+assertive: +inter- rogative: +tonal]	EQ
4:12	σὺ δὲ τίς εἶ ὁ κρίνων τὸν πλησίον;	τ-Q [+assertive: +inter- rogative: +elemental]	EQ

BIBLIOGRAPHY

Adamson, James B. *James: The Man and His Message*. Grand Rapids: Eerdmans, 1989.

Allison, Dale C., Jr. *A Critical and Exegetical Commentary on the Epistle of James*. ICC. New York: Bloomsbury, 2013.

Althusser, Louis. "Ideology and Ideological State Apparatuses (Notes Towards an Investigation)." In *Essays on Ideology*, 1–60. New York: Verso, 1984.

Aune, David E. *Apocalypticism, Prophecy, and Magic in Early Christianity*. 2006. Reprint, Grand Rapids: Baker, 2008.

Bakhtin, M. M. "Discourse in the Novel." In *The Dialogic Imagination*, edited by Michel Holquist, 259–422. University of Texas Press Slavic Series 1. Austin: University of Texas Press, 1981.

Batten, Alicia. "God in the Letter of James: Patron or Benefactor?" In *The Social World of the New Testament: Insights and Models*, edited by Jerome H. Neyrey and Eric C. Stewart, 49–61. Peabody, MA: Hendrickson, 2008.

———. "Ideological Strategies in the Letter of James." In *Reading James with New Eyes: Methodological Reassessments of the Letter of James*, edited by Robert L. Webb and John S. Kloppenborg, 6–26. LNTS 342. London: T. & T. Clark International, 2007.

———. *What Are They Saying about the Letter of James?* WATSA. New York: Paulist, 2009.

Berger, Peter L., and Thomas Luckmann. *The Social Construction of Reality*. New York: Anchor, 1966.

Bourdieu, Pierre. *Outline of a Theory of Practice*. Translated by Richard Nice. Cambridge: Cambridge University Press, 1977.

Brim, Orville G. "Adult Socialization." In *International Encyclopedia of Social Sciences*, 14:555–61. New York: Macmillan, 1968.

Cargal, Timothy B. *Restoring the Diaspora: Discursive Structure and Purpose in the Epistle of James*. SBLDS 144. Atlanta: Scholars Press, 1993.

Coker, K. Jason. "Calling on the Diaspora: Nativism and Diaspora Identity in the Letter of James." In *T&T Clark Handbook to Social Identity in the New Testament*, edited by J. Brian Tucker and Coleman A. Baker, 441–53. London: Bloomsbury, 2016.

Davids, Peter H. *Commentary on James*. NIGTC. Grand Rapids: Eerdmans, 1982.

———. "James and Paul." In *Dictionary of Paul and His Letters*, edited by Gerald F. Hawthorne et al., 457–61. Downers Grove: IVP, 1993.

Dawson, Zachary K. "Language as Negotiation: Toward a Systemic Functional Model for Ideological Criticism with Application to James 2:1–13." In *Modeling Biblical Language: Selected Papers from the McMaster Divinity College Linguistics Circle*, edited by Stanley E. Porter et al., 362–90. LBS 13. Leiden: Brill, 2016.

———. "The Rules of 'Engagement': Assessing the Function of the Diatribe in James 2:14–26 Using Critical Discourse Analysis." In *The Epistle of James: Linguistic Exegesis of an Early Christian Letter*, edited by James D. Dvorak and Zachary K. Dawson, 155–95. Eugene, OR: Pickwick, 2019.

deSilva, David A. *An Introduction to the New Testament: Context, Methods, and Ministry Formation*. Downers Grove, IL: IVP, 2004.

———. *Honor, Patronage, Kinship & Purity: Unlocking New Testament Culture*. Downers Grove, IL: IVP, 2000.

Dibelius, Martin. *James: A Commentary on the Epistle of James*. Revised by Heinrich Greeven. Translated by Michael A. Williams. Hermeneia. Philadelphia: Fortress, 1976.

Dvorak, James D. "Edwin Judge and Wayne Meeks." In *Pillars in the History of New Testament Interpretation, Volume 2: Prevailing Methods after 1980*, edited by Stanley E. Porter and Sean A. Adams, 179–203. MBSS 2. Eugene, OR: Pickwick, 2016.

———. "John H. Elliott's Social-Scientific Criticism." *TrinJ* 28 (2007) 251–78.

———. "'Not Like Cain': Marking Moral Boundaries through Vilification of the Other in 1 John 3:1–18." *Dialogismos* 1 (2016) 1–19.

———. "'Prodding with Prosody': Persuasion and Social Influence through the Lens of Appraisal Theory." *BAGL* 4 (2015) 85–120.

———. "The Interpersonal Metafunction in 1 Corinthians 1–4: The Tenor of Toughness." PhD diss., McMaster Divinity College, 2012.

———. "To Incline Another's Heart: The Role of Attitude in Reader Positioning." In *The Language and Literature of the New Testament: Essays in Honor of Stanley E. Porter's 60th Birthday*, edited by Lois K. Fuller Dow et al., 599–624. BIS 150. Leiden: Brill, 2016.

———. "'Why Would Anyone Want to Do That?' The Function of Questions in the Negotiation of Values." Paper presented at the annual meeting of the SBL. Boston, MA, November 18, 2017.

Elliott, Gregory. "Ideology." In *A Dictionary of Cultural and Critical Theory*, edited by Michael Payne and Jessica Rae Barbera, 340–45. 2nd ed. Malden, MA: Blackwell, 2010.

Elliott, John H. *Beware the Evil Eye, Volume 3, The Bible and Related Sources*. Eugene, OR: Cascade, 2016.

———. "Envy, Jealousy, and Zeal in the Bible: Sorting Out the Social Differences and Theological Implications—No Envy for YHWH." In *To Break Every Yoke: Essays in Honor of Marvin L. Chaney*, edited by Robert B. Coote and Norman K. Gottwald, 344–64. SWBA 3. Sheffield: Sheffield Phoenix, 2007.

———. "Patronage and Clientage." In *The Social Sciences and New Testament Interpretation*, edited by Richard Rohrbaugh, 144–56. Peabody, MA: Hendrickson, 1996.

———. "The Epistle of James in Rhetorical and Social Scientific Perspective: Holiness–Wholeness and Patterns of Replication." *BTB* 23 (1993) 71–81.

———. *What is Social-Scientific Criticism?* GBS. Minneapolis: Fortress, 1993.

Esler, Philip F. "Social-Scientific Approaches." In *Dictionary of Biblical Criticism and Interpretation*, edited by Stanley E. Porter, 337–40. New York: Routledge, 2007.

Estes, Douglas. *Questions and Rhetoric in the Greek New Testament*. Grand Rapids: Zondervan, 2017.

Fairclough, Norman. *Analysing Discourse: Textual Analysis for Social Research*. London: Routledge, 2003.

———. *Critical Discourse Analysis*. 2nd ed. Longman Applied Linguistics. London: Longman, 2010.

———. *Discourse and Social Change*. Cambridge: Polity, 1992.

———. *Language and Power*. 3rd ed. Abingdon: Routledge, 2015.

Fitzmyer, Joseph A. *First Corinthians*. AB 32. New Haven: Yale University Press, 2008.

Gass, Robert H., and John S. Seiter. *Persuasion, Social Influence, and Compliance Gaining*. 2nd ed. Boston: Allyn and Bacon, 2003.

Goatly, Andrew. *Critical Reading and Writing: An Introductory Coursebook*. London: Routledge, 2000.

Halliday, M. A. K. *Halliday's Introduction to Function Grammar*. Revised by Christian M. I. M. Matthiessen. 4th ed. London: Routledge, 2014.

———. *An Introduction to Functional Grammar*. 2nd ed. London: Arnold, 1994.

———. "Language as Code and Language as Behaviour: A Systemic–Functional Interpretation of the Nature and Ontogenesis of Dialogue." In *The Semiotics of Culture and Language, Volume 1: Language as Social Semiotic*, edited by Robin P. Fawcett et al., 3–35. OLS. London: Frances Pinter, 1984.

———. *Language as Social Semiotic: The Social Interpretation of Language and Meaning*. Baltimore: University Park Press, 1978.

Hart, Christopher. *Discourse, Grammar, and Ideology*. London: Bloomsbury, 2014.

Hauerwas, Stanley. *A Community of Character.* Notre Dame: University of Notre Dame Press, 1981.

Hodge, Robert, and Gunther Kress. *Social Semiotics.* Ithaca, NY: Cornell University Press, 1988.

Hodges, Zane. *The Gospel Under Siege.* Dallas: Redención Viva, 1981.

Hood, Susan. "The Persuasive Power of Prosodies: Radiating Values in Academic Writing." *JEAP* 5 (2006) 37–49.

Hunston, Susan, and Geoff Thompson. *Evaluation in Text: Authorial Stance and Construction of Discourse.* Oxford Linguistics. Oxford: Oxford University Press, 1999.

Hunt, Benjamin B. "Brothers, Sisters—Adulteresses." In *The Epistle of James: Linguistic Exegesis of an Early Christian Letter,* edited by James D. Dvorak and Zachary K. Dawson, 246–78. LENT 1. Eugene, OR: Pickwick, 2019.

Johnson, Luke Timothy. *Brother of Jesus, Friend of God: Studies in the Letter of James.* Grand Rapids: Eerdmans, 2004.

———. "James 3:13—4:10 and the *Topos* περὶ Φθόνου." *NovT* 4 (1983) 327–47.

———. *The Letter of James: A New Translation with Introduction and Commentary.* AB 37A. New York: Doubleday, 1995.

Kluckhohn, Florence, and Fred L. Strodtbeck. *Variations in Value Orientations.* New York: Harper and Row, 1962.

Köstenberger, Andreas J., et al. *The Lion and the Lamb: New Testament Essentials from The Cradle, the Cross, and the Crown.* Nashville: Broadman and Holman, 2012.

Laws, Sophie. "Does Scripture Speak in Vain? A Reconsideration of James iv, 5." *NTS* 20 (1973) 210–15.

———. *The Epistle of James.* BNTC 16. 1980. Reprint, Peabody, MA: Hendrickson, 1993.

Lemke, Jay L. *Textual Politics: Discourse and Social Dynamics.* Critical Perspectives on Literacy and Education. Abingdon: Taylor and Francis, 1995.

Lockett, Darian R. "Wholeness in Intertextual Perspective: James' Use of Scripture in Developing a Theme." *MJT* 15 (2016) 92–106.

Louw, Johannes P., and Eugene A. Nida. *Greek-English Lexicon of the New Testament Based on Semantic Domains.* 2 vols. New York: United Bible Societies, 1988.

Malina, Bruce J. *Christian Origins and Cultural Anthropology: Practical Models for Biblical Interpretation.* 1986. Reprint, Eugene, OR: Wipf & Stock, 2010.

———. "Collectivism in Mediterranean Culture." In *Understanding the Social World of the New Testament,* edited by Dietmar Neufeld and Richard E. DeMaris, 17–28. London: Routledge, 2010.

———. "Early Christian Groups: Using Small Group Formation Theory to Explain Christian Organizations." In *Modelling Early Christianity: Social-Scientific Studies of the New Testament in Its Context,* edited by Philip F. Esler, 96–113. London: Routledge, 1995.

———. "Faith/Faithfulness." In *Handbook of Biblical Social Values,* edited by John J. Pilch and Bruce J. Malina, 61–63. 3rd ed. Matrix 10. Eugene, OR: Cascade, 2016.

———. "Honor and Shame." In *Handbook of Biblical Social Values,* edited by John J. Pilch and Bruce J. Malina, 89–96. 3rd ed. Matrix 10. Eugene, OR: Cascade, 2016.

———. "Humility." In *Handbook of Biblical Social Values,* edited by John J. Pilch and Bruce J. Malina, 99–100. 3rd ed. Matrix 10. Eugene, OR: Cascade, 2016.

————. "Love." In *Handbook of Biblical Social Values*, edited by John J. Pilch and Bruce J. Malina, 106–9. 3rd ed. Matrix 10. Eugene, OR: Cascade, 2016.

————. "Meekness." In *Handbook of Biblical Social Values*, edited by John J. Pilch and Bruce J. Malina, 109–10. 3rd ed. Matrix 10. Eugene, OR: Cascade, 2016.

————. *New Testament World: Insights from Cultural Anthropology*. 3rd. ed. Louisville: Westminster John Knox, 2001.

————. "Patronage." In *Handbook of Biblical Social Values*, edited by John J. Pilch and Bruce J. Malina, 131–34. 3rd ed. Matrix 10. Eugene, OR: Cascade, 2016.

————. *The Social Gospel of Jesus: The Kingdom of God in Mediterranean Perspective*. Minneapolis: Fortress, 2001.

Malina, Bruce J., and Jerome H. Neyrey. *Calling Jesus Names: The Social Value of Labels in Matthew*. Foundations and Facets. Sonoma, CA: Polebridge Press, 1988.

————. "Conflict in Luke–Acts: Labelling and Deviance Theory." In *The Social World of Luke–Acts: Models for Interpretation*, edited by Jerome H. Neyrey, 97–122. Peabody, MA: Hendrickson, 1991.

Martin, J. R. *English Text: System and Structure*. Philadelphia: John Benjamins, 1992.

Martin, J. R., and P. R. R. White. *The Language of Evaluation: Appraisal in English*. London: Palgrave Macmillan, 2005.

Martin, Ralph P. *James*. WBC 48. Waco: Word, 1988.

Mathewson, David L., and Elodie Ballantine Emig. *Intermediate Greek Grammar: Syntax for Students of the New Testament*. Grand Rapids: Baker, 2016.

McKnight, Scot. *The Letter of James*. NICNT. Grand Rapids: Eerdmans, 2011.

McVann, Mark. "Change/Novelty Orientation." In *Handbook of Biblical Social Values*, edited by John J. Pilch and Bruce J. Malina, 14–16. 3rd ed. Matrix 10. Eugene, OR: Cascade, 2016.

————. "Compliance." In *Handbook of Biblical Social Values*, edited by John J. Pilch and Bruce J. Malina, 30–32. 3rd ed. Matrix 10. Eugene, OR: Cascade, 2016.

————. "Family-Centeredness." In *Handbook of Biblical Social Values*, edited by John J. Pilch and Bruce J. Malina, 64–66. 3rd ed. Matrix 10. Eugene, OR: Cascade, 2016.

Meeks, Wayne A. *The Moral World of the First Christians*. LEC 6. Philadelphia: Westminster, 1986.

————. *The Origins of Christian Morality: The First Two Centuries*. New Haven: Yale University Press, 1993.

Moo, Douglas J. *The Letter of James*. PNTC. Grand Rapids: Eerdmans, 2000.

Moule, C. F. D. *An Idiom Book of New Testament Greek*. 2nd ed. Cambridge: University of Cambridge Press, 1959.

Moyise, Steve. "Quotations." In *As It Is Written: Studying Paul's Use of Scripture*, edited by Stanley E. Porter and Christopher D. Stanley, 15–28. SBLSS 50. Atlanta: SBL, 2008.

Neyrey, Jerome. "God, Benefactor and Patron: The Major Cultural Model for Interpreting the Deity in Greco-Roman Antiquity." *JSNT* 27 (2005) 465–92.

————. "Loss of Wealth, Loss of Family and Loss of Honor: The Cultural Context of the Original Makarisms in Q." In *Modelling Early Christianity: Social-Scientific Studies in the New Testament in Its Context*, edited by Philip F. Esler, 139–58. London: Routledge, 1995.

————. "Questions, *Chreiai*, and Challenges to Honor: The Interface of Rhetoric and Culture in Mark's Gospel." *CBQ* 60 (1998) 657–81.

———. "Wholeness." In *Handbook of Biblical Social Values*, edited by John J. Pilch and Bruce J. Malina, 175–78. 3rd ed. Matrix 10. Eugene, OR: Cascade, 2016.

Nock, A. D. *Conversion: The Old and the New in Religion from Alexander the Great to Augustine of Hippo*. Baltimore: Johns Hopkins University Press, 1933.

Nystrom, David P. *James*. NIVAC. Grand Rapids: Zondervan, 1997.

OpenText.org. http://www.opentext.org.

Ortlund, Jr., Raymond C. *Whoredom: God's Unfaithful Wife in Biblical Theology*. NSBT. Grand Rapids: Eerdmans, 1996.

Osiek, Carolyn. "Ordering." In *Handbook of Biblical Social Values*, edited by John J. Pilch and Bruce J. Malina, 124–25. 3rd ed. Matrix 10. Eugene, OR: Cascade, 2016.

Palmer, F. R. *Mood and Modality*. 2nd ed. CTL. Cambridge: Cambridge University Press, 2001.

Penner, Todd C. "The Epistle of James in Current Research." *CurBS* 7 (1999) 257–308.

Peoples, James, and Garrick Bailey. *Humanity: An Introduction to Cultural Anthropology*. 10th ed. Stamford, CT: Cengage Learning, 2015.

Perdue, Leo G. "Paraenesis and the Epistle of James." *ZNW* 72 (1981) 241–56.

———. "The Social Character of Paraenesis and Paraenetic Literature." *Semeia* 50 (1990) 5–39.

Pfuhl, Edwin H. *The Deviance Process*. New York: Van Nostrand Reinhold, 1980.

Pilch, John J. "Interpreting the Bible with the Value Orientations Model: History and Prospects." *BTB* 32 (2002) 92–99.

———. *Introducing the Cultural Context of the New Testament*. 1991. Reprint, Eugene: Wipf and Stock, 2007.

———. "Power." In *Handbook of Biblical Social Values*, edited by John J. Pilch and Bruce J. Malina, 137–39. 3rd ed. Matrix 10. Eugene, OR: Cascade, 2016.

———. "Trust (Personal and Group)." In *Handbook of Biblical Social Values*, edited by John J. Pilch and Bruce J. Malina, 173–75. 3rd ed. Matrix 10. Eugene, OR: Cascade, 2016.

Pilch, John J., and Bruce J. Malina. "Introduction." In *Handbook of Biblical Social Values*, edited by John J. Pilch and Bruce J. Malina, xix–xxxviii. 3rd ed. Matrix 10. Eugene, OR: Cascade, 2016.

Porter, Stanley E. *Idioms of the Greek New Testament*. BLG 2. 2d ed. London: Continuum, 1999.

———. "Systemic Functional Linguistics and the Greek Language: The Need for Further Modeling." In *Modeling Biblical Language: Selected Papers from the McMaster Divinity College Linguistics Circle*, edited by Stanley E. Porter et al., 9–47. LBS 13. Leiden: Brill, 2016.

———. *Verbal Aspect in the Greek of the New Testament, with Reference to Tense and Mood*. SBG 1. New York: Peter Lang, 1993.

Reed, Jeffrey T. *A Discourse Analysis of Philippians: Method and Rhetoric in the Debate over Literary Integrity*. JSNTSup 136. Sheffield: Sheffield Academic Press, 1997.

Robertson, A. T. *A Grammar of the Greek New Testament in Light of Historical Research*. 4th ed. Nashville: Broadman Press, 1934.

Rohrbaugh, Richard L. "Gossip in the New Testament." In *Social Scientific Models for Interpreting the Bible*, edited by John J. Pilch, 239–59. BibInt 53. Atlanta: SBL, 2001.

———. "Honor." In *Understanding the Social World of the New Testament*, edited by Dietmar Neufeld and Richard E. DeMaris, 109–125. New York: Routledge, 2010.

Schaefer, R. T., and R. P. Lamm. *Sociology*. 4th ed. New York: McGraw Hill, 1992.

Seeman, Chris. "Zeal/Jealousy." In *Handbook of Biblical Social Values.* 3rd ed. Matrix 10. Eugene, OR: Cascade, 2016.

Sire, James W. *The Universe Next Door.* Rev. ed. Downers Grove, IL: IVP, 1988.

Stanton, Graham N. "Jesus Traditions." In *Dictionary of the Later New Testament and Its Developments,* edited by Ralph P. Martin and Peter H. Davids, 565–79. Downers Grove, IL: IVP, 1997.

Tajfel, Henri, and J. C. Turner. "An Integrative Theory of Intergroup Conflict." In *The Social Psychology of Intergroup Relations,* edited by William G. Austin and Stephen Worchel, 33–47. Monterey, CA: Brooks/Cole, 1979.

Theissen, Gerd. *A Theory of Primitive Christian Religion.* Translated by John Bowden. London: SCM, 1999.

Thiselton, Anthony C. *The First Epistle to the Corinthians.* NIGTC. Grand Rapids: Eerdmans, 2000.

VanGemeren, Willem A. *Interpreting the Prophetic Word: An Introduction to the Prophetic Literature of the Old Testament.* Grand Rapids: Zondervan, 1990.

Varner, William. *The Book of James: A New Perspective: A Linguistic Commentary Applying Discourse Analysis.* The Woodlands, TX: Kress Biblical Resources, 2010.

Vološinov, Valentin N. *Marxism and the Philosophy of Language.* Translated by Ladislav Matejka and I. R. Titunik. Studies in Language 1. New York: Seminar Press, 1973.

Wachob, Wesley Hiram. *The Voice of Jesus in the Social Rhetoric of James.* SNTSMS 106. Cambridge: Cambridge University Press, 2000.

Wall, Robert W. "James, Letter of." In *Dictionary of the Later New Testament and Its Development,* edited by Ralph P. Martin and Peter H. Davids, 545–61. Downers Grove, IL: IVP, 1997.

White, P. R. R. "Beyond Modality and Hedging: A Dialogic View of the Language of Intersubjective Stance." *Text* 23 (2003) 259–84.

Wortham, Stanton, and Angela Reyes. *Discourse Analysis Beyond the Speech Event.* London: Routledge, 2015.

Wuellner, Wilhelm H. "Der Jakobusbrief im Licht der Rhetorik und Textpragmatik." *LB* 43 (1978) 5–66.

Young, Richard A. *Intermediate New Testament Greek: A Linguistic and Exegetical Approach.* Nashville: Broadman and Holman, 1994.

9

Brothers, Sisters—Adulteresses!

Establishing and Maintaining Tenor Relations in James

Benjamin B. Hunt

INTRODUCTION

THE FORMS OF ADDRESS in the Epistle of James are ubiquitous and diverse.[1] Including the initial designation of the addressees in Jas 1:1 (i.e., ταῖς δώδεκα φυλαῖς ταῖς ἐν τῇ διασπορᾷ), the writer uses between eight and ten different forms of address, and he uses these forms of address some nineteen to twenty-one times.[2] Moreover, it is difficult to observe many of these forms of address without suspecting that they

1. Throughout this essay I use the designation "forms of address" to designate the forms in the Greek language that indicate *to whom* an instance of language is being spoken or written. Formally, these are grammaticalized as nouns and adjectives in the vocative and nominative cases, and can be accompanied by modifiers. I view the nominative and vocative forms as functionally equivalent based on James Moulton's observation of the interchangeability of the case-forms in address (*Prolegomena*, 71). See also, Turner *Syntax*, 34–35, who makes it difficult to articulate a distinction between the two cases in forms of address during the Koine period. Nevertheless, some have attempted the task, including Moulton himself (*Prolegomena*, 70), as well as J. P. Louw ("Linguistic Theory," 80) and Porter (*Idioms*, 87). I, however, am of the understanding that both nominative and vocative forms of address were capable of grammaticalizing the same kinds of semantics.

2. The following forms of address are used in James: ἀδελφοί μου (1:2; 2:1, 14; 3:1, 10, 12; 5:12, 19); ἀδελφοί μου ἀγαπητοί (1:16, 19; 2:5); ὦ ἄνθρωπε κενέ (2:20); μοιχαλίδες (4:4); ἁμαρτωλοί (4:8); δίψυχοι (4:8); ἀδελφοί (4:11; 5:7, 9, 10). Also, οἱ πλούσιοι (5:1) and οἱ λέγοντες followed by the content of speech (4:13–14) might also be considered as forms of address.

function in James in some kind of intentional manner. It is difficult to imagine a situation in which an author addresses a community as both ἀδελφοί μου ἀγαπητοί and as μοιχαλίδες without concluding that the forms of address were deliberately employed for some purpose. If the writer of the Epistle of James was intentional about the forms of address he employed, as one can reasonably assume, then what was their purpose?

In this essay, I want to explore how the forms of address utilized in the Epistle of James may have contributed to the relationship between James and the addressed community. One particularly helpful method of such an exploration would be a linguistic study of the way forms of address might have affected interpersonal relationships in a first-century Mediterranean context. The systemic functional linguistic (SFL) theory associated with M. A. K. Halliday is the theoretical framework that this study will use due to its emphasis on language as a *social* semiotic, where language is understood as a social activity through which meanings are exchanged between people in some kind of actual or prescribed relationship.[3] The procedure of this essay is two-fold: first, I will develop a linguistic model detailing the interpersonal semantic choices available to a person speaking Greek in the first century when addressing another person or a group of people; second, I will examine forms of address in James as indicators of the relationship James is attempting to prescribe between himself and the addressed community.[4] In light of this examination I will argue that James strategically employed forms of address as reminders of the addressees' status in relation to himself in order to maximize the probability that his direction and teaching would be accepted.

SYSTEMIC FUNCTIONAL LINGUISTICS, TENOR, AND INTERPERSONAL SEMANTICS

SFL, as stated above, understands language use as a form of social activity. Most systemic functional linguists speak of the social aspect of language use in terms of Register Theory.[5] As a beginning point, Michael Halliday

---

3. See Halliday, in Halliday and Hasan, *Language, Context, and Text*, 12.

4. Due to the nearly limitless combinations of lexemes that can be used in forms of address, the model I develop should not be taken as exhaustive, but as a general description of the kinds of interpersonal semantic possibilities available in the Greek language.

5. Register Theory seems to have as many conceptions as linguists who discuss it. However, a notable difference can be seen between the Register Theory posited by

recognized that any use of language takes place within a particular mix of social and material settings, which he called the context of situation. In order to more delicately describe the features of the context of situation, Halliday divided the context of situation into three contextual categories (field, tenor, and mode), each consisting of particular kinds of extra-linguistic factors that had bearing on the language used between partici-pants. Furthermore, Halliday also theorized that the relevant features of these three contextual categories are evinced in the semantics exchanged between the participants.[6] Thus, Halliday developed the theory of the metafunctions, which are the three semantic categories of ideational meaning, interpersonal meaning, and textual meaning, and these cor-respond respectively to the contextual variables of field, tenor, and mode. The metafunctions realize the *relevant* features of their corresponding contextual categories in the meanings exchanged.[7] Halliday called the combination of these three metafunctions the register of the text. Thus, register is a semantic concept, which attempts to describe the realization of contextual factors in the meanings exchanged between participants in a communicative event.

This brief description of Register Theory forms the basis for this study of the forms of address in the Epistle of James, as well as how they contributed to the relationship between the addressed community and himself. For the sake of brevity, however, it is appropriate to discuss only the contextual category of tenor and the corresponding interpersonal metafunction, which are the most germane to the topic of this paper.[8] When considering tenor between human participants in a communica-tive event, the linguist looks at those participants in the communicative event and the statuses and roles of these participants with respect to one another (e.g., whether the participants were equals, whether they were well acquainted with one another, etc.). The interpersonal metafunc-tion, according to Halliday, details the relevant features of tenor precisely because interpersonal semantics attest to language as a social activity

---

Michael Halliday and that of another notable systemic functional linguist, J. R. Martin. For a helpful overview of such differences, see Dvorak, "Tenor of Toughness," 29–33.

6. Halliday, *Language as Social Semiotic*, 21–22.

7. See Halliday, in Halliday and Hasan, *Language, Context, and Text*, 15–43.

8. For a more thorough description of the three categories of context of situa-tion, see Halliday, in Halliday and Hasan, *Language, Context, and Text*, 3–14.

whereby roles and relations are enacted and/or constructed through the creation of meaning.[9]

Register Theory has been used for various purposes in systemic functional linguistic study, and here I will contrast two of these. The first is to study language use as a depiction of an already known context. Conversely, biblical scholars using SFL have recognized that Register Theory can be utilized to posit a context of situation (traditionally, *Sitz im Leben*) based on a study of the language used. The present study is in this second vein. I want to note first that both types of linguistic study operate under the understanding that language is a veritable window into the reality of the context of situation. However, when language is used it also has the potential of *influencing* and *changing* the context of situation.[10] This is important to recognize because when James wrote his epistle, he would have changed, whether intentionally or unintentionally, a host of variables of the context of situation. He could have established a new tenor with roles and relationships previously nonexistent. Similarly, James may have maintained an established tenor, or even modified it is some way. What seems to be at risk in the Epistle of James is whether the addressed community might alter their behavior based on James's teaching and commands. It is true that one factor that could determine whether such an alteration might take place is the addressees' acceptance of the role prescribed to them; however, I am unconcerned with the historical realities of the context of situation. Whether this prescribed tenor was historical fact is beyond the scope of this study. Rather, I want to know the answer to this question: how did James attempt to make his role known, as well as the role(s) expected of the addressed community, in order to initiate change in the context of situation? I believe that the forms of address in the Epistle of James can contribute significantly towards answering this question.

GREEK FORMS OF ADDRESS

Prior to fleshing out a systemic-functional model for forms of address, I will first briefly discuss how Greek grammarians have traditionally treated forms of address. While none of the grammarians discussed in this section operated within the SFL framework, it is still worthwhile to discuss the ways in which Greek grammarians described forms of address

9. Ibid., 20.

10. See Hasan and Martin, *Language Development*, 8.

in conversation with the ways SFL describes the various functions of language. By doing this we can more plainly see the benefits of using SFL in advancing our understanding of the Greek language. A survey of modern grammarians would seem to indicate that forms of address in Koine Greek have not been described in terms of interpersonal semantics. There does, however, appear to be one notable exception with the use of ὦ with forms of address. In reading these grammars, one might get the impression that forms of address were not able to grammaticalize interpersonal semantics (to use SFL's terminology) without the presence of ὦ, and at least one grammarian suggests as much.[11] The particle ὦ is said to have contributed an interpersonal sense to forms of address that might not otherwise be present in those forms without ὦ—whether "politeness,"[12] "solemnity,"[13] or any other emotion "of a lesser ... or greater degree."[14] For my own part, I think it is possible that the paucity of ὦ with forms of address in Koine Greek has led many grammarians to reason that ὦ was the only component of forms of address by which SFL's interpersonal semantics might have been realized.[15] Nevertheless, as stated above, these grammarians do not operate within the bounds of SFL and its terminology, so this survey of modern grammars cannot be taken as the final word on the issue.

The ancients themselves appear to have acknowledged that forms of address could have affected what SFL proponents understand as tenor relations. One notable example comes from Apollonius Dyscolus (second century CE) in his work *On Syntax*. During a lengthy engagement with Tryphon, who reasoned that the nominative form of σύ should have *always* been considered a form of address due to its usage with second-person verbs, Apollonius concedes that nominative σύ *may* have been

11. Wallace, *Greek Grammar*, 67–68. However, Wallace briefly mentions his view that the *articular* nominative form of address can be an address to an inferior (*Greek Grammar*, 57).

12. Smyth, *Greek Grammar*, §1284; and BDF §146.

13. Robertson, *Grammar*, 463–64.

14. BDF §146. Turner provides examples of what he believes are emotive uses of ὦ within the New Testament (*Syntax*, 33). See also Wallace, *Greek Grammar*, 56 and 68.

15. The particle ὦ appears a mere seventeen times in the NA28, which can be compared to the nineteen or twenty forms of address found in James alone. For a more thorough discussion, see Turner, *Syntax*, 33; Dickey, "Greek Address System of the Roman Period," 500–501.

used as a form of address. However, Apollonius counters that, "address-ees are likely to be annoyed (δυσανασχέτως ἔχουσιν) at being called by means of the pronoun [i.e., σύ], since naturally they want to hear their own name when called."[16] Such words from a prominent ancient grammarian suggest that forms of address could influence tenor relations, even to the point that a form of address might jeopardize previously amicable relations between participants.

Forms of address are also found throughout ancient Greek writing, and the insights of many other scholars indicate that these forms might realize the kinds of relations SFL subsumes under tenor—although, again, most do not work within the bounds of SFL and its labels. For instance, Jeremy Hultin's programmatic study of obscene speech in the ancient world indicates that forms of address were common forms of abusive speech.[17] Likewise, classicist and linguist Eleanor Dickey has argued the point that forms of address were used to indicate all manner of social relations in the Roman period (first-century BCE–third-century CE).[18] Through an extensive investigation into Latin and Koine addresses in sub-literary letters from this period, Dickey argues that the Koine forms of address found in the Egyptian documentary papyri were influenced by Latin forms of address, which "allowed far more scope for flattery, expressions of friendly affection, and recognition of subtle differences in status."[19] Dickey argues well that many Greek forms of address were appropriated to conform with those found in Latin because Greek speakers wanted to capture the nuanced social relations the Latin forms of address could capture.[20] In one notable example Dickey convincingly reasons that the term δεσπότα/δέσποινα was an "inappropriate" translation of the Latin term *domine/domina* because *domine/domina* bore connotations of politeness, while δεσπότα/δέσποινα bore connotations of servitude.[21] Dickey also argues that the Greek term κύριε/κυρία came to be used for its general lack of reference to servitude to another.[22] Her

---

16. Apollonius Dyscolus, *On Syntax*, 218.9.

17. Hultin, *Ethics of Obscene Speech*, 20–27.

18. See Dickey, "Greek Address System of the Roman Period," 494–527; Dickey, "Ancient Greek Address System," 1–13.

19. Dickey, "Greek Address System of the Roman Period," 526.

20. Ibid., 511–19.

21. Ibid., 511.

22. Ibid. Dickey was careful to note that κύριε/κυρία is used to convey politeness

analysis also articulates that the so-called "kinship terms," such as ἀδελφέ, ἀδελφή, πάτερ, μῆτερ, υἱέ, θύγατερ, and τέκνον, were utilized in texts in which a favorable disposition—not necessarily a familial relation—between participants was existent or desired (e.g., family members, friends, business colleagues, etc.).[23] In sum, Dickey's studies support the claim that Koine forms of address spoke to what SFL proponents understand as tenor relations.

Tenor Relations and Greek Forms of Address

In order to describe tenor relations, SFL proponents have developed a two-axis model of tenor relations in which both axes represent the fundamental features of tenor relations, namely, power and solidarity.[24] The power axis speaks to the characteristics of (in)equality between participants in a communicative event. Participants may be of equal or unequal status and, if unequal, one participant may exert the power differential over the other(s).[25] Cate Poynton has observed that in English the (in)equality in power between participants may be measured with reference to the principle of the reciprocity of linguistic choice (e.g., whether one participant is expected or permitted to dominate the conversation, whether one participant has more right to address the topic at hand based

in the manner of *domine/domina* as it pertains to human relations. Though mentioning κύριε/κυρία is applied to the Divine, Dickey does not make any remark that might speak to the social relations conveyed by κύριε/κυρία in human-divine relations (ibid., 511, 523).

23. Ibid., 512–16.

24. In the description that follows, I have utilized a host of sources that are regularly cited for this end. Whether the terms "power" and "solidarity" are used in a given discussion of tenor relations will depend largely on the linguist one is reading. The present terms are found in Martin and White, *Language of Evaluation*, 29. However, J. R. Martin and David Rose use "status" and "solidarity" (*Genre Relations*, 11–12); Cate Poynton uses "power" and "distance" ("Address," 90–93), and Ruqaiya Hasan, in Halliday and Hasan, uses "power" and "social distance" (*Language, Context, and Text*, 57).

25. The terminology associated with this power axis does not need to be read pejoratively. Instead, power may also be recognized as a social good, especially when wielded by a person who has legitimately come into a power position by social consent or by social recognition as someone who is able to achieve (see Fairclough, *Language and Power*, 26–27). Such recognition can be based on a host of factors, such as force, authority, status, and expertise (Poynton, *Language and Gender*, 76–77). My thanks go to James D. Dvorak for his help in clarifying these issues (for more, see Dvorak, "Prodding with Prosody," 88–89).

on expertise, etc.).[26] Because SFL associates (in)equality and reciprocity with power, the power axis is typically depicted as a vertical cline in attempts to visually represent the "vertical" dimensions of human relationships (e.g., supervisor-worker, parent-child, professor-student, etc.). Conversely, solidarity refers to the characteristics of the level of (un)familiarity between participants, and can include the emotional bond that characterizes the language users' relationship.[27] Solidarity is depicted, then, as the horizontal cline of the tenor relation axis model. Poynton has also hypothesized that the horizontal cline of English-speaking cultures is measured by the principle of proliferation, the amount of linguistic work needed to accomplish the communicative task based on the social relations between communicative partners.[28] Based on these characteristics and principles, presentations of tenor within SFL attempt to represent the wide array of complex relations between human beings by arguing that they are co-occurring in all communicative events. When presented visually, power and solidary form an X-Y axis graph on which plotted points represent the particularities of the tenor relations grammaticalized by language use in modern English-speaking societies.

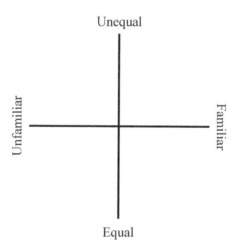

Figure 1: Tenor Relations in Modern English-Speaking Society

26. Poynton, "Address," 74–78.

27. Poynton, "Names as Vocatives," 27–30.

28. Ibid., 1–34, esp. 27–30. My favorite example of proliferation comes from J. R. Martin and P. R. R. White, who state the following: "For outsiders, Stevie Ray Vaughan might be introduced as *Texas Bluesman Stevie Ray Vaughan* . . . whereas for hardcore fans [SRV] will do" (*Language of Evaluation*, 31).

Now, while this two-axis conception of tenor relations is a help-ful starting point for this study, I do not think that it should be adopted wholesale as an accurate description of the tenor relations that can be communicated by forms of address in Koine Greek. This is because there are vast differences between modern English-speaking cultures and that of the first-century Mediterranean world. Any theoretical explanation of Koine Greek forms of address should consider the social values of the first-century Mediterranean world, rather than the values of modern Western culture. For instance, the characteristics and principles of power in my own culture may not fit well within a description of the first-centu-ry Mediterranean in which one's honor/shame status relied very heavily on the social evaluation of others. Similarly, while levels of acquaintance most certainly existed in the first-century Mediterranean human rela-tions it appears that such aspects of human relations were understood by the ancients in terms of honor and shame.[29] Thus, power and solidarity, as discussed above, do not appear to delineate the particular and complex nature of tenor relations in the New Testament world. So, how should we come to understand this complexity within a SFL framework? We need to furnish the horizontal and vertical clines of tenor relations with the pivotal social dynamics of first-century Mediterranean society. When utilizing the work of Eleanor Dickey it becomes apparent that forms of address spoke to three types of relations: (1) those between members of differing social levels; (2) those between family members (whether con-jugal, extended, or fictive families) and group members; and (3) those between strangers.[30] Of significant note is that these relations were con-cerned with some of the pivotal values of social interaction in the first-century Mediterranean world, which have long been determined to be honor/shame and group orientation by those involved in social-scientific criticism of the first-century Mediterranean world. Examining these rela-tions through the lens of social-scientific criticism, these pivotal social values can provide a framework by which they might be better compre-hended. It will also provide the generalizations necessary to develop a SFL model regarding tenor relations in the first-century Mediterranean world, as well as how forms of address relate to tenor relations.

It is important to understand how the relations evinced in Greek forms of address were based on evaluations of honor and shame, which,

29. Malina, *New Testament World*, 140–41.

30. Dickey, "Ancient Greek Address System," 5–6.

as a result, requires a description of honor and shame in the first-century Mediterranean world. According to Bruce Malina, honor in the New Testament era involved the group- or society-validated claim to worth or power; shame, on the other hand, could be viewed both positively and negatively. Positively, shame can refer to one's sense of shame, a sensitivity to one's reputation and others' opinions; to *have* shame is good.[31] Negatively, one can *be* shamed if one aspires to a status that is rejected by public opinion for some reason; this is synonymous with being dishonored.[32] One's honor was recognized, in part, by the evaluation of a host of factors such as a person's family, authority, gender, and humility.[33] Thus, as David deSilva helpfully points out, honor was recognized in an individual "on account of accidents of birth or grants by people of higher status," making one's lineage a pivotal factor determining one's status.[34] More than this, however, honor could also be achieved or lost based on a group's or society's assessment of an individual's embodiment of group values.[35] Regarding the social relations between persons of different social levels, people operated within a culturally sanctioned balance between honor and shame, in which the person of higher worth or power was the person of honor, and the person of lesser worth or power was viewed as shameful. This is because the level of one's honor was defined in terms of another's.[36] In relations within families and groups, honor statuses were recognized and accepted by all members, unless the gender, authority, or behavior of one of the members indicated that more honor or shame was to be recognized in that member.[37] And finally, it appears that strangers were viewed as *non*-honorable and *non*-shameful precisely

31. Malina, *New Testament World*, 48–49.

32. Ibid., 50.

33. Ibid., 48–51.

34. deSilva, *Honor, Patronage, Kinship & Purity*, 28. Another such "accident" or unchangeable facet of a person's existence that affected their honor/shame status was their gender. For example, daughters/females embodied the shame of the family or group, while sons/males embodied the honor (see, Elliott, *Conflict, Community, and Honor*, 58). This does not mean, however, that honor was "better" than shame, as shame could be viewed positively in the sense that it was the recognition of one's place and status, and the actions taken to ensure this status was not harmed. My thanks to James D. Dvorak for his input on this matter.

35. deSilva, *Honor, Patronage, Kinship & Purity*, 28–29.

36. Malina, *New Testament World*, 89–90.

37. Ibid., 36–37.

because they were unknown; in fact, it was not until the stranger had been tested as to whether they would adhere to group values that the stranger was ascribed honor, but until then the stranger was a "guest" whom a host and the host's family or group were to restrain from shaming.[38] In sum, a person's honor status was a considerable component of how that person related to others.

It must be understood, likewise, that the relations between strangers, family members, and members of differing social statuses also involved group orientation. The honor/shame value was contextually based, specific to "what in a given social *group* or *society* count[ed] as honorable behavior."[39] For honor to be acquired by a person, it had to have been sanctioned by the group(s) to which a person was oriented (e.g., family, religious cult, guild, etc.). In this manner, honor was bestowed when group members evaluated an individual's adherence to the complex values expected of him or her by the group. For instance, when subordinates accepted and respected the power that their superiors had over their lives, honor was socially recognized as belonging to the superiors.[40] Further, as stated above, honor was shared among familial groups, but if group members deviated in some way from the group's values, they could still be shamed. And lastly, it appears that strangers were strangers in part because it was not known to what group or family they belonged.[41] Thus, a person's orientation to a group and his or her adherence to its values factored largely into that person's relations to others.

As can be seen, social relations evinced by forms of address can be helpfully understood within the theoretical framework of social-scientific criticism, and, I argue, this understanding fits well within the theoretical framework of SFL as it pertains to depictions of tenor relations. In particular, the social values associated with these relations speak volumes to the relevant characteristics of tenor relations in the first-century Mediterranean world. As the discussion above indicates, a person's honor/shame status and orientation to a group were considered when a person engaged in social interaction with others. For this reason, I find it helpful to see honor/shame and group orientation to be the primary aspects of tenor relations in the New Testament era, which does not replace, but

38. Malina, "Hospitality," 115–20.

39. Plevnik, "Honor/Shame," 108 (emphasis mine).

40. Pilch, "Power," 158.

41. Malina, "Hospitality," 115–20.

simply nuances, the relations of power and solidarity typical in this kind of discussion.

There are some additional principles by which tenor relations were measured, and these need some discussion. The first principle is one I will refer to as *recognition*. Joshua Jipp convincingly demonstrates the operation of this principle when he details the brief suspension of judgment people take when they meet strangers.[42] If nothing was known about another person—that is, if they were strangers whose group orientations and concomitant honor statuses were unknown—then the ancients suspended judgment on that person, albeit for a very short period, until more was known of that person.[43] So, it appeared that the ancients had to consider their level of recognition of an individual in order to make a determination about their honor status and group orientation. Recognition likely boiled down to whether one had knowledge of another's honor status within his or her group. This principle is particularly evident in the forms of address utilized by Greek language users of the time. If the language user was incapable of conveying their recognition of the addressee, the language user could use lexis that was ambiguous in terms of honor/shame and group orientation (e.g., ἄλλος, ἀλλότριος, ξένος, παρεπίδημος, ἄνθρωπε)—that is, lexis that depicts the addressee as a stranger. What is described here is the ancient practice of deferring judgment to strangers until more was known about them.

A second principle is the principle of *inclusion/exclusion* in relation to group orientation. Malina summarizes well the importance given to group orientation when he writes the following:

> For the collectivistic personality [of the first-century person], interpersonal behavior remains purely impersonal, without some sort of perception that he or she and another person are somehow attached to each other, somehow related to each other. In other words, a basic prerequisite for a truly interpersonal exchange is that I, as a collectivistic personality, and another human being mutually believe that we have some common personal bonds, from shared blood to mutual acquaintances to common ethnic heritage. We have to come to see that somehow we are "brothers and sisters" or "kinsmen." We thus perceive each other as members of the same group, an in-group. Should

42. See Jipp, *Divine Visitations*, 59–130, esp. 62–72.

43. For a similar definition of "stranger," see Elliott, *Home for the Homeless*, 24–25.

there be nothing in common between us except our common humanity . . . then our interactions should remain impersonal.[44]

This signals that the horizontal nature of first-century Mediterranean tenor relations can be understood with reference to principles of inclusion and exclusion. A person was either included in a family (again, whether conjugal, extended, or fictive) or a group, excluded from membership, or viewed as a stranger, and all of these possibilities factored into the type of communication that could take place between language users, including the roles each could assume in their linguistic exchange. Therefore, I will refer to the horizontal cline of tenor relations as the group orientation cline, because this term captures the inclusion/exclusion principle that shaped the horizontal tenor relations in the New Testament world.

A third principle is concerned with the vertical cline of tenor relations in the first-century Mediterranean world. It is not difficult to see a "vertical" characteristic of tenor as operative within the limited good society in view here. Life was a zero-sum game; as someone's honor increased, someone else's decreased.[45] But, the nature of the value placed on honor in the New Testament world seems to indicate that the act of evaluating others may be key factor in describing the vertical nature of first-century Mediterranean tenor relations. As indicated in the section above, honor was ascribed to, or acquired by, a person based on evaluations of that person's family, authority, gender, and humility, as well as the group's evaluation of that person's adherence to group-ordained values. Thus, as with the group orientation cline, I want to propose that the vertical cline (henceforth the honor/shame cline) can be helpfully seen to operate in terms of the principle of *evaluation*.

Interpersonal Semantics of Greek Forms of Address

Having articulated what I believe to be the primary social features by which the tenor relations of the first-century Mediterranean operated, I will now describe how Greek forms of address grammaticalized interpersonal semantics. For this purpose, I have detailed what I believe to be the system of choices that was available to Greek language users in the first-century Mediterranean world (see Figure 2). As may be noticed, this

44. Malina, *New Testament World*, 63.
45. Ibid., 89–90.

semantic system correlates to the honor/shame and group orientation clines outlined above, only these systems broadly articulate how those relations were instantiated in Greek forms of address. In outlining these semantic possibilities, I have followed the conventions of SFL system networks.

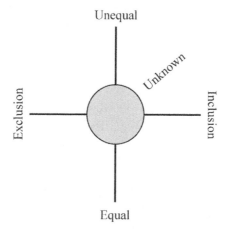

Figure 2: The Greek Interpersonal System of Address Making

Summary

With this discussion I have begun to lay out the complex interpersonal semantics of Greek forms of address by theorizing the first few interpersonal semantic choices with which those in the first century considered when attempting to recognize tenor relations. While the system network could undoubtedly be detailed with more delicacy in terms of semantic choice, I have been careful to emphasize that my goal is to present a basic picture of the semantic choices available to Greek language users when addressing others. The choices were theorized based on a brief consultation of contemporary grammarians, linguists, and social-scientific critics. Of great importance here was the work of Eleanor Dickey, as well as some social-scientific critics of the New Testament. In what follows, I will utilize this semantic system to describe the tenor relations prescribed in the Epistle of James. More than this, however, I will document how James leveraged tenor relations to bring about his rhetorical goal.

FORMS OF ADDRESS AND TENOR RELATIONS IN JAMES

At the outset of this study, I stated that the forms of address in James are ubiquitous and diverse. The second of these qualities I count as surprising, given that these forms of address appear to have been applied to the same people. I will soon argue what tenor relations the writer of James was likely creating through these forms of address. But, this first requires explaining how James situated himself in relation to the addressees, and so I will begin by investigating the greeting of James's letter.[46]

Establishing Tenor Relations in James

James began his letter with the following self-designation: Ἰάκωβος θεοῦ καὶ κυρίου Ἰησοῦ Χριστοῦ δοῦλος.[47] The first word of the greeting identified the writer as an unspecified James. To be sure, there is considerable debate over the authorship of this letter, but scholars have recently come to a consensus that the James mentioned here was *intended* to refer to James, the brother of Jesus, also known as James the Just and James of Jerusalem.[48] I find the arguments that have led to this opinion convincing, and so I adopt this position here. The implication is that James, the brother of Jesus, as the presumed author of this letter, was a man of a significant status in the early Church, and the addressees of this letter were expected to acknowledge James as such.[49]

But the tenor relations between James and the addressees relied on more than simple name recognition. Indeed, James's ensuing self-presentation, when viewed in tandem with the initial presentation of the addressees, demonstrates that James was claiming elevated honor in relation to the addressees. James's assertion that he was a "slave of God and of the Lord Jesus Christ" was likely a claim to special honor in the

---

46. I acknowledge that there is, and has been, serious debate initiated by Martin Dibelius concerning whether James is a true letter (see Dibelius, *James*, 1–2). I will note here, however, Richard Bauckham's observations that "the only really essential formal feature of a letter was the letter opening, consisting of at least the parties formula, normally also a greeting" (Bauckham, "Pseudo-Apostolic Letters," 471; see also White, "Greek Documentary Letter Tradition," 91).

47. All Greek from James is from the NA28.

48. For an overview, see Batten's discussion on authorship of James (*What Are They Saying*, 28–34).

49. For the role of this James in the early church, see the thorough presentation in Bauckham, *Jude and the Relatives of Jesus*, 45–133.

vein of Moses and the prophets.[50] More significantly, however, James as a slave cannot be fully appreciated without reference to his depiction of the addressees as a diaspora community (ταῖς δώδεκα φυλαῖς ταῖς ἐν τῇ διασπορᾷ). There are several suggestions throughout scholarship discussing the precise meaning of the lexeme διασπορά here, but I am most persuaded by the suggestion of Timothy Cargal. According to Cargal's structural semiotic reading of James, James's use of diaspora language was used to intimate that the addressees had "wandered away from the truth" (Jas 5:19).[51] Further, in some Jewish literature, a slave of God was depicted as an agent who returned from a diaspora community (Neh 1:5–11; Isa 49:1–6). Though the use of διασπορά here does not appear to be a form of address, I suspect that the use of this word grammaticalizes something very near to the semantics of [+recognition], [+power], and [+inclusion], as articulated above. Thus, the addressees are a group characterized by shame for having "wandered" from the group values shared by the people of God. This depiction is, of course, relative to James's honor for being one capable of restoring the diaspora, a "slave of God." James here seems to have instantiated an unequal honor/shame tenor relation between himself and the addressees, who are members of his group that have not adhered to group values.

Maintaining Tenor Relations in James

Turning now to the forms of address in the remainder of James's epistle, it will be interesting to see whether or not James attempted to maintain the tenor relations he established in the epistle's greeting. In investigating this, I will discuss the forms of address as they appear in the text and their contribution to the immediate co-text and then to the discourse to track the linear progression of tenor relations in the unfolding text.[52]

50. Contra Edgar, *Has God Not Chosen the Poor*, 45–50, esp. 46–47.

51. Cargal, *Restoring the Diaspora*, 45–49, esp. 49. For a critique of Cargal's proposal, see Edgar, *Has God Not Chosen the Poor*, 97.

52. Edgar has a similar tactic in *Has God Not Chosen the Poor*. There, however, he presented a topical discussion of the social relations conveyed by the following forms of address: (1) "Brothers"; and (2) "Adulteresses, Sinners, and Double-minded" (*Has God Not Chosen the Poor*, 101–5). I am appreciative of Edgar's presentation, but I find that his topical presentation does not convey the potential dynamism in tenor relations in James that comes from following them in the unfolding discourse.

James 1:2–18

Within this first section, we encounter two forms of address: ἀδελφοί μου and ἀδελφοί μου ἀγαπητοί. It is worth noting that forms of address containing ἀδελφοί are among James's favorites.[53] The term ἀδελφοί is a familial term; it "marks out the addressees as members of a fictive kin group of which the author is also a member," expressing "a co-belonging to the People of God."[54] The literature on familial language as boundary-markers of fictive kin groups is vast, and many commentators do well to note such writings.[55] It is clear, then, that James here grammaticalizes [+recognition] and [+inclusion] in an attempt to articulate in part what he wanted the tenor relations between himself and his addressees to be—that they were members of the same group (group orientation cline).[56] However, there is often an argument that this realization of group orientation by ἀδελφοί speaks to an "equality of relationship" on the honor/shame cline between an author and the addressees.[57] I believe this assumes too much too quickly for the use of ἀδελφοί in James, primarily because it would lead to the conclusion that James almost immediately abandoned the tenor relations he attempted to establish in 1:1.[58] More convincing are the implications of research into the relationship between brothers and sisters in the ancient Mediterranean basin, whether in conjugal or fictive kin groups, in which it is difficult to understand "siblingship" as a relationship of equality on the honor/shame cline.[59] Paul's assertion of his

53. Four times as ἀδελφοί (4:11; 5:7, 9, 10); 7 times as ἀδελφοί μου (1:2; 2:1, 14; 3:1, 10, 12; 5:12, 19); three times as ἀδελφοί μου ἀγαπητοί (1:16, 19; 2:5).

54. Edgar, *Has God Not Chosen the Poor*, 101.

55. Ibid., 102 n. 23. A great study to this effect is Harland, "Familial Dimensions of Group Identity," 491–513.

56. See Aasgaard, *My Beloved Brothers and Sisters*, 91–92; Burke, *Family Matters*, 122; and Hellerman, *Ancient Church*, 35–51.

57. Edgar, *Has God Not Chosen the Poor*, 101–2.

58. Intriguingly, Edgar himself acknowledges this difficulty when he writes that the author of the epistle "clearly expects the acknowledgement of his authority, even among equals" (ibid., 102). See David Horrell's similar conclusion to Edgar's regarding Paul's use of ἀδελφοί ("From ἀδελφοί to οἶκος θεοῦ," 299–303).

59. See Aasgaard, "Brothers and Sisters in Faith," 291; Aasgaard, *My Beloved Brothers and Sisters*, 91–92, 308–10. Indeed, Paul (1 Cor 8:1–13) and at least one of his philosophical contemporaries, Plutarch, acknowledged that there were varying levels of honor/shame status among siblings in their first-century contexts, which appeared to be dependent upon adherence to group-advocated values (*Frat. Amor.* 13–15). On various interpretations of the differing honor/shame statuses of the "knowledgeable"

own apostolic authority in Romans, 2 Corinthians, and Galatians, where many of Paul's "ἀδελφοί" addresses are found can be proffered as evidence of the inequality of siblingship. Perhaps even James's own assent to the authority of teachers in Jas 3:1 shows that fictive brothers and sisters were not always equal on the honor/shame cline of tenor relations.[60]

The question remains of what seems to be taking place with ἀδελφοί forms of address in terms of the semantics they could grammaticalize in the evaluation and inequality systems. In reviewing the literature on sibling relationships noted above, one detail emerges: the tenor relations realized by ἀδελφοί forms of address appear to have been continuations of the tenor relations on the honor/shame cline as dictated by co-text or context. That is, when a Greek language user addressed another as a sibling, such an address grammaticalized the semantics associated with a culturally prescribed tenor relationship. Thus, regarding ἀδελφοί μου in 1:2, the semantics of [+power] seem to be realized with reference to the previously established tenor relations in 1:1.[61] If this is correct, then James used ἀδελφοί to maintain the tenor relations he previously established—he and his addressees are members of the same group (group orientation cline), but James is a more honorable member within it (honor/shame cline).

Regarding the longer forms of address with ἀδελφοί (ἀδελφοί μου and ἀδελφοί μου ἀγαπητοί), I think that many biblical scholars are very close to the mark in their assessments that the addition of the pronoun μου, and the further addition of the adjective ἀγαπητοί signify "signs of affection," or something very much like that.[62] These assessments point to the understanding that μου and αγαπητοί realize what appraisal theorists

---

and "weak" brothers and sisters in 1 Cor 8:1–13, see Neyrey, *Paul*, 125; Meeks, *First Urban Christians*, 69–70.

60. Contra Edgar, who cites this text as proof of his "authority, even among equals" interpretation (*Has God Not Chosen the Poor*, 102 n. 19).

61. Please note that this conception of semantic realization views semantics as the cumulative outworking of an interface between co-textual, contextual, and lexico-grammatical choices—that is, semantics are possibilities of meaning constrained by co-text, context, and lexico-grammar simultaneously. See Dvorak ("Evidence," 4–6) for a concise presentation of such a view on semantics. My thanks to Zachary Dawson for urging clarity on this point in a previous version of this paper.

62. Martin, *James*, 14. See also Varner, *Book of James*, 69–70; Davids, *Epistle*, 111. Ropes takes the more general stance that these addresses were "inserted for emphasis" (*Epistle of James*, 193).

call semantic graduation, or semantic up-scaling or down-scaling.[63] Specifically, with the use of μου, James seems to have graduated the semantics of [+inclusion] realized by ἀδελφοί, bringing this relational term into sharper focus, which contributes to creating solidarity with his addressees. Furthermore, when ἀγαπητοί is added this harkens to the first-century Mediterranean understanding that to be "beloved" (ἀγαπητός) meant that one was viewed as attached to another or to a group.[64] With ἀδελφοί μου ἀγαπητοί, then, James scales the semantics of [+inclusion] in an attempt to establish even greater solidarity with his addressees in terms of the group-orientation cline.

The first form of address is used in James's explanation of what he thinks is the addressees' beliefs about the source of their testing/temptation:[65] "You consider it pure joy,[66] my brothers and sisters [ἀδελφοί μου], when you face temptations of many kinds, thinking that the testing of your faith produces endurance, and [thinking that[67]] endurance must have its full effect so that you may be complete and whole, lacking in nothing (1:2–4)." This system of belief appears to be derived from the "piety of the poor" worldview found in Jewish wisdom traditions. In this belief system it is thought that God sends divine reprimand upon a person as a means of producing greater faith, or as a means of giving to that person their desired gift.[68] The use of ἀδελφοί μου here helps to control the tenor because in invoking a term that orients James as part of the group he addresses, he can speak from a social position that allows him to describe the beliefs of the addressees without appearing overly presumptuous. But why does James bring up his addressees' belief system? Surely numerous explanations can be offered, but I am convinced

---

63. See Martin and White, *Language of Evaluation*, 135–53. For examples of graduation within Greek, see Dvorak, "Interpersonal Metafunction," 94–104.

64. See Malina, "Love," 127–30.

65. For a detailed treatment on reading Jas 1:2–4 as an enumeration of the addressees' system of belief, see Cargal, *Restoring the Diaspora*, 57–72.

66. This translation understands the verb ἡγήσασθε as expressing indicative mood, rather than imperative. I recognize that I take a minority view here, but my analysis serves as my defense for holding this view. See also Cargal, *Restoring the Diaspora*, 61–63.

67. This translation renders the δέ in 1:4 as *extending* the content of the addressees' presumed thoughts. See Hunt, "Meaning in Bulk," 394–405.

68. See Cargal, *Restoring the Diaspora*, 65, who cites Gerhard Von Rad, *Wisdom in Israel*, 195–206.

that James believed that this belief system was misguided. There are three reasons for my position on this matter. First, James immediately counters this system with a different means to attaining the desired gift: rather than believing that experiencing temptation will land them some divine gift, the addressees should instead simply ask God for "pure joy" (1:5). Second, James articulates the conception of God and his gifts, which opposes the divine reprimands evinced in the "piety of the poor" worldview. James even states that God "gives to all generously, without reprimand," (1:5) which directly contrasts with the "piety of the poor" worldview. These first two points are given greater credence in light of 1:16–17, in which James specifies that God is the source of all gifts, and to believe otherwise is to be deceived. Third, James openly critiques the thought that trials/temptations come from God; "God is unable to be tempted with regard to evil, and he tempts no one" (1:13). Temptations come from within the individual (1:14). Thus, the "piety of the poor" worldview, according to James's presentation, is built on faulty theology.

Still, James's opposition to the "piety of the poor" worldview appears to come from more than its perceived theological inaccuracy. The divisive attitudes and practices this belief system has produced among the addressees' community seem to be equally unfavorable in James's eyes. Take as evidence of this divisive activity James's instruction for the one seeking wisdom to ask God "without distinguishing herself or himself [as more honorable]" (μηδὲν διακρινόμενος) in 1:6.[69] To be sure, this understanding of μηδὲν διακρινόμενος will have its detractors, but I believe it is accurate for two reasons. First, it conveys the potential reflexive semantics realized by the middle voice, which illuminates the requestor's role in giving him- or herself a distinguished place on the honor/shame cline. Second, and most importantly, it squares well with the use of διακρίνω in 2:4 where distinctions are clearly being made on the honor/shame cline. Elsewhere in the letter (2:1–4), James suggests that some among the addressees were motivated by their place on the honor/shame cline. What is most significant, however, is the perceived link between divine gifts and social status. James's instruction in 1:6 suggests that some within the community were entranced by their place on the honor/shame cline, and apparently so much so that they would align themselves with whatever

---

69. I agree with Peter Spitaler that there is no reason to hold to the tradition that διακρίνω takes on a special meaning in the middle voice, as it appears here, to mean something like "doubt." See Spitaler, "Doubt or Dispute," 201–22; Spitaler, "Διακρίνεσθαι," 1–39.

gave them a more prominent position. It is for this reason that James called such individuals "double-souled" (δίψυχος).[70] This pre-occupation with attaining prominence appears to have come at the expense of the unity of the group. The sad irony of the actions of these members is that, according to James, status achieved through any means is inconsequential, because status is ever-changing by nature (1:9–11).[71]

It is significant that, in the reading of James I am proposing, the second form of address (ἀδελφοί μου ἀγαπητοί [1:16]) appears with the first direct appeal to all of James's addressees, not just a subset of status-motivated members. To reiterate: Jas 1:16–18 seems to be an attempt to re-orient the theology of the addressed community. Gifts come straight from the "Father of lights," states James, not from the endurance of trials/temptations. Significantly, this is one of the first positive, constructive teachings from James's pen. The form of address again marks a re-emphasis of James's assumed honorable status (honor/shame cline) within the group (group orientation cline). All of this means that James has utilized this form of address at the precise moment that he begins to re-orient the theology of the addressees so that the group's integrity may be maintained. If the tenor relations prescribed by this form of address are upheld by the addressees, James's corrective will hit its mark. Indeed, if the presentation of 1:2–18 proposed above is correct, then James is relying mainly on forms of address to manage the tenor relations with his addressees in the first section of his letter.

JAMES 1:19–27

The function of the single form of address in this section of the letter is intriguing. Note the formal ambiguity of the verb ἴστε, which precedes the form of address (ἀδελφοί μου ἀγαπητοί) in 1:19; this form can be either imperative or indicative. Although most scholars favor the imperative mood-form,[72] I favor the indicative, reading 1:19–20 as a maxim already known to the addressees: "You know, my beloved brothers and sisters, [that] every person must be quick to listen . . . [and] slow to wrath, for

70. On a similar view of δίψυχος, see Porter, "Dipsuchos," 473–84. I am not convinced, however, by Porter's assessment that the two uses of the term in James (1:8 and 4:8) have such disparate meanings as he proposes.

71. See Reicke, James, 15; Cargal, Restoring the Diaspora, 74–75. See also, Alicia Batten, "Degraded Poor," 65–78.

72. See Varner, Book of James, 74.

wrath does not produce the justice of God."[73] Coming off the heels of a substantial theological corrective (1:2–18), this maxim reminds the addressees of their principle to remain attentive without biting back in anger.[74] If this presentation is correct, James's use of ἀδελφοί μου ἀγαπητοί in 1:19 makes a great deal of sense because it realizes the semantics of [+inclusion] and the semantics of [+power], maintaining James's honorable status within the group. James thus asserts his role as one capable of reminding the addressees of their knowledge and as one capable of quelling potential rebuttals. The remaining verses (1:21–27) similarly take advantage of James's established tenor role, because James is seen advocating the abandonment of previous modes of behavior (ἀποθεμένοι) and commanding the reception and enactment of the "implanted word, which is able to save [their] souls."

JAMES 2:1—3:12

James continues to adjust tenor relations throughout Jas 2:1—3:12, vacillating between ἀδελφοί μου and ἀδελφοί μου ἀγαπητοί another six times in order to realize the graduated semantics of [+inclusion] as well as the semantics of [+power]. In each case, these addresses add a kind of rhetorical punch to the argument, which manages the tenor relations at risk because James begins to aim weighty criticisms at the addressees regarding their inconsistencies.[75] Such inconsistencies come in several forms and can be organized into three sections: (1) being inconsistent with the Royal Law (2:1–13); (2) being inconsistent with faith and works (2:14–26); and (3) being inconsistent with controlled speech (3:1–12).[76] Significantly, the forms of address peppered throughout 2:1—3:12 appear at times when it would be good for the addressees to be reminded of their relationship with James. Forms of address precede commands in 2:1; 3:1, 10, for which James's higher place on the honor/shame cline needs to be accepted, and questions in 2:5, 14; 3:14, where James presumes to have knowledge of the addressees' beliefs, implying James's place on the group orientation cline. In light of this, James's forms of address appear to be small, intentional reminders of his asserted role within the group

---

73. This reading allows the διό in 1:21 to exercise its greatest utility, which is to point the addressees to the practical outworking of this known maxim.

74. See Edgar, *Has God Not Chosen the Poor*, 162–64.

75. See Cargal, *Restoring the Diaspora*, 93–136.

76. See ibid., 139–42

to which he is writing. If his role is accepted by the addressees, such frequent reminders could have increased the likelihood that his rhetorical aim would have been met.

Nevertheless, James may have placed his tenor role in jeopardy with his "unquestionably harsh" address ὦ ἄνθρωπε κενέ, because this address has no clear external referent.[77] This individual is routinely referred to as an "imaginary interlocutor," the identity of whom is a matter of considerable debate. It is curious to me that the addressees are rarely identified as an option, despite there being many reasons to do so.[78] First, following Davids, it is clear that the formula ἀλλ᾽ ἐρεῖ τις in 2:18, where the interlocutor referenced in 2:20 is introduced, makes this interlocutor an objector or opponent.[79] Further, it can be argued that τις identifies this person with an oppositional person among the addressees, for James has previously used τις to invite the addressees to engage in self-reflection (1:5, 23, 26; 2:14, 16). If this is the case, the inclusion of κένος in this address seems to invoke the semantics of [+power], which would elevate James's place on the honor/shame cline while simultaneously lowering that of the addressees, because James claims this person has a "lack of capacity for understanding."[80] Of greater insult may be the use of ἄνθρωπος in this address, which, though innocuous in some respects,[81] denotes the language user's lack of knowledge regarding the honor/shame status or group orientation of the addressed. Thus, James appears to realize the semantics of [-recognition], effectively disassociating himself from this oppositional member of the addressees. James could be claiming that he can have no part with one who argues for the divorce of faith and works. The addressees may take offense at this, and so James may have put his rhetorical aim in jeopardy. However, James is quick to remind the addressees of their place within his group more than once in 3:1–10.

JAMES 3:13—5:6

The next section of James moves into synthesis of, and presents an alternative to, the *modus operandi* of the addressees, which James criticizes in

77. Ibid., 128.

78. A way through the maze is detailed in ibid., 123–26.

79. Davids, *Epistle of James*, 124.

80. This is the title of the sub-domain under which Louw and Nida classify the term "κένος" (*Greek-English Lexicon*, 2:388).

81. Dickey, "Greek Address System of the Roman Period," 526.

2:1—3:12. My position is that 3:13—4:6 comprises a transitional paragraph whereby James synthesizes the grounds upon which a rebuke can be made,[82] and James 4:7—5:6 can be viewed as a kind of prophetic call to repentance.[83] Viewing 3:13—5:6 as a single, unified section is admittedly somewhat unorthodox, though it is perfectly within the tradition of arguing about the boundaries of distinct sections in James.[84] However, the following presentation indicates that this schema works well within the rhetorical aim of the letter.

The transitional paragraph (Jas 3:13—4:6), at first glance, appears to address disparate topics (wisdom, envy, self-promotion, group conflict, infidelity, hatred) making it difficult to see how this paragraph can be called a synthesis. But, by appealing to the system of patronage and reciprocity within the cultural context of the first-century Mediterranean, the link between these topics in the context of the addressees' community becomes clearer. Patronage involved social relations whereby individuals received some kind of mutual benefit based on the practice of reciprocation of gifts or goods-and-services,[85] and it existed in almost every kind of relationship, most of which involved participants of unequal statuses (patron-client relations such as husband-wife, divine-human, etc.).[86] Already in James the addressees have been informed that God is a giver of gifts (1:17), establishing God as patron to whom the addressees are clients. What is more, wisdom—or more likely, its associated status—appears to have been the gift most sought by the addressees (1:5–8; 3:1). According to James, the addressees have indeed received a gift from a patron, but their gift is not "from above" (3:14–15). The wisdom they possess is

---

82. Johnson, "James 3:13—4:10," 332. See also the similar conclusion of Edgar (*Has God Not Chosen the Poor*, 181–83). Indeed, it may be appropriate to attach this paragraph to 2:1—3:13 as a summation of James's discourse to this point. However, my understanding that James utilizes the development here in his rebuke (4:7—5:6) leads me to include it in this section.

83. See Johnson, "James 3:13—4:10," 333; Laws, "Does Scripture Speak in Vain," 210–15. Edgar (*Has God Not Chosen the Poor*, 187–88) posits that a new section begins in 4:11 with the re-use of ἀδελφοί; however, despite his arguments to the contrary, the condemning tone is also prevalent in 4:11—5:6.

84. See Johnson, "James 3:13—4:10," 327–32.

85. Malina, "Patronage," 151–55.

86. Friendship often had the pretense of equality between participants (Johnson, "Friendship," 214), though I am not convinced that such equal relations often existed in reality (see Meeks, *Origins*, 40).

seen in their actions of bitter jealousy and "self-promotion"[87] (e.g., those things for which James previously criticized the addressees in 2:1—3:12), whereas the wisdom from God would be peaceable, unhypocritical, and impartial (3:16-17). Indeed, it is the self-promotion of the addressees, their desire to obtain the status concomitant with wisdom, that causes the divisions within their community (3:18—4:3).[88] In sum, the community appears to have divided because the addressees have sought the patronage of the world, rather than that of God (4:4). Now, because they have "desired enviously" against the witness of Scripture,[89] the addressees are included among the number God opposes (4:5-6). In brief, the conduct of the addressees and its divisive effect on the community betray their true allegiance to a patron other than God.

It is in this context that James is able to accuse the addressees of infidelity by way of the only form of address in the transitional paragraph— μοιχαλίδες (4:4). The image evoked by "adulteresses," is one of wives who have been unfaithful to their husband and patron, God.[90] Beyond the precedent for this image in the Hebrew Bible, the use of the grammatical feminine gender is provocative and surely would have scandalized both male and female members of the addressees' community. Female members would have recognized that James had claimed they had engaged in a shameful activity against the cultural ideal of their chastity; male members may have been doubly shamed by the assertion that they had engaged in womanly activities.[91] The address μοιχαλίδες then can be seen as a summary of the critique James has lobbied against the addressees.

---

87. Louw and Nida, *Greek-English Lexicon*, §88.167.

88. I interpret the syntax of 4:2–3 in such a way that the violent actions (φονεύω, μάχομαι, and πολεμέω) function as the *result* of their passions (desire and jealousy). See also Mayor, *Epistle of St. James*, 136, who is followed by Ropes, *Epistle of St. James*, 254; and Johnson, "James 3:13—4:10," 329–30. For a group-oriented explanation of ἐν τοῖς μέλεσιν ὑμῶν (4:1), see Edgar, *Has God Not Chosen the Poor*, 191; Martin, *James*, 145; Ropes, *Epistle of James*, 253.

89. Here I follow Laws's suggestion that 4:5 ought to be rendered as two leading questions that should be answered negatively: "Do you think the scripture speaks vainly? Does it say the indwelling spirit within us desires enviously?" (Laws, "Does Scripture," 210–15).

90. Schmitt has attempted to problematize the standard reading that adultery in this case refers to the people of God as God's unfaithful wife ("You Adulteresses," 331–32), but Edgar's critique of Schmitt's proposal is well founded (*Has God Not Chosen the Poor*, 103 n. 26). See also Ropes, *Epistle of James*, 260; Dibelius, *James*, 219–20.

91. See Westfall, *Paul and Gender*, 7–24.

Their envy, self-promotion, group conflict, infidelity, and hatred demonstrate that they have been unchaste with regard to their patron, God. Indeed, their adultery is engaging in activities that will garner them favor and prestige with a new patron—the world.

This is a grave accusation and it is possible that, with the semantics realized by μοιχαλίδες, James has put the chances of achieving his rhetorical goal at significant risk. The semantics of μοιχαλίδες could have been interpreted by the addressees as an accusation to have shamefully transgressed the bounds of a fictive family group, realizing the semantics of [+exclusion] and [+power]. In this view James would be seen to have the authority necessary to exclude the addressees from the group based on a lack of adherence to group-ordained norms. But, this would be a substantial departure from the tenor relations previously maintained in the letter, in which James appears to be reminding the addressees of their orientation to the group. On the other hand, each form of address may realize the semantics of [+inclusion] and [+power]. In this reading, James either maintains the tenor relations previously prescribed, or alters them slightly, in hopes that the addressees will recognize James's authority. This allows for the forms of address in 2:1—3:12 to function as frequent reminders of James's and the addressees' orientation to the same group, allowing μοιχαλίδες to serve expressly as a disclosure of the severity of the addressees' infidelity. The second option may have been James's intention, yet the first option should be kept in mind, for it is possible the addressees interpreted James in this way. Such accusations could have jeopardized James's rhetorical aim, particularly if the addressees chose to disregard the tenor roles James prescribed based on these accusations. However, the ensuing "call to repentance" (4:7—5:6) demonstrates that James wanted the addressees to be faithful members of the group.

I think a convincing reading of James 4:7—5:6 is as a prophetic call to the addressees to abandon their "adulterous" life, and return to demonstrating faithfulness to their patron, God. Indeed the first clause of 4:7 functions as a kind of thesis statement for the section: "Submit, therefore, to God." The forms of address that appear in 4:8, ἁμαρτωλοί (sinners) and δίψυχοι (double-souled), also hint at the deplorable state of the addressees, yet the co-text invites them to repent. "Sinners" (ἁμαρτωλοί) is unquestionably negative and accuses the addressees of denying the group and its patron, God, their rightful honor by transgressing group-ordained boundaries.[92] "Double-souled" (δίψυχοι)—despite debates over its mean-ing—gives the clearest indication of the addressees' sin, showing that their allegiance is split between God's patronage and that of the world.[93] The addressees have been "leading lives which are divided, instead of be-ing wholly committed to God."[94] As with μοιχαλίδες, it is possible for James to have intended to maintain tenor relations with the semantics of [+inclusion] and [+power], yet the addressees took James's words as overly critical. But, the imperatives to "clean your hands" and "pu-rify your hearts" are invitations to the addressees to reinvigorate their commitment to God and the boundaries of the addressees' community. James's use of these negative forms of address demonstrates his attempts to maintain tenor relations in which James is an honored member of the community, while showing that the addressees are dangerously exceed-ing the proper bounds of their group.

The fourth form of address in this section, ἀδελφοί, has posed some difficulty in the interpretation of its co-text, because the form of address seems to conflict with the condemnatory tone in 3:13—5:6. It is possibly James's recognition that he had negatively affected the tenor relations be-tween himself and the addressees, or simply an indication that ἀδελφοί is James's default form of address. Varner helpfully explains, however, that this form of address intentionally highlights the ensuing call to avoid slandering other members of the group, other ἀδελφοί.[95] Thus, James can be seen to realize the semantics of [+inclusion] and [+power] as an intentional reminder of the tenor relations of the group, which he then utilized as a basis for discontinuing unjust judgment against others of the community. Again, the form of address solidifies James's desire for the addressees to retain their group membership by repenting of the behav-ior that caused them to transgress group boundaries.

The last calls to repentance feature only one form of address, which is οἱ πλούσιοι in 5:1.[96] The previous verses (4:13–17) function as a call to the well-to-do to abandon "a blatant desire to become rich," and to seek

92. Malina, *New Testament World*, 59–60.

93. Again, see Porter, "*Dipsuchos*," 473–84.

94. Edgar, *Has God Not Chosen the Poor*, 104.

95. Varner, *Book of James*, 158.

96. It is possible that οἱ λέγοντες (4:13), as well as the content of the speech which comprises most of 4:13 and all of 4:14, could be considered a form of address. How-ever, the length of the formulation has made me disregard it here.

instead the will of God when planning for the future.[97] Extending this call, James now enjoins the "rich" (οἱ πλούσιοι) to mourn the state to which they have attained through hoarding their wealth (5:2–3), and by withholding due wage to those who have brought them a life of luxury (5:4–6).[98] The form of address οἱ πλούσιοι would be ambiguous were it not for the surrounding co-text that constrains its meaning. Certainly one could be honorably rich in the first-century Mediterranean world, but within these limited-good societies the accumulation of wealth meant to deprive another of their standard of living.[99] Thus, the form of address functions to demonstrate that the addressees are acting out of step with the societal values the group has appropriated. Reasonably, James can be seen to realize the semantics of [+inclusion] and [+power] yet again in an attempt to reiterate James's tenor relation with the addressees. He exerts some control over the addressees as an honorable member of the group, and he is therefore able to condemn the addressees and call them to repentance. As with the other forms of address in this section, James's intention may have been poorly received by the addressees, who have been labelled heavily in this section, and thus, James's rhetorical aim may be compromised. But, the remainder of the letter appears to attempt to mitigate any such difficulty.

JAMES 5:7–20

This final section of James in the reading I have proposed deals with how James, as a "slave of God" intends to restore the addressees' community that has "wandered from the truth" (5:20). It is important to note that each of James's teachings here has a corollary within the theological system of the addressees, which James critiques in 1:2—3:12. James's insistence that God blesses those who endure so that they might fulfill God's purposes (e.g., the prophets and Job), which is found in 5:7–11, directly opposes the theology of those who seek out temptation as a means of gaining the honor that comes with wisdom (1:2–18). Similarly, James's call to simple, ethical speech (5:12) combats the uncontrolled speech so highly criticized in 3:1–12. The call to remember the community-oriented ethic of the addressees (e.g., prayer for one another, praise with one another, and confession to one another) in 5:13–18 is the proper conduct for the

---

97. Martin, *James*, 165. See also Cargal, *Restoring the Diaspora*, 175–76.

98. Batten, "Degraded Poor," 75–76.

99. Malina, *New Testament World*, 89–90.

addressees rather than the favoritism discussed in 2:1–13. It is through enforcing these things within the community that errant members of the addressees may be "restored" (5:19–20). Remarkably, this section has a very high concentration of forms of address—five in just thirteen verses, all of which are derived from James's beloved "ἀδελφοί" form of address (5:7, 9, 10, 12, 19). In line with the other forms of address of this type, James likely intended to grammaticalize the semantics of [+power] and [+inclusion]. They are indeed members of the same group; the address-ees simply need to be restored, and James empowers them to do so.

CONCLUSION

In this essay, I wanted to enter a conversation that is often ignored. Forms of address are easily overlooked, but they are capable of contributing much to a discourse. The analysis above of the Epistle of James demonstrates that seemingly innocuous words may indeed jeopardize the intended aim of a discourse. It is for this reason that I wanted to present an overview of the possible interpersonal semantics realized by forms of address, and the way these semantics can correlate to tenor relations. As I stated above, the theoretical framework is broad and, through the course of analyzing the text of James, it is clear that the semantic system needs to be defined in more detail. This will allow this system to more accurately reflect the complex interplay of social relations in the first-century Mediterranean world, and it will help describe the everchanging tenor relations within a discourse. I believe the present theory has presented a fine starting point, but much work needs to be done. With regard to the Epistle of James, I have attempted to demonstrate that forms of address may have impacted the effectiveness of James's rhetorical aim. While he spent a good deal of time attempting to garner positive affect through the tenor relations he prescribed, some of his forms of address, particularly those 3:18—5:6, may have impeded his rhetorical aim. Fortunately, the historical recep-tion of James's letter demonstrates that James's letter was at least partially effective in reaching its goal.[100] Perhaps social name-calling is alright in some circumstances.

---

100. My thanks to Cynthia Long Westfall for this insight.

BIBLIOGRAPHY

Aasgaard, Reidar. "Brothers and Sisters in Faith: Christian Siblingship as an Ecclesiological Mirror in the First Two Centuries." In *The Formation of the Church*, edited by Jostein Ådna, 285–316. WUNT 1.183. Tübingen: Mohr Siebeck, 2005.

———. *'My Beloved Brothers and Sisters!' Christian Siblingship in Paul.* JSNTSup 265. London: T. & T. Clark, 2004.

Bauckham, Richard J. *Jude and the Relatives of Jesus in the Early Church.* Edinburgh: T. & T. Clark, 1990.

———. "Pseudo-Apostolic Letters." *JSNT* 107 (1988) 469–94.

Batten, Alicia J. "The Degraded Poor and the Greedy Rich: Exploring the Language of Poverty and Wealth in James." In *The Social Sciences and Biblical Translation*, edited by Dietmar Neufeld, 65–78. SBLSymS 41. Atlanta: SBL, 2008.

———. *What Are They Saying About The Letter of James?* WATSA. New York: Paulist, 2009.

Burke, Trevor J. *Family Matters: A Socio-Historical Study of Kinship Metaphors in 1 Thessalonians.* LNTS 247. London: T. & T. Clark, 2003.

Cargal, Timothy B. *Restoring the Diaspora: Discursive Structure and Purpose in the Epistle of James.* SBLDS 144. Atlanta: Scholars, 1993.

Davids, Peter H. *The Epistle of James: A Commentary on the Greek Text.* NIGTC. Grand Rapids: Eerdmans, 1982.

deSilva, David A. *Honor, Patronage, Kinship & Purity: Unlocking New Testament Culture.* Downers Grove, IL: InterVarsity, 2000.

Dibelius, Martin. *James: Commentary on the Epistle of James*, edited by H. Koester. Revised by H. Greeven. Translated by M. Williams. Hermeneia. Philadelphia: Fortress, 1976.

Dickey, Eleanor. "The Ancient Greek Address System and Some Proposed Sociolinguistic Universals." *LS* 26 (1997) 1–13.

———. "The Greek Address System of the Roman Period and Its Relationship to Latin." *CQ* 54 (2004) 494–527.

Dvorak, James D. "'Evidence that Commands a Verdict': Determining the Semantics of Imperatives in the New Testament." Paper presented at the Annual Meeting of the Society of Biblical Literature, San Antonio, TX, November 19–22, 2016.

———. "'Prodding with Prosody': Persuasion and Social Influence through the Lens of Appraisal Theory." *BAGL* 4 (2015) 85–120.

———. "The Interpersonal Metafunction in 1 Corinthians 1–4: The Tenor of Toughness." PhD diss., McMaster Divinity College, 2012.

Edgar, David H. *Has God Not Chosen the Poor? The Social Setting of the Epistle of James.* JSNTSup 206. Sheffield: Sheffield Academic, 2001.

Elliott, John H. *Conflict, Community, and Honor: 1 Peter in Social-Scientific Perspective.* Cascade Companions 2. Eugene, OR: Cascade, 2007.

———. *A Home for the Homeless: A Social-Scientific Criticism of I Peter, Its Situation and Strategy.* Philadelphia: Fortress, 1981.

Fairclough, Norman. *Language and Power.* London: Longman, 1989.

Francis, Fred O. "The Form and Function of the Opening and Closing Paragraphs of James and 1 John." *ZNW* 61 (1970) 110–26.

Halliday, M. A. K. *An Introduction to Functional Grammar.* Revised by Christian M. I. M. Matthiessen. 3rd ed. London: Hodder Arnold, 2004.

————. *Language as Social Semiotic: The Social Interpretation of Language and Meaning.* Baltimore, MD: University Park, 1978.

Halliday, M. A. K., and Ruqaiya Hasan. *Language, Context, and Text: Aspects of Language in a Social-Semiotic Perspective.* 2nd ed. Oxford: Oxford University Press, 1989.

Harland, Phillip A. "Familial Dimensions of Group Identity: 'Brothers' (ΑΔΕΛΦΟΙ) in Associations of the Greek East." *JBL* 124 (2005) 491–513.

Hasan, Ruqaiya, and J. R. Martin. *Language Development: Learning Language, Learning Culture.* Advances in Discourse Processes 27. Meaning and Choice in Language: Studies for Michael Halliday. Norwood, NJ: Ablex. 1989.

Hellerman, Joseph H. *The Ancient Church as Family.* Minneapolis: Fortress, 2001.

Horrell, David G. "From ἀδελφοί to οἶκος θεοῦ: Social Transformation in Pauline Christianity." *JBL* 120 (2001) 293–311.

Householder, Fred W. *Apollonius Dyscolus: The Syntax of Apollonius Dyscolus.* Amsterdam Studies in the Theory and History of Linguistic Science III. Studies in the History of Linguistics 23. Amsterdam: Benjamins, 1981.

Hunt, Benjamin B. "Know Your Enemies: Rhetorical Semantics in the Epistle of Jude." MA thesis, McMaster Divinity College, 2014.

————. "Meaning in Bulk: The Greek Clause Complex and 1 Peter 1:3–12." In *Modeling Biblical Language: Selected Papers from the McMaster Divinity College Linguistics Circle,* edited by Stanley E. Porter et al., 391–414. LBS 13. Leiden: Brill, 2016.

Hultin, Jeremy F. *The Ethics of Obscene Speech in Early Christianity and Its Environment.* NovTSup 128. Leiden: Brill, 2008.

Jipp, Joshua W. *Divine Visitations and Hospitality to Strangers in Luke-Acts: An Interpretation of the Malta Episode in Acts 28:1–10.* NovTSup 153. Leiden: Brill, 2013.

Laws, Sophie. "Does Scripture Speak in Vain? A Reconsideration of James 4:5." *NTS* 20 (1973–74) 210–15.

Louw, J. P. "Linguistic Theory and the Greek Case System." *AC* 9 (1966) 73–88.

Louw, J. P., and E. A. Nida. *Greek-English Lexicon of the New Testament Based on Semantic Domains.* 2 vols. 2nd ed. New York: United Bible Societies, 1989.

Malina, Bruce J. *The New Testament World: Insights from Cultural Anthropology.* 3rd ed. Louisville: Westminster John Knox, 2001.

————. "Hospitality." In *Handbook of Biblical Social Values,* edited by John J. Pilch and Bruce J. Malina, 115–18. Peabody, MA: Hendrickson, 1998.

————. "Love." In *Handbook of Biblical Social Values,* edited by John J. Pilch and Bruce J. Malina, 127–30. Peabody, MA: Hendrickson, 1998.

Malina, Bruce J., and Jerome H. Neyrey. "Conflict in Luke–Acts: Labelling and Deviance Theory." In *The Social World of Luke–Acts: Models for Interpretation,* edited by Jerome H. Neyrey, 97–122. Peabody, MA: Hendrickson, 1991.

————. "Jesus the Witch: Witchcraft Accusations in Matthew 12." In *Social-Scientific Approaches to New Testament Interpretation,* edited by David G. Horrell, 29–67. Edinburgh: T. & T. Clark, 1999.

Malina, Bruce J., and Richard L. Rohrbaugh. *Social-Science Commentary on the Synoptic Gospels.* Minneapolis: Fortress, 1992.

Martin, J. R., and David Rose. *Genre Relations: Mapping Culture.* London: Equinox, 2008.

Martin, J. R., and P. R. R. White. *The Language of Evaluation: Appraisal in English.* New York: Palgrave MacMillan, 2005.

Martin, Ralph P. *James*. WBC 48. Waco, TX: Word, 1988.

Mayor, Joseph B. *The Epistle of St. James*. 3rd ed. London: MacMillan, 1909.

Meeks, Wayne A. *The First Urban Christians: The Social World of the Apostle Paul*. 2nd ed. New Haven: Yale University Press, 2003.

Moulton, James Hope. *A Grammar of New Testament Greek*. Vol. 1. *Prolegomena*. 3rd ed. Edinburgh: T. & T. Clark, 1908.

Neyrey, Jerome H. "Deception." In *Handbook of Biblical Social Values*, edited by John J. Pilch and Bruce J. Malina, 40–45. Peabody, MA: Hendrickson, 1998.

———. *Paul, in Other Words: A Cultural Reading of His Letters*. Louisville: Westminster John Knox, 1990.

Pilch, John J. "Power." In *Handbook of Biblical Social Values*, edited by John J. Pilch and Bruce J. Malina, 158–61. Peabody, MA: Hendrickson, 1998.

Pilch, John J., and Bruce J. Malina, eds. *Handbook of Biblical Social Values*. Peabody, MA: Hendrickson, 1998.

Plevnik, Joseph. "Honor/Shame." In *Handbook of Biblical Social Values*, edited by John J. Pilch and Bruce J. Malina, 106–15. Peabody, MA: Hendrickson, 1998.

Porter, Stanley E. *Idioms of the Greek New Testament*. 2nd ed. BLG 2. Sheffield: Sheffield Academic, 1994.

Poynton, Cate. "Address and the Semiotics of Social Relations: A Systemic-Functional Account of Address Forms and Practices in Australian English." PhD diss., University of Sydney, 1990.

———. *Language and Gender: Making the Difference*. London: Oxford University Press. 1989.

———. "Names as Vocatives: Forms and Functions." *NLC* 13 (1984) 1–34.

Reicke, Bo. *The Epistles of James, Peter and Jude*. AB 37. Garden City, NY: Doubleday, 1964.

Robertson, A. T. *A Grammar of the Greek New Testament in the Light of Historical Research*. 4th ed. Nashville: Broadman, 1934.

Ropes, James Hardy. *A Critical and Exegetical Commentary on the Epistle of St. James*. ICC. Edinburgh: T. & T. Clark, 1916.

Schmitt, John J. "'You Adulteresses!' The Image in James 4:4." *NovT* 28 (1986) 327–37.

Smyth, Herbert Weir. *Greek Grammar*. Revised by Gordon D. Messing. Cambridge, MA: Harvard University Press, 1956.

Spitaler, Peter. "Doubt or Dispute (Jude 9 and 22–23): Rereading a Special New Testament Meaning through the Lens of Internal Evidence." *Bib* 87 (2006) 201–222.

———. "Διακρίνεσθαι in Mt. 21:21, Mk. 11:23, Acts 10:20, Rom. 4:20, 14:23, Jas. 1:6, and Jude 22—the 'Semantic Shift' That Went Unnoticed by Patristic Authors." *NovT* 49 (2007) 1–39.

Turner, Nigel. *A Grammar of New Testament Greek*. Vol. 3. *Syntax*. Edinburgh: T. & T. Clark, 1963.

Varner, William. *The Book of James: A New Perspective: A Linguistic Commentary Applying Discourse Analysis*. The Woodlands, TX: Kress Biblical Resources, 2010.

von Rad, Gerhard. *Wisdom in Israel*. Nashville: Abingdon, 1972.

Wallace, Daniel B. *Greek Grammar beyond the Basics: An Exegetical Syntax of the New Testament*. Grand Rapids: Zondervan, 1996.

Westfall, Cynthia Long. *Paul and Gender: Reclaiming the Apostle's Vision for Men and Women in Christ*. Grand Rapids: Baker Academic, 2016.

White, John L. "The Greek Documentary Letter Tradition Third Century B.C.E. to Third Century C.E." *Semeia* 22 (1981) 89–106.

10

Ἰακώβου *Contra Mundum*
Anti-Language and the Epistle of James

JONATHAN M. WATT

INTRODUCTION

IN A BARELY POST-HIPPIE era article that appeared in *American Anthropologist*, M. A. K. Halliday proposed that "special forms of language generated by some kind of anti-society" can emerge in counter-cultural, non-prestige communities, which effectively reinforce the group's identity and distinct values and warrant a classification of *anti-language.*[1] After reviewing Halliday's conception of the term and his supporting case studies, this chapter will explore the potential of applying the concept to the New Testament Epistle of James. The direction taken will hinge on both sides of the *anti*-equation: the formal features of anti-language as defined by Halliday, and the functional reality of the sub-culture that creates, and is reinforced by, this kind of speech code.

FEATURES AND FUNCTIONS OF ANTI-LANGUAGE

Three language situations attracted Halliday's attention and led him to develop the concept of anti-language: vagabond speech of Elizabethan England,[2] along with the twentieth century underworld codes of Cal-

1. Halliday hyphenated the word in his defining essay, so I use the hyphenated form throughout this essay for my own use and its non-hyphenated form only in direct quotations that have it otherwise.

2. Harman, *Caveat or Warening.*

cutta[3] and of Polish prisons.[4] The non-prestige status of each sub-group and the specific activities, values, and circumstances that defined them were instrumental to the development of these codes; the codes were dependent upon the sub-community's identity in distinction from the majority population, while at the same time their code helped maintain that distinction. The defining mark of Halliday's construct was disarmingly basic: "The simplest form taken by an anti-language is that of new words for old; it is a language relexicalized,"[5] though he added, "Typically this relexicalization is partial, not total." (He noted as an exception "mother-in-law" language within the Australian Aboriginal language, Dyirbal.) Halliday observed this phenomenon would be "no more than the technical and semitechnical features of a special register" unless other factors came into play.[6] With anti-language, the new vocabulary shows up "only in certain areas, typically those that are central to the activities of the subculture and that set it off most sharply from the established society."[7] The code, he went on to explain, would only have been a "register" were it not for the tendency to overlexicalize, and thus to create a picture of things "larger than life"; for example, Calcutta's underworld had 21 words for "bomb" and 41 for "police,"[8] while Polish prison social hierarchy was bifurcated into those designated either as one of two types of "people" or relegated to one of three levels of "suckers."[9] Lexical specialization known only to insiders is a defining feature of this phenomenon.

Halliday's discussion made it clear that anti-language involves more than form. Leaning on sociological constructs from the likes of Peter Berger and Basil Bernstein, he argued that such codes tend to be definitive and formative, effectively reinforcing a sub-culture by re-socializing the speaker and framing a person's new identity through the marked conversation of a new "society that is set up within another society."[10] Halliday argued that a sub-culture uses its own perceptive world as a framework for designating definitions of their new terminology, which constitutes

---

3. Mallik, *Language of the Underworld*.

4. Podgorecki, "'Second Life' and Its Implications."

5. Halliday, "Anti-Languages," 571.

6. Ibid.

7. Ibid.

8. For this, Halliday drew from Mallik, *Language of the Underworld*, 22–23, 27.

9. Podgorecki, "Second Life," 7.

10. Halliday, "Anti-Languages," 570.

"a never ending search for originality, either for the sake of liveliness and humor or . . . [for the purposes of] secrecy,"[11] and this search that Halliday postulates leads one to ask why originality was so highly valued by social sub-groups. To answer this, Halliday proposed that, along with secrecy, a certain "communicative force" and "verbal art" seemed to play into the picture, and whatever ingredients were considered essential to the brew, secrecy was a byproduct, a "necessary strategic property . . . [though it was] unlikely to be the major cause" of what he dubbed "folk anti-linguistics."[12] He saw it as a "feature of the jargon rather than a determinant" of it.[13]

Consequently, the social aspect of the anti-language picture became an essential puzzle piece. Citing Podgorecki, Halliday noted that these communities "need to maintain inner solidarity under pressure," their anti-language then becoming the means of identity maintenance and the "reconstruction of the individual and society" with their "alternate reality."[14] An "anti-language is the vehicle of such resocialization"[15] with a "reality-generating force . . . and . . . power to create and maintain social hierarchy"[16]—a surprising attribute of power to a code that was "no one's mother tongue" yet able to provide the "means of realization of a subjective reality: not merely expressing it, but actively creating and maintaining it."[17] Halliday's anti-language is *defensive* in its maintenance of an alternate reality and *offensive* in its expression of protest against prevailing majority standards.

Despite the fact that the communities Halliday used to define the paradigm were secretive, he suggested that the prevalence of scholars' interest in them was more than fanciful. The essence of the matter was sociological; these codes go with groups diametrically opposed to the societal majority,[18] and while they may be associated with caste or class, they also may be generational (one thinks of 1960s hippie jargon), economic, sexual, or even religious. They promote and maintain an alternate

11. Ibid., 571.
12. Ibid., 572.
13. Ibid.
14. Ibid., 573.
15. Ibid., 575.
16. Ibid., 574.
17. Ibid., 576.
18. Ibid., 580.

social order and are therefore unflinchingly hierarchical,[19] and essentially metaphorical, for not only do they contain metaphors (a staple of language communities everywhere), but their "regular patterns of realization" offer metaphorical compounding, metatheses (he cited Mallik's description of thirty phonological processes in Calcutta underworld argot),[20] and rhyming alternations (for which Cockney slang comes to mind).[21]

Some observations about the anti-language proposal are appropriate. First, and most important, is the surprising fact that Halliday used only criminal case studies for defining his paradigm. This seems unnecessarily, if accidentally, limiting to further applications. Whatever social elements may be shared between Polish prisoners and economic, generational, or religious societies is never discussed by Halliday, other than a brief assertion that "the early Christian community was an anti-society, and its language was in this sense an anti-language,"[22] which appeared without elaboration.

The second observation involves the essentially oral nature of the phenomenon, at least as Halliday framed it. To be sure, the life of language is in its native and spoken use, and of course spoken language is routinely represented in writing, whether it is done by careful or by casual observers (or practitioners). However, key to Halliday's identification of the concept was the connection of artifact with worldview, a nexus more concretely identified when a code's speakers can be interviewed with regard to nuance and motivation (as documented by Mallik's study in India and Podgorecki's in Poland, upon which he was leaning). Quoting Berger and Luckmann, Halliday agreed that "the most important vehicle of reality-maintenance is conversation."[23] Consequently, this present essay will necessarily come to a tenuous solution, because it has to draw from a limited manuscript base (e.g., first-century apostolic writings) and no interview is possible for assessing insider language perceptions. Thus, a significant distance remains between original usage and modern evaluation.

19. Ibid., 580–81.
20. Ibid., 576–78.
21. Ibid., 579.
22. Ibid., 575.
23. Ibid., 574.

Third, while anti-language was defined centrally as a lexical matter, how could it not have morpho-phonemic, if not syntactic, anomalies? In fact, Halliday addressed this area from a developmental point of view (e.g., the way Mallik had discussed Hindi-infused Bengali, which undergoes metathesis and back formation of phonological segments), but morpho-phonemics should be considered a defining element of the equation. "New" words spoken by isolated communities ordinarily develop morpho-phonemic particularities, even if only in their suprasegmentals, such as nasality in the Italian-English mobster jargon of New York City or the rising intonations common to Irish-English within Australian convict jargon.

Fourth, there seem to have been two significant omissions of well-documented language situations with codes that could have been helpful in definition, as well as facilitative for further application, of Halliday's seminal essay. One is nineteenth-century Australian convict jargon, the other being East London Cockney—situations certainly familiar to a British linguist who taught and researched in Australia. Many books have described the sub-culture of transported "government men," and nearly two centuries and numerous studies have come and gone since the first mentions of criminalized antipodean speech, while Cockney is familiar even to non-specialists. It is unfortunate that the speech of these sizeable counter-cultural language communities was absent from Halliday's defining essay.

CASE STUDIES IN ANTI-LANGUAGE

Despite Halliday's limiting choice of foundational case studies, his idea of anti-language has attracted interest, even if the meanderings have been more like a stream than a river. After all, identifying instances of a distinct code in which "nobody's 'mother tongue' . . . exists solely in the context of *re*socializiation, and the reality it creates is inherently an alternate reality . . . constructed precisely in order to function in alternation"[24]—*and* which has been recorded or at least documented—is no simple task for researchers. However, the task receives inspiration these days in the form of persuasion, for anything that influences a social reality necessarily aims to be persuasive. James Dvorak has suggested that:

---

24. Ibid., 575.

> Every attempt at persuasion among human beings is at once en-
> abled and constrained by two key dimensions of social relations:
> *power* and *solidarity*. *Power* . . . describes one's ability to exercise
> control over and gain compliance from another with regard to
> the other's beliefs, attitudes, behaviors, etc. *Power relations* range
> from equal to unequal, and the basis of one's power derives typi-
> cally from more than one of the following factors: force, author-
> ity, status, and expertise. . . . *Solidarity* . . . describes the social
> distance or strength of relatedness between the members of a
> group, the measure of which is how strongly they adhere to the
> group's core values.[25]

As it relates to the question of anti-language and James, then, some
attention will be directed toward the issue of influence as discussed in
persuasion theory. For now, it will be observed that the anti-language
construct has been connected by various writers to additional speech
communities, one of the most energetic being that of the sectarian Jewish community residing at the site of Qumran on the northwest coast of
the Dead Sea. The initial connection between anti-language and Qumran
Hebrew came from William Schniedewind, who argued from the manuscripts connected to the community since the original 1947 discoveries
that "The purpose of the peculiar orthography seems . . . to be to mark
off the sectarian texts from other Jewish literature,"[26] collating such
uniqueness with what he called their "studied avoidance" of Aramaisms
in an attempt to keep their Hebrew language "pure"—the ironic result
being an "artificial language." Schniedewind influenced James Charlesworth[27] in the same direction and, in the words of Gary Rendsburg,
thereby "launched a new approach to Qumran Hebrew, understanding
the unusual grammatical features and lexical usages to reflect a purpose-
ful linguistic ideology."[28]

Rendsburg explained that the Hebrew of most Dead Sea Scrolls
represents "a different Hebrew register from all other Hebrew varieties
known to us" and appropriately locates the reasoning for its use within the
interests of language ideology.[29] He expanded upon the criminal examples that constituted the origins of Halliday's term to include the realm of

25. Dvorak, "Prodding with Prosody," 88–89.

26. Schniedewind, "Qumran Hebrew," 248.

27. Charlesworth, *Pesharim and Qumran History*.

28. Rendsburg, "Qumran Hebrew," 131.

29. Ibid., 81.

prostitutes, in-community gay terminology, and African American word usages, along with drug culture, and he cautiously suggested parallels with modern cults. Additionally, Rendsburg noted that linguistic archaisms, real or manufactured, supplied a "patina of antiquity" for Qumran anti-language, while "most strikingly, the dialect is relatively devoid of [Aramaic, Persian, or Greek] loanwords," which falls alongside what he calls "the very strange Qumran Hebrew usage of adding -*a* to pronoun forms."[30] So, whether or not Catherine Hezser is correct that Qumranic Hebrew (QH) was solely a written scribal code and not actually used in day-to-day speech,[31] the concept may nevertheless be applicable (see below for further discussion). Steven Weitzman concurred with the anti-language position on QH,[32] as did Martin Abegg, who noted that various scrolls gave evidence that their scribes had taken pains to contrast the "strange speech and a strange tongue" or the "blasphemous language" of non-sectarian Jews with the self-perceived purer language that was constructed as "a purposed reaction" on the part of the Qumran community.[33]

An additional angle relating to the QH discussion differs from Halliday's even as it builds upon his proposal: Schniedewind, citing Halliday's observation that "An anti-language may be 'high' as well as 'low' on the diglossic spectrum,"[34] proposed that the "classicizing tendency" of QH classifies it as a high register code.[35] In other words, Halliday conceived of possibilities for highbrow anti-language despite the consistently low social spectrum examples he used to make his original case. The "high" status of the code would be reinforced by what Emanuel Tov saw in QH's inconsistent, "unique and peculiar" details of orthography, which represented a "learned attempt at archaism," something Frank Cross also was seeing in QH.[36]

However, what remains squarely in league with Halliday's conception throughout the variety of QH/anti-language discussions appears to be the belief that the use of anomalous language encodes and promotes

---

30. Ibid., 82–83.

31. Hezser, *Jewish Literacy*, 228 n. 13.

32. Weitzman, "Why Did the Qumran Community Write in Hebrew," 35–45.

33. Abegg, "Hebrew Language," 461.

34. Halliday, "Anti-Languages," 583.

35. Schniedewind, "Qumran Hebrew," 245 n. 45.

36. Ibid., 247–48, citing Cross, "Some Notes," 5, and labeling the features "anomalous." See also Tov, "Orthography and Language," 31–57.

identification with a counter-cultural community of some sort. Though Chaim Rabin did not invoke the anti-language lens in particular, he noted that QH is "more like that of the Bible, and has only a few traits of the spoken language. This effort at purism was probably not a function of superior linguistic training, but part of the self-identification of that group with the generation of the Exodus from Egypt and the will to imitate not only the latter's religious customs, but also their way of speaking."[37] Put another way, the whole anti-language proposal was a concept born slightly before its time. It fit into a sociolinguistics field that had been sown in the latter half of the twentieth century, but had affinity with the corner of that field that came to be identified as language ideology, which dates to the 1980s. As Woolard and Schieffelin would explain it, "Ideologies envision and enact links of language to group and personal identity, to aesthetics, to morality, and to epistemology. Through such linkages, they often underpin fundamental social institutions . . . [and] social institutions . . . hinge on the ideologization of language use,"[38] and that is surely the stuff of anti-language. Particular language choices arise because of identity and belonging, and simultaneously affirm and promote it among its speakers, or as Halliday had put it, anti-language "is the means of realization of a subjective reality: not merely expressing it, but actively creating and maintaining it."[39] What set his approach apart from the ideology corner of the field was not only timing, but the fact that he was describing a code that was not a part of any speaker's natural repertoire, but rather a manufactured alteration.

Other applications of the anti-language concept have appeared, some with and others without data support. Rendsburg, for example, suggested that ancient Samaritans might have had their own anti-language to distinguish themselves from general Judaism, though evidence was not forthcoming.[40] Additionally, R. M. Frazier, who once quipped that Classical philosophical works are routinely packed with jargon and field-specific definitions routinely found baffling by non-specialists, went on to give the example that Neo-Pythagoreans between the second century BC and the first century AD demonstrated a penchant for obscure hyper-lexicalization that tended to baffle those unfamiliar with their te-

---

37. Rabin, *Short History of the Hebrew Language*, 37.

38. Woolard and Schieffelin. "Language Ideology," 55.

39. Halliday, "Anti-Languages," 576.

40. Rendsburg, "Qumran Hebrew," 83.

nets.[41] Another case, with firsthand descriptions available for support, involves the Jacobean "dialect" of the early Quaker movement, sometimes labelled "God-talk," with its use of King James-vintage "thee/thou" personal addresses in the daily speech of adherents. As some have put it, in the Quaker tradition, "dress is simple and speech is biblical," and that kind of constructed speech demarcated their line of divergence from the societal majority.

A number of studies in sixteenth- and seventeenth-century English criminal cant actually overlap with Halliday's defining essay. Daniel Heller-Roazen, for example, discussed various criminal codes including those of twelfth-century European beggars, fifteenth-century Burgundian bandits (self-named *Coquillars*, i.e., "People of the Shell"), along with the speech of English vagabonds that had been part of Halliday's essay.[42] Though Heller-Roazen explicitly affirmed the anti-language concept, he suggested that "Strictly speaking, they [i.e., the underworld codes in question] constitute not so much secret languages … as secret uses of languages," proposing instead that these are "parasitic languages" since they "borrow" from the phonetics, morphology, and syntax of standard language and "submit them to an 'abnormal transformation,'" to produce "cryptic jargons … made of new words and phrases."[43]

Various works, historical and linguistic, have described nineteenth-century Australian convict jargon/argot. The earliest plenary description of it has frequently been reprinted, referenced or incorporated in some way, the substance being the autobiographic *Memoirs of James Hardy Vaux* (a.k.a. "Flash Jim" Vaux, 1782-c. 1841), which, in its first printing in 1819, was accompanied by a second volume titled the *New and Comprehensive Vocabulary of the Flash Language*, both emanating from none less of a self-admitted recalcitrant and thrice-transported offender.[44] A couple of things bear noting here, including the fact that the author could clearly alternate between a more standard English and his presumed ability to use the terms defined there; the subtitle of the book, "*written by himself*," makes this contrast evident (and the original publisher noted in his introduction that he himself made few editorial changes to Vaux's manuscript). A second matter of note is that many of Vaux's entries are

41. Personal conversation.

42. Heller-Roazen, *Dark Tongues*.

43. Ibid., 38.

44. Vaux, *Memoirs of James Hardy Vaux*.

demonstrably loanwords from working class Irish English; their special status lay in the mind of the "new" users and hearers, and, in contrast to scholarly observation on the noteworthy *lack* of Aramaic or Greek loanwords in Qumran Hebrew, Australian convict argot (like the one-time property of its speakers) was frequently on loan.

So, whether specifically by the use of the term *anti-language* or by generally amenable descriptions, the literature has shown interest in connecting Halliday's now-forty-year-old concept with language situations that formulate connections between special uses of sub-community language code and the values and separateness of the communities they represent, and so they help differentiate their speakers from the majority (and typically more law-abiding) environment.

CAN THE CONSTRUCT OF ANTI-LANGUAGE APPLY TO THE NT?

Bruce Malina made an early application of the anti-language model to the New Testament, particularly involving the Gospel of John, and it was published along with critical responses from participants of a colloquy.[45] His work built upon Halliday's assertion that the early Christian community was an anti-society with its own anti-language, and argued for its relevance to the fourth Gospel.[46] However, Malina conceived of the Johannine community as a socially vulnerable group (even if it lasted some centuries) that was resistant to a collage of close yet competing religious groups, including even rival Christian groups. Drawing on Halliday's characterizations that included language as not merely relexicalized but *over*lexicialized, Malina utilized Halliday's ideational, interpersonal, and textual modes of meaning, and pointed to punning and ambiguity in John.[47] Malina then argued that the gospel writer's penchant for using synonyms (for nouns and verbs), and the new social and structural forms being promoted by the fourth gospel, supported the impression that John's gospel "orient[s] toward the interpersonal and textual modes of the linguistic system" and foregrounds new social values, which John is advocating for to help believers "maintain inner solidarity under pressure."[48]

---

45. Malina, *Gospel of John*.

46. Ibid., 11.

47. Ibid., 12–13.

48. Ibid., 13–14. See also Malina, *Christian Origins and Cultural Anthropology*.

One problem with Malina's approach seems to be the jump he made from Halliday's original case studies involving criminal elements and groups (ancient or modern) that promote views that stand diametrically opposed to a larger society to new views advocating moral and ethical circumspection. Furthermore, Halliday's work had been constructed around oral events that were relatively close to those documenting them, i.e., in time and firsthand experience. In any attempt to do this with a New Testament gospel or epistle we have precious few outside sources with which to contrast the wording. For example, metaphors may abound in mainstream speech communities without rendering them anti-communities; how does one distinguish a frequent resort to metaphor in speech without it all being considered "metaphorization"? And, as Stephen Breck Reid posed in his response to Malina, a counter-cultural group might use anti-language only in some contexts but not when addressing an outsider, for people and groups often have a multi-code repertoire with choices being made that are dependent upon each social speech situation encountered by the speaker.[49] Additionally, it could be argued that many metaphors apply qualities expected of one entity to another of unlike kind: automobiles can be lemons, a human can be a nutcase, an insect can bear the sting of death, and a kingdom can be a mustard seed. When it comes to metaphors, by their nature one shall know them.

Interestingly, Malina turned the tables on the original concept by suggesting that "the process of socialization and solidarity maintenance makes special demands on the antilanguage" since it must now promote affective ties between the authority most able to "influence the collectivity as well as with significant others in the group"[50]—something accomplished by reporting a conversation Jesus had with someone which then becomes a monologue that is itself then directed to the reader/hearer. Nevertheless, Malina acknowledged that anti-language arises from within groups since it "exists solely in a social context of resocialization ... it is a means of realizing the cultural script of the group in question, a means of expressing perceptions of the reality mediated by that script by actively creating and maintaining that reality by means of language."[51] Thus, the tension between society and anti-society is highlighted because "it implies an emphasis on new core values and an attempt to create stan-

---

49. Response section in ibid., 30.

50. Ibid., 14.

51. Ibid., 14–15.

dards and structure to implement those values."[52] He offered up some of the well-known Johannine dualisms in support of this claim, e.g., "spirit/above" vs. "flesh/below," and John's writing on proper vs. unacceptable behaviors. And while overlexicalization takes place (e.g., he noted that "bread" and "fruit" can both mean "food" in John's Gospel), some of the new terminology bears no relationship to the customary or mainline meanings, e.g., "before Abraham was, I am," and the pre-existent Word of God.[53] And building on Halliday's point of metaphor-in-language, Malina argued that "Metaphorization takes place when some common, often implicit, quality proper to one entity is predicated on another" that may be a quite different entity, e.g., Jesus's "I Am" statements describing him as bread, light, a door, a vine, etc., concluding that "in antilanguage, metaphorical modes of expression are the norm."[54]

David Lamb's revised publication of his doctoral dissertation also formulated a sociolinguistic approach to analysis of the Johannine Community hypothesis, and dealt with how text connects to the context that "bred" it.[55] Offering the most involved discussion (that I am aware of) of the anti-language concept in connection with the New Testament, Lamb devoted a full chapter to the issue, beginning with discussions of the theoretical parameters of the community in the literature including modern concepts of its interactions and separation from outsiders.[56] He moved next to the work of Malina, describing him as "the pioneer" in Johannine anti-language studies and noted, among other things, Malina's identification of that community as occupying a "weak group/low grid social location" and belief that Halliday's concept was typified by the Johannine writings.[57]

Lamb headed in a different direction, however, both in his rejection of those who invoked the anti-language concept so as to construe an allegedly secular Johannine community model, and in taking issue with the Hallidayan concept that he observed "has not been widely adopted in the

---

52. Ibid., 15.

53. Ibid., 16.

54. Malina in Malina and Waetjen, *Gospel of John*, 16.

55. Lamb, *Text, Context and the Johannine Community.*

56. See ibid., 103–44, which is the fifth chapter of his book titled "The Antilanguage Antisociety."

57. Ibid., 114.

field of sociolinguistics."[58] His extensive discussion challenged those who would use the concepts of anti-language and society in order to construct a secular model of the community, arguing that they misused Halliday's working concept, which he said was in decline anyway.[59] He critiqued reliance on such concepts as re- and over-lexicalization because they may "carry the prestige of scientific rhetoric" even as they fail to account adequately for the ways actual language is socially couched, adding there is no direct link between anti-language and anti-society.[60] The empirical evidence also runs short, according to Lamb, who asked "Is there any linguistic evidence, outside of the Jn writings, to support this process as indicative of antilanguage? Halliday does not offer any, neither do any of the Jn commentators I have considered."[61] For Lamb, John and anti-language was hardly a match made in heaven.

DOES JAMES USE ANTI-LANGUAGE?

Certain difficulties, then, haunt the conception and the application of Halliday's anti-language construct in general. Yet its potentials are intriguing, and so we turn next to the question of an early Christian writing to further consider its usefulness. We will need to consider both the social situational front pertaining to the community James addressed, and the linguistic front encoded in the language of James's epistle. Judith Irvine considered both of these in her description of language ideology, since it involves "the cultural system of ideas about social and linguistic relationships, together with their loading of moral and political interests."[62] These prongs shall guide the approach that follows here.

The Social Situation of James

The Epistle of James, usually dated to the central third of the first century, was intended primarily for a Palestinian audience and likely had Palestinian Jewish believers in Jesus in mind. Though the traditional identification of the writer of this epistle as a family member (brother

58. Ibid., 115.

59. See particularly ibid., 116 n. 58, which referenced earlier and more diverse applications of the concept in the scholarly literature that had appeared both before and after Halliday's own mid-70s publication.

60. Ibid., 139–40.

61. Ibid., 142.

62. Irvine, "When Talk Isn't Cheap," 250.

or step-brother) of Jesus suggests Galilee as a potential venue, Josephus (and Acts 15) connected him most directly with Jerusalem to the south in Judaea. Ralph Martin demonstrates considerable affinity between James's epistle and the Matthean tradition, again implying a Palestinian Jewish linkage that is being assumed here, whether or not the hypothesized secondary link to Antioch holds true.[63] Regarding linguistic environments, Hughson Ong explains with regard to Galilee, the Decapolis, Perea, and Syria that there is evidence of interaction between speakers of Hebrew, Aramaic, Greek, and Latin to such a degree that the population was predominantly multilingual.[64] Since the most widespread of these languages (Greek) evidences substantial interaction of Jews (including Jewish believers in Jesus) with the populations and speech codes of the greater Mediterranean social environment, it would have been entirely appropriate for the writer of this epistle to either write in Greek while located in Palestine or to write in Greek with a Palestinian Jewish audience in mind.[65] So whether one wished to address Palestinian Jews—or another contemporary ethnic group in the Mediterranean world—it made sense to select as the language of an epistle the Greek that was likely to be understood by the most people groups.

The values shared by these groups, for the purposes of this study, might be considered along the lines discussed by Pilch and Malina, i.e., many would be the shared values, ranging from specific doctrinal beliefs to altruism (e.g., as shown to the poor) to compassion to justice to sin and shame.[66] And these values can be assumed of the majority community despite the older criticisms of James's epistle as being allegedly non-Palestinian because of its affinity with standard Hellenistic language.[67] Perhaps James could even visualize such people, since it has been suggested that the higher/lower sitting positions referred to in Jas 2:3 implied their presence in the synagogues, many of which had staggered bench rows around their periphery, such as those in Masada and the Herodion, which is suggestive of believers maintaining their connections to the Jewish community even as they worshipped in the name of Jesus.

---

63. On which see Martin, *James*, lxxvi–lxxviii.

64. Ong, *Multilingual Jesus*, 198–214.

65. See ibid., 214–17, for details on the import of the cross-linguistic interaction.

66. Pilch and Malina, eds., *Handbook of Biblical Social Values*.

67. See discussion in Davids, *Epistle of James*, 10–13.

However, a specifically Jewish-Christian community located within the Mediterranean environment would be doubly marked, first for its Jewishness and second for its minority status within that Jewish matrix. To what extent, though, do the epistle's themes and lexicon set this sub-group apart as a counter-culture? The epistle is a suitable place to query this since, as James Adamson captured it, James's epistle "takes us better than any other NT book back to the infancy of the Christian Church, to the purple dawn of Christian enthusiasm and the first glow of Christian love."[68] The writer talks of God the Creator who is good (1:16–17) and includes a Christology embodied in a phrase like "our glorious Lord Jesus Christ." He discusses deeply embedded human sinfulness, refers to a παρουσία (5:7) of God and links it with judgment (5:1–11)—this, and more, directed to people swept up in trials and testing (1:2–4), perhaps circumstances linked in some way to the testimony James sealed with his own blood.[69] If one accepts with Martin that James was based in Jerusalem[70] and was a "Jewish Christian pietist and leader caught in a delicate position,"[71] then Halliday's concept of anti-society remains a viable consideration.

Also interesting in these identifications is the application of Halliday's characterization of language as a "vehicle for resocialization" that has a "reality-generating force" and the "power to create and maintain social hierarchy,"[72] given that James conveys much community-directed paraenesis that rails not at the unregenerate so much as the refinement of poorly-behaving insiders/believers who are summoned, among other things, to avoid double-mindedness (1:8), to calibrate their tempers and tongues (1:13–20; 3:1–12), to cease their interpersonal conflicts (4:1–12), and to renounce materialism and social injustice (5:1–6). In other words, James's subject matter is consciously and unrelentingly *in*-house as it lunges at perceptions and behaviors that fall short of noble standards of Jewish-Christian piety and from which faithful believers must distinguish themselves.

---

68. Adamson, *Epistle of James*, 21.

69. Josephus, *Ant.* 20.197–203; cf. *War* 4.314–25.

70. Martin, *James*, lxvii–lxix.

71. Ibid., lxviii.

72. Halliday, "Anti-Languages," 574–75.

The Language of James's Epistle

However, even if the concept of anti-society seems commensurate with the societal situation, we must question next whether the epistle's vocabulary (including its idioms) offers evidence of Halliday's thesis, including such things as relexicalization, originality, and "liveliness." To be sure, its language style has been described as typical of Greek koine, though with "some ambitions toward rhetorical flourish," being not as "idiosyncratic as the Greek of Paul and far more polished that that of John . . . comparable in quality, if less complex in texture, to that of Hebrews."[73] The epistle's wording betrays affinities with the LXX, sometimes citing it directly (e.g., 2:8–11, 23; 4:6) and other times alluding to it (e.g., 1:11; 2:25; 5:4–5, 17, 20). There is frequent parataxis and asyndeton, and use of the articular infinitive, which taken together with other features may indicate Semitic language influence. Sentences tend toward shortness, and its paraenesis is supported by a hortatory style, with roughly half of its 108 verses containing a total of 59 imperatives. Luke Timothy Johnson has also noted that James's rhetorical style occasionally includes poetic meter, pleonasms, alliteration, and other forms of wordplay.[74]

Moreover, with regard to the lexis of the epistle, Stanley Porter addressed the question of whether or not James's use of δίψυχος (lit. "double-souled"), which makes two appearances in James (1:8; 4:8), can properly be called a uniquely "Christian" word.[75] Though he did not raise the anti-language question *per se* in this article, he documented how this word and its cognates recurred in Christian writings from the late first through twelfth centuries while seeming never to be in secular usage prior to, nor during, those centuries. Porter's cautious conclusion, leaning on "the evidence as a whole *at this stage of investigation*" (italics mine), is that the word δίψυχος is "probably one originating with the book of James,"[76] its author being "a creative user of the Greek language, probably himself inventing a lexical item to express a concept he wished to grammaticalize in a single lexical form, which had subsequent widespread though exclusive use within a Christian linguistic environment."[77]

---

73. Johnson, *Letter of James*, 7.

74. Ibid., 8.

75. Porter, "Is *dipsuchos* a 'Christian' Word," 469–98.

76. Ibid., 498.

77. Ibid., 474.

Especially helpful for our purposes are Porter's establishing criteria, namely, whether one can establish that a word originated within the New Testament and its writers while being conspicuously absent from pagan sources. As he noted, subsequent evidence may reveal surprises that upset a tentative conclusion, and even apart from such, a unique word or idiom in James or anyone else may represent nothing more than idiolect.[78] Porter's cautionary flag (beware what lurks in a yet-to-be-identified bin), combined with the fact that a word like δίψυχος would be more properly classified as "neologism" than "relexicalization," leaves the anti-language and James question still unsettled.

The next field ripe for the hunt is the use of inter-sentential linkages. Johnson observed that a number of James's sentences are linked via catchwords, i.e., a word in one sentence is repeated, usually in a different grammatical form, in the subsequent sentence (e.g., θρησκός/θρησκεία [1:26–27]; κρίνεσθαι/κρίσεως [2:12–13]; καρπῶν/καρπός [3:17–18]; κριθῆτε/κριτής [5:9a–b, 12]; ἐπιστρέψῃ/ἐπιστρέψας [5:19–20]).[79] This technique is likely mnemonic, as are the frequent occurrences of alliteration and a few instances of rhyming and of punning, and it supports a Greek original that would lend itself well to an oral didactic method. Add to this James's frequent use of vocative address forms (1:2, 16, 19; 2:1, 5, 14; 3:1, 10, 12; 5:12, 19), "my (beloved) brothers," along with second-person address forms, use of an imaginary interlocutor (who is sometimes criticized), the posing of curt questions promptly answered or rhetorical questions arranged in fast staccato style, and it is apparent that James practices a dialogic style bordering on diatribe.

Additionally, it should be observed that there are a number of terms that recur in James's epistle. The first of these is τέλειος (1:4a, b; 1:17, 25; 3:2). It occurs only nineteen times in the New Testament, and is used five times in this one letter, typically designating the mature or developed person in contrast to the double-minded (δίψυχος, 1:8; 4:8), and indicating that mature people produce a perfect outcome to their efforts (1:4). Another word of central importance to James is "wisdom" (σοφία) that specifically emanates "from above" (ἄνωθεν, 1:17; 3:15, 17)—something to be expected of a writing that shows affinity with Old Testament wisdom literature. To Jewish ears, the adverb would have been acceptably redundant; to Greek, perhaps it was viewed in antithesis to classical/

78. Ibid., 472.

79. Johnson, *Letter of James*, 8–9.

cultural tradition. Furthermore, James is ripe with metaphor and imagery: people can be tossed like waves (1:6) or withered under a relentless sun (1:10–11); faith can be dead (2:26); one's tongue/speech can be a fire-inducing spark (3:5–6), fresh or bitter water (3:11), or sweet like fruit (3:12); human life is like vanishing mist (4:14) and its wealth like moth-eaten clothing (5:2); and, wealth corrodes and will eat one's flesh like fire (5:3). James's analogies include the power of the tongue exceeding one's ability to control horses (3:3) or guide ships (3:4) or tame wild animals (3:7), while there is much to be learned from farmers who wait for rain (5:7), as well as from the exemplary behavior such as that seen in Old Testament heroes (2:21–25; 5:10–11, 17–18). These analogies of James often carried vivid imagery, such as God giving birth (1:18), demons shuddering (1:19), tongues that were on fire like Gehenna (3:6), and inner desires that waged warfare (4:1); or they were framed paradoxically, as in the idea of boasting from a humble position (1:10). There is some evidence here for anti-language, but a firm verdict is hardly forthcoming.

So we return to consider James's means of persuasion. Appraisal Theory (of which Dvorak is a recent exercise)[80] identifies three operative sub-systems: *attitude*, involving the resources for expressing feelings (and includes judgment and appreciation); *engagement*, which includes resources for interacting with interlocutors; and *graduation*, which includes up- or down-scaling in the intensity of propositions.[81] These coalesce in the practice of power and solidarity. The classic New Testament epistolary tokens of power and authority—affinity with Christ who equips and commissions representatives—find their realization in James's explicit identification as θεοῦ καὶ κυρίου Ἰησοῦ Χριστοῦ δοῦλος ("of God and of [the] Lord Christ Jesus, servant") in the opening verse, not to mention his implicit reputation for leadership in Palestinian Judaeo-Christianity. The orientation of the entire epistle around the two axes of Jewish piety—faith in God and righteous behavior directed toward one's fellow man—taken along with the (above mentioned) 59 imperatives in just 108 verses, underscore the strongly paraenetic tone of the letter and speak volumes about assumed authority. If we add to these James's citations of the Jewish Scriptures (Lev 19:18 in 2:8; Exod 20:14 in 2:11; Gen

---

80. Dvorak, "Prodding with Prosody," 85–120. But see also Dvorak "Interpersonal Metafunction," his doctoral dissertation, which was the first, and still most thorough, appropriation and application of Appraisal Theory for Hellenistic Greek.

81. On the development of the Appraisal Theory for English see esp. Martin and White, *Language of Evaluation*.

15:6 in 2:23; Num 23:19[?] in 3:5; Prov 3:34 in 4:6) as he draws on the divine word to strengthen immediate counsel, James ranks high on the index of persuasiveness.

Yet James also breathes solidarity, not least in the form of fraternal appeal, notably ἀδελφοί [μου] ("[my] brothers," 1:2; 2:1, 14; 3:1; 4:11; 5:7, 9, 12, 19) along with the commonality fostered by first person pronominals such as "our" father Abraham (2:21), "we all stumble" (3:2) and "we bless" (3:9), and by second-person direct appeals such as "you see" (2:22, 24), "who among you is wise?" (3:13), and "Come now, you who. . ." (4:13; 5:1), all of which are mechanisms for linking writer with hearer/reader persuasively. Taken together, what makes a "persuasive message" persuasive, says Dvorak, is its strong appeal to core values set into a highly cohesive form of solidarity, even when framed in an unequal power relation (e.g., an apostolic circle member speaking to 'rank-and-file' believers).[82]

James's language style is demonstrably lively, colorful, vivid, and memorable, an example of what Halliday would call "verbal art," parallel to (but not as macabre) as Australian convict jargon, which pictured execution by hanging with such imaginative phrases as "to take a leap in the dark," "to be in a deadly suspense," "to have a hearty choke [artichoke] and caper sauce," or "to piss when you can't whistle"—speech Robert Hughes described as "brusque, canting defiance."[83] The language of James, on its own terms, is fast-paced and invasively imaginative.

CONCLUSIONS ON JAMES AND ANTI-LANGUAGE

So the language of James's epistle shows affinities with Halliday's anti-language construct when it comes to sociology: the early Jewish-Christians James addressed were marginalized and culturally non-conformist. On that score, the anti-language concept has traction. But on the linguistic flank, Halliday's narrowly derived definition comes up short, linguist and apostolic leader appearing to be connected by thread rather than bound by rope. The tenuous application of anti-language to the Epistle of James is clarified further by comparison with Beier, who queried whether sixteenth- and seventeenth-century English underworld canting (which he also labels "underworld slang" and "criminal argot") should properly be identified as "anti-language" at all, or "simply another instance of a

82. Dvorak, "Prodding with Prosody," 88–90.

83. Hughes, *Fatal Shore*, 33.

jargon, a specialized vocabulary."[84] He critiqued what he regarded as less-than-vigorous research methods that proceeded from the *a priori* assumption that canting was actually spoken, and that it was static in form and meaning; and he argued that "Until 1985 no student of canting had ever established from sources other than literary ones that it was in fact *spoken* by anyone in early modern England."[85] And though he allowed that, on the basis of judicial records, it was in fact "used in the underworld . . . the argot [being] . . . a learned vocabulary and a tool of the trades of thieving and begging"[86] and pertained to "a criminal world cut off from respectable society that was urban rather than rural,"[87] he nevertheless admitted that "Even non-criminal uses of jargon can express alienation from a hegemonic order,"[88] citing a study of similar speech today used by mostly white South African secondary school students who aim to defy prevailing social norms. Beier's objections facilitate a cautious contrast:

> There is no doubt that the literature of roguery and its lists of cant vocabulary fostered the belief that an anti-society of criminals stood ready to destroy good order in sixteenth- and seventeenth- century England. But the terms "create," "demarcate" and "construct" impart a degree of teleology that is perhaps unwarranted. The idea that canting developed because it served a purpose is partly true. But above all it assisted the canting elements to disguise their speech and crimes . . . In the process boundaries were demarcated, but we should be wary of reifying the experience of criminality, just as we should that of class . . . [C]anting would be more accurately described as a counter-experience rather than a counter-reality.[89]

The diachronic details of Beier's comparative statistics (something that might be considered with respect to early Jewish-Christian writings if sufficient literary evidence could be assembled) support the impression that cant was gradually going mainstream and becoming jargon in wider usage. A cautionary conclusion when it comes to something so strident as underworld cant may be wisest when one considers James. If

84. Beier, "Anti-language or Jargon," 64.

85. Ibid., 69, emphasis mine.

86. Ibid., 73.

87. Ibid., 89.

88. Ibid., 90.

89. Ibid., 91.

the anti-language package fails to match even a criminal product, then it will prove even more challenging to align it with redemptive paraenesis, so if the glove doesn't fit one shouldn't commit.

Thus, we can bring these considerations together under four headings. First, although it is possible to construe the nascent Christian community of first-century Jewish Palestine as an anti-society, some of its people may have been quite integrated (e.g., at Jerusalem, and out of necessity) even if others were insular (e.g., Ebionites). Still, its doctrinal beliefs and social values were incessantly counter-cultural; their Christology put them at odds with prominent exponents of the Jewish tradition from which they had sprung while their social standards triggered pushback from many Greco-Roman neighbors, as Roman historians have amply recounted. This part of the early church was opposed to majority *and* minority communities in their immediate and greater environments, and this would have made for an uncomfortable opposition with complex implications. Halliday's view that anti-language is defensive in its maintenance of an alternate reality, and offensive in its protest against prevailing majority standards, seems like a possible match with James, but not necessarily with Palestinian believers on the whole. The match is imperfect, if not messy.

Second, Halliday conceived of anti-language as "the means of realization of a subjective reality: not merely expressing it, but actively creating and maintaining it."[90] However, this is the stuff of language ideology in general; after all, which language choices do *not* actualize perceptions and priorities? The lively language that permeates James's epistle is unlike that of thieves and vagabonds even if it is replete with vivid metaphor and rhetorical technique. It does not seem possible to characterize the epistle as overlexicalized, or even to find a way to measure that when this text-out-of-context is relatively short. This appears to be the greatest gap between theoretical essay and practical epistle.

Third, one must be cautious when attempting to construct a bridge between esoteric underworld argot and the speech of a self-perceived morally upright community, even if they do share as a common goal lexicalization that fits the values and central defining topics of their respective communities. One wishes that Halliday had diversified his paradigm cases, for this might have adjusted the shape of his conception and surely would have made it more applicable to other language communities. The

90. Halliday, "Anti-Languages," 576.

hallmark feature of anti-language, a distinct vocabulary, is also the stuff of professional specialists, teen cliques, military personnel, and academics. The "verbal art" he saw in underworld jargon is visible in the liveliness of James' language, but how far the parallel can be drawn is unclear. It would be preferable to construe a code continuum that ranges from standard daily speech with its various registers and styles to jargon and over to folk phrasings, then over to cant, and finally on to diametrically-opposed codes (anti-language). The oral world of James's community is hard to gauge through writing, especially when the primary source has only 1740 Greek words. More importantly, James's words surely were meant to embrace outside hearers winsomely and openly—something underworld communities rarely attempt.

Fourth, there is in James a concern for maintenance of a new identity and, to use Halliday's language, he offers a "reconstruction of the individual and society" with an "alternate reality";[91] his language is a "vehicle of such resocialization" and presents a "reality-generating force . . . [with] power to create and maintain social hierarchy."[92] Admittedly, it cannot be said that James's speech was "no one's mother tongue,"[93] as it has been judged well within the range of typical Koine. Yet this rural Galilean had become situated in the historical city of his ancestral faith, only to find himself *contra mundum* with regard to Jews *and* Greeks. The vehicle for galvanizing opposition was language that captured the truths of an emergent counter-community, but "lively" is not the same as "anti-."

CONSIDERATIONS FOR ONGOING STUDY

So it seems preferable at this stage of the game to approach the concept of anti-language like that of diglossia: the narrow paradigm articulated in a seminal essay will need to flex if it is going to have a chance at illuminating imperfectly matched speech situations.[94] If the discussion of the language of the Epistle of James is going to progress with reference to the anti-language construct, at least two greater contexts will need to be advanced. The first relates to the matter of linguistic criticism, which by

91. Ibid., 573.

92. Ibid., 574–75.

93. Ibid., 576.

94. For discussion of this need for flexibility in the application of Fergusonian diglossia, see Watt, "Current Landscape of Diglossia Studies," 18–36; Watt, "Some Implications of Bilingualism," 9–27; Watt, "Living Language Environment," 30–48.

its nature involves cross-linguistic considerations. Whenever one moves beyond description and aims to delve into the perceptions and motivations of an original speaker/writer (especially if that person is no longer available for interview) it is necessary to keep in view the apparatus of language performance and cognition. What is understood to occur in modern living language situations *may* apply to an ancient one and be useful for its analysis, so long as contextual factors align. The value of modern linguistics is evident in its diversity of theories and methodologies, and in its reach at balancing consideration of the phenomena of a particular language (or ancient text) by juxtaposing it with other languages. As Porter notes, linguistic analysis often differs from classical philology because of its strong empirical base (which has been advanced by the potentials of computer assisted research), its concern with the systematicity and structure of language, its particular interest in synchronic issues (albeit with appreciation for diachronic influences), and its descriptive freedoms (in contrast with prescriptive judgment).[95] Whether the anti-language concept survives will be up to scholars who decide which constructs have been sufficiently helpful for understanding modern situations so they may possibly see retroactive application to ancient ones.

The second matter of context, located within the first, has been out on the table for about three decades, and that pertains to language ideology, which addresses the aims of speaker-writers in creating linkages between language and such things as personal identity, morality, and social institutions,[96] and institutions such as religious groups and churches, which on their part rely on the ideologization of language. We noted above that the author of the Epistle of James indeed expresses his ideological views via such mechanisms as hortatory, metaphoric, and other rhetorical expressions; however, whether these classify as anti-language will depend on whether scholars find application for the concept to communities *other than the underworld*. Though counter-cultural thieves maintain their separate identity by constructing an alternate reality with supporting language, this does not mean that all counter-cultural communities will generate anti-language in order to do so.

---

95. Porter, *Linguistic Analysis*, 83–84.

96. As noted by Woolard and Schieffelin, "Language Ideology," 55, and quoted previously.

What options other than anti-language are promising, given the apparent interests James pursued that included solidarity of believers set apart from the world around them? It is often argued that the theme of James is perfection, a quite reasonable conclusion given the frequent mention of "maturity/completion" using τελ-words in the epistle (as indicated above). Maturity involves, among other things, recalibrating one's relationship with the κόσμος, understood as location as well as system. Richard Bauckham showed that one of the ways this is accomplished is through a change of worldview with reference to wealth and status: "Since material goods and social status were connected with honor . . . the poor were generally treated with contempt in the ancient world," noting by way of contrast that "James' accusation that they [believers] are dishonoring or shaming the poor (2.6) reverses the evaluations of the dominant social values."[97]

Or one might consider the role of holiness in James's epistle, the concept carrying for Jews and Jewish Christians implications of purity and separation. The concept would encourage identification and solidarity with other pure persons even as it promoted some degree of separation from the world and its impurities. To this end, Darian Lockett has taken up the seminal work of Mary Douglas[98] in support of his contention that "James employs the line-drawing language of purity/pollution to map out a proper construal of reality—labeling the values associated with ὁ κόσμος as impure or 'dangerous,'" in contrast with a God-ordained worldview, which is pure and undefiled (e.g., Jas 1:27).[99] He noted that, "even if it [purity language] is metaphorical, such language should be understood as an integral part of the author's construction and perception of reality—a distinct means of charting social and theological territory."[100]

Consequently, it appears that even though James is demarcating a counter-cultural lifestyle for a distinct people, concepts identified by words like "maturity," "purity," and "integrity" were being indicated by lexical diversity but hardly by *re*lexicalization. Even though James surely aimed to do what Halliday had contended anti-language accomplished—forming in-group solidarity along with separation of social spheres—the ancient writer appears to have done this using standard terminology.

97. Bauckham, *James*, 189.
98. Douglas, *Purity and Danger*.
99. Lockett, "Unstained by the World," 73.
100. Ibid., 51.

Either the concept of anti-language has to be re-construed along expanded lines with a measurement standard for gauging relexicalization, or other rhetorical mechanisms and interactional dynamics will render the construct superfluous to the discussion.

BIBLIOGRAPHY

Abegg, Martin G., Jr. "Hebrew Language." In *Dictionary of New Testament Background*, edited by Craig A. Evans and Stanley E. Porter, 459–63. Downers Grove, IL: InterVarsity, 2000.

Adamson, James. *The Epistle of James*. NICNT. Grand Rapids: Eerdmans, 1976.

Bauckham, Richard. *James: Wisdom of James, Disciple of Jesus the Sage*. New Testament Readings. London: Routledge, 1999.

Beier, Lee. "Anti-language or Jargon? Canting in the English Underworld in the Sixteenth and Seventeenth Centuries." In *Languages and Jargons: Contributions to a Social History of Language*, edited by Peter Burke and Roy Porter, 64–101. Cambridge: Polity, 1995.

Burke, Peter, and Roy Porter, eds. *Languages and Jargons: Contributions to a Social History of Language*. Cambridge: Polity, 1995.

Charlesworth, James H. *The Pesharim and Qumran History*. Grand Rapids: Eerdmans, 2002.

Cross, Frank Moore. "Some Notes on a Generation of Qumran Studies." In *The Madrid Qumran Congress: Proceedings of the International Congress on the Dead Sea Scrolls, Madrid 18–21 March, 1991*, edited by Julio Trebolle Barrera and Luis Vegas Montaner, 4–5. Vol. 1. STDJ 11. Leiden: Brill, 1992.

Davids, Peter H. *The Epistle of James*. NIGTC. Grand Rapids, MI: Eerdmans, 1982.

Doriani, Daniel M. *James*. Reformed Expository Commentary. Phillipsburg, NJ: P&R, 2007.

Douglas, Mary. *Purity and Danger: An Analysis of the Concepts of Pollution and Taboo*. London: Routledge & Kegan Paul, 1966.

Dvorak, James D. "'Prodding with Prosody': Persuasion and Social Influence through the Lens of Appraisal Theory." *BAGL* 4 (2015) 85–120.

———. "The Interpersonal Metafunction in 1 Corinthians 1–4: The Tenor of Toughness." PhD diss., McMaster Divinity College, 2012.

Halliday, M. A. K. "Language as Social Semiotic: Towards a General Sociolinguistic Theory." In *The First LACUS Forum*, edited by Adam Makkai and Valerie Becker Makkai, 169–201. Columbia, SC: Hornbeam, 1975.

———. "Anti-Languages." *AA* 78 (1976) 570–84.

Harman, Thomas. *A Caveat or Warening for Common Cursetories Vulgarely Called Vagabones*. London: Wylliam Gryffith. 1567.

Heller-Roazen, Daniel. *Dark Tongues: The Art of Rogues and Riddlers*. New York: Zone, 2013.

Hezser, Catherine. *Jewish Literacy in Roman Palestine*. TSAJ 81. Tübingen: Mohr Siebeck, 2001.

Hughes, Robert. *Fatal Shore: The Epic of Australia's Founding*. New York: Vintage, 1988.

Irvine, Judith. "When Talk Isn't Cheap: Language and Political Economy." *AE* 16 (1989) 248–67.

Johnson, Luke Timothy. *The Letter of James.* AB 37A. New York: Doubleday, 1995.

Kochman, Thomas. *Rappin' and Stylin' Out: Communication in Urban Black America.* Urbana, IL: University of Illinois Press, 1972.

Lamb, David A. *Text, Context and the Johannine Community. A Sociolinguistic Analysis of the Johannine Writings.* LNTS 477. London: Bloomsbury T. & T. Clark, 2014.

Lockett, Darian. "'Unstained by the World': Purity and Pollution as an Indicator of Cultural Interaction in the Letter of James." In *Reading James with New Eyes: Methodological Reassessments of the Letter of James,* edited by Robert L. Webb and John S. Kloppenborg, 49–74. LNTS 342. London: T. & T. Clark International, 2007.

Malina, Bruce J. *The Gospel of John in Sociolinguistic Perspective: Protocol of the Forty-eighth Colloquy, 11 March 1984.* Edited by Herman C. Waetjen. Vol. 48. Berkeley, CA: Center for Hermeneutical Studies in Hellenistic and Modern Culture, 1985.

———. *Christian Origins and Cultural Anthropology: Practical Models for Biblical Interpretation.* Atlanta: John Knox, 1986.

Mallik, Bhaktiprasad. *Language of the Underworld of West Bengal.* Research Series 76. Calcutta: Sanskrit College, 1972.

Martin, J. R., and P. R. R. White. *The Language of Evaluation: Appraisal in English.* New York: Palgrave MacMillan, 2005.

Martin, Ralph P. *James.* WBC 48. Waco, TX: Word, 1988.

Ong, Hughson T. *The Multilingual Jesus and the Sociolinguistic World of the New Testament.* LBS 12. Leiden: Brill, 2015.

Pilch, John J., and Bruce J. Malina, eds. *Handbook of Biblical Social Values.* Peabody, MA: Hendrickson, 2000.

Podgorecki, Adam. "'Second Life' and Its Implications." Mimeograph, 1973.

Poirier, John C. "The Linguistic Situation in Jewish Palestine in Late Antiquity." *JGRChJ* 4 (2007) 55–134.

Porter, Stanley E. "Is *dipsuchos* (James 1,8; 4,8) a 'Christian' Word?" *Biblica* 71 (1990) 469–98.

———. "Linguistic Criticism." In *Dictionary of Biblical Criticism and Interpretation,* edited by Stanley E. Porter, 199–202. London: Routledge, 2007.

———. *Linguistic Analysis of the Greek New Testament: Studies in Tools, Methods, and Practice.* Grand Rapids: Baker Academic, 2015.

Rabin, Chaim. *A Short History of the Hebrew Language.* Jerusalem: Haomanim, 1974.

Rendsburg, Gary A. "Qumran Hebrew as an Anti-Language." Accompanying notes to Lecture 21 in the Course Guidebook for *The Dead Sea Scrolls.* Great Courses Series. The Teaching Co., 2010.

———. "Language at Qumran (with a Trial Cut [1QS])." In *The Dead Sea Scrolls at 60: The Scholarly Contributions of NYU Faculty and Alumni,* edited by Lawrence H. Schiffman and Shani Tzoref, 217–46. Leiden: Brill, 2010.

Schniedewind, William M. "Qumran Hebrew as Antilanguage." *JBL* 118 (1999) 235–52.

Tov, Emmanuel. "The Orthography and Language of the Hebrew Scrolls Found at Qumran and the Origin of These Scrolls." *Textus* 13 (1986) 31–57.

Vaux, James Hardy. *Memoirs of James Hardy Vaux.* 2 vols. London: John Murray, 1819.

Watt, Jonathan M. "The Current Landscape of Diglossia Studies: The Diglossic Continuum in the First-Century Palestine." In *Diglossia and Other Topics in New Testament Linguistics,* edited by Stanley E. Porter, 18–36. JSNTSup 193; SNTG 6. Sheffield: Sheffield Academic, 2000.

―――. "Some Implications of Bilingualism for New Testament Exegesis." In *The Language of the New Testament: Context, History, and Development*, edited by Stanley E. Porter and Andrew W. Pitts, 9–27. ECHC 3; LBS 6. Leiden, Brill, 2013.

―――. "The Living Language Environment of Acts 21:27–40." *BAGL* 4 (2015) 30–48.

Weitzman, Steven. "Why Did the Qumran Community Write in Hebrew?" *JAOS* 119 (1999) 35–45.

Woolard, K. A., and B. B. Schieffelin. "Language Ideology." *ARA* 23 (1994) 55–82.

11

Conclusion

Linguistic Exegesis of the Epistle of James with Reference to Exegetical Commentary Writing

Zachary K. Dawson and James D. Dvorak

INTRODUCTION

IN 2013, THE SAME year Dale Allison published his commentary on James, Scot McKnight published an essay in a festschrift honoring Grant Osborne in which he surveyed many of the major commentaries on James published over the last century.[1] His evaluation of all of them was overwhelmingly positive (including Dibelius's), and he expressed the opinion that "there are never enough" commentaries as long as there are "independent and fertile and careful minds to do serious work on the books of the Bible."[2] Meanwhile, in another part of the same volume, Stanley E. Porter wrote an essay in which he surveyed sixteen commentaries in major exegetical commentary series (ICC, NIGTC, WBC, and BECNT), four each for four different New Testament books (Matthew, Romans, James, and Revelation), with the purpose of evaluating the linguistic competence of each commentary. One key criterion in Porter's evaluative scheme was the extent to which a given commentary critically engaged and/or utilized "linguistically appropriate methods" in the

---

1. McKnight, "James and His Commentaries," 405–19. McKnight begins with J. B. Mayor's commentary published in 1913 and surveys twenty other commentaries chronologically, ending with his own in 2011.

2. McKnight, "James and His Commentaries," 405.

analysis of the biblical text in its original language.[3] Porter recognizes that it would be unfair to evaluate whether or not commentaries that were written in, say, the 1800s were "linguistically appropriate" by what qualifies as such in the twenty-first century. In an attempt to avoid this anachronism he creates a framework in which he divides the history of Greek grammatical study into three approximate periods of time: (1) the rationalist period, which lasted up until around 1885, of which Winer's grammar is representative; (2) the comparative-historical period, characterized by comparisons to classical Greek, discovered papyri, historical origins, supposed Semitic influence, and the like; and (3) the modern linguistic period, which in biblical studies began in 1961 with James Barr's *The Semantics of Biblical Language*, but also includes works involving discourse analysis in addition to other linguistic topics such as verbal aspect, lexicography, and other matters.[4] Porter then assesses whether and to what extent each commentary critically engaged "the best scholarship available to them at the time of composition," and how, if at all, such interaction impacted their interpretation of the biblical text.[5]

Porter's conclusion was not as optimistic as McKnight's. Porter found that "whereas earlier commentators virtually always showed themselves linguistically informed of the latest and most important work in Greek . . . language study, the same cannot be said of later commentators."[6] The commentaries on James were no exception. Of the four commentaries on James that Porter surveyed, McCartney's 2009 commentary received the harshest criticism because, apart from a few articles, "he seems to know of no other linguistically informed works."[7] This critique counteracts McKnight's welcoming invitation for "careful minds" to continue writing commentaries because, at least with respect to being *linguisti-*

3. Porter, "Linguistic Competence," 38–51. Other criteria included the style and presentation of information (e.g., terseness v. verbosity), the use of non-English commentaries and other sources, and the use of original languages (ibid., 33).

4. Porter, "Linguistic Competence," 39–40. See also, Campbell, *Advances*, 29–50, who describes the same history, but uses less descriptive and even confusing labels to mark off time periods. For instance, he names one period "Modern Linguistics" and the following period "The Modern Era." The confusion comes from mixing the history of advances in the wider field of linguistics with the use of linguistics in biblical Greek studies, which has usually lagged several decades behind. For this reason Porter's description is more useful.

5. Porter, "Linguistic Competence," 38–39.

6. Ibid., 51.

7. Porter, "Linguistic Competence," 50. See McCartney, *James*.

cally minded, commentators have shown a trend of becoming increasingly less competent, and this will not have a positive impact on biblical scholarship. Admittedly, most of the commentaries McKnight surveyed were categorized as historical-critical and were evaluated as such, but even if the method used in an exegetical commentary is historical-critical, this does not excuse the failure to adequately describe the Greek text in relation to the current state of Greek studies, especially since exegetical commentaries purport to be based on the Greek text itself.

If Allison's replacement of James Hardy Ropes in the ICC series had appeared a year earlier, then both Porter and McKnight likely would have considered it in Osborne's festschrift. Instead, the ICC commentary Porter surveyed was Ropes's now century-old commentary on James, which he found to be quite linguistically competent for its time.[8] Allison's 790-page commentary, on the other hand, has yet to be evaluated according to comparable criteria, and given its length and the enduring reputation of the ICC series, it would be interesting to see how it measures up with its predecessor and how it compares with the trend in declining linguistic competence that Porter details. Several reviews of Allison's commentary have been written over the past five years, some even giving passing and uncritical praise to Allison's attention to grammatical detail;[9] however, the verdict is still out on whether Allison brings the latest advances in biblical Greek studies to bear on the Epistle of James. Therefore, as a means of demonstrating the exegetical payoff of the various essays of this volume it seemed suitable to us to bring them into dialogue with the practice of contemporary exegetical commentary writing as represented by Allison's recent commentary on James.

A LINGUISTIC EVALUATION OF ALLISON'S COMMENTARY ON JAMES

Allison's Use of Linguistic Resources

Some initial observations of how Allison's commentary compares with Ropes's earlier ICC commentary on James can orient this evaluation. In his commentary, Ropes makes frequent reference to the latest Greek grammarians of his day, including Moulton, Blass and Debrunner, and

8. Porter, "Linguistic Competence," 41.

9. Darian Lockett's review, for instance, makes the grand statement that Allison's "detailed study of James's Greek grammar and style rivals Joseph Mayor's magisterial commentary first published in 1892" (Review of *Epistle of James*, 446).

Burton, all of whom had published their grammars within two decades of Ropes's commentary. When we compare Allison's commentary in this respect the results are revealing. From the date of publication, Allison does not cite a single Greek grammar published within the last fifty years. The most recent grammar cited is the second edition of C. F. D. Moule's *An Idiom Book of New Testament Greek* published in 1959, a grammar that was 54 years old when Allison's commentary came out.[10] Further, Allison makes use of BDF more than any other grammar; it would seem that BDF is the authority in his eyes. The only other grammar consulted at all in Allison's commentary is the second edition of A. T. Robertson's grammar (1914), which was published twenty years before its final fourth edition (1934). Thus, Allison only consults grammarians who worked in the comparative-historical period of Greek studies, and then only selectively and not always with the latest edition of the works. It would appear, then, that Allison is either unaware or unconcerned with the advances in Greek grammar since the turn of the modern linguistic era.

The linguistic competence displayed in Allison's work can also be assessed by observing the reference works he chooses to use (and not use). The reference works he cites most often are BDAG and *TDNT*; there is no reference in the commentary to any other New Testament lexicons such as Louw and Nida, which presents a much more linguistically sophisticated approach to lexicography than the two reference works Allison favors.[11] This is somewhat surprising given that Allison's approach to detailing the structure and cohesion of units in James (no definition of what constitutes a "unit" is provided) is based on how words "draw on" or "connect back to" other uses of the same term or general topic.[12] If this is to be a main criterion for identifying cohesion in James, then the Louw-Nida lexicon, being based on semantic domains would have been a valuable resource to group lexemes together, rather than simply identifying the use of duplicated lexemes and relying on one's own intuition on which words have related meanings and which ones do not. The method used in Stanley E. Porter's essay on cohesion in James contrasts with Al-

10. Even though Funk's translation was published in 1961, we still consider Moule's grammar to be the most recent for the very reason that BDF is a translation of Blass and Debrunner's older German grammar.

11. The only other reference works Allison avails himself of are two additional lexicons, one on the Greek of the Septuagint and the other on the Greek in Patristic literature. See Muraoka, *Greek-English Lexicon*; Lampe, *Patristic Greek Lexicon*.

12. See, for example, Allison, *Epistle of James*, 165.

lison's commentary here because Porter uses Louw and Nida's semantic domains in his linguistic method for calculating the degree of cohesion in the text. Because Porter applies a method using the most up-to-date resources, he is able to demonstrate by means of his linguistic method and the credibility of his data that the entire Epistle of James contains a high degree of cohesion.

Allison should not be critiqued *per se* for using Kittel's *TDNT*; he does not appear to commit the theological fallacies that Barr identified,[13] and which continue to plague much New Testament scholarship today. His primary use of the dictionary is to gain quick access to instances of word usages in Greek sources to survey their range of senses. Despite being dated, *TDNT* can still be a useful resource in this regard, and in no way does Allison restrict himself to the sources referenced in this dictionary. His thoroughness in cataloguing usages of words and phrases in Greek, Hebrew, and Aramaic primary sources is quite extensive, although he has no explicit method for discriminating which sources are relevant and why. Nevertheless, this is where methods of intertextual analysis are useful and even necessary for explaining how words and phrases relate to other texts in a speech community. Xiaxia E. Xue and Ji Hoe Kim's essays in particular demonstrate that when writers use words and phrases they depend on, respond to, or in some way take into account the thematic meanings that such language has accumulated from other texts, along with the values and beliefs with which they are associated.

Allison's Linguistic Competence Demonstrated in His Exegesis

When analyzing the way in which Allison comments on grammatical details throughout his commentary, there is a very clear agenda that emerges: he incessantly tries to demonstrate the Semitic character of James's Greek and goes to great lengths to discover allusions and parallels to other Jewish sources that show that James was steeped in Jewish tradition. The reason for this is established in the initial matters of the commentary. Conforming to the tradition of commentary writing, Allison starts by addressing the typical areas of discussion such as author, date, genre, etc. In doing so, he establishes a number of positions that he then seeks to support in the exegetical part of the commentary. Allison sets out to argue that James is a pseudepigraphon written between 100–120 CE by

13. Barr, *Semantics*, 206–62.

a Christian Jew.[14] Allison also takes the view first argued by James Hope Moulton that, contrary to popular thought, the letter of James was written to Jews rather than to Christians.[15] The content of the letter as well as the style and grammatical features of James's Greek help to identify the letter's *Sitz im Leben* as an environment highly influenced by Jewish tradition and Semitic languages. According to Allison, James is written mostly in idiomatic Greek, but "Wifstrand was justified to conclude: 'the author was a man who knew ordinary *koine* Greek as it was written by people of some education, but as soon as he felt a need to rise into a higher stylistic sphere, he had no Greek mode to follow, but had recourse to the higher style that he was really master of, the Semitic one.'"[16] Thus, Allison sides with Wifstrand that James's Greek is best characterized as "the language of the Hellenistic synagogue."[17] This position then drives how Allison addresses grammatical matters in the commentary; he often attempts to explain unnatural Greek[18] by translating the Greek into a Hebrew equivalent followed by a search for such equivalent phrases in Jewish literature to support the view that James is writing in "the language of the Hellenistic synagogue." The following is an example from Allison's commentary of Jas 1:13 of just such a case:

> λέγω (Jas: 7x) introduces authoritative citations in 2.23; 4.5, 6, but here, as in 2.14 and 4.13, it prefaces faulty opinions. Although μηδεὶς λεγέτω is a Greek idiom otherwise absent from Jewish sources, the Hebrew equivalent, אל יאמר אדם, is attested, and James' μηδεὶς λεγέτω is the rough equivalent of μὴ εἴπῃς (= אל תאמר), which commonly prefaces defective remarks in the LXX wisdom literature, including Ecclus 15.11–12, which likely lies behind our text.[19]

14. Allison, *Epistle of James*, 28–29.

15. Allison spends ten pages discussing a range of various views about the audience of James, taking time to point out all of their weaknesses before turning to Moulton's view (*Epistle of James*, 32–41).

16. Allison, *Epistle of James*, 82, quoting Wifstrand, "Problems," 176.

17. Allison, *Epistle of James*, 82. Allison never defines the meaning of "the language of the Hellenistic synagogue." Based on my understanding of Allison, this would probably be comparable to a variety of Greek or a code that blends various Semitic influences with the common Greek language, but Allison does not demonstrate any linguistic awareness to identify what he means as such.

18. Allison uses the adjective "unGreek" (*Epistle of James*, 82).

19. Allison, *Epistle of James*, 239.

Much more can be said regarding this example. The number of il-logical steps Allison took with James's phrase μηδεὶς λεγέτω to argue for a Jewish background text in this example is alarming. First, the fact that Allison admits up front that μηδεὶς λεγέτω is idiomatic Greek should have been enough to prevent forcing a Hebrew phrase behind it. Second, there is no commonly occurring thematic phrase in Jewish literature that would prompt one to perceive a Jewish tradition behind μηδεὶς λεγέτω. Third, the notion of constructing equivalent phrases in another language, as any modern Bible translator would recognize, is problematic in its own respect, especially when "equivalent" is left undefined as it is here. Languages are neither coterminous nor do they have identical semantic systems, and so what constitutes an accurate translation is ultimately left to the sensibilities (and hopefully linguistic expertise) of the one doing the translating. It would be more appropriate to discuss which phrase(s) in Hebrew has a similar application as the Greek phrase and to have left the notion of "equivalency" out of the discussion.[20] Fourth, the same issue of "equivalency" arises when Allison states that μηδεὶς λεγέτω is roughly equivalent to μὴ εἴπῃς, which apparently is exactly equivalent (note the "=" symbol) to תאמר אל. This statement is inaccurate for several reasons. Μηδεὶς λεγέτω and μὴ εἴπῃς have multiple semantic differences that make them distinct. The main distinction is that λεγέτω is a third person present imperative and εἴπῃς is a second person aorist subjunc-tive—they differ in three of the Greek verb semantic systems, which is not linguistically insignificant. Such semantic oversight is typical throughout Allison's commentary where no mention is ever made of verbal aspect (or even the outmoded time-based understanding of traditional grammars), and grammatical number and verbal mood are rarely considered.[21] Fifth, to then claim that μὴ εἴπῃς *equals* the Hebrew phrase אל תאמר, which occurs in Sir 15.11–12, not only has the same problems just identified, but is flawed by the very fact that James does not use this Greek phrase. In other words, by putting "bits" into James's mouth, Allison controls his "tongue" to support the agenda that James is using "Hellenistic synagogue

20. See Lyons, *Theoretical Linguistics*, 434.

21. There are a few occasions where the significance of the imperative is con-nected to the Stoic diatribe or some other historical influence. For example, Allison makes the ambiguous statement regarding πλανᾶσθε in Jas 1:16 that "It is often said that the imperative is from Stoic diatribe" (*Epistle of James*, 263).

language." This not only demonstrates a linguistic inattentiveness on Allison's part, but also a great deal of eisegesis.[22]

The use of a clearly defined method, linguistic or otherwise, helps critical analysis in that it restrains one from selecting evidence ad hoc to support a preformulated thesis. Christopher D. Land's essay has even shown that other conclusions, which are arguably more coherent than the ones Allison makes, can be drawn from Allison's own understanding of the *Sitz im Leben* of the Epistle of James. There are several essays in this volume that have explained contextual features of the context of situation in James from the constraints of linguistic models and methods, namely the essays by Zachary K. Dawson, James D. Dvorak, and Benjamin B. Hunt, who all investigated different aspects of the tenor relations at work in the letter, which in turn reveal various values, beliefs, and social relations at risk in the text. Such analyses exemplify that insights into the context of the Epistle of James can result from a bottom-up priority to analysis, and one does not have to begin with a thesis that must then be argued from the content of the letter.

Given that Allison's positions on the style of James and the *Sitz im Leben* of the letter depend so much on Semitic language influence and a Jewish tradition, it is also surprising that he does not enlist any theories of bilingualism. Much work has been done in the field of sociolinguistics on this topic, but there is also a body of literature in biblical studies that has brought much linguistic insight to New Testament Greek on topics such as bilingualism, language varieties, diglossia, regional dialects, and the like.[23] Instead, concerning the character of James's Greek the commentary exemplifies a perspective analogous to Nigel Turner's view that New Testament Greek reflects "a distinct type of Jewish Greek."[24] This is seen in Allison's commentary by his cataloguing numerous apparent Semitisms and his discussion of these in the exegetical sections of each chapter.[25] Support is given to this view by means of citing various secondary sources, including Turner's work, along with citing as many "paral-

---

22. An equally confusing discussion for many of the same reasons as the quotation on Jas 1:13 above can be observed in Allison's discussion of the phrase πᾶς ἄνθρωπος in Jas 1:19 (*Epistle of James*, 300–301).

23. See, for example the chapters by Jonathan Watt, Stanley Porter, and Christina Bratt Paulston in Porter, ed., *Diglossia*. See also Silva, "Bilingualism," 198–219.

24. Turner, *Grammatical Insights*, 182.

25. For examples, see Allison, *Epistle of James*, 235, 250, 286, 296, 762, 776, among numerous other instances.

lels" as possible from Jewish literature of Hebrew or Aramaic derivative words, phrases, and grammatical structures. However, no explicit argument for the so-called "Semitic-Greek hypothesis" is given, nor are any of the critiques of this view ever acknowledged.[26] As indicated above, a more linguistically informed approach to questions regarding the style, dialect, idiolect, or other influences that bear on James's language would draw from the field of sociolinguistics, which is how Jonathan M. Watt has attempted to advance the conversation for Jacobean studies. While cautious of the unrestrained use of Halliday's theory of anti-language, Watt demonstrates the kind of linguistic analysis necessary to understand James's language in relation to his linguistic environment.

Matters of Structure

One last area that invites comment on Allison's linguistic competence concerns his approach to the structure of James, which is an area of Jacobean scholarship notorious for its lack of consensus. It is also a good subject on which to gauge linguistic competence because it entails analyzing structures of discourse along with categories such as cohesion and coherence. This is how Allison states his approach to this matter: "This commentator largely agrees with Bauckham: 1.1 is the prescript, 1.2–27 serves as an introduction of sorts, and 2.1–5.20 is the main body, or at least the rest of the letter. Regrettably it is hard to say much more."[27] In other words, Allison provides no method for determining the structure of James, but simply adopts Bauckham's very simple structure, bypassing all consideration of the many methods used to propose structures of the letter. This is an undeniably weak attempt to address one of the major problematic areas of Jacobean scholarship. The structure of individual units is then discussed throughout the commentary, but the criteria for determining the structure cannot be said to be linguistically sophisticated. Units are delineated, as far as we can tell, by three main criteria: catchwords;[28] liter-

---

26. For example, Moisés Silva's assessment of the characteristics of Palestinian Greek does not appear in the bibliography. Silva explains that the style of each individual's use of Greek can be evaluated based on Semitic influence, but Semitic influences did not have a permanent influence on Greek. Therefore, Silva's conclusions would validate assessing James's language based on Semitic influence, but they would also falsify the notion that the "Greek of the Hellenistic synagogue," or Jewish Greek was an established dialect ("Bilingualism," 215–16, 219).

27. Allison, *Epistle of James*, 78. Cf. Bauckham, *Wisdom*, 63–64.

28. Allison describes catchwords similarly to how linguists define the textual

ary devices such as parallelism (including chiastic structures), assonance, consonance, and alliteration; and Allison's own intuitions on where a unit begins and ends, for which he then finds support in secondary literature. Only a couple of works that actually use linguistic methods are ever cited in these sections, but they only appear to support the structures that Allison finds in the text.[29] Here the essay written by Cynthia Long Westfall shines by contrast; the structure of Jas 1:2–27 is not only shown to be much more than "an introduction of sorts," but rather shows that "the first chapter is mapped on a series of comparisons that serve to summarize the readers' problems and ethical failings, which encompass most of the major themes in the rest of the discourse, and serve to urge the readers to make life-giving choices in each case."[30] Such an analysis not only speaks to the integrity of the Epistle of James as a coherent text, but has the practical payoff of providing the structure of the letter for those who wish to teach, preach, or otherwise study James according to its own patterns of organization.

CONCLUSION

Based on the matters considered above, there can be no doubt that Allison's commentary does not provide a sufficient replacement to Ropes's commentary in regard to linguistic competence. Allison only uses a couple of Greek grammars that postdate Ropes's commentary, but they are all outdated by several decades. No linguistic frameworks or methods are enlisted in the commentary to lend support to the arguments about

---

feature of lexical cohesion. See Allison, *Epistle of James*, 82–83. "Lexical chain" is a common name for repetitive uses of words; they are a legitimate criterion for establishing cohesion in discourse. However, linguists would extend the notion of lexical cohesion beyond the repeated use of the same lexeme to synonyms, near-synonyms, superordinate words, general terms, and pronouns. See Halliday and Hasan, *Cohesion in English*, 277–82.

29. Periodic references are made to the linguistic works of Mark Taylor and William Varner for this purpose. See Allison, *Epistle of James*, 222 n. 50, 323 n. 32 for a couple of examples of how he references these works along with other non-linguistic works to support his interpretive decisions. Cf. Varner, *Book of James*; Taylor, *Text-Linguistic Investigation*. Moreover, Allison also makes unsure statements about the structure of the letter, such as "The section may be analyzed this way . . ." and "This commentary tentatively suggests three main parts" (*Epistle of James*, 292, 593). Such uncertainty would prompt even an uncritical reader to doubt Allison's competence in dealing with matters of structure.

30. Westfall, "Mapping the Text," 12.

the style of Greek in James, in which Allison invests much to demonstrate the Jewish character of James's Greek and to further his argument that James was steeped in Jewish tradition and was written to Jews rather than to Christians. Last, with matters of structure, a major area of contention in scholarship, Allison demonstrates no linguistic competence at all. Thus, Allison's commentary continues to perpetuate the trend of declining linguistic competence that has characterized the enterprise of commentary writing in recent years. By contrast the essays in this volume address the critical questions surrounding the Epistle of James in a much more linguistically competent manner, some of which even suggest new insights into the makeup, content, and social aspects of the letter. This goes to show that more projects such as this, where all the essays are unified under a functional linguistic model, have the potential for advancing New Testament studies in ways that commentaries, generally speaking, no longer seem to achieve.

BIBLIOGRAPHY

Allison, Dale C., Jr. *A Critical and Exegetical Commentary on the Epistle of James.* ICC. New York: Bloomsbury, 2013.

Barr, James. *The Semantics of Biblical Language.* Oxford: Oxford University Press, 1961.

Bauckham, Richard. *James: Wisdom of James, Disciple of Jesus the Sage.* New Testament Readings. London: Routledge, 1999.

Campbell, Constantine R. *Advances in the Study of Greek: New Insights for Reading the New Testament.* Grand Rapids: Zondervan, 2015.

Halliday, M. A. K., and Ruqaiya Hasan. *Cohesion in English.* ELS 9. New York: Longman, 1976.

Lampe, G. W. H. *A Patristic Greek Lexicon.* Oxford: Clarendon, 1968.

Lockett, Darian. Review of *A Critical and Exegetical Commentary on the Epistle of James*, by Dale C. Allison, Jr. *JETS* 57 (2014) 446–49.

Lyons, John. *Introduction to Theoretical Linguistics.* Cambridge: Cambridge University Press, 1968.

McCartney, Dan G. *James.* BECNT. Grand Rapids: Baker Academic, 2009.

McKnight, Scot. "James and His Commentaries." In *On Writing of New Testament Commentaries: Festschrift for Grant R. Osborne on the Occasion of His 70th Birthday*, edited by Stanley E. Porter and Eckhard J. Schnabel, 405–19. TENT 8. Leiden: Brill, 2013.

Muraoka, T. *A Greek-English Lexicon of the Septuagint.* Rev. ed. Louvain: Peeters, 2009.

Porter, Stanley E. *Diglossia and Other Topics in New Testament Linguistics.* JSNTSup 193. Sheffield: Sheffield Academic, 2000.

———. "The Linguistic Competence of New Testament Commentaries." In *On Writing of New Testament Commentaries: Festschrift for Grant R. Osborne on the Occasion of His 70th Birthday*, edited by Stanley E. Porter and Eckhard J. Schnabel, 33–56. TENT 8. Leiden: Brill, 2013.

Ropes, James Hardy. *A Critical and Exegetical Commentary on the Epistle of St. James.* ICC. Edinburgh: T. & T. Clark, 1916.

Silva, Moisés. "Bilingualism and the Character of Palestinian Greek." *Biblica* 61 (1980) 198–219.

Taylor, Mark E. *A Text-Linguistic Investigation into the Discourse Structure of James.* LNTS 311. London: T. & T. Clark, 2006.

Turner, Nigel. *Grammatical Insights into the New Testament.* Edinburgh: T. & T. Clark, 1965.

Varner, William. *The Book of James: A New Perspective: A Linguistic Commentary Applying Discourse Analysis.* The Woodlands, TX: Kress Biblical Resources, 2010.

Wifstrand, Albert. "Stylistic Problems in the Epistles of James and Peter." *ST* 1 (1947) 170–82.

Westfall, Cynthia Long. "Mapping the Text: How Discourse Analysis Helps Reveal the Way through James." In *The Epistle of James: Linguistic Exegesis of an Early Christian Letter*, edited by James D. Dvorak and Zachary K. Dawson, 11–44. LENT 1. Eugene, OR: Pickwick, 2019.

Index of Modern Authors

Index of Ancient Sources

Made in the USA
Coppell, TX
10 July 2020

30512418R00193